THE WARWICKSHIRE SCANDAL

THE WARWICKSHIRE
SCANDAL

ELIZABETH HAMILTON

MICHAEL RUSSELL

© Elizabeth Hamilton 1999

The right of Elizabeth Hamilton to be identified
as the author of this work has been asserted by her
in accordance with the Copyright, Designs
and Patents Act, 1988

First published in Great Britain 1999
by Michael Russell (Publishing) Ltd
Wilby Hall, Wilby, Norwich NR16 2JP

Typeset in Sabon by The Typesetting Bureau
Allen House, East Borough, Wimborne, Dorset
Printed and bound in Great Britain
by Biddles Ltd, Guildford and King's Lynn

Indexed by the author

TO
ALICE, HATTIE, IMOGEN,
GABRIELLA, ANNA
AND FREDDIE

Contents

List of Illustrations

Acknowledgements

The story of the Warwickshire Scandal is largely based on letters and documents concerning the Mordaunt case in my husband's family collection. I am indebted to Mr Jeens, the Warwickshire County Archivist, and to his staff for their help in sorting out the documents; to Mr Robert Bearman, Senior Archivist at the Shakespeare Birthplace Trust; to Dr Kate Harris, Librarian and Archivist to the Marquess of Bath; to the Blair Charitable Trust, Blair Castle, Perthshire, for permission to quote from letters, and to Mrs Jane Anderson, the Archivist at Blair Castle; to the Trustees of the Edward James Foundation at West Dean and to Sharon Kusonoki, the Archivist at West Dean; to the Curator of the Wellcome Institute for the History of Medicine for permission to quote from Dr Tuke's Case Book, and to the Readers' Services Staff for all their help. Quotations from records in the Longleat Archives are included by permission of the Marquess of Bath, Longleat, Warminster, Wiltshire, and quotations from Alice Miles, *Every Girl's Duty*, ed. Maggy Parsons, by permission of André Deutsch Ltd.

Dramatis Personae

Albert Edward, Prince of Wales, afterwards King Edward VII
Queen Victoria, his mother
Princess Alexandra, his wife
Prince Arthur, Prince Leopold, his brothers
Victoria, 'Vicky', the Crown Princess of Prussia, his sister
Princess Louise, 'Loosy', Duchess of Argyll, his sister

HIS FRIENDS

Francis Knollys, Christopher Sykes, Sir Frederic Johnstone,
Sir William Gordon-Cumming, Sir Ernest Cassel

The Moncreiffes

Sir Thomas Moncreiffe
Lady Louisa, his wife
Lady Kinnoull, his mother-in-law

HIS CHILDREN

Louisa, Duchess of Atholl
Helen Forbes and Evie, her daughter
Georgina, Countess of Dudley,
  'Georgy'
Harriett, Lady Mordaunt
Blanche, 'Bunchy'
  'Francie'
Selina 'Lina'
Mary
John, 'J.A.', his eighth son

FRIENDS AND RELATIONS

Lord Newport, a cousin
Gerald Arbuthnot, a cousin
Captain Farquhar, a friend
Lord Cole, a friend
George Forbes, 'Georgie',
  brother-in-law to Helen
Alice Miles, a young lady about
  town
Louisa Scott, best friend to Lady
  Mordaunt

The Mordaunts

Sir Charles Mordaunt
John and Osbert, his brothers
The Dowager Lady Mordaunt
Harriett, Lady Mordaunt
Violet, her daughter

HIS UNCLES

Revd Francis Murray
Robert Murray
Herbert Murray and Mrs Murray

MORDAUNT EMPLOYEES

Mr Cobb, the agent
Mr Bird, the butler
Mrs Caborn, the housekeeper
Mrs Stephens, the cook
Jessie Clarke, the lady's maid
Frederick Johnson, the footman
Mr Bracebridge, the gardener

LADY MORDAUNT'S ATTENDANTS

Mrs Hancox (the midwife)
Mrs Carruthers (the 'lunatic' nurse)
Jane Laing, Miss Parsons,
Mrs Keddell ('attendants')
Sarah Barker (nurse and maid)
Nurse Archer

The Doctors

Dr Priestley
Sir James Simpson
Dr Tuke
Dr Alderson
Dr Gull
Dr Harris of Worthing
Dr Hughes of Bromley
Dr Orford of Wellesbourne
Dr Jones of Leamington Spa

Dr Solomon of Birmingham
Dr Reynolds
Dr Burrowes
Dr Tyler Smith
Dr Forbes Winslow
Dr Wynter
Dr Maudsley
Dr Barnes
Dr Wood, 'the referee'

The Lawyers

Lord Penzance
Judge Ordinary of Her Majesty's Court for Divorce

Benbow and Saltwell
Sir John Coleridge, the Solicitor-
    General
Dr Deane

Haynes, Hannay and Haynes
Mr Benjamin Hunt
Mr Serjeant Ballantine
Mr Inderwick

The Clergyman

Revd Edward Cadogan

I

The Prince

When Prince Albert died in November 1861 and Queen Victoria became engulfed in widowhood, not the least of her worries was the behaviour of her eldest son, Albert Edward Prince of Wales, known to his family and friends as Bertie. In spite of the rigorous education inflicted on him, and in defiance of the guidance provided by his parents concerning the choice of suitable companions, the Prince had already, by the age of twenty, revealed a marked preference for dissolute company and, more worrying still, for young ladies of doubtful reputation. The clandestine introduction of the actress Nellie Clifden into the Prince's bed at the Curragh barracks in Ireland had caused his parents much concern, and it was the Queen's unshakeable belief that this episode had precipitated her husband's death. She was unable to forget 'that heavenly face of woe and sorrow which was so dreadful to witness' when the news arrived that was to break her angel's heart.

Demented with grief though she was, the Queen recovered her mental stability sufficiently to apply her mind to the only remedy which might halt her son's decline into debauchery. The search for a suitable mate had been initiated before Prince Albert's death and was now intensified as the Queen instructed her daughter Vicky, the Crown Princess of Prussia, to search for a suitable bride among the royal families of Europe. The choice of Princess Alexandra of Denmark seemed in every way suitable, for by all accounts she was lovely enough to meet with Bertie's approval and virtuous enough to please his mother. In fact, to the Queen, Alexandra was 'one of those sweet creatures who seem to come from the skies to help and bless poor mortals'. Bertie conveniently fell in love with her, and on his wedding day in March 1863 he looked 'blissful, beaming and radiant', while his mother watched the proceedings from an upper gallery dressed as ever entirely in black. Love, she was sure, had 'spread its sunshine on these two dear young hearts' and it was noticeable how at ease and happy they seemed in each other's company, 'so comfortable and at home together', in the Queen's description. She felt sure that the

Princess would bring out the best in her son, for there was little doubt that he possessed many good qualities, most notably his considerable charm and what Disraeli had described as his 'singularly sweet manner'. Although the intensity of his schooling had removed any inclination he might have had to study, he was endowed with many of the social graces and was an amusing conversationalist, talking with the slightly guttural German 'r' which was a relic of the time when his father had encouraged his children to converse in German. Although somewhat short of stature, he was considered handsome, and he as yet showed no signs of the obesity which was to afflict him in later life, nor had he begun to go bald. It was perhaps because of these qualities that the Queen was to be disappointed in her hopes of seeing her son settle down into a quiet life of sombre domesticity. She became increasingly dismayed as the young couple established themselves at Marlborough House in Pall Mall and entered into a glittering round of dinner parties, balls and visits to the theatre, as well as informal house parties enlivened by practical jokes and other japes.

The Queen admitted that she herself was at this time totally incapable of bearing joyousness and merriment. She did not encourage frivolous conversation, and at the Palace or at Balmoral the guests habitually returned to their rooms after the hushed formality of meal times. The Prince on the other hand was an excellent host, making sure that his guests enjoyed themselves as much as he did himself. In every way he had reacted against the restrictions of his austere upbringing, all the more so as his mother avoided giving him any responsibility or meaningful occupation, firmly rejecting the idea that he could in any way fill the gap left by his father. Restless by nature, he was the antithesis of his recluse-like mother with her widow's weeds and her shattered nerves. Whereas she preferred to stay at home, Bertie was always on the move, altogether overdoing what the Queen referred to as 'this visiting and going about'. While she found smoking obnoxious, Bertie was seldom to be seen without a cigar, and his frequent visits to the races as well as his love of a mild flutter were equally distasteful to one who had never been known to place a bet. The Queen shunned society and particularly disliked those she described as 'bumptious', but to her disgust Bertie chose his companions with a careless disregard for the proprieties, frequently entertaining those she described as the aristocratic 'high borns', those 'horrid people' who dedicated their lives to pleasure and set a bad example to everybody else. She was to become increasingly concerned about the excesses of the 'higher classes with of course exceptions and honourable ones', thinking them to be

> so frivolous, pleasure-seeking, heartless, selfish, immoral and gambling that it makes one think ... of the days before the French Revolution. The young men are so ignorant, luxurious and self-indulgent – and the young women so fast, frivolous and imprudent that the danger really is very great, and they ought to be warned ... or some dreadful crash will take place. What I can, I do and will do – but Bertie ought to set a good example in these respects by not countenancing even any of these horrid people.[1]

The appearance of the young royals on the London scene gave a new impetus to the fun-loving people who had languished when Victoria and Albert set the tone with their abstemiousness and stern adherence to the proprieties. Now it seemed that times were changing as the Prince and Princess introduced a new regime where enjoyment was the watchword. In fashionable circles, as a new generation began to flout the conventions, there was a sense of liberation among the girls and young men alike. They felt free to indulge in the dangerous delights of flirtation, with all the paraphernalia of exchanged glances, of gentle caresses on gloved hands and even the occasional kiss.

For over a decade the female form had been surrounded by the iron cage of the crinoline, but already this fashion was in decline, giving way to the bustle and on summer occasions to delightfully feminine dresses in white muslin decorated with pink or blue ribbon. The Princess had at her wedding set the seal on the use of fresh flowers for trimming, her bridesmaids' outfits festooned with fragrant blooms and her own hair beautifully adorned with musk roses and orange blossom. It is true that one observer, Lord Clarendon, had been of the opinion that her dress had been 'too sunk in the greenery', but his wife told him that he was wrong, and the fashion had become established with the help of all the myrtle and exotic blooms provided by the conservatories of the rich.[2]

The flowers lent a delightful scent to the dresses they decorated as well as setting off beautiful shoulders to perfection. The more daring among the new generation, bored with the staid propriety of square dances such as the quadrille, much preferred the excitement and close bodily contact of the waltz. Whirling round the dance floor brought a healthy glow to delicate complexions, and this often necessitated a

withdrawal to the conservatory to cool off. There the young could
flirt on a cane sofa placed conveniently out of sight in the shadow of a
potted palm or a bank of ferns. 'Fast little dots' just out of the schoolroom entered this exciting world confident of their ability to look
after themselves out of range of chaperones or duennas. No longer in
fashion were the downcast eyes, the statuesque beauty of girls with
impeccable morals, and now a new breed emerged, as bright and
sparkling as the champagne they sipped.

As for the young men, they fell into several categories, ably
analysed by a young debutante, Alice Miles, who was brought over
from Paris for the London season in 1868.[3] First of all there were the
cousins, a category covering anybody able to claim the flimsiest
relationship as the excuse for an easy familiarity. Then there were the
'drones' or 'retrievers' who had no occupation of any kind except to
follow dog-like at a girl's heels and to attend to her every need,
carrying parasols and any other impedimenta. Handsome young
Guardsman could, it was true, be called away to their duties in the
barracks at the most inconvenient times, but at least they could be
relied upon to acquire tickets for the Blues ball and similar entertainments. Such admirers were useful as escorts, but when it was a
question of marriage, a young girl was taught to ignore those they
referred to as 'the contemptibles', in other words the impoverished
and often frivolous younger sons, as well the heirs destined to wait
years before they came into their inheritance. A girl's duty was to
search among the 'eligibles' for older men with titles, large rent rolls
and houses both in the town and in the country.

Anthony Trollope had some of his heroines questioning whether
there should be more to a girl's life than marrying sensibly and
raising two children, but in the end they all had to accept the
limitations of their role. As Violet Effingham, the young heiress in
Trollope's *Phineas Finn*, aptly put it to her friend Lady Laura
Standish:

> I like a roué myself, while a prig who sits all night in the House,
> and talks about nothing but church-rates and suffrage, is to me
> intolerable. I prefer men who are improper, and all that sort of
> thing. If I were a man myself, I should go in for everything I
> ought to leave alone, I know I should. But you see I'm not a
> man, and I must take care of myself. The wrong side of a post –
> or a woman is so very much the wrong side. I like a fast man,

but I know that I must not dare to marry the sort of man that I like.[4]

For fathers with daughters to spare, the dangers of a roué were more than apparent. A daughter deflowered was an asset squandered, and a father who normally did little more in the way of chaperonage than to hand his daughter into her carriage at five o'clock in the morning, would be stirred into greater watchfulness if a man with a bad reputation decided to pay her undue attention. Many girls were quite ignorant about the hazards of kissing and caressing and in general leading a man on. Alice Miles for example was awakened to the dangers when one evening in the course of a country house party, a young man challenged her to come out onto the landing after she had officially retired to bed, to prove to him that her coiffure did not rely on any help from false hair pieces. She was taken aback to find that the sight of her luxuriant tresses falling over her shoulders provoked in him a look which she compared to a Royal Bengal tiger about to pounce on its prey, and this made her beat a hasty retreat into the safety of her bedroom.

The Prince and his companions were in the forefront of the new liberation movement, and already there were whispers among the older generation that he himself was not to be trusted. Some mothers may well have been torn between the glamour of royalty and fears for their daughters' safety, but there was little doubt all the same that invitations to the 'small evenings' which the Prince and Princess held at Marlborough House were greatly prized. The young royals had style, they were leaders in the field of fashion, and wherever they went they generated laughter and excitement.

Already the Prince had gathered round him a group of close companions who in return for being chosen were expected to be loyal as well as discreet. Among them was Christopher Sykes, the son of a Yorkshire squire, Sir Tatton Sykes, referred to in the novels of Robert Surtees as 'Old Tat, or 'Tatters'. Sir Tatton had been something of a martinet to his sons, but reacting like the Prince against his strict upbringing, Christopher had grown up determined to devote his life, not to horse and hound, but to the social world of the metropolis. Tall, slender and slightly effete, with fine features, a melancholy expression and drooping eyelids, he sported a blonde beard like his royal friend, and he soon became known as one of the most fashionable men in town. In spite of himself, Old Tat had been impressed by his son's social success, and by his savoir faire when it came to such things as handing young ladies into a carriage. 'Ee's a regular Broomel is Chris' said the Yorkshireman proudly.

Sykes certainly had his uses. His father had set him up in a Jacobean manor house which was conveniently near Doncaster and the St Leger race meeting. The house was enlarged to accommodate the royal party, and everything was laid on for the Prince's entertainment, whether it was gambling, dancing, hunting or shooting. Sykes was adept at arranging just the right mix of people, 'a solid groundwork of historic peerages' with a few 'fast men' and a smattering of vulgarians, the nouveaux riches, whom the Prince always liked to include. In addition Sykes took a London house in King Street which the Prince frequently visited, declaring that no host could compare with 'dear old Christopher'. Becoming over the years increasingly demanding, the Prince would order his friend to arrange ambitious dinner parties, sometimes with only a day's notice.[5]

The Queen was exasperated by her son's choice of companions. In particular she mistrusted the Duchess of Manchester, believing that she was worldly and fast, but this did not prevent the royal pair from gravitating towards the 'Manchester set' and they often went to stay with the Duchess at Kimbolton Castle in Huntingdonshire. The Duchess's lover, the Marquess of Hartington, nicknamed 'Harty Tarty', was to become one of the Prince's closest friends. Nor did the Prince limit his visits to Kimbolton, and soon he had found for himself a string of country houses both in England and Scotland where he knew he would be unstintingly entertained by the rich and the great, whether in old manorial houses or fine modern palaces. Provided there was a railway station nearby, and a racecourse within easy reach, the Prince was more than ready to grace the establishment with his presence. Most important of all, of course, was the need for good company, for pretty ladies, and for a host who would enter into, or at least condone, those activites so dear to the Prince's heart. The climate had to be right for the encouragement of flirtations and even '*affaires*', for it was considered far safer to consort with a society lady than with a woman of the streets.

Anything was acceptable, provided it was kept discreet. The guests spent their evenings in back-slapping merriment, collapsing into helpless mirth at jokes which were usually made at somebody else's expense. Often theatricals and music would be laid on, with tableaux, 'statues', and 'attitudes', and later in the evening the entertainment would become more lively. No part of the house was safe from the evening romps; even the bedrooms were invaded for pillow fights and games of hide-and-seek. A favourite pastime was to toboggan downstairs on a tray. This sport became so popular that one titled host had ordered his butler to lock away all the silver trays in the house in case they should get spoilt. And when the un-suspecting guest finally retired to his room he would find, at best, an apple-pie bed to greet him, or, pushed between the sheets, surprise items such as a dead bird or a doormat. Hats would be knocked off, soda siphons squirted, and everything greeted with paroxysms of laughter. The unfortunate Sykes became the prime butt of endless jokes and japes, achieving fame by uttering the immortal phrase 'As Your Royal Highness pleases' when the Prince emptied a bottle of brandy over his head.

For the ladies, house parties could have their longueurs. The days sometimes seemed endless when there was nothing much to do except to eat large meals and frequently change their clothes as they awaited the menfolk to return from the woods or the moors. The Countess of Warwick described such weekends as intolerably boring; after break-fasting at ten o'clock when there would have been enough courses in silver dishes on the sideboard to 'last a group of well-regulated di-gestions for the whole day', the ladies sat around at spindly-legged tables writing letters and discussing their neighbours. The only con-solation was that often included in the party were a few unsporting men known as the 'darlings', whose purpose in life was to entertain the women with their witty and amusing conversation.[6]

Within a year or two of their marriage the life of the royal pair had fallen into a predictable pattern. They would spend the months of November and December at Sandringham, taking up residence at Marlborough House after Christmas where they entertained lavishly, attended innumerable dinner parties and were often to be seen at the opera or the theatre. In the spring the Prince would go off *en garçon* with his friends to Paris and the south of France.

When the Prince returned to England, the royal pair would enter into the summer season which each year became more glittering and more packed with events. The rich and the powerful would sweep up marble staircases into crowded ballrooms night after night until, just before Goodwood, came the most elegant of all the balls, described by Trollope as 'the great culminating crush in July'. During the Goodwood week the town would empty, clearing out everybody except those whom Alice Miles described as 'a few wretched Foreign Office attachés and disconsolate guardsmen who couldn't get leave'.[7] This was followed by Cowes week and thereafter many families would travel north by train to immerse themselves in all the delights of the Scottish season.

Queen Victoria's romantic love of the Highlands had been born during the visits she had made to Scotland with her adored husband. Her appreciation of the magnificent scenery was matched by her admiration for the people she met on their travels, from the dukes they had stayed with to the fine strong men who lifted her onto her pony and led her along the narrow mountain tracks. The loyal welcome she received was calculated to warm her heart, and over and over again she recorded in her journal the very special nature of a Highland welcome, for example, at Inveraray where the landing place was ornamented with heather and the Duke of Argyll's pipers walked in front of the carriage on the way up to the castle. Then there was the Gathering at Braemar, 'with the Highlanders in their brilliant and picturesque dresses, the wild notes of the pipes, the band, and the beautiful background of mountains' which the Queen found extremely exciting. The Farquharson, Duff and Forbes men would march onto the ground and after the hammers and cabers had been thrown, the royal party would watch the strenuous race of the young men up the hill of Craig Cheunnich. The Prince had often enjoyed these occasions in the company of his parents and he too became enamoured of the Scottish way of life. When he was old enough he was granted his own establishment at Abergeldie, just down river from Balmoral. Each year, after paying a therapeutic visit to one of the German spas, he would set off for the north where he was able to enjoy good sport in the daytime on the hills and lochs, followed by cheerful entertainment in the evening. There were formal balls, as well as parties for the servants, when the Prince would join in with gusto, dancing reels and in general making himself agreeable.

For the Prince there was more to Scottish life than the tossing of the caber, and he soon found that it was possible to extend the London social round with a pleasant itinerary that took him from Deeside to Donside, and from Dunrobin to Dupplin. Many noble lairds had in the past entertained his parents, but it was a fact that his mother often much disliked their progeny who were inclined to be rather wild. The Queen deprecated their influence, but the Prince, as usual, took little notice of his mother's preferences.

In 1842 the Prince's parents had headed north after landing at North Queensferry, rejoicing as the mountains began to appear, and in particular enjoying the beautiful view of Moncreiffe Hill. After changing horses at Bridge of Earn they had gone on to lunch with Lord Kinnoull at Dupplin Castle, described by the Queen as 'a very fine modern house with a very pretty view of the hills on one side and a small waterfall close in front'. Following in his parents' footsteps, but without the maternal presence, the Prince too had found his way to Dupplin on many occasions, his friendship with the Kinnoulls opening up all kinds of delightful social avenues. Dalhousie, their house just outside Perth, was only a short distance from Moncreiffe House at Bridge of Earn, where Lady Kinnoull's daughter Lady Louisa Moncreiffe lived with her husband Sir Thomas and their tribe of children.[8]

Moncreiffe House was beautifully set below the hill which had once been the dry stone stronghold of the Pictish kings, and the Moncreiffes were an ancient family, their ancestor Sir Matthew having been confirmed in his lands by royal charter in 1248. In spite of this proud heritage, Sir Thomas was feeling the financial strain of bringing up his large family, and for him the task of marrying off his eight daughters was a very serious business. It was imperative that they should marry well and marry young, thus releasing more funds to meet the cost of providing governesses for his other daughters and tutors for his sons. Young men of impeccable pedigree, among them the Prince of Wales, were encouraged to visit Moncreiffe, and there was an easy enjoyable atmosphere there. Some people were of the opinion that the daughters were 'educated' to be flirtatious to help Sir Thomas's task of matchmaking, and it was said that one of the Moncreiffe governesses had given in her notice after complaining that education was impossible when there were always so many young men coming in and out of the schoolroom.

Friendships made during the Scottish season could be cemented at balls and parties held later in the year in London. Working within this social context, Sir Thomas had already successfully disposed of two of his daughters, the eldest, Louisa, having married the young Duke of Atholl, while the second, Helen, was the wife of Charles Forbes of Newe near Gartley in Aberdeenshire, the heir to a baronetcy and the castle that went with it. By the summer of 1865 plans were already well ahead for the marriage of the third daughter, the exceptionally lovely Georgina, to the rich Earl of Dudley. That year, the fourth daughter Harriett Sarah, now seventeen years old, had just emerged from the schoolroom. With her large grey eyes and her vivacious manner, she had already attracted several admirers, including the Prince of Wales.

Thanks to their wide circle of relations, the Moncreiffe daughters were well endowed with admirers in the cousinly class and there were great advantages in knowing young men who by virtue of the family connection were allowed to be on the kind of affectionate Christian name terms which normally would have been considered improper. As Trollope put it, there were restrictions which made it impossible for a girl to enjoy the full flow of friendship with a man until after matrimony, but the cousinly relationship provided some escape from the hardship of such rules.

> Cousins [Trollope wrote] are Tom, and Jack, and George and Dick . . . Cousins have romped with you and scolded you, and teased you when you were young. Cousins are almost the same as brothers, and yet they may be lovers. There is certainly a great relief in cousinhood.[9]

Young men such as their second cousin Lord Newport, the Earl of Bradford's heir, or George Forbes,[10] their sister Helen's brother-in-law, were on just such terms with the Moncreiffe sisters and the summer of 1865 was an exciting time for Georgy and Harriett in their happy unattached state, as they exchanged photographs for their albums, and roamed in the hills, and had endless carefree fun. 'Dear Moncreiffe, I think it is the nicest place I ever was at' wrote George Newport after his visit had sadly come to an end. 'I was so sorry to say goodbye to you all that morning and I hope I may be asked to pay you another visit next year.' He was twenty years old and a subaltern in the Life Guards; his grandfather had married Sir Thomas's great-aunt Georgina Moncreiffe, and there was an extra connection to draw the families together since his grandfather had married, as his second wife, the widow of their grandfather, Sir David Moncreiffe. With such close connections Lord Newport was understandably treated as one of the family. After he left, some of them had travelled up to the Black Mount for a house party, where they were the guests of the Earl of Dudley. When George Newport wrote Harriett what he described as 'a horrid stupid letter all about photographs', he expressed the hope that she was amusing herself there. 'How is Georgy's ankle?' he inquired, and went on

None the worse I hope for that nice walk we had this day last week up the hill. Please give her my love. This photograph I am sending you is I think a horrid thing not half good enough for your book. Remember I am looking forward to getting one from you. Will you tell Bunchy [Harriett's younger sister Blanche] that I will send her the one I promised her when I go to Windsor which will be in a few days, as I have got no more here. Don't *quite* forget me Harriett and believe me

ever your affectionate cousin

NEWPORT

On 29 September he wrote again from Weston Park, Shifnal, his father's seat in Shropshire:

My dear Harriett

Thanks very much for the photograph and letter which I received last night. I like the photo very much though I must say I don't think it is nearly pretty enough for the original. Naughty girl, to say that you think your letters could be dull or that I could get tired of Moncreiffe news.

It had become evident to George Newport by this time that the visit to the Black Mount had been more than a purely social occasion. The Earl of Dudley, the host, was a man in his late forties, and had been a widower ever since his wife had died in childbirth only seven months after their wedding in 1851. It had taken him years to recover from the shock of discovering that when he married her, his wife had been with child by another man. He was something of a hypochondriac and for a time had been considered a little mad, but he was so 'fabulously rich' that any girl would have been a fool to turn him down. When he began 'nibbling' at the lovely Georgina, her father could only approve.[11] Lord Dudley's assets included some coalfields in Staffordshire, a mansion in Park Lane where the food was served on gold plate, and a large estate in Worcestershire, where the house, Witley Court, had recently been remodelled in the Italian Renaissance style.

Georgina became engaged soon after her visit to the Mount, and as soon as he heard the news George Newport wrote to Harriett expressing his surprise. He obviously found it hard to imagine the youthful Georgina being tied down to a man nearly thirty years her senior. 'I must say I was very much surprised to hear of Georgie's marriage, but wonders will never cease and I am sure I hope she will be very happy.'

Harriett had told him that she was doing some knitting for him. 'How nice of you making me some stockings' he wrote, adding

> you know how I shall like them. I am obliged to be at Windsor for duty on the 1st Decr, so I hope I may see you in London which would be very nice. I have been travelling about all over the country, shooting; last week I was in Norfolk at the Duke of Grafton's partridge shooting. We had wonderful sport but I don't know that I enjoyed it much more than our pigeon shooting at Moncreiffe though I only killed one bird I think. I have not heard from Georgie Forbes lately. I suppose he will be going to Moncreiffe soon. How I envy him. I should think you will have great fun at the Perth meeting. I am just going out shooting now, 'all by my own self' so goodbye. Please give my love to your sisters and believe me your very affec Cousin, NEWPORT

The letter suggested that Lord Newport, although on familiar terms with all the family, had a special affection for Harriett, and it is probable that she was attracted to him, since she only knitted stockings for those who were particularly favoured.[12] But she had other admirers, some of them far more eligible than a subaltern of twenty years old living on an allowance from his father. All the signs were that Harriett, with her lively nature and exceptional good looks, would be able to take her pick.

In November of that year, 1865, Harriett received an invitation to join the Waleses at Sandringham and the fact that the Prince had singled her out as a suitable recruit for his circle of friends was an indication of her value. Her parents, who regarded the Prince as a family friend, apparently made no objection, flattered that the heir to the throne had bestowed such a favour on their daughter. Many of the older generation, however, viewed with deep suspicion the house parties which had become so fashionable, believing, as did the formidable Lady Lufton in Trollope's *Framley Parsonage*,[13] that they tended to harbour such undesirable characters as 'gamblers, Whigs, atheists and men of loose pleasure'. It was far better, in the opinion of the dowager, to live 'without contamination among hunting squires'.

This was certainly the kind of country life that the Earl of Dudley envisaged for his young wife, with some limited and discreet participation in the London season. He was a man of the old school, and he did not much care for the free and easy atmosphere of Moncreiffe. Chastened by his earlier experience, he had no intention of exposing his second wife to the dangers of a dissolute society. Perhaps aware that she was already in love with another man,[14] he married Georgina without delay in November, and from then on she had to accept the restrictions, as well as the advantages, of becoming the mistress of a large household. He treated her well and the marriage was to be happy. Georgy bore him six sons and a daughter, and later nursed him with loving care after he fell ill in his latter years, although this did not mean that she was immune to other admirers who were less old-fashioned and staid than her husband. Harriett rather rudely labelled her brother-in-law 'frizzle wig', while Lord Dudley viewed her in return with some disapproval, probably scenting danger when she was invited to Sandringham. He himself had no illusions about the Prince's character.

At Sandringham the royal couple, and particularly the Princess, were at their happiest. The house was small and cluttered with furniture, potted plants and knick knacks, and there was always a delightfully informal atmosphere. The Princess felt at home there from the start, appreciating the flat lands around the house which reminded her of her native Denmark. She was fond of riding and often went out hunting which was considered quite daring for a lady at that time. She had also invested in a pony carriage and pair, and she would drive around the estate at speed, looking extremely dashing. It was probable that she also drove herself about in London. Certainly, one observer, seeing a little phaeton with a pair of ponies being driven by a very pretty young lady somewhere near Marble Arch, was convinced that he had caught a glimpse of the Princess.[15] Soon other young ladies began to model themselves on the stylish Alexandra, making their husbands buy them the equipage which provided them with a kind of 'happy emancipation' as they drove themselves about at will. Trollope pictured his Lady Glencora Palliser in a little low carriage drawn by two small horses, which was 'the sweetest thing you ever saw'.[16] It was still considered somewhat shocking for a young lady to drive herself in town, but as Lady Glencora put it, what was the harm in looking fast, so long as one did nothing improper? Nobody cared at Sandringham, and driving around made a welcome pastime for the Princess while her husband and the other men were out during the day time in their tweed knickerbockers enjoying a day's shooting.

Although always elegant and dignified in public, the Princess was able to relax among her friends, wandering through the rooms at Sandringham doing her knitting, with several dogs at her heels. She would join in the 'romps', the practical jokes and the tray tobogganing as enthusiastically as her husband. The Queen sometimes found her daughter-in-law rather 'stiff and cold', but things were different at Sandringham. 'Bertie and Alix are the most amiable hosts and seem so happy here at Sandringham' wrote the Queen, adding, 'The improvements made about the place are charming, and I am so glad to see Bertie taking so much interest in these things and showing so much taste in building and planting – occupation of that kind is so good for him.'[17]

The Prince was in his prime, enjoying life to the full, with an immense appetite for food and drink. He now sported a luxuriant moustache and beard which camouflaged his rather ugly mouth and his receding chin. His blue eyes, large and slightly protuberant like his mother's, were perhaps his best feature, and they were tailor-made for the popular sport of catching a girl's eye in a crowded room. Always fashionably dressed in clothes of impeccable cut, he was polite to everybody, of whatever class, finding more pleasure in talking to a gardener about his begonias than he did discussing affairs of state with men of importance. At the dinner table he liked to arrange matters so that he always had the prettiest and most vivacious ladies on either side of him and Miss Moncreiffe was just the type of girl to fill this role.

After she left Sandringham, Harriett wrote to the Prince, using the usual photographic exchange as an excuse to start up a correspondence. He replied to her from Marlborough House

Dear Miss Moncreiffe,
    Pray accept my best thanks for your letter and I shall be only too happy to receive another photograph from you if you will kindly send it to me. Believe me,
                                        Very sincerely yours,
                                        ALBERT EDWARD

Harriett duly sent her photographs and received a formal letter from the Prince's equerry:

Sandringham
King's Lynn
December 11th 1865

Lt Colonel Keppel presents his compliments to Miss Moncreiffe and has been desired by the Prince of Wales to thank her for the photographs with which His Royal Highness is much pleased.

His Royal Highness proceeded to invite Miss Moncreiffe to Marlborough House on several occasions, and she was also asked to join the Prince and Princess and their friends when they went to the theatre, sitting with them in the royal box. The letter writing continued, as did the exchange of photographs. 'According to my promise,' the Prince wrote, 'I send you the last photograph that has been taken of me, and I hope that you will think it better than the one I gave you at Sandringham in the winter.' And so the Prince's photograph too found its way into Harriett's album, joining the portraits of Lord Newport and other admirers. Although she had become involved with people whom the Queen described with chilling opprobrium as 'fast', this did not make her any less popular in other circles and she was universally liked, even adored, for her charming nature as well as her good looks. She was, in fact, basking in the light of universal adulation.

In London, Lady Kinnoull made her Moncreiffe granddaughters welcome at her house in Belgrave Square. She was a lively character – 'larky' was the word that Harriett used to describe her – and she was not above entering into their 'japes'. Nor was she too energetic as a chaperone, and Harriett was allowed to attend the Prince's intimate dinner parties without anybody enquiring too closely what went on. In any case, Harriett would probably have been too headstrong and determined, 'stiff-necked' to use the contemporary term, to listen to any advice. The Queen, for her part, could do nothing to influence her son except to complain about his behaviour, volubly and at length, in her letters to her daughter Vicky.

Not everybody approved of Harriett's goings-on, and certainly by the time the summer season was in full swing, some of the more observant, including her brother-in-law, Lord Dudley, were beginning to feel apprehensive about her behaviour, and particularly about the fact that she was encouraging the Prince in his attentions. As one fashionable ball followed another, Harriett would be seen with his group of friends, laughing and joking and taking bets, and on one

occasion when she and the Prince indulged in the usual light-hearted
betting, Harriett won and demanded the settlement of a wager. The
Prince duly obliged by sending her a bouquet of flowers. It was
delivered to her on the morning of the Dudley House Ball, with a
note which ran

Dear Miss Moncreiffe,
   As you desired me to settle what the bet was to be which we
had the other night, I have come to the conclusion that a bouquet might perhaps be an acceptable offering and I shall be
much pleased if you will use it this evening at the Ball and
hoping to have the pleasure of seeing you at Dudley House.

Harriett had every excuse to attend the ball given by her sister
Georgy and her husband, and afterwards she pressed some flowers
from the bouquet and wrapped them carefully in a piece of paper, on
which she wrote in pencil 'Flowers out of the Prince of Wales bouquet, June 18th 1866. Given me for the Dudley House Ball.' These she
kept in her 'private box'.

It is unlikely that the host at Dudley House, old 'frizzle wig', was
unaware of the significance of the bouquet or that he failed to warn
her parents of the attentions being paid to his sister-in-law by the heir
to the throne. Perhaps for this reason Harriett was sent back to Scotland before the town emptied for Goodwood, in the hope that she
would be out of harm's way among the simpler pleasures of life
at home. Up at Moncreiffe there was as usual much coming and
going of relations and friends, among them George Newport, whose
brotherly affection for his cousin had blossomed during the winter
season into a deeper attachment.

2

The Hunting Squire

There was another cousinly visitor at Moncreiffe in August 1866, a young man formed in a rather different mould from Harriett's other admirers, George Newport and Georgie Forbes. Sir Charles Mordaunt of Walton in Warwickshire, thirty years old, slight in build and diffident in manner, was Harriett's second cousin, and he had known her from her earliest years, seeing her grow from an enchanting child into one of the most admired young women of her day. Each year he had visited Moncreiffe on his way to remote Corrour Lodge which was situated north of Rannoch Moor, on the Road to the Isles.[18] Although not by any means on the same easy terms as George Newport, he seemed, this summer, to be taking a more than usual interest in Harriett and she had not discouraged him. They had exchanged photographs, and when he went off to Corrour for the stalking, Sir Charles left his album in her safe keeping. This gave him a good excuse to return to Moncreiffe at a later date.

Harriett's father accepted Sir Charles as a significant contender in the marriage stakes. Nobody could quarrel with his pedigree. The Mordaunts had come over to England with William the Conqueror, settling at Turvey in Bedfordshire where there are some fine tombs in the church with recumbent figures of the first and second Barons Mordaunt. Later members of the family were ennobled as the Earls of Peterborough. It was in the sixteenth century that a younger son, Robert Mordaunt, married the Walton heiress Barbara L'Estrange, and his heirs had made Walton their home from that time onwards. Through his mother, born Caroline Sophia Murray, and his grandfather, George Murray, Bishop of Rochester, Sir Charles was descended from the 3rd Duke of Atholl, while his grandmother, the Bishop's wife, was a daughter of the 10th Earl of Kinnoull, who was also Harriett's great-grandfather.

Sir Charles had succeeded to the baronetcy, first conferred on his ancestor L'Estrange Mordaunt in 1611, when he was only nine years old after his revered father had died following a shooting accident. On coming of age he had built himself an impressive new house at

Walton near Warwick to the design of the fashionable architect Sir
Gilbert Scott. He also owned lands in Norfolk, Northamptonshire and
Somerset which all added up to an impressive rent roll. Known to be
virtuous and of a steady nature, preferring country pursuits to the
social life of the city, he was already a Member of Parliament for
South Warwickshire, having been re-elected the previous year after a
very 'severe' contest with the Earl of Camperdown. Although he could
hardly be termed handsome, with his rather large nose and somewhat
thin mouth, he could certainly be classed among the 'eligibles'.

If Harriett's father had hoped that she would be out of range of the
Prince's attentions in Scotland, he was to be disappointed, for before
long she received an invitation to a royal ball at Abergeldie. This was
what the Prince described as a 'quality' ball and he had written to his
younger sister Princess Louise inviting her to join the party and to
come over from Balmoral for the evening if their Mama would allow
it. 'We have the Fifes, Farquharsons, Forbes etc' he told her 'as we
thought it better to get the smart dance over first – before the ghillies'
balls later.'

An invitation from the Prince was difficult to refuse, but Harriett
was well chaperoned by her relations when she went to Abergeldie.
Her mother stayed at home as she was expecting yet another child the
following October, but her father took her up to Newe and they went
on from there with Charles and Helen Forbes and other members of
the family. The Earl of Dudley had, however, wisely taken Georgy off
to the remote safety of the Black Mount.

After the ball, on her return to Moncreiffe, Harriett was pleased to
find a letter awaiting her from Sir Charles, which she replied to on 2
September, telling him that among the guests staying at Moncreiffe
had been Dr Priestley and his wife, who had just left that afternoon. Dr Priestley was a fashionable London doctor who attended
many society ladies in their confinements and advised them on their
gynaecological problems. On this occasion he was mixing business
with pleasure since he was able to advise his hostess about the
progress of her fourteenth pregnancy.

My dear Sir Charles [Harriett wrote],
    Thank you so much for your nice letter that I received on
arrival here from Newe. I was so glad to get it as not knowing
that the letters took such a long time to reach you, I was afraid
that I had mistaken the direction and that my letter had been

lost. Helen will be sorry to hear of your not being able to go to Newe next week as she leaves there next Friday on her way to pay Georgy a visit at the Black Mount. We left Blanche with Helen at Newe till Friday when she comes back here. Papa and I came home on Friday after the ball the night before at Abergeldie which perhaps you heard of. All the Newe party went except Helen Newport[19] and the Dudleys, the latter of which had left earlier in the week and it was too far for Helen to drive. It was a very jolly dance but I had such a fearfully bad headache that I could not enjoy it. Princess Louise and Prince Arthur came over from Balmoral for the dance and went back afterwards. I am so glad to hear that you are having good sport. I shall be very glad to see you back here again in September if you can come. Papa, Mama and I are off to Blair tomorrow morning for a fortnight or so, Blanche joins us there on Saturday ... It is very uncertain weather now, showery but not cold. I am taking great care of your Photo books – they are quite safe up in my room where I am writing now, they are waiting for your return here. I am afraid it is time to dress for dinner so I must leave off writing. I suppose this letter will still find you at Corrour Lodge so I will send it there. If you write will you send my letter to Blair Castle, Blair Atholl where I shall be for the next ten days at least. With kind remembrances from all here. Believe me

Ever yours, most sincerely,

HARRIETT MONCREIFFE

At Blair Atholl, the young Duke and Duchess, whose first child, a daughter, had been born the previous March, were entertaining a large family gathering. Harriett's brother-in-law Iain, who had come into the dukedom on the death of his father two years before and was still only twenty-five years old, was a very different proposition from 'old frizzle wig' and Harriett was on such good terms with him that he did not hesitate to give her a brotherly kiss from time to time, while she included him among the most favoured by knitting him a pair of stockings. It is probable that by now the possibility of a marriage between Sir Charles and Harriett was being openly discussed in family circles. She herself was hesitant, for although to the older generation Sir Charles must have seemed an eminently suitable choice, to a young girl who had only recently begun to enjoy the delights of the London season, the idea of being tied down to a sober hunting squire was bound to cause her some dismay. He could certainly be classed as one of the 'humdrum' young men described by Trollope's Violet Effingham, who tended to have nothing on their minds beyond foxes, pheasants, church rates and suffrage. As yet she hardly knew him and certainly could not pretend that she loved him, and in such circumstances it might have seemed unwise to rush into matrimony. Even the Queen was of the opinion that it was 'a thousand times better never to marry than to marry for marrying's sake'.

There were other considerations, of course. Marriage to a landed gentleman brought with it considerable status as well as a greater freedom. A married lady could dispense with chaperones and was no longer dependent on her family. Georgie Forbes, who was also staying at Blair, had visited Walton as Sir Charles's guest during the hunting season, and was able to tell her how pretty it was, and what beautiful horses Sir Charles kept there. The handsome mock Gothic house was splendidly equipped for house parties, with a conservatory full of hot-house plants, a billiard room, and all the accoutrements deemed necessary in fashionable society. Sir Charles, himself addicted to all the sporting pastimes, would be able to provide her friends with everything they needed for their enjoyment and there was no good reason why she would not be able to entertain them. In addition, as a Member of Parliament, Sir Charles would of necessity spend much of his time in town, which would enable her to accompany him and join in the social round in London. Provided she avoided flouting the proprieties, a young married woman did not necessarily have to go into retirement, and, above all, marriage to Sir Charles would bring a release from the penury of living in a family of thirteen children in straitened financial circumstances. Sir Thomas made sure, when he discussed terms with Sir Charles, that he set the price very high for the young man who was aspiring to marry his lovely and much sought after daughter.

When Harriett was still at Blair Atholl, George Newport wrote to her from Longshaw Lodge in Sheffield. He may have had some inkling of what was in the wind.

My dear old thing

I cannot resist enclosing a note in my letter to Georgie to ask you how your dear self is. You have never written to me as you promised, unkind girl, but don't bother yourself about it as I know you have too many other things to think of just now. I was so sorry to say goodbye to you all the other day and to you most of all my old pretty. What fun we did have up there didn't we? I have never heard a word about the Abergeldie Ball, how did it go off? I am coming back to Scotland in a few days to Black Mount. I wish you were going to be there but I suppose we shall meet in October. Francy and Lina [Harriet's sisters Frances and Selina] were so glad to see me at Moncreiffe the other day, they are great ducks. Goodbye my pet. I wish I could give you one more kiss.

Yours, NEWPORT

Harriett wrote to him in reply, prompting another affectionate letter written from his family home, Weston Park, Shifnal, on Sunday 16 September 1866:

My dear Harriett,

It is too nice of you having finished my stockings and I look forward immensely to putting them on, but I think you had better keep them at Moncreiffe till I come there as it will be more appropriate for me to wear them there for the first time. I am looking forward immensely to going there and seeing you all . . . We have had nothing but rain here, it has been too beastly. I hope you will be able to read this scrawl but I have got such a bad pen that I can scarcely write. Hoping to see you soon,

Believe me

Ever your affectionate Cousin,

NEWPORT

The next day, 17 September, he wrote to her again:

My own pet

Just one line to thank you for your dear letter and to give you my best love. I often think of you and hope that you are amusing yourself and are happy. I wonder if (even with the party that you said you were going to have now) you ever think of your old friend. I believe, you naughty thing, that it is very much a case of 'Out of sight, out of mind' with you. We had a very jolly week except that I lost all my money at Doncaster races. I am going up to Black Mount on Friday. I shall be so glad to get into Scotland again. What fun we had at Newe. I shall never forget how nice you were there. I should think that Freddy Villiers will be rather a bore at Moncreiffe, poor fellow. He lost a good deal more than he can afford at Doncaster. I wish you were coming to the Black Mount next week. I wonder where you will be and how the world will be 'jogging on' with you. I have not heard anything of Georgie Forbes for a long while. I wish I knew where to write to him. I must not write any more, my duck. Isn't that other a very correct and proper letter? Goodbye my dear old thing, think sometimes of your affectionate N.

These letters reached Harriett when she returned to Moncreiffe from Blair Atholl. Her father meanwhile had arranged a meeting with Sir Charles who, eager to secure the glittering prize, had agreed to a settlement of £2,000 a year which more than satisfied Sir Thomas. Sir Charles was granted permission to propose without delay.

When he broached the subject, Harriett explained to him how daunting it was for a young girl who had been leading a carefree existence among her friends to be thrown into matrimony and separated from her family and the way of life she had come to accept. She told him that she was sure she could not commit herself unless she was sure that this would not happen. With the prize so nearly in his grasp, Sir Charles was ready to promise anything, and he assured her that he was prepared to invite to his house as many of her friends and family as she wished. But she wanted more than that; she would still turn him down unless he could give her his word that he would never be jealous if she talked to other men, even danced with them. Anxious and infatuated, he gave her his solemn oath that he accepted her conditions, and would never be jealous of her attentions to others. Granted this assurance, Harriett agreed to marry him, and on 19 September she wrote to the Duke of Atholl to give him the news:

I write you one line as I promised to tell you that I am going to marry Sir Chas Mordaunt, it was all settled yesterday. I have already written to Papa so perhaps he will have told you before you read this letter, only I thought I should like to write a line to tell you myself as I should like your approval! I feel quite happy about it now it is all settled. I think I shall perhaps be able to finish your stockings to send by this afternoon's post as I have only a very little bit to do but if not I will send them tomorrow as I have such a lot of letters to write today. Goodbye now dear Iain and with love

Ever yours affectionately,
HARRIETT MONCREIFFE

The news of her engagement was to come as unwelcome news to Harriett's other cousinly admirer. There was little doubt that her relationship with Newport must now change. As Trollope put it in *The Vicar of Bullhampton*, when his heroine became engaged to a man other than her cousin: 'There must be no more laying of her head upon his shoulder, no more twisting of her fingers through his locks, no more looking into his eyes, no more amorous pressing of his lips against her own.'[20]

Newport took the news as well as he could, and as he put it to Harriett when he wrote to her from the Black Mount:

You will have thought me very unkind not to have answered your dear letter before but I have been up at the Iron House and only got it yesterday, so you must forgive me and I shall only be able to write you a few lines now as we are just starting off to the great drive. Dear child, far from disliking your writing to me which would be impossible I am only too delighted that you still care to confide in me and I can only assure you that if ever you should happen to want a friend (which I hope you never may) you may know where to find one to whom it would be the greatest pleasure to do anything in the world for you. I will come to Moncreiffe Harriett if you wish it, though I had half intended not to. I think I shall like to see you there once more. I cannot write more now as they are calling me to be off, so goodbye my darling,

Ever yours, NEWPORT

Harriett also received a letter from the Prince of Wales. He had evidently received the news of her engagement with equanimity for he knew by now that matrimony did not always mean that an enjoyable flirtation would be curtailed.

Dunrobin Castle,
Sutherland
September 27th /6

My dear Miss Moncreiffe,
As I have just heard that you are engaged to be married to Sir Charles Mordaunt, I am anxious to be one of the first to offer you my heartiest and most sincere congratulations and amongst the many good wishes that you will receive from so many relations and friends none will I think be more sincere than mine.

We have been here since Monday last and are enjoying ourselves very much and have beautiful weather. We spent a very
pleasant time at Abergeldie since I last saw you and I killed
seventeen stags before we left.

The Princess joins with me in offering you our best wishes for
your future happiness.

I remain, Yours very sincerely,

ALBERT EDWARD

Harriett was delighted with this letter, and showed it to Jessie Clarke,
her lady's maid. Nobody could take exception to it, as it had all the
appearance of coming from somebody who was no more than a
family friend. All the same, Harriett put it away, and kept it. She did
not show it to Sir Charles.

A few weeks after their engagement, Harriett and Sir Charles,
known to his family and friends as Charlie, dined with Lady Kinnoull
in Belgrave Square, and at some stage in the evening Lord Dudley
took his future brother-in-law aside, warning him that Sir Thomas
and Lady Louisa had allowed an intimacy to exist between the Prince
of Wales and Harriett which he, Lord Dudley, thought most imprudent. He warned Sir Charles 'in marked terms' about the corruptness
of the Prince's character. When he asked Sir Charles whether the
Moncreiffes had ever mentioned this intimacy, Sir Charles replied
that they had not. 'Ah, I thought so,' remarked Lord Dudley, 'just
like them, it was not likely that they would.'

In the weeks following their engagement, Harriett seemed to be
testing Charlie out as she flirted and danced with other men. Several
people told Sir Charles that they thought she was going to the fur-
thest extent in her flirtations in order to try him. If he did make any
remark about her behaviour, she would simply reply reasuringly that
he need not worry, as 'everybody did it'. There was always the hope
that she would settle down once she was married, and if he expressed
any fears that she might be lonely when he was busy in the House of
Commons, or immersing himself in his country pastimes, she replied
that she would never complain about his pursuit of pleasure provided
he did not interfere with hers.

Harriett's parents saw no need to delay the marriage, although they
had to allow enough time for Lady Louisa to recover from the birth
of her sixth son, Malcolm, who arrived on 29 October. The wedding
was fixed for 7 December and it was perhaps fortuitous that the

Prince of Wales happened to be out of the country at this time, attending his sister-in-law's marriage to the Grand Duke Alexander, later Tsar Alexander III. Princess Alexandra was expecting her third child in the New Year and so had been unable to accompany him. He returned to England on 8 December, and although he could not attend her wedding, he did send Harriett the present of a diamond and emerald horseshoe ring, which perfectly complemented the pendant on a pearl necklace given her by Sir Charles, also in diamonds and emeralds.

3
The New Bride

The marriage took place on a cold winter's day at St John's, the episcopal church in Perth. A number of Sir Charles's relations made the journey to Scotland including his sister Alice and her husband the Revd Walter Portman and several of the Murray family. Sir Charles's younger brother John had accompanied their mother and sister Mary, who was to be one of the bridesmaids. Many friends and relations of the Moncreiffes were there, including the Dowager Lady Kinnoull, although Georgina and Helen were absent as both were expecting a child, Helen in January, and Georgina in May. Georgie Forbes was in the congregation; Lord Newport sent a wedding present but did not attend.

The time of the ceremony had been fixed for 12 o'clock but long before that the church had become crowded with spectators and the crush was so great that seats set aside for the invited party were only kept clear with great difficulty. A large crowd also gathered in the street outside.

At Moncreiffe, the bride put on her dress of white velour trimmed with Brussels lace and her Brussels lace veil which was held in place with a wreath of orange blossom. A little after eleven o'clock she was ready to leave Moncreiffe. With her father beside her, she was driven under the fine floral arch which had been put up at the main gates and decorated with the mottoes 'Health and Happiness' and 'Long Life and Prosperity'. They were greeted by enthusiastic cheering from the villagers here and along much of the route to Perth.

Meanwhile the bridesmaids had taken up their places on either side of the porch near the font. The bridegroom had also arrived. He and his best man, Robert Duff[21] of Fetteresso, a friend of both the families, were dressed in ordinary morning suits. Among the bridesmaids were Harriett's four unmarried sisters, Blanche, Frances, Selina and Mary, her Kinnoull cousins Lady Constance and Lady Evangeline Hay, and Miss Mary Balfour. They were all wearing bonnets of white tulle with dresses of white glacé silk trimmed with cerise velvet and white jessamine. Each had been given by the bridegroom a diamond-shaped gold locket with the initials H and C M in coloured enamel. Waiting ready robed were the Right Revd the Bishop of St Andrews, the Revd William Blatch, the incumbent of St John's, and Sir Charles's uncle the Revd Francis Murray, Rector of Chislehurst in Kent, who were to officiate at the service.

Leaning on the arm of her father and followed by the eight brides-maids, the bride made her way up the aisle, and soon the marriage vows had been said and the irrevocable step into matrimony had been taken. After the usual signing ceremonies in the vestry, the bridal pair left the church by the main entrance and faced the cheering crowds outside, hearing many shouted good wishes as they drove away in their carriage and four. From the Mordun top, twenty guns thundered out a salute and the assembled visitors by the triumphal arch gave them a hearty welcome as did over 160 children from the schools in Bridge of Earn who were drawn up along the avenue to the house, each holding a small banner and managing to look cheerful in spite of the cold.

At Moncreiffe House, sixty guests sat down to a handsome *déjeuner* with the band of the Perthshire Rifles playing a selection of appropriate music. After the reception, the bride and groom travelled by train to Brechin Castle, the seat of the Earl of Dalhousie, where they were to spend their short honeymoon.

That evening the principal inhabitants of Bridge of Earn met at the Moncreiffe Arms and proposed the health of the bride and groom. In Warwickshire the bells of Leamington, Stratford-on-Avon, Henley-in-Arden and Wellesbourne had been sounding out 'in merry peals' throughout the day, and at Stratford the Mayor caused the corpora-tion banner to be hoisted on the Town Hall.

The bride and groom started their journey south on the Monday, spending that night at Preston. Meanwhile, at Walton and Welles-bourne the preparations for their arrival were well under way. Mr Cobb, the agent, was busy organising everything and many houses had put out banners. Holland of Warwick were responsible for the triumphal arches and other decorations. There was no bell-ringing in Walton 'for the best of all reasons', as the local paper put it, 'that the Church of St James boasts of no steeple and only a single bell', but the sound of bells as far away as Sherbourne near Warwick was borne along on the breeze. The last of the evergreens were tucked into the triumphal arches, and over the classical porch of the little Grecian-style church the finishing touches were added to a floral decoration encircling the motto 'God bless thee and make his light shine upon thee'.

Towards tea time, in the gathering dusk, a large crowd of local residents gathered on the lawn in front of the house, all wearing a white favour. The estimated time of arrival came and went, and the suspense mounted.

The bridal pair had in fact missed their connection at Rugby which accounted for the delay, but on their arrival at the Avenue Station in Leamington they found Sir Charles's barouche drawn by four handsome greys from the Regent Hotel waiting to convey them to Walton. The bells rang out as they drove through Warwick, and they were given a royal welcome by the crowds in Barford and Wellesbourne who were waiting on either side of the road. Wellesbourne, not to be outdone by the Bridge of Earn, was elaborately *en fête*, with magnificent arches of flowers and evergreens at both ends of the village. In the Kineton road the 7th Troop of Horse of the Warwickshire Yeomanry, of which Sir Charles was Captain, was drawn up to meet him, headed by his brother, Lieutenant John Mordaunt. They then drove out of the village towards Kineton to the little yellow stone lodge at the foot of Friz Hill where a triumphal arch had been erected decorated with the coats of arms of both families. Here, on the margin of the estate, the sun suddenly came out and the clouds dispersed, which was thought to be a very good omen. The estate workers who had been waiting at the lodge removed the horses and dragged the carriage down the drive to the house, preceded by the band of the Second Warwickshire militia playing tunes such as 'The Campbells Are Coming' and 'Home Sweet Home'.

It was by now very chilly and there were flurries of snow as the workers pulled the young master and mistress down the road below the Bath Wood, then across the great meadow and down the valley where the Dene brook meanders between the hawthorn bushes and willows. To their right lay the village, a cluster of cottages which Sir Charles was rebuilding in a more modern style for the benefit of his workers. The bridge over the River Dene was spanned by an arch decorated with a rose, a thistle and a true lover's knot. It was then that the young bride would have seen for the first time, strikingly set at the heart of the valley, the imposing house that was to be her home, a mass of yellow- and ochre-coloured stone, with its tall chimneys, its spire and towers outlined against a steely sky, its grey roof-tiles dusted with snow, its windows glimmering from the gaslight within.

Sir Charles and his bride were greeted by the cheers of the tenantry gathered on the lawn in front of the house. The Sunday school children, dressed in the red cloaks which had been given to them by Sir Charles's mother, lined the path to the door throwing flowers into the path of the bride, who, everybody agreed, was as beautiful as she was young. The laurel bushes were decorated with festoons of evergreens, and in spite of the cold there was no mistaking the warmth of the welcome. The Vicar of Walton, the Revd Edward Cadogan, a contemporary of Sir Charles's at Christ Church, Oxford,[22] stood in the pillared porch and made a speech, thanking Sir Charles for the 'kindly and fostering protection' of the house of Mordaunt, and, addressing the bride as this 'fair and gentle' lady, expressing the hope that the good will of all those at Walton would 'soften the trial of parting from her home of earlier years'. Sir Charles replied on behalf of his bride, saying that he was sure she would long remember 'with peculiar pleasure' their acclamations. He then thanked everyone for their presents and he was greeted with cheers and a 'bumper' for Lady Mordaunt.[23]

A phalanx of servants was drawn up in the impressive galleried entrance hall, cathedral-like with its polished marble columns and Gothic arches. The gaslight glowed on the stained glass windows which proudly trace the armorial history of the family back to the time of the Conqueror. Most of those waiting to greet the bride had been in the service of the Mordaunt family for years, and were firmly entrenched. Head of the household was the bachelor steward, Henry Bird, who had come to Walton as a boy nearly forty years before from Edinburgh, and had kept a fatherly eye on the young baronet since the tragic death of his father. Almost as powerful was Mrs Sage Ann Caborn, one of the Cobb tribe who had been in the service of the Dowager Lady Mordaunt's father, Bishop Murray, in the see of Sodor and Man and later at Rochester. Mrs Caborn, coming to Walton as Lady Mordaunt's personal maid, had worked her way into a position of authority as housekeeper, in charge of an army of housemaids; she had been with the family for forty years, and claimed to have been in the room when Sir Charles was born. Her brother, Frederick Cobb, who had started as an under-gardener, now lived in the agent's house and he too, as steward to the estate, was an important figure.

Most of the servants could remember the day when Sir Charles's father, Sir John, had been carried in bleeding after the shooting accident which was to be the cause of his death, leaving his son fatherless at the age of nine. The sadness of that terrible event had hung about the old house, cancelling out the happier memories of those times when the kindly Sir John had played cricket with his young sons, ridden with them or walked across the fields to the plantations which had been his special care. Now the sadder memories could perhaps be laid to rest as a new era began with the arrival of a bride; soon there would be a new generation of children to bring laughter into the house.

As the *Leamington Courier* put it:

> Oh happy they, the happiest of their kind,
> Whom gentler stars unite and in one fate,
> Their hearts, their fortunes and their beings bind.

There were many excitements for Harriett in the early days of her life at Walton. First there was the house to explore, the tenants to meet and the pleasure gardens, the kitchen garden and the hot-houses to visit. Then there were the wedding presents to examine, including a clock from the inhabitants of Wellesbourne with the message, 'We pray that with your honoured husband you may long be spared to perform the duties, exercise the hospitalities and dispense the graceful charities which belong to your high station'. The Walton villagers had clubbed together to give her a bible, saying that they had spent their lives under the kind care of the house of Mordaunt, and they hoped the book would prove a comfort under all circumstances. An epithalamium for Sir Charles, marked out in gold thread with coloured capital letters, was decorated by two doves bearing a ring and a verse which read

> Round Walton's heir and round his youthful bride
> Diffuse the nuptial blessing far and wide,
> Archived in splendour let their union be
> Upholden, grant they generations see.

In her lovely boudoir with its large windows looking out onto a stone balustraded balcony and across the lawns to the ha-ha and the fields and woods beyond, Harriett wrote enthusiastically to her friends, thanking them for their presents and inviting them to come and see her new home for themselves. Georgie Forbes and George Newport were at the top of her list, but, not knowing of the conditions that Harriett had laid down when she agreed to marry Sir Charles, they were wary of accepting her invitation so soon after the wedding. George Newport was clearly alarmed both by the invitation and by the indiscreet way it had been addressed. In his letter he wrote:

I am sorry to say that I cannot possibly get away from London. I had promised to go down to Witley for Xmas but find that I cannot even get away for that, so I am afraid I must refuse. What could have made you [send it] direct to Belgrave Square instead of Regents Park Barracks! I read the account of all your doings in the Morning Post, and I am so glad to hear you are so well and so happy.

Georgie Forbes was more forthcoming and just ten days after the wedding he wrote, not without some hesitation, to accept her invitation

9 King William Street,
City
December 17th.

My dearest Harriett,
Thanks very much for your letter and for asking me to come to Walton on the 8th and then you say if it would suit me better I may come the week before. Now its awfully good of you old thing, but I really want you to tell me exactly what you think and wish, and I am going to have the cheek to tell you what I should like to do, which is to come to you from Witley where I go on Saturday to stay till the 31st Monday. Now altho' you were good enough in your letter to ask me to come that week, you may perhaps change your mind or he might not like me to come so soon, therefore for goodness sake write and say no if it is the least little bit inconvenient. I shan't consider you any friend of mine if you don't say exactly what you think but as I do consider you one, I trust to your telling me to go to the D . . . l if you would rather be alone. Thanks very much for sending me the Leamington paper. Isn't it a stunning account, how I should have liked to have seen it all. London is so beastly dull & so am I after all the fun I've had since I have been away. I came to town on Thursday but have seen nobody, and not even any one in the streets except old Newport who I saw at Charles's [his brother Charles Forbes's] house on Friday. I hope he will accept your invitation but he has never said a word to me

about it and there is a chance of his not being able to get away
as I know he can't go to Witley for that reason, but I hope he
will be able to go to you. I am so glad you like Walton so much,
I knew you would. I think it quite charming, and hasn't he nice
horses. Horace Farquhar and I dine with Helen tonight and go
to the St James's to see *Hunted Down* which I hear is capital. I
am going to have tea with Lady Fife this evening in her new
house in Cavendish Square . . . I hope Mordaunt has had good
sport. Helen [Forbes] was dining at Broom Wood on Saturday
and is awfully well and not a bit the worse for her journey up
from Scotland. I am just going to leave the City and as Tommy
Kingscote is waiting for me I must shut up.

Ever yours affectionately,
GEORGE

Reassured by Harriett's reply Georgie Forbes paid a visit to Walton
in the new year. Sir Charles remained true to his promise that he
would welcome her friends and made no objection. A large party of
relations assembled for the Hunt Ball in the Town Hall at Stratford
on 9 January. Harriett's parents and sisters, as well as Sir Charles's
mother and sister, joined the 450 guests, among them many of the
great of the county – Lord Willoughby de Broke and Lord Guernsey,
the Earl of Aylesford's heir, with Colonel Little from Newbold Pacey,
the Granvilles and Paulets from Wellesbourne, the Gregory-Hoods
from Loxley, and Sir Robert Hamilton from Tiddington, hero of the
Indian Mutiny, who had undertaken all the arrangements with Mr
Starkey and Mr Allfrey. The stairs to the upper room were taste-
fully decorated with striking festoons of flowers, and the walls were
covered in crimson and white fluted drapery, while on the landings
there were clumps of gorse from which peeped out foxes, 'an excellent effect', according to the local paper.

On 14 January, after the family party had gone, Sir Charles took his
wife to the Warwickshire Yeomanry Cavalry Ball, organised by his
younger brother Johnny at the Shire Hall in Warwick, which was
decorated with draped mirrors and flags. By that time the weather
had turned cold and because of the frost the oyster table was 'con-
spicuous by its absence', the loss of this 'accustomed and invigorating
relish' causing much regret. Major Wise opened the dancing with Lady
Mordaunt which was the measure of her status within the county.
Throughout the evening the band played the waltz, quadrille, galop

and contre-dance 'in gay succession'. It was nearly six o'clock before Mr Superintendent Hickling, who was in charge of the police arrangements, had the satisfaction of seeing the last carriage take its departure.

Attendance at the Yeomanry Ball had been disappointing, and in general the Warwickshire winter season had declined since the days when Sir Charles's parents had engaged in a busy and seasonable round of charity balls and other events during the first month of the year. The family Harriett had married into, like many other county families of the time, had established a tradition of good works, the men mindful of their duties in the neighbourhood, taking the lead in local affairs, the women too, in the intervals of childbearing, playing their part in ministering to the poor, having been brought up in the belief that privilege must be balanced by good works and care for the less fortunate. This was the kind of dedication that Disraeli's hero Coningsby had admired in Lady Everingham, 'the graceful energy, and thorough acquaintance with details' with which she superintended schools and organised societies of relief. Sir Charles's father Sir John had been tireless in his public duties, serving on innumerable committees and subscribing liberally to charity. He had enjoyed his sporting activities but had been less dedicated to them than Sir Charles who devoted himself to hunting, shooting, fishing and cricket with an almost religious fervour. Political opponents had already begun to make capital out of the fact that Sir Charles, in his pursuit of fur and feather, was happy to absent himself from the House of Commons from July onwards and head for the moor and loch. Now he had acquired a wife who, youthful and pleasure-seeking as she was, hardly seemed cast in the philanthropic mould, and it was difficult to imagine her settling down and devoting her life to dispensing soup and flannel petticoats to the needy.

Sensing, perhaps, that the agent Mr Cobb and the butler Bird and housekeeper Mrs Caborn were too firmly entrenched to welcome interference, Harriett made little attempt to assert herself or to make any sweeping changes in the running of the household, which she left in the capable hands of Mrs Caborn, seldom giving directions but earning the respect of all the servants with her kind and polite manner. Mrs Caborn, touched by her youth and inexperience, later insisted that she had done everything she could to help the new bride and make her comfortable, 'she being so young'. Bird felt that he got on with her well, and he liked the way she would always thank him politely as he handed her the newspaper when she came in from her drive each day.

He very much appreciated the fact that she always treated him with kindness. The head gardener, William Broadbridge, for his part, was pleased by the interest that she took in the gardens. Whether alone or in company, for she frequently came out into the pleasure grounds with friends or family who were staying in the house, she would always stop and chat to him about the plants. She also got on well with her mother-in-law and was soon on intimate, friendly terms with Alice Cadogan, the clergyman's wife, taking her out driving and often visiting the Parsonage where she was a great favourite with the children.

Those who visited Walton were struck by the couple's happiness and their apparent affection for each other. Sir Charles went out of his way to please his wife by making her family and friends welcome. Her parents appreciated his efforts, and in their turn were kind and friendly towards Sir Charles. It did seem as if in the choice of his beautiful and charming wife Sir Charles had at last excelled. Up to now, in spite of his wealth and privilege, he had often seemed insecure, relying on his more handsome and more confident brother Johnny. When Charlie left Eton, his housemaster had written 'I am glad to have had the benefit of his example and influence in my house for the last five years', adding, however, that although he was amiable by nature, he suffered from a certain diffidence, unlike Johnny, who lacked exertion when it came to academic work but was infinitely more self-assured. Charlie's enthusiasm for games was not always matched by success; on the cricket field it was his younger brothers who could boast of the highest scores. But the housemaster had been sure that in spite of his diffidence Charlie would grow up to be an estimable man[25] and now that he had reached the age of thirty, there were few who would deny that the prediction had come true.

Admirable though Sir Charles certainly was, there must have been times when he seemed a trifle dull if compared with the more poised and 'detrimental' young men Harriett had known before her marriage. She certainly had no compunction about continuing her flirtatious behaviour which some observers found distinctly puzzling. They said nothing at the time, although later they recalled, and reported, what they had seen.

For example, one evening in the January after Lady Mordaunt's first Christmas at Walton, Broadbridge the gardener came upon her at dusk in the kitchen garden with Georgie Forbes, who was holding her hand and also had one arm round her waist. Broadbridge was only a few yards from them, and when they saw him, they immediately separated and Lady Mordaunt started talking to him about violets, her face colouring up as she did so. Broadbridge, not unnaturally, was somewhat surprised at this encounter.

Harriett's brother-in-law Johnny was equally startled one day, when he was alone in the library at Walton reading a book, to see her enter the room on her own, everybody else having gone to church. Apparently without preliminaries, she said to him 'Charlie kisses all my sisters, and I don't see why you should not give me a kiss.' This he did 'as a brother might a sister', and said he hoped they would be good friends. A few weeks later, when Sir Charles and some others went over to Staple Hill where Johnny lived, his brother having rebuilt and extended the farm house for him, Harriett joined the lunch party. Afterwards all the gentlemen, with the exception of Johnny who was indisposed, went off to join a pigeon shooting party in Wellesbourne. When Harriett was left alone with Johnny in the drawing-room, she threw herself into his arms and kissed his hands. He was quite taken aback by her behaviour and did not give her any encouragement, but from that time he did not go over so much to Walton as he had in the past. He said nothing about the incident to his brother, for fear of upsetting him.

Since neither his brother nor Broadbridge saw fit to tell Sir Charles what they had seen, he remained oblivious, always remembering his promise to trust his wife. Although he had told her that he would respect her privacy and would not expect her to show him all her letters, she did let him see the majority, although the ones that came from George Forbes and Charles Newport she locked away secretly in her escritoire. She had written to the Prince thanking him for his present, which was 'proper' enough, although it was perhaps less correct to have sent him a small present in return, thus putting him under the obligation to reply. She had to wait some time before she heard from him, and it was not until 13 January that he wrote to her from Sandringham. He had returned from his enjoyable six weeks' trip to the wedding in St Petersburg, where he had been a great success with the Russian ladies, to find his wife very unwell, and it had soon become evident that her indisposition could not solely be accounted for by the fact that she was expecting a child in February. As she became wracked with pain, rheumatic fever was diagnosed, and there was much anxiety in royal circles, even though the Prince managed to remain as cheerful and as ebullient as ever, as his letter to Harriett reveals:

My dear Lady Mordaunt,

I am quite shocked never to have answered your kind letter, written some time ago, and for the very pretty muffetees, which are very useful this cold weather. I had no idea where you had been staying since your marriage, but Francis Knollys[26] told me that you were in Warwickshire. I suppose you will be in London for the opening of Parliament, when I hope I may perhaps have the pleasure of seeing you, and of making the acquaintance of Sir Charles. I was in London for only two nights, and returned here on Saturday; the rails were so slippery that we thought we should never arrive here. There has been a heavy fall of snow here, and we are able to use our sledges, which is capital fun.

Believe me, yours ever sincerely,

ALBERT EDWARD

Parliament had been prorogued until 5 February, so there was still some time to wait before Harriett had a chance of meeting her old friends in London. Meanwhile the cold weather referred to by the Prince had spread all over the country; near Moncreiffe, trains had become stuck in snowdrifts, and in Warwickshire too the rivers and lakes were frozen and there were many accidents on the ice. Fortunately the thaw had set in by the time the hounds met at Walton on 28 January, and Harriett wrote off for the second time to invite Newport to come down, her husband having offered him a horse for the occasion. He replied in a much less stilted tone than he had before, Georgie Forbes perhaps having told him that nothing had changed and that Harriett was ready to carry on old friendships as before. In his earlier letter he had addressed her as 'My dear Harriett', but when he wrote again from the Regent's Park Barracks, he reassumed all his old cousinly familiarity.

You nice Harriett,

It really is too duckish of you asking me again to Walton though I hate your saying you think it might be a bother to me to write an answer to you when you know there is nothing I like so well. I know you will think me a brute for I cannot come, as I have arranged to go down to Weston on Tuesday for the last three days of the shooting season and have got two friends going with me. Will you thank Sir Charles very much for offering to mount me and tell him that I am very sorry that I cannot accept it. I am so glad to hear that you are coming up to London and shall count the days to the time. I saw Georgie Forbes yesterday and we talked a good deal about you. I am orderly today and he is coming up here presently to see me, I know. I know who I should like to be coming instead.

Goodbye darling, I shall be so glad to see your nice old face again.

Ever yours affectionately,
NEWPORT

The meet at Walton attracted a large field, Mr Lucy of Charlecote bringing six fine greys, one of which unfortunately died during the run. The hounds found in a spinney near Wellesbourne Wood and after dodging about the country for some time, lost the scent in the neighbourhood of Charlecote.

The Queen opened Parliament that year dressed in plain black silk with the ribbon and star of the Garter, wearing the Koh-i-noor diamond on a necklace at her throat. She was attended by her daughters the Princesses Helena and Louise and by her son Prince Arthur who wore the very plain uniform of the Royal Military Academy. The Prince of Wales did not attend. It was on 11 February that Mr Disraeli rose amidst loud and continual cheers from the ministerial benches to make his promised statement about his proposals for reform, and for many weeks there were eloquent debates on this subject. During the first week in March there was much excitement in parliamentary circles as Lord Derby explained the details of the Reform Bill to his supporters, and Disraeli made a speech to the House about the Bill, with the debates continuing well into April.

Sir Charles took his wife up to London for the opening of Parliament as the Prince had hoped. They stayed at the Alexandra Hotel, Hyde Park Corner, Sir Charles attending the important debates, and Lady Mordaunt doubtless finding many opportunities to meet her friends, including the Prince of Wales.

On 21 February Princess Alexandra gave birth to a daughter, Princess Louise,[27] but she remained seriously ill. When her mother came over to see her in March she was greatly shocked by her daughter's appearance; Alix looked thin and was still in pain, crippled by the inflammation in her joints, her left knee being particularly badly affected. The Prince was concerned enough to move his desk into the invalid's room so that he could be with her when he was attending to his correspondence, but he made no effort to curtail his social activities and he was often out until very late at night, even when his wife was at her worst. The Princess would lie awake, refusing to take her opiates for fear of missing him when he returned. By the end of April, she had begun to make some progress and was sleeping better at night, the swelling on her knee having subsided, but she was still immobilised and far from well so that there was considerable criticism when the Prince made plans to go to Paris as usual. He had developed a love of this spirited city from the earliest age. There he could enjoy what Sir William Knollys politely but disapprovingly called 'the female Paris notorieties', the *demi-mondaines* or *grandes cocottes*, Blanche d'Artigny, Cora Pearl, Madame Barucci, to name but a few, who could be courted well away from watching English eyes. The Prince also consorted with delightful actresses such as Hortense Schneider, while the attractive Princesse de Sagan, although separated from her husband, made her house freely available whenever he wanted it.

Harriett had been working on Sir Charles in the hope that he would take her to Paris. This he obligingly did, but their visit did not coincide with the Prince's. However, when he heard that Lady Mordaunt was going to Paris, the Prince charged her with the task of buying him a lady's umbrella. The thought of the innocent Sir Charles accompanying his wife round the streets of Paris while she carried out the Prince's commission would have caused much ribaldry among the Prince and his friends. A lady's umbrella, to the lewd mind, could be construed as a symbol of male incompetency, which was relevant in view of the fact that Lady Mordaunt had not yet conceived after nearly six months of marriage. This opened the way for raucous suggestions that one of their set could easily succeed where Sir Charles had failed. The Prince, however, was as discreet as ever when he wrote to Harriett from Sandringham on 7 May.

My dear Lady Mordaunt,

Many thanks for your letter, and I am very sorry that I should have given you so much trouble looking for the ladies' umbrella for me at Paris. I am very glad to hear that you enjoyed your stay there. I shall be going there on Friday next; and as the Princess is so much better, [I] shall hope to remain a week there. If there is any commission I can do for you there it will give me the greatest pleasure to carry it out. I regret very much not to have been able to call upon you since your return, but hope to do so when I come back from Paris, and have an opportunity of making the acquaintance of your husband.

Two weeks later the Prince was back in London. He seemed unconcerned that the London gossips were linking his name with Hortense Schneider and the Princesse de Sagan. Embarrassingly, the Princesse had recently given birth to a son, her first child for nine years, and although she had managed to engineer a timely, if brief, reconciliation with her husband, the dates somehow seemed to tie up with one of the Prince's visits to Paris.[28] The Queen, reading reports of her son's relationship with Hortense Schneider in the sedate columns of *The Times*, was concerned enough to suggest that he should avoid further trouble by keeping well away from the festivities of the forthcoming London season. But as usual he took no notice of her advice, reminding her that since she spent most of her time out of London, it was essential for him to remain and fulfil the public duties which she should have been undertaking herself.

4
The Season of 1867

In May Sir Charles set up a town establishment at 15 Chesham Street, not far from Lady Kinnoull's establishment in Belgrave Square. He had perhaps become aware by this time that his lovely wife was turning out to be an expensive acquisition. It was clear that she did not intend to do the London season by halves and a new footman, Frederick Johnson, had been taken on to accompany her when she went out, standing at the back of the carriage whatever the weather, and waiting for her in the servants' hall until the carriage was called to take her home. Johnson joined Sir Charles in Warwickshire on 15 May where they remained for a week before going up to London.

On 24 May the Prince was granted his long-awaited chance to meet Sir Charles. The carriage had been called that day for nine o'clock in the morning in order to take Sir Charles and Lady Mordaunt to the grand review of the Horse Guards. Afterwards they were invited back to Dudley House where they met the Prince. The day did not end there, for that evening there was a visit to the Covent Garden opera, followed by a sortie to the house of Lord Derby, the Prince's friend.

The following day Georgy gave birth to her first baby, a son called William. The Earl of Dudley, prostrate with anxiety, retired to bed himself as he was to do for all his wife's seven confinements. Earlier in the year Helen Forbes had also had a son, and Duchess Louisa a second daughter. On 29 May Harriett visited Georgy and the baby on her way to the theatre. Her brother-in-law Iain, Louisa's husband, dined at Chesham Street alone with Harriett on 30 May, on a night when Sir Charles was home late as the House of Commons did not rise until after two in the morning.

Soon the season was in full swing and night after night the carriage was called to convey Lady Mordaunt with Johnson in attendance to parties given by the Duke of Devonshire, Lady Emhurst, Lady Londonderry, and by the Duke of Montrose at 45 Belgrave Square. There was also a fancy dress ball at the home of Mrs Washington Hibbert. Lady Londonderry, one of the great hostesses of the day, had invited to her house in Park Lane an impressive contingent of royalty, including the Prince of Wales, the Duke of Teck, son-in-law to the Duke of Cambridge, and Prince Edward of Saxe-Weimar, a nephew of Queen Adelaide. On this particular night Johnson waited in the servants' hall until ten past two in the morning for Lady Mordaunt's carriage to be called and as always he was expected to accompany his mistress on her morning visits the next day.

Frederick Johnson soon realised that he had undertaken an arduous task. Indefatigable as she was in the pursuit of pleasure, Lady Mordaunt expected him to work long hours with little or no respite. During the course of the next six weeks the carriage was called out in the evening twenty-eight times, mostly returning around two o'clock in the morning, and sometimes even later. This was usually on top of a heavy day spent calling on various people, or driving around the Park. When she was driven out, Lady Mordaunt was sometimes accompanied by one of her young lady friends, Miss Louisa Scott or one of Lord Vivian's daughters.[29] Occasionally there were visits to places of interest, such as the Kensington Museum of Arts, or the Hall of Arts and Sciences to see the Queen lay the foundation stone. One Saturday the carriage was out for eight hours, mainly driving around the Park seeing and being seen, arriving back at seven and going out again at nine to the opera. Sundays were rather less strenuous, with at most a dinner party in the evening at the grandmother's house, which would mean an early night – to Johnson's relief. Occasionally he was allowed one complete day off, when he enjoyed himself staying at home 'doing nothing but reading and thinking'. In spite of his long hours, however, Johnson did find time to keep a diary in which he noted down the details of every expedition. This was a common practice among footmen who were anxious to improve their writing skills and in general to 'better' themselves. It was also a well-known fact that such diaries could command a high price as evidence in a case of matrimonial conflict. Lady Mordaunt, whose reputation for flightiness was already firmly established among the servants, was just the kind of lady whose past activities might one day come under scrutiny.

On 4 June the Mordaunt carriage took a party from Chesham Street to Waterloo for the journey to Ascot. The Prince also attended the races, and caused some of the 'fashionable female celebrities' to be invited. The crowds gave the Prince a very 'flat reception'. They would far rather have seen his beautiful wife.

Shortly after her return to London that evening, Lady Mordaunt again called the carriage, and Johnson did not get to bed until mid-night. The next day her ladyship had to be conveyed to Paddington so that she could take the train to Epsom, but at least she did not go out again that evening, and for once Johnson was able to get to bed by eleven. 'Wonderful' he commented.

During the week of 10 June, as Sir Charles had no parliamentary duties, he removed his wife from the London scene and took her down to his Northamptonshire estate at Wicken. Leaving home at three o'clock, they travelled to Buckingham station from Euston, arriving at half-past seven. Johnson recorded that they were met by all the 'Phesentry' who lined the avenue to Wicken Park. There was the inevitable triumphal arch, and the horses were as usual taken out of the shafts so that the workers could have the doubtful pleasure of dragging the carriage up the road. Johnson described how 'the bells rang out a merry peal of welcome and Sir Charles and my lady were so pleased'. The next day they went out in a hired chariot visiting all the farmers and driving through the villages of Perry and Grafton. 'It was so jolly' wrote Johnson who evidently preferred this style of life to the gruelling social round in London. The following day they had time to look at the village and the church, and Johnson himself enjoyed a very pleasant country walk with Jessie Clarke the lady's maid. On Tuesday 13 June they posted through Stony Strat-ford to Wolverton where, as Johnson put it 'the poor people met her Ladyship with bokeys of flowers'. They left for London at eleven o'clock, and that evening, without giving herself or Johnson any time to recover from the journey, she called the carriage out and ordered the coachman to convey her to a ball in Grosvenor Square. She ar-rived home at two in the morning.

In the course of the next two weeks, Johnson saw the Prince several times, noting that he was present at a ball held by the Earl of Brad-ford, Lord Newport's father, on Saturday 15 June, as well as at Lady Molesworth's 'rout' in Eaton Place a few days later and at Lady Rendlesham's.[30] The Princess never appeared, for she was still vir-tually immobile, with the leg which had been particularly badly af-fected by her illness now in a splint and a sling. Many people were critical of the fact that the Prince still continued to abandon her in the evenings. They were also shocked by rumours that in Paris he had consorted with undesirable women in the least reputable parts of the capital and that in addition he had been seen in England 'spooning' with an English titled lady.[31] The fact that he was now determined to enjoy the London season while his wife languished at home did not endear him to the more sober members of society. It seems that for the general public, the Princess, slim and beautiful, with her large eyes and 'sly sideways look',[32] was far more popular than her husband. They felt cheated when the Prince appeared without her, believing that the real truth about her illness was being kept from them.

As for Sir Charles, he was probably happy to let his wife go her own ways in the stuffy ballrooms of the great while he kept out of her way at the House of Commons. Like many wives she would have been pleased for him to be otherwise engaged in the afternoon as well as in the evening, and she certainly encouraged him to occupy any free time he might have had shooting pigeons at Hurlingham where rock doves imported by train from Scotland were used as targets.[33] That she spoke to the Prince on the subject is revealed in one of his letters:

> My dear Lady Mordaunt
>
> When I had the pleasure of seeing you on Saturday last you mentioned to me about a new Gun Club for Pigeon shooting in which your husband takes an interest and wishes me to become a Patron of it.
>
> If he will call on me some afternoon I shall be only too happy to talk the matter over with him.

We do not know whether Sir Charles took up this offer; most likely he did not. It was still his policy to steer clear of the Prince and he encouraged his wife to do the same, remembering the warning given him by his brother-in-law Lord Dudley.

Sir Charles had never made a habit of staying in London for the whole of the season, in fact for at least eight years he had abandoned his parliamentary duties in late June and travelled to Norway for the salmon fishing, remaining in London for only a few days before going up to Walton and then on to the shooting lodge at Corrour. He would have liked this pattern to continue and had hoped that his wife would accompany him to Norway. However she made it clear that she could hardly be expected to leave London with the season still in full swing. So he had to content himself with pigeon-shooting in the afternoons and then listening to long debates in the Commons on such important matters as the representation of the people and the question of suffrage, topics which did not interest his wife at all.

On only one occasion did Johnson record fetching Sir Charles to a ball attended by his wife. It was on Monday 17 June that the carriage had been called to take Lady Mordaunt to Kingston House in Prince's Gate, the home of Lord Listowel, who, at thirty-three years old, with a young wife and a baby, was one of the more youthful hosts that season. Johnson's orders were to fetch Sir Charles from Westminster after delivering Lady Mordaunt, but as the House did not rise until twenty-five past one, Johnson recorded that he had to wait there for two hours before going on to Lord Listowel's with Sir Charles and waiting there in the servants' hall until the small hours.

While her son had remained in London, enjoying himself among his friends, the Queen had immured herself at Balmoral. She occasionally emerged, to the delight of the locals, on an expedition, and on one occasion she drove through Braemar to the Falls of Corriemulzie in bright warm weather. She returned to London in June but was less than willing to show herself in public. The absence of the Queen from the evening ball at Buckingham Palace on 25 June was explained officially as being due to the fact that agitation, or worry, or too much talking in the evenings, always caused her sleepless nights, distressing sick headaches and a sense of great exhaustion.

The Prince of Wales, conversely, suffered from none of these symptoms. He had no difficulty in sleeping and was able to rise early however late he had been up the night before. On one occasion, hearing that his sister Vicky's little son Sigismund had died of meningitis, he sent Harriett a note telling her that in consequence he was very sorry to say that he would not have the pleasure of seeing her at the ball that evening. This sad event did not, however, curtail his enjoyment for long, and he was among the guests at Lady Rendlesham's house at 42 Grosvenor Square, when the dancing lasted almost until dawn, the long-suffering Johnson waiting until ten to five in the morning for his mistress to call the carriage. This was, as he put it with commendable restraint, 'a bother'. Sir Charles was probably not present on that occasion, the House of Commons being counted out at ten past two, and Johnson making no mention of taking him to the party. The following day Johnson recorded for the first time that the Prince called at the house in Chesham Street, Sir Charles being out at the time, probably doing some pigeon-shooting. The Prince took tea with Lady Mordaunt alone. Nobody told Sir Charles about the visit, so no complaints were made. That evening Sir Charles did accompany his wife to Buckingham Palace for a state ball attended by the Prince. Neither the Queen nor Princess Alexandra put in an appearance.

Towards the end of the month, the festivities worked up to a crescendo, the carriage being out all day, and in the evenings going from one great house to another mainly at the invitation of the Prince's friends, so that Harriett had plenty of opportunities to meet him. On 28 June she dined at 48 Grosvenor Street with the Aylesfords, whose heir, Lord Guernsey, later to earn the nickname of 'Sporting Joe', was one of the Prince's racing partners as well as his personal friend. After dinner the party continued at the Countess of Bradford's and then most people went on to Lady Hoare's ball in Kensington. On 1 July the evening started at six o'clock with another visit to Lady Hoare and then on to the houses of Lady Derby and the Duchess of Westminster followed by a visit to the Duchess of Buckingham at Chandos House.

It is probable that the Earl of Dudley was too preoccupied with his wife and infant son to take as much notice of his sister-in-law's behaviour as he normally would have done. Sir Charles, still mindful of his promise to be tolerant of her activities, perhaps paid less attention than was wise. Even if Princess Alexandra had begun to realise what was happening, there was little she could do about it, except to be patient and long-suffering. 'She is very fond of Bertie, tho' not blind,' wrote the Queen who was, however, of the opinion that there were faults on both sides. 'I am sorry too for Bertie' she wrote; 'I don't think she makes his home comfortable; she is never ready for breakfast – not being out of her room till 11 often, and poor Bertie breakfasts alone and then she alone. I think it gets much worse instead of better; it makes me unhappy and anxious.'[34]

Sir Charles, aware that his wife was consorting with the Prince and his friends, was no doubt as worried as the Queen. 'Hopes there cannot be!!,' Victoria had burst out in the early days of her son's marriage, convinced that Alix's frenzied life style was preventing her from bearing children. Sir Charles could well have uttered the same cry. Although Harriett never confided in him fully, Sir Charles knew that she had been consulting Dr Priestley and he was led to believe that she was being treated for 'irregularities' and an ulceration of the womb. He had also begun to realise that she was highly strung and that she could become quite hysterical, especially at certain times of the month. The doctor certainly thought that she was short of sleep and that the endless late nights were undermining her health.

He advised Sir Charles to take her abroad as soon as possible and meanwhile to cut down on the social activities. Sir Charles therefore made arrangements to set off for Switzerland in July and for several days before they left he kept Harriett at home with a succession of what Johnson described as 'heavy' dinner parties. Harriett did, however, have one last chance to see the Prince. Johnson recorded that she attended a ball 'to meet the Prince and the Pashe of Egypt' on 7 July, going on afterwards to a second ball at Lady Willoughby de Broke's and arriving home at three in the morning.

George Newport, observing Harriett with the acuteness of a man who was still deeply fond of the girl he had loved since childhood, did not fail to notice how sad she sometimes looked, and especially now that she was to be taken away from the heat of London to cool off among the glaciers. 'Darling,' he wrote, 'I was so, so sorry for you last night.' After she had left for Switzerland he wrote to tell her that he intended to travel up to Scotland in August

> I hope to get away in time for the 12th. You poor old dear, I was so sorry for you the other day – you looked in such low spirits. However you may console yourself as there is not a single soul left here. I came from Goodwood today . . . I feel so dull here almost all by myself that I don't know what to do. Write to me again if you have nothing better to do. After Monday direct to Weston Shiffnal.

In spite of everybody's fears that she would find Switzerland dull, Harriett enjoyed herself there far more than she expected, the beautiful scenery and her adoring husband proving an acceptable substitute for the hectic social life and her more racy companions. For Charlie there can only have been considerable relief in having her to himself, well away from sophisticated friends with their spicy talk and the 'fie-fie' stories which he himself found rather distasteful. He was at times shocked by his wife's conversation, as well as by the 'naughty' books she was in the habit of reading. The openness with which she discussed topics and used words which he would not have expected to hear from a young lady's lips also surprised him. However, he dismissed any apprehensions he might have felt and continued to humour her, even if he at times regretted her choice of companions.

After seeing off the master and mistress from Victoria Station on 9 July, Johnson and the rest of the staff packed up all the luggage before leaving for Warwick. Johnson spent a day paying bills and in

the evening enjoyed a visit to the Sun Music Hall. The next night he
went to the 'Pervillian', which he found 'very jolly'. His diary entry
for 13 July ran: 'finished packing then came down to Warwick. Thus
ends the London season of '67.'

5
Life in the Country

There was some respite for the staff while the master and mistress were abroad and Johnson enjoyed the weeks at Walton. Among the entertainments he joined in were the cottagers' flower show at Ettington with tea and dancing to a band in the Park. 'Came home by moonlight, lovely, enjoyed it much,' he wrote. He also went to the Alveston flower show which was held in the grounds of Avoncliffe, Sir Robert Hamilton's house on the river at Tiddington, and after that looked over the house that Shakespeare was born in, describing it as a 'very nice place'.

Soon after they returned from Switzerland, Sir Charles and Lady Mordaunt left for Scotland, accompanied by Bird and Johnson and by the lady's maid Jessie Clarke. Meanwhile, members of the royal family were assembling at Balmoral without much enthusiasm. 'You must summon your courage and energy now for the amusements of your approaching Highland life,' Prince Arthur told Princess Louise, adding that it would all be rather a bore if the weather turned out to be wet, 'a thing which *occasionally* happens in Scotland'.[35]

Lady Mordaunt, for her part, had no intention of sitting on her own in a shooting lodge while Sir Charles spent his days in the hills, and when he went off to the wilds of Corrour, she made arrangements to spend a fortnight at Newe with her sister Helen, who had arranged a house party which included some of the Prince's closest friends – among them Captain Arthur Farquhar, a Forbes relation, and Count Maffei, Chief Secretary at the Italian Embassy.[36]

After leaving Newe, Harriet went on to stay with the Atholls, Iain and Louisa, at Blair Castle and in mid-August she left for Moncreiffe. Her family met her at Perth station and Charlie joined her at Moncreiffe soon afterwards. During this time Jessie Clarke was allowed some leave of absence which she spent with friends in Scotland. From Moncreiffe Harriett and Charlie, with Bird, Johnson and Clarke, went on to Sir William Scott's house in Roxburghshire, the home of Harriett's best friend Louisa Scott.[37] After a few days Captain Farquhar arrived there, and Harriett introduced him to her husband for the first time, describing him as a friend of the family. Bird observed that the Captain appeared to be with Lady Mordaunt more than the other guests, and although he himself did not notice anything particularly untoward there was certainly some talk among Sir William's servants about his behaviour.

The fact that Arthur Farquhar was approved of by the Moncreiffes gave him, in Sir Charles's eyes, the stamp of respectability. Sir Charles trustingly invited him to Walton for the shooting and made him welcome there. He had after all promised his wife that he would be hospitable to her former acquaintances.

They arrived home from Scotland on 24 September and were joined two days later by Count Maffei who stayed for three or four days. On 28 September Captain Farquhar came for a more prolonged visit of several weeks. There were other guests in the house, including one of Charlie's Warwickshire friends, George Wise, who gained Johnson's approval by giving him a tip of five shillings when he went away.

The servants were not impressed by Captain Farquhar. They soon noticed that he was much less interested in the normal country pursuits than the other gentlemen, and he was always happy to remain behind when the rest went shooting. He and Lady Mordaunt were often seen together and it was not long before this became a topic of conversation. The servants noticed that on one particular Sunday when Sir Charles, the guests and almost all the servants went to church as usual, Lady Mordaunt and Captain Farquhar stayed behind in the house. Jessie Clarke was aware that the Captain was frequently alone with Lady Mordaunt in her boudoir which was next to her bedroom, and on one occasion when he had not realised that Jessie was about, he came into the bedroom and took some flowers from Lady Mordaunt's toilet table. In the same way Broadbridge saw them in the garden together one day when Sir Charles and two other guests had gone out hunting. He observed Lady Mordaunt putting flowers into her hair and asking the Captain's opinion as to which suited her best. Captain Farquhar made a reply, but he spoke in an undertone and the gardener was not able to hear what he said. Although there was nothing improper in either of these incidents, yet there was something not entirely correct either, and the servants felt uneasy about the relationship, labelling the Captain 'sneaky Farquhar'.

Johnny Mordaunt already had some cause to be suspicious of his sister-in-law's character, and he did not fail to notice that one day when his brother had arranged to shoot over the farm at Staple Hill, Captain Farquhar did not join in the morning shooting and arrived later with Harriett for luncheon. Alice Cadogan, the clergyman's wife, found that when Lady Mordaunt had her own friends staying at the Hall, she did not invite the Cadogans down to meet them nor did she make her usual informal visits to the Parsonage. Young and frivolous as she was, she had not as yet made any strenuous efforts to take on charitable responsibilities and she clearly felt that the social life of the neighbourhood was not worth cultivating. Johnson's diary lists various shopping expeditions, including one into Leamington for the purpose of buying half a dozen pairs of socks, and Lady Mordaunt did on one occasion order the carriage for a visit to Warwick Castle. She had, of course, what fashionable ladies described as their 'work', which mainly encompassed various forms of needlework. Also, in common with other ladies in the neighbourhood, she was trying to develop her wood-carving skills. In Thomas Kendall's atelier in Warwick, classes were held for aspiring lady wood-carvers and there were plenty of examples of Kendall's own work at Warwick Castle and at Walton too, for he had designed a magnificent sideboard for Sir Charles's dining-room.[38] Although Lady Mordaunt could hardly aspire to imitate Thomas Kendall's fine carving, she certainly bought a collection of tools, which she kept in her boudoir, and it seemed that she welcomed any muscular help that she could get. On one occasion when Bird went into the boudoir, he found Captain Farquhar there with Lady Mordaunt and he noticed that they were sitting rather close together, surrounded by the wood-carving tools.

Sir Charles, of course, was frequently absent, either hunting or shooting or playing his part in local affairs. On the evening of 9 October Johnson accompanied him to a large public dinner in Stratford and heard 'some very good speeches', which provided the footman with a welcome change from the more tedious expeditions organised by Lady Mordaunt.

Having shown his wife to the Wicken tenants in the summer, Sir Charles had now arranged a visit to his Somerset estates, and on 16 October they left together for Frome from Warwick Station at eight o'clock in the morning. They stayed for a couple of days at the Royal Hotel in Weston-super-Mare and drove about showing Lady Mordaunt off to the tenants around Badgworth and other villages, passing through 'the most lovely country by Cheddar Cliffs' as the footman appreciatively put it. On 24 October they came home through Bath, Swindon, Didcot, Oxford and Banbury. On their return, Johnson once again became involved in his more mundane task of accompanying her ladyship on various visits, for example to her mother-in-law at Goldicote. He very much appreciated a day off which he spent with Cobb the steward and Mrs Caborn the housekeeper looking over Warwick Castle, which he described as 'the loveliest place I ever saw; had my photograph taken and returned home early'.

The Prince, meanwhile, had been doing his duty by accompanying his wife, his two small sons and his infant daughter on a trip to Wiesbaden. Official bulletins concerning the Princess's health had insisted that reports of her deafness were much exaggerated, and that she was in fact making a good recovery. The usual observers of royal doings, however, crowding round the royal yacht Osborne at Wool-wich and indulging in the 'natural desire to catch a glimpse of the royal visitors', could not avoid noticing that the small invalid car-riage in which the Princess was sitting, had to be carried, 'sedan chair like' into the saloon of the boat which demonstrated only too well her continuing immobility. At Wiesbaden there was certainly some improvement in her condition, and it was reported that she had begun to put on weight and to walk about a little in her room, her recovery no doubt assisted by the fact that she had her beloved Bertie with her. Restless as ever, however, the Prince left her to come home on her own and the Queen was shocked when she saw her in Novem-ber, noting how thin and frail she looked. 'The poor leg is completely stiff and it remains to be seen whether it will ever quite get right again' wrote the Queen who was afraid that Bertie's whole existence would become 'deranged' as a result. She need not have worried. The Prince had no intention of letting his wife's immobility and deafness curtail his own pleasures.

Soon after his return to England, Harriett had re-established con-tact by writing to the Prince about some grey ponies they had evi-dently discussed at a previous meeting. It seems that she had already expressed some interest in acquiring them. The Prince replied on 1 November from White's:

My dear Lady Mordaunt, – Many thanks for your letter, which I received this morning. I cannot tell you at this moment the exact height of the ponies in question, but I think they are just under

14 hands; but as soon as I know for certain I shall not fail to let you know. I would be only too happy if they will suit you, and have the pleasure of seeing them in your hands. It is quite an age since I have seen or heard anything of you; but I trust you had a pleasant trip abroad, and I suppose you have been in Scotland since. Lord Derby[40] has kindly asked me to shoot with him at Buckenham, on the 9th of next month, and I hope I may perhaps have the pleasure of seeing you there.

Believe me, yours ever sincerely

ALBERT EDWARD

6

The Hunting Season

Sir Charles had no intention of accepting any invitations that might bring his wife into contact with the Prince, and if Lord Derby did send them an invitation to Buckenham it was refused. As far as Sir Charles was concerned there was little point in leaving Walton at this time of the year since he could get all the sport he wanted at home. Harriett seemed contented enough, and to his delight she had become increasingly loving towards him. There were even signs, at last, that she was expecting his child. It came as something of a surprise to him when at the beginning of November she suddenly announced that she intended to go to London to order some carpets and to make some other purchases. She said that she had also fixed to see Dr Priestley. Charlie made no objection, and offered to accompany her, but she said that she preferred to go alone, telling him that he would only be in the way. Charlie had by now fallen into the habit of letting her do as she liked in order to avoid a scene. Knowing that she could be in the early stages of pregnancy, he was anxious to avoid a confrontation or to put any obstacles in her way.

Harriett had booked for two nights at the Palace Hotel, Buckingham Gate, and she and Jessie Clarke were given rooms sixteen and seventeen on the first floor of the hotel, which went with number eleven sitting-room. The bedrooms were not adjacent to the sitting-room but were situated a little way further up the passage. They were booked in by the hall porter, and that evening dinner was brought to Lady Mordaunt in the private sitting-room. Jessie was called at about half past ten to prepare her mistress for bed, and Lady Mordaunt then told her that she could retire as her services would not be required any more that evening. Jessie was startled as she went back to her own room to meet Captain Farquhar on the landing as she had no idea he had arrived at the hotel.

Next morning Lady Mordaunt ordered breakfast in her bedroom, and when Jessie went to the sitting-room to ring the bell, the waiter asked her whether the gentleman the lady had dined with also required breakfast. Jessie replied that she had received no orders to that effect. She was by this time beginning to suspect that Captain Farquhar and her mistress had slept together, but she could see nothing in the room to confirm her suspicion, although she did notice that some of the furniture was arranged differently and some books had been moved. That morning Lady Mordaunt was absent in town until lunch time and in the afternoon she went out again, leaving Jessie behind at the hotel. In the evening she dined between six and seven, after writing a quick letter to her husband:

> My darling Charlie,
>   One line in great haste to say that I shall not be able to leave here by the 12 o'clock train tomorrow, but will come by the one that leaves Paddington at 3.50 if you will send the brougham to meet me. I felt horribly dull all by myself yesterday evening but have not had much time as yet today as I have had such lots to do. I have seen Priestley and will tell you about it when I come home.
>
> Ever your affectionate wife,
HARRIETT MORDAUNT

Lady Mordaunt went out that evening about half-past six, saying that she was going to the theatre with Princess Soltikoff. She told Jessie not to wait up for her. Jessie went to bed at half past ten, by which time Lady Mordaunt had not returned.

The next day they left for home, and shortly afterwards Lady Mordaunt was taken ill during the night. Dr Orford, the Wellesbourne physician,[41] was called in and he told her firmly that she must stay in bed as he believed that she had suffered a miscarriage. Mrs Cadogan came down from the Parsonage to see her and was puzzled when she asked whether there were rumours circulating in Warwickshire concerning Charlie's inability to father a child. 'Certainly not' Mrs Cadogan replied. Harriett then said Dr Priestley had told her that some of her Warwickshire neighbours had asked him if there was ever likely to be an heir at Walton and he had assured them that there was every probability of an heir and that there was no reason whatever why Sir Charles and Lady Mordaunt should not have a large family.

On the first day that Lady Mordaunt was able to leave her bedroom and go to her sitting-room, Jessie noted, while arranging the toilet-table, a letter which was almost hidden under a pincushion. The letter was dated 9 November 1867, the day that Lady Mordaunt had left London, and the lady's maid was unable to resist reading it. It was headed 'The Tower, Saturday' which was bound to arouse her interest, as Lady Mordaunt had told her that Captain Farquhar was currently stationed there.

> Darling – I arrived here this morning, about a quarter to nine o'clock, very tired and sleepy, as you may suppose.
>
> I have seen the *Morning Post* and found my name entered among the arrivals at the Palace Hotel – Farmer, instead of Farquhar. So it is all right, darling. I was afraid Charlie would be suspicious if he saw my name in the arrivals at the hotel with you ...
>
> Yours,
ARTHUR

There were also references in the letter to people they had seen at the theatre, which proved that she had been accompanied by Captain Farquhar rather than the Princesse she had named to Jessie Clarke.

Jessie had already told Bird about the Captain's appearance at the hotel, and had pointed out the entry in the *Morning Post*. She now took the letter and showed it to him, before returning it to its place under the pincushion. Later she noted that Lady Mordaunt showed signs of surprise when she caught sight of the letter and quickly snatching it up put it on the fire, saying that she had not realised there were any letters about. Henry Bird, having seen the letter, managed to acquire two copies of the *Morning Post*, one of the 7th and one of the 9th, and kept them, seeing that the name of 'Captain Farmer' was indeed among the list of guests at the hotel. By this time Lady Mordaunt's behaviour had become a 'topic of conversation' between Jessie Clarke, Henry Bird and Mrs Caborn, the housekeeper. They frequently talked about it. Jessie felt reasonably sure that her mistress had committed adultery, but did not want to discuss her misgivings, afraid always of gaining a reputation for prying and as a result endangering her future employment prospects. Henry Bird for his part was not entirely convinced. Meanwhile, Sir Charles, going about his life as usual, appeared to have no suspicions. A few days after Harriett's return, some carpets were delivered to Walton, which confirmed her original story.

Winter had by now set in and the weather had turned foggy and unfit for hunting. In spite of this there was a meet at Walton on 11 November, and although the fog was so dense that the hounds did not 'throw off', Johnson recorded that 500 people turned up to take advantage of Sir Charles's hospitality. In the hall tables were laid for 100 guests and Lady Mordaunt was very upset when Dr Orford told her that she was still too unwell after her miscarriage to go downstairs and must be content to watch the proceedings from the gallery above.

The chances of another visit to London were now remote, and for Harriett there was the prospect of several long weeks in the country, with little in the way of entertainment except the occasional dinner party and the humdrum daily drive out in her carriage with nobody except the clergyman's wife for company. To combat 'dullness' she had definitely decided she would badger Charlie to buy the Prince's white ponies so that she could drive herself out whenever she pleased in imitation of Princess Alexandra. Charlie probably appreciated the fact that in view of her recent miscarriage driving was at least a safer option than riding to hounds. In any case the ponies were bought, Sir Charles only insisting when they first arrived that his wife went out several times accompanied by Johnson to make sure that she was proficient. She practised her skill driving the footman on a shopping expedition to Leamington.

The Prince wrote to Harriett on 30 November telling her that he was very glad to hear she had bought the two ponies. 'I also trust' he went on 'that they will suit you, and that you will drive them for many a year. I have never driven them myself, so I don't know whether they are easy to drive or not.'

The Prince had recently travelled from Sandringham to Evesham, where he had hunted with the Worcestershire and enjoyed some shooting in the Woodnorton covers. Georgina Dudley and her husband had been among the welcoming party at Evesham Station, and the Prince told Harriett that he thought her sister was looking very well. Harriett herself was given no opportunity to meet the Prince that autumn and had to be content with a gossipy letter about the first shooting party at Sandringham and about their mutual friends, 'the great Oliver' and Lord Blandford, who had been making plans for going abroad, although they still had not decided 'to what foreign clime' they were going to betake themselves. The Prince told Harriett that he was sorry she would not be going to Buckenham at Lord Derby's invitation.

'It is such an age since I have seen you' the Prince complained, adding 'If there is anything else (besides horses) that I can do for you, please let me know.' Harriet must have written almost by return, prompting a swift answer from the Prince, written at Sandringham on 5 December, warning her to be careful when she drove the ponies out.

My dear Lady Mordaunt,
    Many thanks for your letter, which I received this evening; and I am very glad to hear that you like the ponies, but I hope that they will be well driven before you attempt to drive them as I know they are fresh. They belonged originally to the Princess Mary,[42] who drove them for some years; and when she married, not wanting them just then, I bought them from her. I am not surprised that you have had no hunting lately, as the frost has made the ground as hard as iron. We hope, however, to be able to hunt tomorrow, as a thaw has set in. We killed over a thousand head on Tuesday, and killed forty woodcocks today. 'Lover' has been in good force, and as bumptious as ever. Blandford is also here, so you can imagine what a row goes on. On Monday next I go to Buckenham, and I am indeed very sorry that we shall not meet there. I am very sorry to hear that you have been seedy, but hope that you are now all right again.
                                        Ever yours sincerely,
                                        ALBERT EDWARD

From now on life began to lose some of its dullness for Harriett, as she drove the fiery grey ponies around, establishing her independence. Then, as Christmas approached, the house began to fill up with family and friends. They included Harriett's parents and one of her brothers, her grandmother Lady Kinnoull, Iain and Louisa Atholl, Helen and Charles Forbes and Lord Murray, who was a cousin to both Harriett and Charlie, as well as Georgie Forbes, George Newport, Louisa Scott and Captain Farquhar. Dr Priestley was also among the guests.
    During the daytime Harriett entertained her sisters by driving them round and showing them the neighbourhood. When the men went out shooting the ladies joined them for luncheon in the Bath House, a romantic folly built by Charlie's great-great-grandfather in the eighteenth century. In the summer time, the Bath House was a favourite destination for walks and picnics, the more intrepid immersing themselves in the cold clear waters of the Roman bath before climbing the stone stairs to take tea in the beautiful octagonal

room above. In the shooting season the food was brought up in hampers and set out in the grotto-like room with its shell-work swags, its cascades of plaster icicles all carried out by the famous Mrs Delany, and its pretty sash windows looking out across the valley. Bird, Johnson and the new under-butler served the food, the gamekeepers and beaters remaining outside. The gentlemen later moved off to new covers.

On 12 December the whole house party went to lunch at Charlecote with the Lucys, and the next day attended the Dispensary Ball at the Warwick Court House, which was the first ball of the season. Lady Mordaunt had been appointed patroness of the event, and the local paper expressed the belief that her influence would certainly help to make it a success. She opened the dancing with Mr James Dugdale who had recently completed the re-modelling of his house at Wroxall, and the ball went on into the small hours 'to the strains of Mr Syner's excellent band' with a large assembly of people.

The family party broke up just before Christmas and on Christmas Eve Harriett and Charlie set off with all their retinue to spend Christmas with the Dudleys at Witley Court. George Newport accompanied them with Lady Kinnoull, and Johnson noted in his diary that they had a four-horse bus to take them from Worcester Station to the Court. Harriett's sister Georgina and her husband were entertaining a large party of relations, and Johnson described Christmas as 'a very jolly day, 50 of us livery servants and girls sat down to a jolly good dinner' which shows there was satisfaction in the servants' hall as well as in the dining room. Witley Court provided a splendid setting for a New Year's Eve ball attended by over 500 people and then, on 2 January 1868, the Walton party left for home, taking the train from Kidderminster to Warwick, posting home from there through a snowstorm.

Once they were back at Walton, all the gaiety began again, with many of Lady Mordaunt's old friends being invited – Georgie Forbes, Lord Berkeley Paget,[43] Robert Duff and Captain Chaplin, the Kinnoull relations the Hon. Mr and Mrs Hay, not to mention Captain Farquhar who stayed for several weeks. The unfortunate Johnson was taken ill on 7 January and although he was allowed to stay in bed all day, he had to get up in order to accompany a large party to a ball the same evening. The next day there was much work to be done because the Mordaunts entertained their guests and friends with a ball at home.

There was a preponderance of young men among the visitors in the house and the servants noted that they did not scruple to enter Lady Mordaunt's private sitting-room whenever they felt like it. Sir Charles did not appear to be worried by this, probably believing that there was safety in numbers. Certainly with the house so full of guests, there were fewer opportunities for Harriett to be alone with Captain Farquhar. All the same, Bird did come upon them unexpectedly when he entered the billiard room one evening and found them standing rather close together near the table. They moved quickly apart as he came in. Johnson also recalled that when he accompanied a party on a visit to Warwick on 20 December, both Lady Mordaunt and Captain Farquhar stayed at home, the Captain pleading illness. And then one day when everybody else had gone out shooting, Johnson was sent up to Lady Mordaunt's private sitting-room with a note. As he walked in, he heard a quick rustle of silk and saw Lady Mordaunt looking rather confused and red in the face. Captain Farquhar was sitting beside her at the table pretending to be busy with the wood-carving work. Lady Mordaunt rebuked Johnson severely for coming into the room without knocking. Later that day, the Captain drove Lady Mordaunt up to join the shooting party for lunch at Walton Wood. Johnson, who waited on the party, heard Lady Mordaunt saying to her husband, 'Where are you going next, Charlie?' and she also made some remark which Johnson did not quite hear or understand, calling her husband 'you old thing'.

Jessie Clarke later recalled an incident which happened late one evening. Sir Charles always remained downstairs until all the guests and the household had gone to bed, making sure that everything was safe and extinguishing the gas lights in the hall himself. On that evening Lady Mordaunt had gone upstairs as usual to prepare for bed, having told Jessie Clarke not to wait up for her. Jessie was in her own sitting-room when Florence Stephens the cook came and told her that she had seen Lady Mordaunt on the landing with a gentleman. Jessie then went up to investigate, remaining in the shadows so as not to be seen. She had a good view of her mistress locked in a long embrace with Georgie Forbes.

It was not only the servants who were worried by Lady Mordaunt's strangely flirtatious behaviour. Sir Charles's brother Johnny had compared notes with one of the Murray cousins, a married man with small children, who had said that when he found himself alone with her, Harriett had treated him with the same effusive affection she had shown to Johnny. They were puzzled by such goings on, but they still avoided saying anything to Charlie, knowing how much he loved and trusted his wife.

There was a ball in Stratford on 10 January, with supper at four in the morning, and then over the next few days the guests began to disperse. When everybody had gone Charlie and Harriett went out to dinner with Johnny and his wife at Staple Hill. A large lunch party was held at the Hall with pigeon shooting, and the hounds met again at Walton. After a good run through the grounds, the fox 'dodged' the hounds 'by running up a tree', which seemed very odd to Johnson, who recorded the incident. One evening Lord Willoughby de Broke and his new bride held a ball at Compton Verney on a beautiful moonlit night.

There was enjoyment for the servants too. Johnson attended the Servants' Ball at Stratford on 5 January when over 200 danced to the Leamington Quadrille Band and Mr Dare of the Shakespeare Hotel provided the refreshments. He also went with Shore, the upper housemaid, to take tea with the servants at Compton Verney, which proved to be 'a very jolly evening'.

According to Johnson, when the hounds met at Goldicote, the home of Captain Smith, Sir Charles's stepfather, and Sir Charles's mother, they had a good run and afterwards thirty or forty people, among them Lord Willoughby de Broke, Lord Aylesford and various other young noblemen, all 'came tumbling in' to have lunch at Walton Hall with the sought-after Lady Mordaunt.

Parliament had reassembled on 13 February after the Christmas recess, and Sir Charles joined the other Members who came up from the shires to debate a new Church Rate Bill. He stayed for a few days at the Palace Hotel and then returned to Warwickshire. The provincial calendar of winter events had almost come to an end, and the round of parties finished with the Bachelors' Ball in Leamington. Once that was over, Harriett could find no very good reason for staying in the country. As soon as Sir Charles returned from London, she ordered Jessie Clarke to pack her bags and she set off without him, catching the 12.40 train from Warwick and arriving at her grandmother's house in Belgrave Square at half past four. She justified her existence in London by going to see Dr Priestley every morning. Sir Charles seemed happy enough to foot the medical bill, although Dr Priestley did say later that Lady Mordaunt often paid the consultation fee herself.

Having visited the doctor, Lady Mordaunt was free to spend the rest of the day as she pleased, and plenty of people were ready to act as her escort. After a few days she sent for her jewellery, which was despatched by rail, Johnson and Jessie Clarke going to fetch it from Paddington Station. There was a considerable panic when the precious diamonds failed to arrive but after Johnson had sent a telegraph they eventually turned up.

Since her carriage was still at Walton, Lady Mordaunt hired a brougham whenever she needed it. She went to the theatre accompanied by Captain Vivian and to a dinner party at Lady Townsend's house where Captain Farquhar was among the guests. On 29 February Johnson had his orders to accompany Lady Mordaunt, Lady Kinnoull and Captain Vivian[44] to the Alhambra Palace in Leicester Square, an expedition to the Music Hall presumably being lent at least some respectability by the grandmother's presence. They left Lady Kinnoull's house at about half past nine in the evening, Lady Mordaunt travelling in her hired carriage, and they stayed on until after midnight into the Sunday morning watching all the entertainments. These included an impressive performance on the tightrope by the acrobat Blondin. During the course of the evening they were joined by Captain Farquhar, and afterwards Lady Kinnoull left with Captain Vivian, allowing Captain Farquahar to travel alone in the covered carriage with Lady Mordaunt, Johnson as usual standing outside on the box. His orders were to put Captain Farquhar down as near as he could to his house in King Street, just a quarter of an hour's drive from Leicester Square, and then to go on to Lady Kinnoull's. Johnson noted that it was a very dark night, but dark or not, he would not have been able to see from his position what was going on inside the carriage, although he could guess. 'Sneaking' was the term he used.

The Prince had by now arrived in town, while the Princess remained at Sandringham, putting off going up to London for as long as possible. 'I cannot say I am looking forward to it much' she confided in her sister-in-law, Princess Louise. Apart from the fact that she was expecting another baby in July, her increased deafness and the stiffness in her leg took much of the pleasure out of the social round and she really preferred to stay in the country. Her absence made it easy for the Prince to pursue his own amusements. He went on a round of visits, frequently calling on Helen Forbes and on the day after the Alhambra expedition he visited Lady Mordaunt at her grandmother's house, arriving at six o'clock in the evening and staying until ten minutes to seven. He was also present at a 'select' party at the Admiralty to which Lady Mordaunt had also been invited.

Eventually the Princess decided to come up to London to join her husband. 'I hate it when he is away' she told her sister-in-law. 'The house seems empty and desolate and lonely.'

Soon Sir Charles too arrived in London. It was important for him to lend his support to the Tory Government's dwindling majority as the atmosphere in the Commmons became increasingly intense, with the two parties locked in conflict over the Irish question and particularly the disestablishment of the Irish Church. Soon after he joined his wife, on 10 March, they were invited to an evening party given by the Prince and Princess at Marlborough House.

The fact that Lady Mordaunt had been openly invited to Marlborough House with her husband gave an air of respectability to her friendship with the Prince. This perhaps masked the fact that they were seeing more of each other than was entirely proper, and Johnson now found himself cast in the role of a go-between, frequently being entrusted with the task of carrying letters to and fro between Belgrave Square and Marlborough House. The footman was very unhappy at finding himself in this position, and since all the late nights were beginning to affect his health he was seriously thinking of changing his job. With a view to bettering himself, he applied for, but did not obtain, the post of butler to the Duke of Richmond. Often he felt depressed and his doctor hinted that if he continued in his present way of life, he well might not have long to live. To add to his difficulties he suffered from toothache and had to have a tooth out at St George's Hospital.

A few days after the party at Marlborough House, Harriett began to feel unwell, and on the Thursday she sent Johnson off with a letter telling the Prince that she would not be able to see him as they had planned. She received the Prince's reply the same day.

My dear Lady Mordaunt,
    I am so sorry to find by the letter that I received from you this morning (Thursday) that you are unwell, and that I shall not be able to pay you a visit to-day, to which I had been looking forward with so much pleasure. To-morrow and Saturday I shall be hunting in Nottinghamshire; but, if you are still in town, may I

come to see you about five on Sunday afternoon? and, hoping you will soon be yourself again,

believe me,

yours ever sincerely,

ALBERT EDWARD

Lady Mordaunt continued to feel ill over the weekend. A local doctor was called in who diagnosed a case of measles. Dr Priestley was also consulted. As the Prince of Wales had been expected for lunch Lady Mordaunt asked Jessie to bring her some writing materials so that she could put him off. She was writing the letter in bed when Lady Kinnoull came in and shortly afterwards Sir Charles was shown into the room. Harriett asked him to wait while she finished the letter which she handed to Lady Kinnoull who passed it on to Johnson who then delivered it to the Prince. When Johnson entered the hall at Marlborough House, he encountered the Princess and he noticed that she went very white when she saw him.

The Prince immediately wrote a letter in reply, expressing his concern.

I cannot tell you how distressed I am to hear from your letter that you have got the measles and that I shall in consequence not have the pleasure of seeing you . . . I have had the measles myself, a long time ago, and I know what a tiresome complaint it is. I trust you will take great care of yourself, and have a good doctor with you. Above all, I should not read at all, as it is very bad for the eyes; and I suppose you will be forced to lay up for a time. The weather is very favourable for your illness; and, wishing you a very speedy recovery,

believe me,

yours most sincerely,

ALBERT EDWARD

Sir Charles meanwhile had been banished to the Palace Hotel and on 17 March Johnson packed up his belongings and saw him off to Walton. Once he had gone, the Prince arrived at Lady Kinnoull's house to enquire after Lady Mordaunt's health. Johnson spent his time travelling about in a hansom cab delivering letters, but at least the evenings were free as Lady Mordaunt was too ill to go out. This meant that he was able to have a social life of his own, and he made the most of his freedom by paying visits to other footmen of his acquaintance. He much appreciated some early nights, but the days were trying, as his mistress was proving extremely demanding, and on 22 March he reported that he was 'about all day with notes, up and down stairs to her Ladyship, very tiresome all day'. The next morning she asked him to post letters to the Prince of Wales, and to Captain Chaplin, Lord Newport and Lord Berkeley Paget.

The newly introduced letter-box was proving a useful innovation for lovers conducting a clandestine correspondence, and posting a letter was certainly less embarrassing for Johnson than taking a note to the house; all the same he felt very put out by the whole situation and as he wrote in his diary he 'gave her Ladyship a bit of my mind about leaving'. After several miserable days attending to his mistress's whims, and getting very worried and tired out, Johnson had definitely made up his mind to give in his notice and return to his family in Oxfordshire.

7
Interlude at the Seaside

On 26 March Sir Charles attended a dinner at the Shire Hall in Warwick in honour of the Master of the Hounds, Mr Spencer Lucy, at which he proposed a toast to the Warwickshire farmers. Two days later he returned to London, booking in at the Palace Hotel. He sent for Johnson to valet him there.

Johnson had by this time decided that he could stand his job no longer and had written to his family announcing his return. Lady Mordaunt, however, made such a fuss when he announced his resignation that he was forced to change his mind, 'the miserablest day I have known and I thought it would be the happiest' he wrote sadly, having sent a letter to his 'dear Sarah' breaking the news that he was not coming home after all. 'Poor dear I did feel for her,' he added.

It had been decided that Lady Mordaunt should go to Hastings to convalesce, which was the last thing she wanted and she put up what Johnson described as 'a regular battle'. Eventually she had to give in and after what he described as a great deal of 'perswation' Johnson was prevailed upon to accompany her. He was sent on in advance to book the rooms and to make sure that everything was comfortable. On the Hastings train he found himself in the company of 'a very agreeable lady' and he helped her with an ingenious ruse when she objected to the presence of several noisy children in their carriage. 'I simply asked their Nurse if she objected to measles, after I had turned up my coat collar and wrapped well up' he wrote, adding that the Nurse gave him a 'harrassing' look and shot out of the carriage at Tunbridge Wells like a scalded cat, taking the noisy children with her.

Johnson thought that Hastings was a very pretty place and he was pleased with his room which looked out over the Castle. The moon was shining on the sea as he sat at the window thinking of Sarah. The only disadvantage was that his wash stand was 'one size too large for a doll and 500 times too small for any human bean [*sic*]'.

Lady Mordaunt's reluctance to leave London and all her friends had only been overcome at a price. As usual her husband had to remember his pre-marriage promise allowing her to entertain her friends, and so he made no objection when a suitable 'darling', in the shape of Lord Newport, was asked to join the party in Hastings, with Lady Kinnoull also going along to provide some nominal chaperonage.

Life in the seaside town was more like a holiday than work and Johnson's health quickly improved as a result. On the first day he went out early onto the beach and the parade; everywhere was crammed with people and there was 'a jolly nice band at play'. He found that he had very few duties apart from taking 'my lady' to the Assembly Rooms one afternoon to see a 'baby actress', whom he described as 'a very interesting little critter and indeed very clever'. He even had time to visit the Castle and was able to explore the smugglers' caves in the company of Jessie Clarke and another lady's maid. On one expedition he discovered the Lovers' Seat at Fairlight and looked round the church and the church yard, gathering primroses and other flowers. On Sunday 6 April, after taking Lady Mordaunt to church at St Leonard's-on-Sea, he was free in the afternoon to ramble along the rocks and cliffs, in the evening going on his own to St Clement's Church in old Hastings, where he heard a very good sermon and found it 'quite a treat to go to a good old church'. He had to admit that he could not stand the High Church 'or rather, Catholic refined', as he put it. On 7 April, after delivering Lady Kinnoull to the station for the London train, Johnson went out in a rowing boat with Lord Newport's valet and another valet who worked for Mr Smith, the Lombard Street banker. They were out for an hour and a half, finishing up with a shrimp tea at the Griffin, and altogether enjoying themselves thoroughly.

Sir Charles went down to Hastings for a few days, which meant that he missed some of the important and animated debates about Ireland which were taking place in the crowded House of Commons. He travelled back to London in order to support Disraeli's Conservative Government in the division, Gladstone having put forward a resolution that the House should go into committee upon the resolutions framed to secure a speedy disestablishment of the Irish Church. After Gladstone's resolution had been passed by a majority of nearly sixty, the House then rose for the Easter recess and Sir Charles rejoined his wife in Hastings where she had been combating 'dullness' in the company of Lord Newport. She was by now completely restored to health and after a few days they all left for London, the Mordaunts spending a night at the Palace Hotel before returning to Walton.

8

A Long Hot Summer

After Easter all the staff began packing up ready for the London season, Sir Charles having taken a house at 6 Chesham Place for the summer. On 15 April the advance party left, 'bag and baggage', followed by Sir Charles a day or two later. Johnson remained behind with Lady Mordaunt, spending a few quiet days and finding time to go to tea with Mrs Padbury, the local baker's wife whom he described as 'a good sort of woman but for her jaw'. On 22 April he accompanied Lady Mordaunt to London and immediately the social round began again with a visit to the Drury Lane Theatre and to the opera, where as Johnson put it, there was 'a horrible crush'. A few days later Johnson finally left Lady Mordaunt's service, and a new footman, Henry Hallett, arrived to take his place.

Before leaving Hastings, Lady Mordaunt had received a letter from the Prince telling her that he was glad she had made such a good recovery, and expressing the hope that on her return to London he would have the pleasure of seeing her. By the time she arrived in London, however, the Prince had left for Ireland on a goodwill visit. In spite of her condition, the Princess had insisted on accompanying him and when she appeared by his side at a state ball she looked as beautiful as ever, wearing a pink satin dress decorated with a flounce of Irish lace. The Prince himself made a good impression on the Irish people, and when he delivered a speech, *The Times* reported that he spoke with 'an unaffected earnestness' which deepened the impression left by his words.

By the time the Prince returned to England the season was in full swing. Soon the weather became very warm, and even before the end of May temperatures had begun to rise well into the eighties, the heat bringing out the delicious scent of the flowers that decorated the ladies' dresses and bonnets. There were choice blooms in all the window boxes outside the open windows of smart houses around the Park and these added their fragrance to secret assignations. The ladies' fashions that year were light and romantic, modelled on the paintings of Watteau, with fresh flowers and lace more in vogue than ever, the dresses made up in white muslin over silk or taffeta with wide blue or rose-coloured sashes. These made the ladies look quite 'fairy-like' in appearance.[45] The *jeunesse dorée* were out to enjoy themselves without thinking too much about the consequences as they sampled in cool drawing-rooms well away from prying eyes the tingling thrill of tender caresses. There was surely no danger for a young lady in allowing her handsome admirers to sit at her feet on a footstool, while stroking her gloved hand and gazing up into her eyes. And there was moral justification, too, for this kind of behaviour, when, as in Lady Mordaunt's case, a husband appeared to put his wife lower on his list of priorities than his parliamentary duties and his sporting activities, and was in any case thought by others to be a dull sort of fellow and something of a killjoy.

Afternoon visits had by now become very fashionable, the gentlemen about town having discovered that husbands and chaperones tended to be out of the house at that time of day attending to business of one kind or another. Lady Glencora, in Trollope's novel *Phineas Finn*, which was coming out in instalments that summer,[46] was not at all pleased to see the Duke of Omnium's carriage parked each afternoon outside the Park Lane house of an eligible widow. She did not think this was at all proper, and it made her fear that the so far childless Duke might be tempted on one of these visits to sire a child who would challenge the right of her own curly-headed son to inherit the dukedom.

In real life, Alice Miles,[47] newly arrived from Paris with every intention of flouting the stricter English conventions, had already shocked her more sedate relations with her readiness to entertain young men alone in her sitting-room. Alice had soon found that she missed so many people by going to the park of an afternoon that she had decided it was far better to remain at home instead waiting for any visitors who might come. Her Aunt Agatha, described by Alice as 'the most straight-laced of all her insupportable relations', had begun to smell a rat as soon as she saw Lord Landsdowne's 'neat equipage with its well-known coronet and prancing horses drawn up most *en evidence* before the door'. Scandalised to find that Alice was alone in the house, both her parents being out, the formidable aunt, accompanied by three children, two nurses and a perambulator, pushed past the servants into the drawing-room where she found Alice leaning back in the softest of easy chairs and, as Alice put it herself, 'the greatest unpardonable sin of the whole deadly catalogue, there at my feet on a low chair, the effect I was producing on him written pretty plainly in his eyes, sat the Marquess of Lansdowne, the man she had been hunting ineffectually the whole season for her own daughter.'[48]

Lady Mordaunt, in the same way, was quite happy to receive her admirers at home, even though her husband was out at the time attending to parliamentary business, or pigeon shooting at Hurlingham. Georgie Forbes and Lord Newport often called on her when Sir Charles was not at home, and that summer another friend of the family, Lord Cole, was a frequent visitor. It was rumoured that Lowry Cole, a lieutenant in the Rifle Brigade, had become engaged to Lady Mordaunt's younger sister Francy, but was unable to marry her as his father, the impoverished Earl of Inniskillen, had told him that he was as yet too young to embark on matrimony. And since he had little means at his disposal it was unlikely that Sir Thomas Moncreiffe had given him any encouragement. Francy could provide nothing in the way of a dowry, but she had one advantage – she was a Moncreiffe, and to be her fiancé gave the rakish Lowry Cole a passport to proximity with Lady Mordaunt. Bird later testified that most of the calls paid by Lord Cole that summer were made in Sir Charles's absence.

The Prince himself was soon visiting Lady Mordaunt in the afternoon on a regular basis, at least once a week. He was careful, of course, not to arrive in a carriage emblazoned with the royal arms, but would step out of a 'common cab', usually around four o'clock. The footman Henry Hallett would answer the door and the Prince always gave him a shilling to pay the cabman. He would then hand Bird his hat, gloves and cane before entering the drawing-room, an indication, according to the social customs of the time, that this was no fleeting visit. When the time came to leave, usually after about an hour and a half, Hallett would be sent out to call a cab for the return journey. Lady Mordaunt had issued strict instructions to the effect that nobody else was ever to be admitted when His Royal Highness was in the drawing-room. What exactly went on in the room, nobody could say, but no doubt the servants were prepared to hazard a guess.

Sir Charles meanwhile was having to spend an increased amount of time in the House of Commons where the question of the Irish Church was being debated with mounting urgency. He managed to take time off to accompany his wife when she attended a levée at Marlborough House but on the whole he left her to her own devices until somebody in the family, probably the Earl of Dudley, gave him a timely warning about the Prince's afternoon visits. As a result he cautioned his wife, telling her that there was a dark shadow in the Prince's past, which should make her wary of consorting with him. He felt that he must speak out about this, in his wife's own interest. However in spite of the warning, when he returned early one afternoon from Hurlingham apparently suffering from a headache and going straight upstairs to his room, it was not long before Bird came up to inform him that His Royal Highness had arrived and was in the drawing-room. Sir Charles went downstairs at once and the Prince left soon afterwards. Harriett, however, managed to persuade her husband that the Prince had come to see her as a family friend and no more. Sir Charles still did not suspect that there was what he described as any 'intrigue' between them.

It must by now have become obvious to the Prince and to Lady Mordaunt that Sir Charles was on his guard and that they would have to be more careful in future. Lady Mordaunt no longer entrusted her letters to the footman, but made sure that she posted them herself. The only time that Bird could remember Lady Mordaunt having spoken to him at all angrily was at about this time. She had told him that she needed some new blotting paper so he had sent the case to the stationers for renewal. Lady Mordaunt then asked him if he had destroyed the old paper which had been in it and when he said no, that had gone to the stationers too, she had said angrily 'Never do that again, you don't know what they might make of it.' She told him always to burn the blotting paper in future.

Sir Charles, for his part, was threatening to wrest his wife away from all the summer enjoyments in London, and plans were well ahead to take her off to Norway for a fishing trip. Her involvement with the Prince and his somewhat doubtful entourage may well have given Charlie an extra incentive to take his wife away to the solitude of the fjords. Not quite understanding her dislike of 'dullness', he felt sure that she would share his enthusiasm for such a beautiful place, and he promised that he would arrange to go with another married couple so that she could have a lady companion. Every possible arrangement would be made for her comfort, even to the extent of chartering a private steamer, which would be far more comfortable than the ordinary passenger boats. He reminded her how much she had enjoyed their visit to Switzerland the previous year, in spite of her initial reluctance, and at first she seemed to go along with the plan, only appearing to change her mind when he had practically

completed the arrangements. She then told him bluntly that she did
not want to go as she had not had enough of London life. He said
that he would rather not go without her, but she encouraged him to
proceed with his plans. Her father supported her, saying that he
would not hear of his daughter going to Norway where the conditions would be unsuitable for a young lady and the accommodation
far too primitive. Although disappointed by her attitude, Sir Charles
did not try to persuade her; he knew by this time that she could easily
become hysterical, and he probably did not wish to risk a scene. As
on previous occasions, she had pulled back only when it was difficult
for him to extricate himself, giving him gracious permission to pursue
his pleasures on his own and no doubt laughing with her friends
about his gullibility. She reminded him that many of her relations,
including three of her sisters, were still in town so that she would not
be lonely. She managed to convince him that he could trust her to
behave appropriately during his absence.

Others did not share Charlie's confidence, and there had been a
great deal of gossip in recent weeks following the recent Norfolk
v. Warwickshire pigeon shooting match at Hurlingham. The Prince
and Sir Charles had captained their respective teams and naturally
the Prince's appearance had attracted a large crowd of fashionable
people who watched the event from drays or the boxes of their car-
riages. Lady Mordaunt had offered to score for both teams, and
nobody could help noticing how anxious the Prince was to help her,
and how there was 'constant communication' between them, the unfortunate Sir Charles being forced to stand by at a slight distance.

Concerned about the fact that tongues had begun to wag, the Earl
of Dudley saw fit to warn his brother-in-law that there would be even
more talk if he were to leave for Norway without his wife. At the
Ascot races, the Earl and Sir Thomas Moncreiffe took Charlie aside
and tackled him on the subject, the Earl saying that he hoped Harriett
would be able to go with him on the trip. Sir Charles replied that she
was not accompanying him because she did not want to make the
journey and he himself felt it was better not to press her. Lord Dudley
again strongly urged him not to leave her behind, saying frankly that
he was sure there would be talk if she remained in London alone at
the same time as the Prince of Wales. Sir Charles, resenting what he
regarded as interference, took umbrage and told the Earl to mind his
own business, saying that he trusted his wife implicitly. Sir Thomas
agreed with his son-in-law that as Harriett was so against going, it

would not do for him to insist on taking her, but he also thought that in order to avoid gossip she should not stay in London once her husband had left for Norway. Charlie then reiterated that he felt he could trust his wife absolutely and had in any case made arrangements for her to go down to Walton in the near future.

Sir Charles told his wife that the whole household would move down to Walton a week after his departure for Norway. She then said that she would prefer to stay on in London for a fortnight. He remained adamant on this point, however, simply asking her whether she would like one of her unmarried sisters to stay with her during her week in town. She replied that it would not be possible for them to be with her all the time, but that one or other of them, or her friend Louisa Scott, would very often be there. He then asked whether Francy and Louisa would go with her to Walton and she replied 'Certainly.'

Sir Charles left London on the Edinburgh train on 15 June. When he said goodbye to his mother-in-law, her parting words about Harriett were, 'I hope she will go on all right.' He did not altogether appreciate the significance of this remark at the time.

As soon as he reached Edinburgh, Charlie settled down to write to his wife:

My darling Harriett,
    We arrived here exactly at the time the train was due and are to sail at 10.30. It blew a gale here until yesterday so we expect a rough passage. I could not sleep all night and am very seedy. Please dearest when you write do not put via Hull and then the letters will go either by Hull or via Denmark according to the day you write as the post goes both ways. Goodbye and God bless you my own precious darling.
                        Ever your most loving husband
                                    C. MORDAUNT

Left at home with a large house and a full staff at her disposal, Harriett made the most of the situation and arranged several lunch parties for her family and friends. On the day that she received Charlie's letter, she had invited her sister Francy to lunch to meet the Prince and his friend Oliver Montagu.[49] After the other two guests had gone, the Prince stayed for over half an hour alone with his hostess.

Sir Charles's clergyman brother Osbert had arranged to stay with

Lady Mordaunt for a day or two following her husband's departure. On the morning he arrived, he noticed that the table was laid for five and although he did not lunch there himself, he was told that there had been several men in the party. In the afternoon he went down to Eton to play cricket and when he returned he discovered that Lord Newport, Georgie Forbes and Francy had been dining at the house and playing whist. Georgie and Francy left at about eleven o'clock, but Newport stayed on and Osbert made a point of staying up until he had gone.

At this time, the servants recalled, the Prince began to call at the house more frequently than ever, in spite of the fact that his wife's baby was due within a few weeks. As for the Princess she was by now becoming used to this sort of behaviour and she had been forced to accept the fact that although Bertie still loved her, yet his love was not strong enough to 'keep him by her side'.[50]

Bird and the other servants had also noticed that Lord Cole, like the Prince, had begun to call more frequently, and he too was often alone with Lady Mordaunt in the drawing-room. On the evening of 27 June he dined there with two ladies and one gentleman who were all described as friends of the family and who all left at around ten or eleven o'clock. Lord Cole stayed on in the drawing-room and was alone with Lady Mordaunt until one o'clock next morning. Bird finally grew tired of waiting up, and to find out whether his lordship had left or not, he took Lady Mordaunt's candle to the table outside the drawing-room and noted that there was still a gentleman's hat on the table. Bird listened at the door but could hear no sounds of conversation so he went back to his room and later heard the front door slam.

Of all this Charlie knew nothing. The letter that his wife wrote to him in answer to his from Edinburgh gave him plenty of reassurance. She told him that in general one of her sisters had been with her all day and that either one of them or Louisa Scott would accompany her when she went down to Walton. There had been some correspondence which she was doing her best to deal with for him; a letter had come from the clergyman Mr Barton begging for the living at Wicken, and another from somebody who wished to be 'got in' as a member at Hurlingham. She would tell them that her husband was out of town and would answer when he got back. She had also approached the agents Goldsmith and Grogan about letting the house and stables in London. In this she had so far met with no success as they had left it far too late, there already being a large number of houses for rent on the market 'begging to be let for nothing almost'. The Hurlingham Ball was to take place the following Friday and she hoped it would be a success. As for a recent match, she reported that 'the Commons won in a walk'. Her letter was full of affection

> My own darling Charlie
> ... I am going to write this to send by Johnny on Monday. I received yours from Edinbro' and was very glad to get it. I hope you did not have a very rough passage and feel very ill. It has been blowing a good deal here until today and it is fearfully hot. I miss you very much but I am getting used to it and do not mind it so much now. I am keeping very well – my time has passed over a little way for certain things and I am expecting it every day ... Antelope's foot is quite well but I would not take him out till yesterday to make it safe. I am doing much the same as usual ... Lina has gone off to Scotland. I ... am going to take this note to Half Moon Street to John to post and to say goodbye to them, as I may not have a chance again before Monday and then I am going from there to the station so I must wind up darling. Hoping that you are quite well and happy and that you will catch plenty of fish and not fidget your old self about me as I am getting on very well and everyone is quite agreeable to me, saying nothing nasty ... I shall write to you again very soon, as soon as the next boat goes and shall hope to hear soon you are all safe at Renade. Believe me, my darling old Charlie.
>
> Ever your loving wife,
HARRIETT MORDAUNT
>
> I have heard from Alice Kenlis asking us to go to them for the 12th of August which I have refused saying we are engaged and cannot manage it. I think that is what you wish dear isn't it, and I think we shall have difficulty in managing it.

The letter certainly gave no hint as to any duplicity on Harriett's part. She told Charlie that she had attended Lady Waldegrave's ball but had not greatly enjoyed it, and assured him that in spite of Lord Dudley's fears there had been no 'nasty talk' about her being left on her own. She had tackled her brother-in-law on this subject, engaging in 'a very satisfactory row' with him and had then 'made friends again'. It seemed that Lord Dudley had almost confessed to being in the wrong, and Harriett told Charlie that there must have been 'a little mistake about what he said to Papa – it must have got a little exaggerated'. Having done her best to set her husband's mind at rest on this point, she told him that she was going to Maidenhead in the afternoon, the first time that she had been down there that year. It sounded the obvious thing to do during a heat wave although Sir Charles might have been alarmed to read Alice Miles's diary entry for 5 July of that year when she recorded that she and her mother spent the day on the river at Maidenhead and 'were the only ones that behaved with the slightest propriety'. Jessie Clarke noted that Lady Mordaunt came back from Maidenhead 'unwell', a fact which Harriett passed on to her husband in a letter.

It soon became apparent that Lady Mordaunt was planning to stay in London for longer than her husband had stipulated. Osbert made a disapproving mental note of the fact, which made its impression, too, upon the servants. In her letter, by way of an excuse for this change of plan, she told Charlie that his uncle, Robert Murray,[51] was very anxious that she should 'bring out' his daughter Eleanor at the ball which the Dudleys were staging for the 'royalties' on the Thursday week. There was a certain irony in the concept of Harriett herself acting as a chaperone, but she told Charlie that if Georgy was ready to issue an invitation to Eleanor, she was quite happy to undertake the task, leaving London the day after as it would be pointless 'to go away and come back again'.

With his wife about to be confined, the Prince was free to go about the town without any fear that she would accompany him. Alice Miles, already proving to be a new star in the social firmament, had caused something of a stir at Lady Pakenham's Ball on 29 June by refusing to dance with the Prince's great friend Francis Knollys, an incident that had caused the Prince much amusement. Alice had snubbed Knollys by telling him with her habitually pretty and disdainful air, that she never danced square dances and so would not partner him in a quadrille. In Alice's opinion quadrilles were 'the invention of the righteous ones to counteract the mischief done by valses' which made the Prince recognise that she was a girl after his own heart; in fact he could not wait to be introduced to her. When Knollys told the story of his rejection to the Prince and his friends, Alice heard that 'the Prince took the story up, laughed at Francis unmercifully, and never meets him now without quizzing him on the subject; of course, everyone else follows HR Highness's example and the unhappy man will never hear the last of it.'[52] Alice hoped that she would be able to meet the Prince at the Blues ball, but her mother, not usually too meticulous in these matters, rejected one or two offers of chaperonage for her daughter – she was unable to obtain a ticket herself – causing Alice to cry herself to sleep with vexation at missing the chance to be introduced to the fascinating Prince.

On 1 July there was a ball at Buckingham Palace attended by several royal Princesses all dressed in the current fashion in lace, white muslin and rose-coloured satin, with chatelaines of pink roses and green leaves, and headdresses of roses and diamonds. The Princess of Wales attended, wearing white tulle over white silk, her satin bodice trimmed with lilies of the valley. This was one of her last appearances before, on the following Monday, 6 July, she gave birth to a daughter, Princess Victoria. The Prince wrote at once to tell Harriett the news:

> My dear Lady Mordaunt
>
> I am sure you will be glad to hear that the Princess was safely delivered of a little girl[53] this morning and that both are doing very well. I hope you will come to the Oswald and St James's Ball this week. There would, I am sure, be no harm of your remaining till Saturday in town. I shall like to see you again.
>
> Ever yours sincerely,
ALBERT EDWARD

In spite of the Prince's assurance that there would be 'no harm' in her remaining in London until the Saturday, Harriett managed to resist the temptation and left London with Jessie Clarke on the Friday. She had already much overstayed the deadline set by her husband. The Prince, for his part, had the decency to remain with his wife on the day after her accouchement, much to the disgust of Alice Miles who was hoping to be introduced to him at a ball that evening. She expressed annoyance at finding he was not there just because 'his stupid little wife chose to go and be confined'. There was at least one compensation for Alice in the fact that Lord Cole vied with Cornwallis West to put her into her carriage at the end of the evening 'and took that privilege on himself'. Alice met him again on 9 July when he was in the same box as her at the opera and talked to her incessantly throughout the performance.[54]

On 7 July Lady Mordaunt duly left Chesham Place for Walton

attended by Jessie Clarke, while Bird and some of the other servants stayed behind to close down the house. At Paddington Station Lord Cole was waiting for Lady Mordaunt to arrive, and as soon as she did so he went off to get the tickets, giving one to Jessie for the second class, and handing Lady Mordaunt into a first class carriage. He then stood outside on the platform as if to prevent anyone else getting in. Just before the train started he entered the carriage, and it was at this moment that Lord Hamilton's valet Hutchings arrived, having been sent by his master with a dog as a present for Lady Mordaunt.[55] When Jessie told him that Lord Cole was in the carriage, Hutchings shook his head, either in disbelief or disapproval. Jessie went to the second class end of the train, and came to the conclusion that Lord Cole had alighted at Reading as she saw him on the platform there before the train moved on.

After her arrival at Walton, Lady Mordaunt invited Mrs Cadogan to accompany her to a croquet party at Warwick Castle and on the way there she divulged to the clergyman's wife that she was expecting visitors the next day. She had already told the servants how many to expect and preparations were made accordingly. Mrs Cadogan was not asked down to the Hall to meet the guests, but she saw them with Lady Mordaunt in church on the Sunday morning. Lord Cole apparently arrived the day after the croquet match, followed by Georgie Forbes, Lord Newport and Louisa Scott. There was no sign of Francy Moncreiffe, who could not have failed to notice by now that the man she was supposed to be engaged to was far more interested in her sister than he was in herself. When Osbert Mordaunt returned to Warwickshire, he called at Walton and was surprised to find Lord Newport there.

The hot weather continued as Lady Mordaunt and her friends enjoyed those few precious days when they were able to have fun without the inhibiting presence of the master of the house. They could laugh and talk, tell naughty stories, play practical jokes and flirt outrageously without fear of discovery. Bird did notice that at least there were fewer opportunities for Lord Cole to be alone with Lady Mordaunt than there had been in Chesham Place.

Meanwhile, nothing had really gone right for Sir Charles. The crossing had been very bad, he was missing his wife, and the fishing was disappointing. To add to his troubles, Mr Gowan, the fishing tackle maker, had sent him out with 'a perfectly useless line of someone else's, mended in three places', instead of the new one he had chosen in the shop. On Friday 19 June he had written from Drontheim:

My own darling Harriett,

I am writing while still in the steamboat, but we are just going to arrive in about an hour all safe but as we are still shaking about a little I am not able to write plainly. We have had a tolerably quick passage but very rough indeed and a good deal of the time it was blowing a gale but the wind was with us or else we should have been out 2 days longer. I have not been sick at all and have been much better than I expected but rather uncomfortable at times. On the second night I was thrown off the sofa where I lay and slept on the floor for the rest of the night. Altogether as far as the voyage is concerned I am very thankful you were not here my most precious darling although I miss you very much. I hope you have been well and happy and that you went to the Ball at Lady Waldegrave's. I was very sorry to hear from Carpenter that poor Antelope was very bad and I told him if necessary the little horse should be sent for. There are six ladies on board but only one able to leave her cabin and that was Lady Ann Coke who is with Lord Leicester and is a very good sailor. I find that the best way for ladies to go out now is through Holland and Denmark when there is only 12 hours sea voyage. Monty Guest came out with two servants and a man cook all for himself, and his luggage consisted of 20 boxes. I am very sorry to find the weather here was so unusually hot in May that too much of the snow melted and the fishing began a fortnight or more since so we shall be too late for the best of it unless we have very hot weather. I find the boats which go from Drontheim home are now loaded with copper and no room for passengers at least not safe in a gale of wind so I shall leave to travel home by land to Christiana leaving on July 26 and arriving at home on Monday the 3rd of August. I am sending this home direct by this boat as the Captain says he will go home at once and so I must say good bye darling, and will write again by the next post after arriving at Renade. I am ever my very own precious darling.

Your most affectionate husband

C. MORDAUNT

I am so thankful I have that nice photograph of you as it is a great comfort to me to look at and I think of you so often.

When he wrote on 25 June, Sir Charles told Harriett again how much he missed her and wished she could be with him 'without having the trouble of that horrid voyage which is the worst part of it'. He was thinking of her all the time and hoping she was well and had been enjoying herself. 'How did the Dudley House Ball go off?' he asked her 'and have you given that Frizzle Wig a little bit of your mind?' As far as reading matter was concerned, he had nearly finished a book called *Little Miss Fairfax* and thought it very 'naughty', and he was even more shocked to find that once the two ladies staying in the house found that out, 'they gave up the books they were reading and commenced it at once'. It seemed to Charlie that the best recommendation for novels nowadays was 'that if they are sufficiently naughty, everybody reads them especially ladies'. In spite of all this he was reasonably comfortable; he had a room to himself and a bed on the floor –

not very comfy and rather hard but I sleep sounder than ever I do in England. We have a French cook who is the fattest man I ever saw. I got up early and went to order some breakfast in the kitchen where he was just getting out of bed so I had a good view of him by accident. There are ten dogs here including Duffy as everybody has three or four. I hope you have not had much difficulty with the horses and that poor Antelope is better. Have you been riding Dandy and I hope that lovely animal is well. I am not quite sure whether to direct this to Walton or not but think it will get to you before you leave London. Please ask Bird to tell Mr Gowan the fishing tackle maker that unless he sends me out a new line directly at his own expense I will never deal with him again . . . I wish the new one to be different from that which I ordered and to be made of the usual prepared stuff instead of Hair Line and not to be too thick. I had paid ready money for the line I chose in the shop. I am afraid darling my letters may have given you some trouble but I hope you will let Bird take as much of it as possible off your hands . . . There is no silver at present at Throndysem worth having but shall get it on my way home at Christiana and hope to bring you back something nice. Since I began my letter the Thermometer went up to 120 and 90 in the shade and I went out and caught only one salmon . . . I must now say goodbye my most precious darling, take care of yourself and I look forward so much to hearing

from you and all about what you have been doing in London
and who is going with you to Walton

I am ever my dearest Harriett

Your most affectionate husband

C. MORDAUNT

In Norway, as in England, the weather had become almost un-
bearably hot, in complete contrast to previous years when Charlie
had fished in a greatcoat and two pairs of stockings and still had not
been able to keep warm. As a result, he had decided to cut short his
stay and return by way of the Continent, sending a telegraph to
inform his wife of the change of plan. He arrived at Dover on Tuesday 14 July and wrote to Harriett as he travelled on the train to
London. His intention was to post the letter in town and to be with
her the following day, catching the ten o'clock train from Paddington
which would arrive at Warwick at 12.45. so that he would be home
by luncheon time.

I am now in the train so am not able to say much as it is shaky.
Since I telegraphed to you a week ago I have travelled day and
night but just missed the boat from Christiana to Hull or I
should have got home on Monday night, so I came by Copenhagen and through Denmark, Belgium and France ... Please
send the trap to meet me my precious darling as I have so little
luggage it will take everything. I am so happy when I think we
shall be together again so soon and we will have such a jolly
month at home before going to Scotland – a sort of honeymoon
over again!

I hope they made no mistake about the telegraph which I sent
a distance of 800 miles directly I had settled to come home as I
thought it would be best to give you all the notice I could.

With my best love dearest

Ever your most affectionate husband

C. MORDAUNT

I have brought home enough salmon to last the winter and
some lovely silver things for you.

In the end, in his eagerness to be reunited with his wife, Sir Charles
decided to alter his plan and to go direct to Walton without spending
the night in London. His telegram had been delayed, and when it
arrived Harriett and her friends realised with a shock that he would

be returning home within two days, a good two weeks before they had expected him. There was a general exodus, Georgie Forbes, George Newport and Lowry Cole departing on Tuesday 14 July and Louisa Scott on the Wednesday morning. This left Harriett, as she thought, a clear day before there was any chance of her husband arriving.

All the time, as Charlie travelled home, the hot weather continued; harvesting was well under way, the labourers working in the broiling sun in temperatures of over ninety degrees, and the granaries already nearly full. At the same time the pasture lands were scorched and the brooks running dry. People were beginning to wonder if there would be enough fodder for the animals through the winter.

Tired after his long journey in the summer heat, but full of pleasant anticipation at the thought of coming home, Sir Charles arrived unexpectedly on the afternoon of Wednesday 15 July. His eagerness soon turned to anger at the sight which met his eyes. There, in front of the house, he saw his wife in the pony carriage drawn by the two enchanting white ponies which had once graced the Prince's stable, as she wheeled them round showing off her driving skills to the gentleman who stood at the door of the house watching her with considerable approval. There was no mistaking the fact that the gentleman was the Prince of Wales.

Such was Sir Charles's rage that had he lived in earlier times he might well have challenged the Prince to a duel, but as one of Trollope's heroines had complained, 'men never fight these days', and in any case it would hardly have been in order to eradicate the heir to the throne.[56] Had he discovered his rival in the bedroom, Sir Charles might have been justified in knocking the offending head against a wall, as John Manners Sutton had done on seeing his wife's lover en route for the marital bed, a scene avidly recounted by Alice Miles in her diary.[57] But to all appearances, the Prince's crime was simply that he had arrived at Walton Hall without an invitation while the master was away and had been caught in the not over-compromising position of watching while a delectable lady trotted round in a pony cart in front of him. Sir Charles's anger was, however, fuelled to white heat by the remembrance of the warnings given to him by Lord Dudley, by his wife's abuse of his trust, and by the Prince's callous exploitation of his absence. It was bitter for the husband to think of the days when he had trustingly fished for elusive salmon in Norwegian waters, totally unaware that any philandering had been going on.

We do not know what was said between the two men, but the Prince departed rapidly the way he had come, up through the wellingtonia-lined avenue to Smatchley Lodge and away to Moreton-in-Marsh station. When he had gone, Sir Charles gave orders to the groom to lead the two ponies onto the lawn below the conservatory. Then he fetched his wife and dragged her down the the steps onto the lawn so that she could watch while the two ponies were shot.

Sir Charles told the grooms to burn the little carriage, and the ponies were buried under the trees at the edge of the garden. But there was no burying the dark secret of his savage act of revenge. The shots that rang out on that summer's afternoon have reverberated around the neighbourhood for over a century. The tale told in all its gory detail by the footmen later that evening in the Peacock Inn in Wellesbourne spread like the proverbial wildfire and flourished unsuppressed. Even the pony carriage survived, the grooms defying orders and selling it to Mr Smith the Stratford glazier and plumber, whose wife happily drove it round the streets of that town for many years to come.

9
The Second Honeymoon

After the departure of the Prince, Sir Charles and his wife were able to enjoy several weeks at Walton in the continuing heat-wave before they left for Scotland. It can hardly have been the idyllic time which Sir Charles had looked forward to; but all the same, they managed to achieve some kind of a reconciliation. Sir Charles's anger, though quick to ignite, was equally quick to die down, and Lady Mordaunt knew by now how to humour him. She could be extra loving when she wanted to be, and she encouraged him to blame everything on the Prince for coming to call without warning. What, after all, is a lady to do, if the heir to the throne takes the trouble to come all the way down from London to see her? It was not the easiest thing in the world to tell a Prince the moment he arrives that he must take the next train back to London, and besides, could it not be said in his defence that he had only come down for the innocent purpose of seeing how the ponies he had sold to Sir Charles were now shaping up?

Sir Charles felt able to accept her explanations, for at this stage he knew nothing about the occasions when the Prince and others had visited his wife in London. His brother Osbert and the servants said nothing, and the gardener Broadbridge did not reveal that one evening after Lady Mordaunt had returned to Walton he had seen the shadowy figures of a lady and gentleman going up in the dusk through the garden towards the Bath House.

Sir Charles probably felt that the killing of the ponies, which were such a symbol of his wife's independence, was punishment enough. Anxious, now, to please her, and to expiate his slaughtering of the animals, he was ready to placate her by letting her accept an invitation to stay with the Farquharsons who lived at Invercauld between Braemar and Balmoral. The Prince had invited them to attend his summer ball at Abergeldie which was only a few miles away. This invitation Sir Charles also agreed to accept, although more reluctantly.

Sir Charles had learnt from the bitter experience of his return to

Walton at least one lesson. He knew now that he must never again leave his wife for such a long stretch of time, thus giving others the advantage over him. In addition he must prove, through his increased attention and companionship, that he did not deserve the jibe that he had neglected her.

It was also important to limit her visits to London, and Sir Charles now began to think seriously about his own involvement in the London scene and about his political future. Although the Queen had at first been reluctant to accept Disraeli's resignation when his Government suffered a defeat over the Irish question, it had by now become clear that there would be an autumn election. This gave Sir Charles the chance to withdraw from parliamentary life. By the end of July there were already rumours that he would not stand again and that John Hardy[58] was likely to offer himself as the new candidate. From the immediate point of view, Sir Charles realised that if he did not become involved in all the business of an autumn election campaign, he would be free to take Harriett away to some destination more lively and more acceptable to her than the fjords of Norway. She was, of course, won over by this possibility, and soon they were discussing plans for a visit to Paris.

It seemed now that they could put the past behind them and look forward to a happier future. Harriett was exceptionally loving at this time, and the few weeks they spent at Walton before leaving for Scotland did seem to develop into the kind of second honeymoon that Charlie had looked forward to. Then one day just before their departure, Harriett confided in Mrs Cadogan when they were out in the carriage together, that she believed she could be 'in the family way'.

At Invercauld, the Farquharsons had gathered together a house party that was very much to Harriett's taste. Her old friend Captain Farquhar was there, as well as Sir Frederic Johnstone, a charming bachelor who was one of the Prince's closest friends. Once or twice, when Sir Charles was out enjoying himself on the grouse moor, the Prince drove over from Abergeldie to join those who had remained in the house. Sir Charles was probably unaware of these visits, and he duly accompanied his wife to the Abergeldie ball, speaking to the Prince briefly during the course of the evening.

By the time they left Invercauld, Harriett had found a new friend in Sir Frederic Johnstone. He and Sir Charles had been contemporaries at Eton, but Sir Frederic was several years younger and they had never met. He was a keen racegoer and racehorse owner and expressed a wish to attend the September races at Warwick, which gave Lady Mordaunt an excuse to invite him to Walton.

After leaving Invercauld, the Mordaunts spent a week with the Atholls and a few days with Helen Forbes at Newe. Afterwards they travelled on to Moncreiffe where Sir Charles's mother-in-law, Lady Louisa, greeted him with her usual affection. This year Sir Charles did not go to Corrour for the stalking, and they returned to Walton at the end of August, Sir Frederic Johnstone joining them there soon afterwards.

The weather was still fine, with the hottest temperatures ever recorded for September, and that year the Warwick races were particularly enjoyable, with many celebrated horses competing, crowds of spectators packing the Common hill behind the course from an early hour each day and many large parties coming in to watch the proceedings from drays. Sir Frederic Johnstone enjoyed himself so much that he returned to Walton some days later for a second visit.

10

A Spate of Letters

Sir Frederick Johnstone turned out to be a pleasant companion and he soon established himself in the role of a 'darling', also acting as the Prince's go-between.

Sir Charles had let the Prince know, in his own melodramatic way, that he did not want Harriett to have any further communication with him. This meant that it had become too dangerous even to put letters in the post, and it seems that Sir Frederic Johnstone was now to act as a messenger, delivering a number of letters that passed between Lady Mordaunt and the Prince in the course of the next few weeks. Harriett wrote first, asking the Prince to put in a word for a friend's son at the Royal Asylum of St Anne's Society, and also telling him about her recent doings at Walton. She did not get her reply until the Prince returned from Scotland to Marlborough House. He wrote from there on 13 October telling her that he was glad that she was 'flourishing at Walton' and adding that he hoped her husband had enjoyed good sport with the partridges. Since he had last seen her he himself had been to Dunrobin, a 'charming stay', followed by a few days with the Grosvenors where he had shot four stags. Most of his cronies had been with him, all wearing the kilt, and the Prince reported that Sam Buckley had looked 'first-rate' in his, while Sir H. Pilly Oliver had not looked as bad as Harriett had been led to believe. They were all enjoying themselves exchanging photographs in the same old way, and the Prince told Harriett that he had received a 'charming epistle' from one of her sisters – he did not say which. Then there was the news that Harriett had referred to in her letter, the engagement of Lord Hamilton who only three months before had sent his valet off to Paddington to present Harriett with a dog. It was perhaps because Hamilton had been one of her own admirers that Harriett had made some rather unfavourable remarks about his bride-to-be. The Prince remonstrated with her, telling her that in fact everyone seemed delighted by the match and, even more important, Hamilton himself seemed to be very much in love, 'a rare occurrence nowadays' as the Prince cynically put it. 'I think you are rather hard on the young lady' he told Harriett 'as although not exactly pretty, she is very nice looking, has charming manners, and is very popular with every one.'[59]

Meanwhile Sir Charles had been pressing on with his plan to pull out of his parliamentary duties. In mid September he wrote a letter expressing his intention of retiring on the grounds of ill health, although there is no evidence to suggest that he was in any way unwell. In fact nobody could say that he had been the most conscientious of Members, since he had only voted 36 times in 164 divisions, whereas his co-member Mr Wise had voted in 126. All the same Mr Wise did his best to persuade Sir Charles to change his mind as he would have liked to retire himself, but Charlie was adamant. 'Since the last election' he wrote in his resignation letter, 'I have supported the present government in passing a measure of reform which will largely increase the constituency and will I believe give additional strength to those constitutional and conservative principles which have been for so long upheld in Warwickshire.'

But now the time had come to stand down. Harriett would probably have liked him to continue, as she would then have had increased opportunities to spend her time in London. There were some who were critical of the prospective candidate, Mr Hardy, since nobody quite seemed to know what he stood for, apart from the fact that he was an ardent champion of the Game Laws. He did at least have the ability to make a speech 'without having anything to say', always an advantage for a politician. The Liberal opponent, Sir Robert Hamilton of Tiddington, near Stratford-on-Avon, on the other hand had a more definite programme and came out boldly as an advocate of the spread of education.

For Sir Charles, such questions now were of less interest than the welfare of his wife and the child she was carrying. The die was cast; he had turned his back on politics, sacrificing the status he had enjoyed as a Member of Parliament, a sacrifice that he had made for her sake. Two things were certain: one was that Sir Charles intended to keep a much closer watch on his wife where the Prince was concerned, and the second that the Prince himself had no intention whatsoever of giving her up. He had read in the papers that she had been in London the previous weekend and was disappointed that she had not let him know as he would have made a point of calling on her. He was in fact finding London boring, as it was very 'empty', although since he had plenty to do, the time did not pass too slowly. 'There are some good plays going on, and we are going the round of them' he told her. He also went down to shoot occasionally at Windsor and Newmarket. The news of her pregnancy had evidently reached him as he said he supposed that she had given up the idea she had told him about of going to Paris in November.

> On the 26th I shall shoot with General Hall, at Newmarket, the following week at Knowsley, and then at Windsor and Sandringham before we go abroad. This will probably be on the 18th or 19th of next month . . . My brother is here, but at the end of the month he starts for Plymouth, on his long cruise of nearly two years.[60] Now I shall say good-bye, and hoping that we may have a chance of seeing you before we leave,
> I remain,
>
> yours most sincerely
> ALBERT EDWARD

Ignoring the dangers of further dalliance with Harriett, the Prince would have liked to meet her again, frustrated as he was by the fact that he had missed her on the only occasion she had come up to town. He was particularly anxious to meet her because he had by now finalised plans to take his wife abroad for the winter. The plan had partly been prompted by the fact that Sandringham was shortly to undergo a refurbishment and would not be habitable for several months.

The Princess had not been in a happy frame of mind since their return from Ireland. She had so enjoyed the Irish visit with Bertie at her side. Everything there, the warmth and enthusiasm of the people and the beautiful scenery, had filled her with happiness. Scotland, by contrast, did not appeal to her, and she had refused to go there this year. She had after all only just given birth to her baby, and in addition, she told Princess Louise, she did not exactly think that the Highlands were the most suitable place for somebody with a stiff leg.[61] She may, however, have regretted her decision after hearing rumours that Bertie had not behaved too well during his stay at Abergeldie. Altogether reports that he had in the past months been unfaithful were gaining momentum. It was all very well for the Prince to insist that the Moncreiffe sisters were family friends and no more. But why should the apparently innocuous Sir Charles have reacted with such violence on finding the Prince standing at his door? And then there was the question of Helen Forbes's baby, Evelyn Elizabeth,

born on 7 October. The gossips delighted to look back to the previous February when the Prince had been in London without his wife
and had spent much time in Helen's company. There was no proof,
of course, which was probably precisely why the Prince preferred to
pay his court to young married ladies who currently cohabited with
their husband. All the same, this could have been a case where it
would have been wise, on looking into the cradle, to take the advice
given by Lady Louisa Moncreiffe to her daughters which was 'never
to comment on a likeness'. And it had by now become common
knowledge that Lady Mordaunt was in an interesting condition, and
the scandal mongers would surely remember about the goings on in
London during Sir Charles's absence in Norway.

The Prince remained confident; provided the husband suspected
nothing, he was safe, and even if anyone did have their misgivings,
they would surely remain silent out of deference to the heir to the
throne. And should anybody intercept his letters, what would they
find in those? No daring use of Christian name terms and nothing
except some expressions of friendliness and a few gossipy titbits as
well as an invitation that might have come from his wife as well as
from himself – 'hoping that we may have a chance of seeing you
before we leave'.

All the same the Prince was making extra efforts to be affable both
to his wife and to the Queen. He was adept at turning on the extra charm when it was needed. In their letters to each other, both
his sister Vicky and his mother dwelt at this time on Bertie's better
qualities, on his kindness and his good heart.

After receiving the Prince's second letter from London, Lady Mordaunt again replied, and again had to wait for an answer until Sir
Frederic Johnstone came down for the November races. The Prince
wrote from the home of Sir William Knollys who lived not too far
from Sandringham

My dear Lady Mordaunt,
    I must apologise for not having answered your last kind letter,
but accept my best thanks for it now. Since the 10th I have been
here at Sir William Knollys house, as I am building a totally new
one.[62] I am here *en garçon* and we have had very good shooting.
The Duke of Cambridge, Lord Suffield, Lord Alfred Paget, Lord
de Grey, Sir Frederic Johnstone, Chaplin, General Hall, Captain
(Sam) Buckley, Major Grey, and myself, compose the party, and

the great Francis[63] arrived on Saturday, but he is by no means a distinguished shot. Sir Frederic Johnstone tells me that he is going to stay with you tomorrow for the Warwick races, so he can give you the best accounts of us. This afternoon, after shooting, I return to London; and tomorrow night the Princess, our three eldest children, and myself, start for Paris, where we shall remain a week, and then straight to Copenhagen where we spend Christmas, and the beginning of January we start on a longer trip. We shall go to Venice, and then by sea to Alexandria, and up the Nile so far as we can go, and later to Constantinople, Athens, and home by Italy; and I don't expect we shall be back again before April. I fear, therefore, I shall not see you for a long time, but trust to find you perhaps in London on our return. If you should have time it will be very kind to write to me sometimes. Letters to Marlborough House, to be forwarded, will always reach me. I hope you will remain strong and well, and, wishing you a very pleasant winter,

I remain,

yours most sincerely,

ALBERT EDWARD

The next day Sir Frederic Johnstone travelled from Sandringham to Walton, taking the Prince's letter with him. The Prince left almost immediately on his travels.

The Calm before the Storm

Now that his wife had given Sir Charles the news that he most wished to hear, he did all he could to make her feel happy and at home in the country. To combat the 'dullness' which would have encouraged her to rush off to London at every possible opportunity, he allowed her to drive herself about without a servant to accompany her, and he also let Sir Frederic Johnstone and Captain Farquhar pay her frequent visits, staying for as long as they liked. His brothers sometimes thought he was being more than a little unobservant. It seemed to Osbert that Captain Farquhar and his sister-in-law were on very intimate terms. They would would often disappear together into Harriett's boudoir, the excuse being that Farquhar was helping her make a screen that had to be finished in time for the Perth bazaar.[64] Osbert also noticed that the Captain sometimes made his health an excuse for spending the day alone with Lady Mordaunt. If he did go out shooting, he usually met the others for lunch in the field, and on the one occasion when he said he would go out in the morning, he kept everybody waiting at the bridge and did not appear until about an hour later. He also tended to be ill on a Sunday morning, and on all his weekend stays at Walton he only went to church once. Strangely enough, Lady Mordaunt always managed to be indisposed at the same time. As Trollope's Duke of Omnium had discovered, Sunday mornings were an excellent time to conduct an affair, with all the household dutifully trooping to worship and leaving the lady of the house on her own.

On one occasion, when Osbert was taking the morning service at Walton Church, he noticed that his sister-in-law's pew was empty and that Sir Frederic Johnstone was also absent. After the service was over, Sir Charles asked Mrs Cadogan to return to the house as his wife wanted to see her. They went across to the Hall and Sir Charles called her name several times. When he failed to get an answer, Mrs Cadogan went upstairs to the boudoir but there was no sign of Lady Mordaunt either there or in her bedroom. Mrs Cadogan then went out into the garden, and Bird joined in the search. Later, as Mrs

Cadogan was leaving to go back to the Parsonage, she met Harriett who appeared rather suddenly and cut across the grass to greet her. She explained that she had been unable to get to church because she had a cold, but Mrs Cadogan was surprised by this as she did not appear to have any symptoms. There was no sign of Sir Frederic.

The brothers still did not say anything to Charlie about his wife's behaviour for fear of making him unhappy. They were in any case quite sure that he would not believe anything bad of the wife to whom he was so much attached. It was well known that a husband could get hysterical, even suicidal, when faced with any suggestion of a wife's infidelity. Louis Trevelyan, for example, in Trollope's novel *He Knew He Was Right*, becomes quite paranoid about his wife's harmless relationship with an elderly friend of the family.[65] All the same, although they said nothing to Charlie, the brothers certainly did at times speculate as to whether or not Harriett had committed adultery with any of her admirers although they really had nothing other than strong suspicions to go on.

The fact that Sir Frederic had for a long time been one of the Prince's closest friends should have put Sir Charles on the alert. Sir Frederic had first met the Prince when they were both at Christ Church, introducing him to the fast set which was famous for its extravagance and womanising. Sir Charles, by contrast, avoided such things, having been trained by his mother to live quietly and frugally. He had spent much of his time at Oxford on the river and he had rowed in the Christ Church eight, discovering that he could save expense when in training as he was not expected to eat too much or have wine for lunch. This was better than cricket where lunches were expensive and matches tended to last all day.

It was Sir Frederic and his cronies who had really opened the Prince's eyes to the possibilities of his position, introducing him, when his formidable guardian General Bruce was looking the other way, to all the 'drunkenness and other evils' which Sir Charles had studiously managed to avoid.[66] They had remained friends, and the Prince frequently stayed with him at Melton Mowbray when he was hunting with the Quorn.

There was no doubt that whatever his past life was like, Harriett found Sir Frederic quite charming. She thought it surprising that he had reached the age of twenty-seven without being ensnared into matrimony, rich, titled and handsome as he was. When she asked her husband if he could explain why this should be, Sir Charles seemed embarrassed and replied that he thought it was something to do with Sir Frederic's health, as he was said to suffer from a disease which prevented him from marrying. Harriett pressed Sir Charles to tell her what disease it was, and he reluctantly did so, at the same time explaining that one form of the disease could affect any children of the marriage.

In the weeks before Christmas, Lady Mordaunt suddenly seemed to become very nervous about her condition. Her brother-in-law John overheard her saying to Sir Frederic that they were promising a very bad year for women in her state. Sir Frederic did not appear to be sympathetic; he spoke to her quite roughly and told her not to talk nonsense, reminding her that there must be about twenty-four million other women in her condition throughout the world so that it would be quite ridiculous to generalise.

At Christmas the household travelled over as usual to Witley Court and immediately after her return Harriett, accompanied by the Duke and Duchess of Atholl, went up to London with Jessie Clarke in attendance. They stayed at the Alexandra Hotel on Hyde Park Corner, where the rooms looked out over Rotten Row and the Park, and where there were elegant coffee-rooms and suites, with an 'ascending room' for visitors. As he walked down the street on the 29 December, the day that the Atholls left, Sir Frederic happened by chance to meet Georgie Forbes who told him where Harriett was staying. He therefore called on her and was asked to dinner the next day. Although he insisted that he had been given no warning that he was to be tête-à-tête, they did in fact dine together.

When she was being dressed for dinner, Lady Mordaunt asked Jessie to call at Bolton's Library in Knightsbridge and order them to send a pack of playing cards to the hotel. She said nothing about entertaining a visitor. Jessie spent the evening out, having ordered the cards, and when she returned to the hotel at about ten o'clock, one of the waiters called her attention to a parcel left for Lady Mordaunt on the hall table. At this moment the man who had waited on Lady Mordaunt at dinner called down the stairs to the waiter in the hall below. 'This is the second time I have told you' he said 'that no parcels are to be taken in Lady Mordaunt's sitting-room as her ladyship does not wish to be disturbed.' Jessie took charge of the packet, and after she had seen Sir Frederic Johnstone leave the private sitting-room at about midnight, she herself went into the room and explained about the parcel, which contained several packs of cards on approval. Lady Mordaunt mildly reproved her for not bringing the cards to her earlier.

During the following two days Lady Mordaunt was out of the hotel most of the time. She did not ask Jessie to go with her but was usually accompanied by Lady Kinnoull's footman. She visited Dr Priestley and then went to one of the most expensive shops in town to order all her baby linen. On New Year's Eve she dined out and on Friday 1 January she apparently ate by herself at the hotel. She paid the final bill, the sum of £10. 19s. 8d., by cheque.

Since Sir Charles had great confidence in the local practitioner, Dr Orford, he had originally made arrangements for his wife to give birth at Walton. However, soon after her return from London she told him that she thought it would be better if the child was born in London under the care of Dr Priestley who was considered to be one of the leading obstetricians of his day, holding the post of Professor of Midwifery at King's College Hospital. After some hesitation, Sir Charles acquiesced, agreeing to take a house in London for the confinement. He demurred at first when she said that she would like him to lease the house for six weeks before 15 April, the date when the baby was expected, but she told him that Dr Priestley thought it would probably be early, adding that as a man Charlie could not be expected to understand such things.

That January Harriett made her condition an excuse to avoid most of the more formal events of the Warwickshire season. She dutifully attended the Hunt Ball, but left it to her neighbour at Compton Verney, the young Lady Willoughby de Broke, to open the dancing at the Yeomanry Ball a few days later. Lady Willoughby was more likely to enjoy participating in a staid quadrille than Harriett for she was cast in a different and far more respectable mould. It was Lord Willoughby's good fortune that he had married a wife who had as little taste for the London life as he had himself.[67] Harriett and Louisa Scott, however, found her altogether too sedate and sober.

Somewhat to her dismay, Lady Louisa had heard that Harriett was to invite all her friends down to a party at Walton, which was particularly unwise in view of the fact that she had recently experienced some nasty 'spasms'. Lady Louisa advised her to treat these with some belladonna linament, imploring her to take care of herself during the party, and adding 'I am afraid, dear child, that you have not much but discomfort to look forward to for the next three months.'

Headstrong, or 'stiff-necked', as she was, Harriett probably ignored her mother's advice to take care of herself. She and her contemporaries refused to be hampered by the conventional restrictions imposed on women 'in a certain condition'. They would go about in tight, light-coloured dresses without even wearing a shawl or scarf, and worse still would dance and 'even valse at seven months!!!!' as the Queen noted with some horror. Vicky wondered how such young women could have 'so little delicacy and dignity' as she felt much too shy of showing herself before the children and the servants, and as for dancing she did not think 'it was nice at all'.[68]

Harriett had invited her younger sister Blanche to come down from Scotland for the party, but her mother explained that this would not be possible as Blanche was helping look after their sister Frances, 'Francy', who had fallen seriously ill. 'Bunch was so sorry for herself not going to you' wrote Lady Louisa. Nevertheless it was perhaps as well that the younger sister was not exposed to the excitements of Harriett's party, as there were certainly some high jinks and japes which ended up with some of the furniture, and notably the doormats, being found in some peculiar places at the end of the day.

Frederic Johnstone, Lowry Cole, George Newport, Robert Duff, Louisa Scott, most of the old gang, were among those who had been invited to the party, which Robert Duff discussed with Louisa when they met at a ball a few days after she returned to London. He had evidently much enjoyed himself, and Louisa told Harriett that he kept asking her 'how I had left the door-mats at Walton at which I looked vacant, but finally I had to roar with laughter. He's not a bit x about it, but evidently much amused.'[69] It had all been what the Prince would probably have described as 'capital fun', especially as it seems that they had somehow arranged for Sir Charles to be out that evening.

Life in London at that moment was not particularly exciting, and Louisa often felt oppressed by her mother who was 'always on the pine' and who disapproved of her fast friends. She had attended Lady Fife's dance which, she reported, had been very jolly; there had been 'every man one knew and rather too many of them'. Dr Priestley had been there too, persecuting one of his female patients, 'Lady H', with reminders, as she 'danced and frisked' the night away, that she should be careful because of her heart condition.

There were big gaps in the social circle. The Prince and Princess were still abroad, about to embark for Egypt, and many people were still out of town, while several of the young men were seriously thinking of matrimony. Lord Hamilton's wedding to Lady Mary Curzon had taken place on 7 January, and it looked very much as if Georgie Forbes was heading in the same direction. Louisa had seen him at Lady Fife's party and thought he looked very jolly and happy. For some time he had been paying his court to Lord Dudley's niece Netty[70] but then there had been some misunderstandings and they had only recently come together again. 'Did you know it was your sister Mrs Forbes who put it straight between Netty and Georgie?' Louisa Scott asked Harriett. 'At least she had told Netty from George that he still wanted to marry her and she said she did ditto, which was satisfactory for him.' Georgie had sobered down somewhat in recent months, but Louisa did what she could to remedy that, telling Harriett that Georgie had come to luncheon the previous Saturday with a big pin in his necktie containing Netty's painted photo 'and we bullied him into his old state of jollity. My father told him as one piece of advice never call your wife "dear" for people never do that till they hate each other.'

With all this talk of matrimony, even Lowry Cole seemed to be getting down to the serious business of finding himself a wife. There had been some tantalising rumours that he was courting the rich but ugly Charlotte Baird of Dumfriess, who with her sister had recently inherited a considerable fortune.[71] Whispers had already reached Alice Miles in Paris. 'Let me tell you' she told her informant

there are all the situations for a drama in what you wrote me of Lord Cole and Fanny Moncreiffe. She, poor girl, was, or at any rate got the credit for, being very much in love with him, but when the hour of trial came, you see the *beaux yeux* and silvery voice of Miss Baird's money chests proved too much for his Lordship's virtue to withstand; and after all I don't know that he is very much to be blamed, for the Enniskillen escutcheon is in pitiable want of regilding, and he may as well do it as anyone else. The Mammon of Unrighteousness is, and as far as I can make out, has always been, undisputed sovereign of this world, and we cannot be surprised when he assumes his rights and engulfs another victim.[72]

Alice had also been told that Harriett's sister had decided to marry another man, Major Arbuthnot, out of pique. Alice applauded this action as a master stroke, 'and sufficiently politic, Arbuthnot being very well off – Mammon again'.

In this Alice was, however, misinformed since it was in fact the other sister, Selina, 'Lina', who had become engaged to Major Arbuthnot. Lady Louisa told Harriett that the couple had apparently met at a ball, and it had been a case of love at first sight. Major William Arbuthnot of the 14th Hussars was a young widower whose wife had died after being struck by lightning. Lady Louisa had originally hoped that he would 'make up' to Blanche who was currently her eldest unmarried daughter, but all the same she was well pleased now that he had revealed the true object of his affections. She had warned him about her daughter's temper, which in any case had much improved, and this had not deterred him. Such were Major Arbuthnot's merits that Lady Louisa could only feel great satisfaction at the match.

> He is the man of all others to suit her as she not only likes him but respects him and he is so nice ... He is about twenty-eight and very good-looking and a good old family, he has £2000 a year now and will have six or seven thousand besides his prospects of promotion in his profession; he soon expects the command of his regiment. He wants Lina to have a season in London which is better, but as the race of men in general go now I think she will be very well off and has every chance of happiness.

On 14 February Harriett received a Valentine card which she opened at breakfast. Charlie was curious, and wanted to know who it was from.[73] She told him that it had been sent by Louisa Scott as a joke. 'Come, that won't do' wrote Louisa when she heard that her friend had put the blame on her, although she was amused by Harriett's pretence.

The news that a house had been booked for the birth on 1 March was by now well known and there were probably other people besides John Mordaunt's wife Elizabeth who had counted the months on their fingers from Charlie's stay in Norway and wondered what was going on. Elizabeth was herself expecting a child in early March and so would naturally have checked the timing. Harriett tried to explain to Mrs Cadogan by saying that she had been led to believe that first babies were always early, but the clergyman's wife said it had not been so in her own case, and left it at that.

Harriett would often visit the Parsonage, usually driving herself up there or if the weather was bad asking the coachman to take her in the carriage. The clergyman's wife was always helpful and sympathetic, for she had noticed that although her young friend appeared to be in good health physically, she seemed at the same time to be tense and anxious about her forthcoming ordeal and was often uncharacteristically silent, as if brooding over something.

It seemed to Sir Charles, too, that his wife sometimes seemed depressed. During the course of his marriage he had become accustomed to her fits of hysteria, but this struck him as something different, and he attributed it to the natural apprehension of a woman approaching her time. She certainly seemed to take every possible chance of attending the sacrament, and had in general become more religious and perhaps less frivolous in her outlook. As far as her physical state was concerned, he realised that she was suffering from some sort of discomfort due to a discharge; she did not say much about it, but he understood that Dr Priestley had given her some remedies. He felt distinctly shocked when she suggested to him that if he felt deprived he should seek his satisfaction with 'one of those women'. When he in his innocence asked what women she meant she replied 'You know, those women in London who everyone goes to.'

Harriett revealed the considerate side of her nature when she sent the ailing Lady Scott a present of some flowers, which Louisa thought was 'tiddumley sweet, kind and dear of her'. To her mother she despatched a bottle of champagne and a large consignment of grapes and to the ailing Francy a smelling bottle – 'just what she wanted so much' Lady Louisa wrote appreciatively. To Lady Louisa herself, although Charlie was not to know this, Harriett had also sent thirty pounds, a very welcome gift when the family resources were distinctly stretched as a result of Francy's illness. To her great consternation, Lady Louisa had discovered that she was pregnant with her fifteenth child when she really believed that she had finally finished. She had made some fairly determined efforts to be rid of it without success and she was feeling extremely tired and unwell. 'It makes me very miserable for every reason and I am feeling very ill but it can't be helped' she wrote. The worst of it was that she had been so sure she would never have any more children that she had done away with every article of clothes into which she could pack 'the little beast', so that it would have to live 'rolled up in a bundle of old flannel petticoats'. To make things worse, Miss Laing the governess had been away on holiday so that Lina had been taking charge of the younger children, but fortunately a new tutor had arrived who was able to take the two boys off her hands. Francy still had to be carried down every day to a bed in the sitting room, either her mother or Bunch sleeping with her at night.

In the circumstances, it was difficult for Lady Louisa to know whether or not she would be able to go down to London for Harriett's confinement. She promised, however, that she would make every effort to be there if Harriett really wanted her. 'Just tell me honestly exactly what you would like and soon dear if you can . . . I suppose as usual I shall manage all I have to do.'

One possible plan was to go to London and then return to Moncreiffe in June just in time to 'land' the baby there. But what with Francy's illness and the expected baby, the family had come to the conclusion that a season in town would be out of the question, and they had therefore decided to let their London house. 'The rent for it is a decided help' Lady Louisa admitted. Meanwhile Harriett's sister Helen assured her that she would do everything she could to help:

> If you would like to have me instead quite as well as Mama of course I shall be only too glad to do anything for you I can and I think I know what sort of things are a comfort to one, but I daresay you would rather have Mama. I have no doubt she would be very glad to come but you had better not write anything more to her about it till after you have seen me as we can talk it over better.

Helen had been charged to buy some muslin curtains for the house where the baby was to be born and she had managed to find some material that was 'pretty and cheap'. She and her husband were going off to stay at Kimbolton with the Duchess of Manchester and would be away when Harriett first arrived in London, but she promised to visit her the moment she arrived back.

Both Helen and Louisa Scott assured Harriett that she was not missing much remaining in the country as there was not a great deal going on in town. All the same Louisa told her that it was to be hoped that she would come up in time to see the latest plays and in general have some fun.

12

The Birth

On Saturday 27 February, just two days before she was due to leave for London, Harriett drove herself up to the Parsonage. Sir Charles was out hunting and she told Mrs Cadogan that she had called in as she was on her way to Wellesbourne to fetch the newspapers. It was while they were talking that she suddenly broke off the conversation and asked if she could go upstairs. After this she drove straight back to the Hall, where she changed her clothes and immediately went out again, carrying out her plan of fetching the papers from Wellesbourne.

Mrs Caborn had been out for the afternoon, but when she returned to the Hall she was told that she was needed upstairs. She found Lady Mordaunt in bed in a state of some agitation. From what she said, Mrs Caborn realised at once that the waters must have broken when she was up at the Parsonage. Lady Mordaunt asked whether she thought she would be able to get to London in time for the birth and the housekeeper replied that she certainly would not.

A messenger was sent post haste to summon Dr Orford. When he arrived, he confirmed that the baby was on the way. Sir Charles was told the news when he returned from hunting, and at about seven o'clock that evening Mrs Cadogan received an urgent note from Mrs Caborn to say that there were 'symptoms'. The housekeeper requested Mrs Cadogan, whose youngest child was just under a year old, to lend everything necessary for the mother and baby as the expensive layette ordered by Lady Mordaunt was not likely to come in time. A makeshift cradle was prepared for the new arrival.

Late that evening an experienced monthly nurse, Mrs Elizabeth Hancox, the wife of Daniel Hancox, a Tysoe stone mason, heard an unexpected knock on her door. She was asked whether she was free to come at once to Walton Hall. Since she had no other commitments she agreed to go, and Sir Charles sent a conveyance to fetch her. She arrived at Walton at about 11.30, and at once began to take charge. At that stage the labour pains had not started in earnest, but all the same Dr Orford decided to sleep in the house. Sir Charles

snatched what sleep he could get on a bed in his dressing-room. Mrs
Cadogan, who had brought down the baby clothes, remained with
Harriett until one o'clock in the morning, trying to soothe her down
as she seemed very frightened and distressed. Mrs Hancox sat up
with her for the rest of the night, later describing her condition as
'poorly'.

Dr Orford, who had been called to the Hall on a number of occasions to attend Lady Mordaunt and to answer questions about
her pregnancy, neverthless noticed that at first she was somewhat
reserved with him. He attributed this to a feeling of 'delicacy'.

Mrs Cadogan went down to the Hall very early next morning
to make sure that everything was all right. Lady Mordaunt seemed
pleased to see her but made it clear that she would like her to leave
the room during the last stages of labour in view of the fact that Dr
Priestley had told her nobody needed to be with her except the doctor
and the nurse. She said she was afraid that under the influence of
chloroform she might start talking 'all sorts of nonsense' and she did
not want to make a fool of herself. Labour began in earnest at about
ten o'clock and when Dr Orford began to administer chloroform at
about twelve, Mrs Cadogan duly went downstairs and did not go
back into the bedroom until about four hours later when Sir Charles
sent her to enquire how things were going. By that time Harriett was
no longer under chloroform and Dr Orford asked Mrs Cadogan to
stay as he wanted her assistance.

A baby girl was born at about five o'clock that evening. The child
was delivered without difficulty; she was remarkably small and somewhat emaciated although perfectly formed. Mrs Cadogan went down
and told Sir Charles that the confinement had gone very smoothly
and that Lady Mordaunt had not suffered too much or become too
exhausted.

At about eleven o'clock that evening, Mrs Hancox noticed as she
settled her down for the night that Lady Mordaunt seemed slightly
agitated.

'I want to ask you one question,' she said.

The midwife imagined that, like all mothers, Lady Mordaunt
wanted to know if there was anything wrong with the baby, and so
she was somewhat startled when Lady Mordaunt asked her if the
child was 'diseased'.

'My lady, you must mean deformed,' said Mrs Hancox.

'You know what I mean' Lady Mordaunt insisted. 'Is it born with the complaint?' Mrs Hancox tried to reassure her, saying that she could not see anything wrong with the child, apart from the fact that it was very small indeed. Mrs Hancox then persuaded Lady Mordaunt to get off to sleep.

Mrs Hancox was puzzled by the mother's attitude, particularly as nobody else seemed worried. The baby was certainly small; with the accuracy of a practised midwife, Mrs Hancox had held it in her hands and guessed that it weighed only three and a half pounds. She later put it onto the scales to confirm that she was right.

Sir Charles went in to see his wife the next morning, and she immediately asked him whether he had put an announcement into the newspaper. He said it would be in the *Morning Post* and *The Times*. She told him to have it put in the other papers, and she asked particularly if he had added the word 'prematurely'. She laid great stress on this and when he replied 'Yes' she said 'That is right.' They then talked about the naming of the child, and she asked whether he thought that Violet was a pretty name. He agreed that it was, and said that he thought one name would be enough, but she said that she wanted the second name to be 'Caroline' after his mother, and as she was very 'urgent' about it, he consented, not seeing any good reason to refuse. When he was later asked if there had been anything strange about her at this time, he replied that she had seemed to him 'perfectly sensible'.

Lady Mordaunt spent a quiet day, but once again, when Mrs Hancox was making her comfortable for the night, she brought up the subject of the child being diseased and asked whether Mrs Hancox had noticed anything wrong.

'Nonsense, what can be the matter with the baby?' Mrs Hancox said.

'Did Mrs Caborn or Mrs Cadogan see anything?'

'What could they see more than is common at birth?'

'Of course you and Dr Orford must know what's the matter with it.'

'All I can say', Mrs Hancox reiterated, 'is that it is near enough to be an eight months baby and don't worry yourself any more about it.'

'How do you know it is an eight months baby?' Lady Mordaunt asked.

'Because it has nails which we don't expect at seven' said Mrs Hancox.

This reply seemed to satisfy Lady Mordaunt and she soon went off to sleep.

13

The Confession

As soon as she heard the news of the birth, Helen Forbes went down to see her sister and was joined by her mother later on the Tuesday. They found Harriett quite calm, but uncharacteristically silent and unwilling to talk. She did not in fact give them a very warm welcome, and seemed indifferent as to how long they stayed. Helen left after a day or two but Lady Louisa decided that she would stay on until the weekend.

Mrs Hancox was really the only person Harriett talked to freely at this time. She was continually seeking reassurance about the state of the child. The midwife was surprised by her knowledge of the difference between the ordinary diseases which many women suffer from, and 'the disease which is caught from men'. Mrs Hancox felt that Lady Mordaunt knew much more than ladies are expected to know on this subject. When she asked whether Mrs Hancox thought she would ever recover from 'the disease', Mrs Hancox told her that it was impossible to understand what she was trying to say, especially in view of the fact that Sir Charles was known to be such a steady quiet gentleman.

'Oh yes, so he is, he is as innocent as possible' said Lady Mordaunt.

Mrs Hancox later testified that she did her best to stop her going on in this vein. Lady Mordaunt, however, said she would go mad if she was not allowed to talk. 'I have something to tell you, and I must and will tell you now and alone' she insisted.

Mrs Hancox said she ought to fetch Sir Charles, but Lady Mordaunt would not let her, saying that she would tell him later. She first of all said 'Hush' to indicate that she was about to reveal a secret. Mrs Hancox, she said, was probably quite right in her assumption that Violet was an eight months child.

'I have been thinking it over' she explained 'and you are quite right for the baby comes from the last week in June when I was in London and Sir Charles in Norway.'

Naturally this revelation startled the monthly nurse. But she pulled herself together and asked the pertinent question: 'How was it that people called when Sir Charles was out?'

'They often do' Lady Mordaunt replied. 'He takes no notice of that.'
She then mentioned that although the Prince of Wales had himself
called on her on a number of occasions, she was sure that the child was
Lord Cole's. Mrs Hancox told her not to talk nonsense and made the
down to earth remark that it was very difficult for a married lady to be
sure about something like that. Lady Mordaunt did, however, appear
to be less agitated now that she had made this final revelation; indeed
Mrs Hancox described her as being quite 'collected'.

In the course of the next few days Lady Mordaunt mentioned Lord
Cole's name several times to Mrs Hancox, although she did not confide in anybody else. Lady Louisa was apparently unaware that there
were any problems, although Charlie was not altogether happy about
his wife's condition. He felt that she did not care for the child as
a normal mother would have done and she was certainly not interested in feeding it, only putting it to her breast on one occasion in his
presence in order to please him. He was later to say that when he spoke
to her about nursing the child – Dr Orford having suggested that he
should persuade her to try to feed it – she shrank from him 'in great
dread'.

On one occasion when he went in to see her, she asked rather
strangely whether he had been crying as his eyes looked red. He told
her that they were watery because he had a cold. She had seemed
worried, and dissatisfied with his reply, and he expressed his uneasiness to his mother-in-law, asking whether she thought that Harriett
could be suffering from milk fever. Lady Louisa replied reassuringly
that she was sure all was well, and she expressed satisfaction with the
care her daughter was getting from Dr Orford and Mrs Hancox. If
Harriett did seem depressed at times, Lady Louisa said, this was not
unusual in women who had given birth, and in fact Georgy had
suffered badly from depression following the birth of her first child. As
usual Sir Charles felt that he got on very well with Lady Louisa and in
the course of the next few days they had many 'amicable' conversations.

Mrs Cadogan visited Lady Mordaunt each day, staying for only a
short time so as not to tire her. She found her rather subdued and was
surprised that she never talked about the baby or made any attempt to
nurse it. Mrs Cadogan only once saw it in bed with her. On the Wednesday, when she went to the nursery, Mrs Cadogan noticed a discharge from the baby's eyes. She told Mrs Hancox to take extra care
and to make sure that Violet was not lying in a draught. She was afraid

the makeshift cradle could be the cause of the trouble. The next day when Dr Orford came he diagnosed ophthalmia and prescribed the customary remedies.

At first nobody told Lady Mordaunt about the baby's eyes for fear of causing her unnecessary anxiety, but as soon as she knew, she became very agitated, and even more so when the eyes deteriorated and Lady Louisa suggested that the advice of an oculist should be sought. Dr Orford agreed to contact Dr Solomon, an eye surgeon practising at the Birmingham Midland Eye Hospital.[74] This did nothing to comfort Lady Mordaunt. She became so worried about the emaciated-looking child, whose eyes were by now quite closed up, that on Thursday 4 March she asked for a message to be sent to Mr Cadogan requesting him to come down at once and baptise the baby privately. When he arrived he asked Lady Mordaunt how she was and she replied that she felt pretty well. His impression was that she was in surprisingly good health. He made a few 'ordinary remarks' about the baby, before christening her in the presence of her parents, Lady Louisa and Nurse Hancox. Lady Mordaunt named the child herself, and then conversed with Mr Cadogan and asked that his wife should come and see her. He told her, however, that he thought she had done enough for one day.

Jessie Clarke resumed her duties in the bedroom on the Thursday after the confinement and Lady Mordaunt made a point of asking her whom she thought the baby was like. Jessie said she thought the child very much resembled her, which seemed to please Lady Mordaunt very much. Sometimes, however, when Mrs Hancox took the baby in to her, and she saw how bad its eyes were, she would start to cry. Obsessed as she had been from the outset that her child would be diseased, she was now convinced that it would go blind. The thought that this could happen was almost unbearable; she said it would be better it should die, and she suggested that Mrs Hancox should give it a dose of laudanum. Mrs Hancox said 'No, not for all the world and you must not think of any such nonsense.'

Although she still did not communicate her worries to anybody else, Lady Mordaunt repeatedly asked Mrs Hancox about her daughter's health, giving the impression that she feared the eye trouble could be her own fault, and saying that she knew Sir Frederic Johnstone was 'a very diseased man'. This introduced yet another element into the story which left Mrs Hancox more perplexed than ever.

On the Friday afternoon Mrs Cadogan paid her usual visit, and Lady Mordaunt was in good enough health to organise a special treat for the children at the Parsonage which proved to be a great success.

My dear Lady Mordaunt

I have just come in and am so cold I can hardly hold a pen. The children send lots of thanks for the buns over which there are great shouts going on. I shall see you tomorrow in the afternoon.

Yours affectionately,
ALICE CADOGAN

Realising that Lady Mordaunt was very worried about the baby's eyes, Mrs Cadogan changed her plan and decided to go down to the Hall in the morning in order to make sure that all was well. From the moment she arrived she felt that there was something wrong. Lady Louisa kept going into the nurse's room and there was constant talk about the child's eyes which was obviously worrying the young mother, particularly as nobody seemed to think of discussing the matter with her. When Mrs Cadogan entered the bedroom, Lady Mordaunt told her that Dr Solomon was coming to see the baby shortly and she was obviously wondering what he would say. When the doctor arrived, he examined the child and reported that he found it 'labouring under ophthalmia' just as Dr Orford had said. He did not seem over-concerned and expressed himself satisfied with the astringent applications recommended by Dr Orford. He did however suggest that a wet nurse should be engaged for the baby, Mrs Hancox having been feeding her up to this time from a bottle. In spite of his reassurances, Harriett remained agitated and asked to see her husband. When Charlie came into the room he begged her to relieve her mind by telling him why she was so distressed, but she refused to say anything. She told Mrs Hancox later that she could not get the words out. They just seemed to choke her.

Seeing how upset she was, Mrs Cadogan decided to stay until the afternoon. Lunch was sent up to the bedroom, but Lady Mordaunt refused to eat anything. Mrs Cadogan reproved her for this, saying that she would get too 'low' if she failed to take any food. She then asked Mrs Cadogan to read the Bible to her, also asking whether Mr Cadogan could come down as soon as possible as she wanted to take the sacrament. It seemed that she was not only anxious about the baby, but about herself as well, mentioning several acquaintances who had died in childbirth or just afterwards and saying that she feared she too would die. Mrs Cadogan felt very sorry for her, and promised to give Mr Cadogan the message. Meanwhile, to soothe her down, she read to her from the Bible, choosing the passage about our Lord curing the blind, which she appeared to understand and appreciate. But she still remained anxious about the child and about herself, and she talked about presents for Jessie Clarke and Mrs Caborn which she said should be given to them in the event of her death.

Dr Orford had so far managed to visit Lady Mordaunt every morning, but on this Saturday he had been held up by another case and did not arrive until the afternoon. He came in and felt Lady Mordaunt's pulse and said 'You are low, you are low.' Mrs Cadogan told him that Lady Mordaunt had eaten nothing. He said 'You must have a glass of champagne.' This was brought to her and she drank it.

Harriett had not wished to see her mother during the morning, but Dr Orford said he would now ask her to come up. He told Lady Louisa about her daughter's state, but she said rather impatiently 'Oh she is only hysterical as her sister Lady Dudley was at her confinement.' Dr Orford contradicted her, insisting that Lady Mordaunt was not in the least hysterical but simply 'low'. The doctor then left, and Lady Louisa went upstairs, by which time Harriett had worked herself up into a state. Lady Louisa did not seem too put out by that as she was obviously used to seeing her daughter having a bout of hysterics. Mrs Cadogan went out leaving mother and daughter together, and as she left she heard Lady Mordaunt cry out 'Mother I have been very silly today.'

Mrs Hancox had begun to wonder whether in view of Lady Mordaunt's troubled condition it would be better if her mother were to stay for a little longer, rather than leaving that afternoon as she intended. When Mrs Hancox suggested this to Lady Mordaunt, she considered it for a while and then said no, her mother had better go. She told Mrs Hancox that she knew she had decisions to make and that she was finding it hard to know what to do next, but she thought she would be better taking whatever steps she had to take on her own and without asking for her mother's help. When Lady Louisa came to say goodbye to her, she did not seem at all put out that she was going. Later, in the middle of the night, she woke Mrs Hancox and said 'I can see it all quite plain now. I have quite made up my mind as to what I shall do, I am going to be poorly. Sir Charles and my father

must make it all right, and I shall go abroad as soon as I can get well.'
She added that the time had come for everything to be told as a result
of the child's eyes.

Having unburdened herself to Mrs Hancox, Lady Mordaunt slept
well for the rest of the night, and when Mrs Cadogan went in the
next day to see her after the morning service, she found her sitting up
in bed looking cheerful and saying that she would like to nurse the
baby. She said Dr Orford was very keen she should do this. Mrs
Cadogan warned her that at this stage, as she had not seriously tried
to feed the baby up to now, it was unlikely that she would have any
milk, but all the same she took the baby in her arms and asked Mrs
Hancox to leave the room. A wet nurse from the village had already
been engaged according to Dr Solomon's orders and she arrived that
morning with her own baby. Mrs Hancox took the child in to show
Lady Mordaunt saying 'Here's a large boy.' Lady Mordaunt laughed
and seemed pleased to see the child.

When Dr Orford arrived to pay his usual call, she clasped his hand
and asked if she could speak to him. He said 'Oh yes.'

'Can I tell you something you won't tell anyone?' she asked.

He promised he would tell nobody.

'Charlie said he could not have any babies, and that I was very
wicked' she told the doctor.

'What on earth do you mean?' inquired the doctor, adding 'I don't
understand you.'

In the afternoon, when Mrs Cadogan visited Lady Mordaunt
again, she was in a very different mood. She said petulantly that the
baby was a silly little thing and that she had given up nursing it.

That evening, when she asked that Sir Charles should come up to
her, Lady Mordaunt appeared to be in a state of considerable excitement. Sir Charles hurried upstairs, and as he entered the room, Mrs
Hancox withdrew as she always did. She went back later and found
that Lady Mordaunt was still over-excited. Mrs Hancox asked what
had been said, and the answer was 'Not much, but the time has come
when I must and will tell him.' Lady Mordaunt complained that Sir
Charles still would not listen to her. After that she had a restless
night.

On Monday 8 March, as the day wore on, Mrs Hancox had the
impression that Lady Mordaunt was becoming increasingly disturbed. When Mrs Cadogan arrived on a visit, she overheard Lady
Mordaunt saying to the nurse 'Oh Charlie, Charlie, confess all to

Charlie, he is so good, confess all to Charlie.' Mrs Hancox went out and nothing more was said on the subject. Mrs Cadogan had brought her knitting and she sat by the bedside for about an hour, talking on all kinds of subjects. Gradually Lady Mordaunt became less agitated and when Mrs Hancox came back into the room she was laughing loudly. 'Well, you see, Mrs Cadogan has cheered you up' the nurse remarked.

Soon after Mrs Cadogan left, Lady Mordaunt asked Mrs Hancox to send for her husband. He came quickly, already worried by the fact that she had seemed in such a strange mental state the previous evening. When he went into the room he saw that she was distressed, but at the same time more composed than she had been the day before. He waited for her to begin the conversation and she cried when she began to speak. She first said 'Charlie, you are not the father of the child. Lord Cole is the father of the child, and I myself am the cause of its blindness.' After that she did not speak for what seemed a very long time, and there was silence between them, Charlie being too dumbfounded to say anything. At last she started to cry as she said, 'Charlie, I have been very wicked. I have done very wrong.'

He asked her with whom.

'With Lord Cole, Sir Frederic Johnstone, and the Prince of Wales,' she told him, 'and with others, often and in open day.' Her voice then died away in sobs, so that she was unable to say more, although Sir Charles believed she would have done had she not been so overcome. He still felt unable to say anything, being himself overwhelmed with grief and horror. In a state of shock he left the room and sent for Dr Orford. His first reaction was that his wife must be suffering from some kind of illness associated with childbirth; perhaps he had been right after all in thinking that she could have contracted milk fever which was making her 'light-headed'.

Dr Orford arrived at about eleven o'clock that night, somewhat surprised by this urgent call, as he had seen Lady Mordaunt that morning and at the time there had been nothing unusual in her condition. Sir Charles told him that his wife was in a very strange state and he wondered whether she had become feverish as she hardly seemed to be in her right mind.

Lady Mordaunt had told Mrs Hancox that she thought she would feel better now that she had done what she meant to do, and when the doctor saw her he thought she seemed very quiet if somewhat prostrate, perhaps as a result of becoming over-excited. She refused to say anything and he was unable to find any signs of fever or delirium. He left her after a few minutes and went back to Sir Charles who then suggested that she might still be suffering from the hysteria that had troubled her at times during her pregnancy. Dr Orford admitted that he had noticed something strange in her manner since the birth and had thought there was some kind of burden on her mind, but he told Sir Charles that for the time being it was best for her to sleep.

There was little possibility of sleep for Charlie on the night of the confession as he mulled over his wife's words. He knew, of course, that the Prince of Wales had been paying her more attention than he should have done, and he knew too that Harriett had friends of the opposite sex who had been entertained in his house, but he could not bring himself to accept that any of them had abused his kindness and trust in this way. Harriett had seemed so loving towards him, telling him repeatedly how she had come to love him more and more, and for him the marriage had been one of pure affection, so much so that he found it impossible to believe anything to her detriment. And yet what can a man think when his wife suddenly announces that her child is not his and that she has committed adultery with several men, one of them the heir to the throne?

Mrs Hancox had slept in Lady Mordaunt's room on the night of the confession, but Jessie Clarke went in to her the next morning and was also struck by her agitated state. At first Jessie took no notice, as she knew that her mistress was naturally excitable. She began to realise there was more to it when Lady Mordaunt said without any preliminaries, 'It is Lord Cole's child', adding that she had confessed everything to Sir Charles. Jessie simply told her that she was talking rubbish, and would soon come to regret it if she carried on in this way. She was obviously in an emotional state, saying things like 'Fetch Lord Cole and Sir Frederic Johnstone.' Later in the day, however, she calmed down, and Jessie never heard her mention Lord Cole again.

Lady Louisa was by now back in Moncreiffe where she received a letter from Sir Charles, informing her that Harriett had not been quite so well as before. 'She has been hysterical and rather nervous and excitable, but without fever' he wrote, adding that Dr Orford was confident that it would all pass off in a day or two.

Mrs Cadogan had promised to keep Lady Louisa informed about her daughter's condition and she too wrote to her that weekend. Lady Louisa replied from Scotland saying that she was tired after her journey and very concerned about the baby, Sir Charles having told her that 'the eyes are gone and the little thing seems weaker'. She was relieved to hear, however, that Harriett's milk had dried up completely, as she was sure that 'her nursery would not have answered'. She finished her letter adding 'There is no saying more as by now all may be over.'

The general feeling was that nobody should wish for the infant to live if she was to end up blind. Sir Charles told Helen that Harriett seemed more or less to have forgotten all about the child and had stopped asking after her, which was perhaps as well as nobody wanted to have to tell her how bad the eyes were. As for Harriett herself, although Dr Orford continued to insist that there was no cause for anxiety, she certainly was not going on as well as everybody would wish. The one good thing was that she continued to sleep exceptionally well, but, Sir Charles wrote, 'She is so excitable and nervous that it is most difficult to keep her quiet and although not at all feverish she wanders a good deal in her mind and cannot understand what is said to her.'

Sir Charles did not tell any of the family about Harriett's confessions, still hoping that these would turn out to be some kind of an illusion. He had, however, given Dr Orford the details of what she had said, in case it could throw some light on her medical state. The doctor became somewhat thoughtful after he heard what Sir Charles had to say, for Lady Mordaunt's confession of infidelity made him see the baby's eye condition in a completely different light. The symptoms could now be interpreted as those of a child infected through a mother suffering from a venereal disease. The ophthalmia certainly seemed to be unusually severe and it was not responding to treatment in the way he might have expected. In addition, he knew that prior to the birth the mother had suffered from 'secretions' which had been severe enough for her to seek advice from Dr Priestley, and which could have had a 'guilty' or an 'innocent' significance. Fearing that the case was becoming more than he could handle on his own, he asked Sir Charles to call in an older and more experienced man, Dr Richard Jones from Leamington, who had been in practice for forty years.[75] Dr Orford felt that if things were later to come out into the open he would like to have somebody to back him up.

Dr Jones was sent for at once and arrived when Sir Charles was at dinner. Dr Orford was also dining and Dr Jones sat down and joined them. It is probable that they discussed the case at the meal, but that Dr Orford did not express any suspicions he might have had as a result of hearing about Lady Mordaunt's confessions. Afterwards Dr Jones went up to the sick room and talked to Lady Mordaunt. As an experienced practitioner he would probably have known at a glance if she had been suffering from the puerperal fever which afflicted so many women after childbirth, but he felt her pulse and skin just to make sure there were no indications of a raised temperature. He then asked the kind of questions normally put to a woman at this stage after her confinement. She answered all of these satisfactorily, but then went silent and he could not get any further replies. Dr Jones had been told that she had not taken any food for some time, so he ordered some beef tea to be brought up. She showed great reluctance to take any of it, although he did his best to persuade her. He then went downstairs and told Sir Charles that as his visit had been somewhat unsatisfactory, he would come again the next day. He visited Lady Mordaunt on the Wednesday and Thursday, and again reported that she was not in any way feverish. He had in his earlier years specialised in cases of women suffering from puerperal fever or mania but he was insistent that he could see no sign at all of these very recognisable diseases. It was extremely puzzling, and because he felt that Dr Orford was keeping something back, he asked him to explain why there was so much mystery surrounding the case.

'I am not at liberty to say, you must find it out for yourself' Dr Orford told him.

'The best thing to do would be to get Lady Mordaunt up and if it were summer instead of winter I would take her for a drive in the park' said Dr Jones, who thought that the most urgent need was for her to be 'roused'.

A chance remark from Sir Charles made Dr Jones wonder if Lady Mordaunt had something on her mind and that this could be the cause of her strange apathy and 'taciturnity'. It also made him wonder whether the baby could be suffering from a gonorrheal rather than a leucorrhoeal discharge of the eyes. He felt unable, however, to make a positive diagnosis, and he put the responsibility squarely back onto Dr Orford's shoulders, expressing the opinion that the best person to give advice was the 'accoucheur and medical adviser' who had been treating mother and child since the birth.

Dr Orford himself still had not told Sir Charles of his suspicions, but he felt increasingly sure that they might prove to be right. He continued to be reassuring about Lady Mordaunt's physical state, and said that she was now well enough to leave her bedroom, recommending that she should be dressed and carried through into her boudoir. He then took the liberty of looking into her medicine cupboard where he found various prescriptions, mostly those habitually recommended for ladies 'in the family way'. The remedies had been prescribed by various medical men; some of them were unsigned and had no date. There were a number of lotion bottles, the prescriptions for these having been written by Dr Priestley, and some of them would have been applicable in the case of somebody suffering from a venereal disease.

In spite of the arrival of a new doctor, Lady Mordaunt had calmed down by the evening of his first visit and she once again slept well. But the next day she was decidedly worse, although nobody could quite account for this sudden deterioration in her mental condition. She became very silent, and strangely subdued. It was difficult to make her take an interest in anything. Jessie Clarke, like everybody else, thought that she was not so well as she had been. When Jessie had seen her a few days after the confinement she had said, 'Clarke, I am going on very nicely', but now she seemed sad and listless. Sir Charles became increasingly worried as she veered between a state of vacancy and inertia to one of extreme agitation, asking him to take her away at night from the house in a brougham and then, when he refused, begging him to pack her into a box and send her away. She told him several times that she thought she was dying, and she talked of coming back to earth with the utmost terror and dread. On one occasion she asked Sir Charles to give her some poison. This lent weight to his belief that the confession she had made could be the fruit of a disordered mind. But Dr Orford reiterated that in his opinion there was nothing wrong with her mental state, and Mrs Hancox believed she was simply carrying out her intention of pretending to be 'poorly' in order to regain her husband's sympathy and to get him to forgive her.

Sir Charles continued to send daily bulletins to Lady Louisa and in the middle of the week he was able to report that there was a slight improvement in the baby's eyes. She had in fact opened them wide for the first time. But if the baby was better, Harriett, unfortunately, was not. Dr Orford continued to be perplexed by her condition and was quite unable to put a name to it. For that reason, Sir Charles told Lady Louisa,

Orford asked me to call in Dr Jones from Leamington who is very clever and he came at once and is coming again today. He says there is no cause for anxiety as long as she continues to sleep so well – she sleeps eight hours every night – also that it is a case where no medicine can be given and he therefore thinks that if she continues to sleep so well her nervous system must get better. The baby has been several times brought to her in order to try and relieve her mind and get her to take an interest in something but she only noticed it for a moment and said it was to be taken away. Caborn and the young nurse look after the baby and the other nurse attends Harriett. Poor darling I am very anxious and distressed about her but feel quite sure that Jones thoroughly understands her case as he says he has seen many similar.

Charlie wrote to Helen in the same vein, describing the baby's eyes as being 'much less inflamed'. He told her too of his anxiety at Harriett's nervous prostration: 'She cannot be roused to do anything or in fact to understand what is said to her and she seems hardly to know me or anyone about her . . . poor darling I am very anxious and distressed about her.'

On the Friday, Charlie was still unable to report any improvement.

My dear Lady Louisa

My darling Harriett remains much the same. She has taken more food and sleeps very well but remains quite still without ever speaking and without understanding anything. She is out of bed and in the sitting room and we have done all that is possible to rouse her from this apathetic state. The doctors say it is entirely hysterical and not in the least dangerous but very distressing to see. The baby gets better and worse alternately and I am afraid the improvement which took place is not decided. A wet nurse is regularly with it.

Ever yours affectionately

C. MORDAUNT

Sir Charles also wrote to Helen telling her how distressing it was to see Harriett in the same state day after day. The doctors, he told her, described the state as 'cataleptic hysteria', and Dr Jones, unable to prescribe any specific remedies, had suggested that it might help to restore her to health if Helen could return to Walton to be with her: 'I hardly like to ask you to come as it is so inconvenient for you to travel all the way again so soon but it would be a great blessing to my poor darling.'

Although Charlie's letters were calm in tone, he was by now in a state of mental anguish over his wife's condition, scarcely knowing where to turn for help. Early next morning he wrote an urgent note which he sent up to the Parsonage, asking Mrs Cadogan to come at once as his wife was in a very odd state. 'I should like you to come and see her very much' he wrote.

Mrs Cadogan had not been down to the Hall for several days, and as soon as she arrived Mrs Hancox brought her up to date with the situation, taking her aside and telling her that Lady Mordaunt had confessed to Sir Charles that the child was not his. This news was distressing enough, but the sight of Lady Mordaunt herself was equally worrying. She was lying there with the blinds drawn, looking totally apathetic. She roused herself enough to say 'How do you do?', and then Mrs Cadogan said briskly 'You are very dull in here, won't you have the blinds drawn back?' but Harriett replied somewhat irritably, 'Shut them.' This was the first time that Mrs Cadogan had seen her take refuge in silence, and although Sir Charles had hoped that Mrs Cadogan would be able to stimulate some response in her, she was quite unsuccessful. Harriett refused to be drawn into conversation and after a while Mrs Cadogan left without having persuaded her to speak. Having heard about the confession, Mrs Cadogan went home convinced that Lady Mordaunt's strange state was caused by a sense of sin and regret for her past behaviour.

Mrs Hancox, for her part, was sure that Lady Mordaunt was still trying to gain her husband's sympathy but that her attempt had gone wrong because her odd behaviour was making him think her confessions were simply the ravings of an unsound mind. The nurse advised her to act sensibly and to prove once and for all whether there was truth in what she had said. To this she replied 'I will, you'll see' and she added 'I shall be better tomorrow morning.'

Rather to his surprise, Sir Charles found that when he visited his wife next day, Saturday 13th, she did in fact show signs of improvement as he told Lady Louisa in his letter that day: 'I am most thankful to tell you there is a change for the better since I wrote last. Harriett has called me by name several times and has said a few words and she is certainly more herself although the change is slight. She takes a good deal more food and sleeps beautifully.' He also said that there was much improvement in the baby's condition.

On the Saturday Sir Charles wrote to Lady Kinnoull.

My dear Aunt Kinnoull

I wrote a few days since to Georgiana at Rome and waited a little before writing to you thinking you would see her letter. Since that time I have been in great distress about Harriett. There is no danger in her state but it has not been at all satisfactory, for although she takes enough food, sleeps well and is out of bed and in her sitting-room she has for a week had what the doctors called cataleptic hysteria. She was quite sensible but never spoke or understood what was said to her, but today she has changed for the better and poor darling called me by name for the first time, but can hardly speak yet. The baby has been very ill with the worst inflammation of its eyes and had to be taken from poor Harriett as she could not nurse it and was not, in the state I have described, able to notice it. Now we have great hopes of it doing well as although often worse it recovers wonderfully and we have had a permanent wet nurse for it all the time. Please shew this with my love to Georgiana and if you would both write to Harriett I am sure by that time she would be able to read a letter and it would be a great comfort to her.

Ever yrs affectly
C. MORDAUNT

In spite of Sir Charles's slightly more hopeful reports to Lady Louisa and Lady Kinnoull, Mrs Hancox thought that on the Saturday Lady Mordaunt was worse rather than better. Mrs Hancox later testified that during the week before when she had appeared to be so apathetic and strange to everybody else, Lady Mordaunt had behaved quite normally with her, which confirmed her suspicions that she was only 'acting poorly' in the presence of her husband, to gain his sympathy. Mrs Hancox, not one to pull any punches, had no hesitation in referring to what Lady Mordaunt had earlier told her and she now brought up the subject of Sir Frederic Johnstone, saying that she wanted to know 'how in the world a lady like Lady Mordaunt could have had anything to do with a man like him'. Lady Mordaunt replied that if she had known as much about him as she did now, she would not have done what she had. Mrs Hancox told her that a young lady like her should know nothing of Sir Frederic

Johnstone or of his complaint, but she gave Mrs Hancox to understand that in London society promiscuity was a common occurrence
and that nobody thought too much about it.

When Mrs Cadogan visited Lady Mordaunt in the late morning,
she found her in a state of 'great grief and trouble'. She was lying on
the sofa and did not answer when Mrs Cadogan spoke to her. Mrs
Cadogan kept the conversation going as cheerfully as possible but
had little response, and after about an hour Sir Charles came and
talked kindly and tenderly to her but was also met with silence. When
he finally gave up and went out, Mrs Cadogan asked Jessie to find
some music and she sat down at the piano and sang some songs.
After a while Lady Mordaunt spoke for the first time, saying 'I like it
so much.' She then began to cry bitterly. Jessie came in to see what
was the matter and took her over to look at one of the pictures to try
to distract her, as if she were a child.

When Sir Charles came back up to the boudoir, Mrs Cadogan went
along to the nursery and started talking to Mrs Hancox. After about
ten minutes they heard Sir Charles calling urgently for the nurse, and
they went out and met him leading Lady Mordaunt upstairs. Mrs
Hancox took her back into her sitting-room, and asked her where she
had been going. Lady Mordaunt replied 'A cold bath would not hurt
me as I would rather meet death in any shape if Sir Charles exposes
me to the world.' Mrs Hancox then told Mrs Cadogan that she was
fairly sure Lady Mordaunt had been 'going to the water' and that Sir
Charles had gone after her and prevented her reaching the river and
throwing herself in.

The irony of the situation was that while Harriett was trying hard
to grab Charlie's attention and, with a threat of suicide, to force him
to forgive and forget, he still resolutely refused to believe that there
was anything to forgive. He was, however, sufficiently shaken by her
half-hearted attempt to end her life in the tranquil waters of the
Dene Brook that he did broach the subject of her confession when he
visited her that evening, hoping perhaps that she would now deny its
truth. But she stuck to her story more emphatically than ever, leaving
him in no doubt that she had deceived him not once but several times
and with different men, several of whom had enjoyed his hospitality.

Sir Charles then said 'Tell me, I implore you, are there any others?'
Although she had not mentioned them in her original catalogue, he
knew that she had enjoyed a long-standing friendship with Captain
Farquhar and Lord Newport, and he specifically asked whether she

included them among the guilty men. When she did not answer, he repeated the question. She again said nothing, but appeared to be so conscience-stricken that he drew his own conclusions.

This interview provided little comfort for Sir Charles. Mrs Hancox recalled that she met him as he left the room, and that he said to her 'Why, Nurse, her ladyship tells me just the same as she told me before; what am I to believe?'

Then, when Mrs Hancox went in to the room, Lady Mordaunt said 'Well, I have made him understand at last.'

'Suppose he goes out and makes inquiries, what then?' Mrs Hancox asked.

'Why,' she replied, 'there'll be an awful row.'

'Whatever you do, send for Sir Charles, and stop him taking this any further. Think what a serious thing an open exposure would be for both of your families' Mrs Hancox urged her. But she said she was sure it would all come out all right as Sir Charles had known all along that the gentlemen had visited her and he had not made any objection at the time. Her defiant mood did not last long, however, for later that evening Mrs Hancox found her out of bed by her dressing-table where several medicine bottles stood, including the laudanum. When Mrs Hancox asked her what she was doing, adding that nothing on the table would do her any good, she said 'Do have pity on me and give me some' and when Mrs Hancox asked 'Give you some what?' she replied 'A good dose of laudanum or anything you like for I cannot stand this and I won't.' Mrs Hancox then locked the bottle away, making a mental note that in future no medicine bottles should be left lying about.

After the morning service next day, Mrs Cadogan hurried over to the Hall to find out the latest developments. When she saw Lady Mordaunt she was immediately struck by the total change in her demeanour. It really did seem as if a great weight had been lifted from her. Mrs Cadogan, who had expected to find her stricken with grief and horror, was rather shocked when she spoke quite lightly about her past behaviour, saying there was no harm in what she had done because she knew that lots of other ladies in London did the same. In any case, she added, she herself had only done it three or four times. Somewhat taken aback, Mrs Cadogan told her that however many times she had done it, she really should ask for her husband's forgiveness. Defiantly, she replied, 'I will humble myself for no man.' Mrs Cadogan thought that she could at least say she was sorry, at which she said, even more shockingly, 'But I am not sorry.' She was quite sure that Sir Charles and her father would be able to work things out between them; she might have to go away for a while, but that was all.

This was the only time that Mrs Cadogan heard an admission of guilt from Lady Mordaunt herself, and what impressed her was how calm she seemed about it. Mrs Cadogan was in fact quite disgusted by her flippant manner; she would have expected her to be overcome with horror at what she had done, but she seemed to be utterly unrepentant.

'I will make it all right with Charlie' she insisted.

'Don't you be too sure' Mrs Cadogan replied.

Startled and upset by the casualness of Lady Mordaunt's remarks, Mrs Cadogan left the room almost immediately.

If his wife seemed relieved and buoyed up by her success in convincing him that she was telling the truth, Sir Charles was totally horrified by his latest interview with her. Harriett had at last convinced him that her confession was more than the fantasy of an hysterical woman and he now knew that he must face up not only to her infidelity but also to the fact that a number of men had humiliated him and abused his trust. On the Sunday morning Dr Orford came over from Wellesbourne at his request and they had a serious discussion about the dates in relation to the appearance of the child at birth and the exact time of Sir Charles's return from Norway. This led them to the conclusion that the child had most likely been conceived when Sir Charles was still abroad. As to the baby's eyes, Dr Orford broke it to Sir Charles that the unusual severity of the condition, together with the revelations concerning Lady Mordaunt's promiscuity, suggested a link with sexual intercourse and venereal disease. This possibility had evidently never occurred to Sir Charles and it came as another devastating blow. Dr Orford later described how at first Sir Charles seemed puzzled and totally unable to grasp the significance of what he had been told. Worse was to come, for when he visited his wife after Dr Orford had left, she adopted the same attitude as she had with Mrs Cadogan. He was appalled when she insisted that there was no harm in what she had done because other ladies in London were in the habit of doing the same. He was still more distressed when she told him that she thought it need have no effect on their life together and that they should co-habit as before.

Sir Charles eventually left the room and went in search of his mother who often came over to the house after the morning service on a Sunday, and stayed for a while walking in the garden or chatting to Mrs Caborn. He told the Dowager what had happened and she went straight up to the boudoir where she found Harriett still lying on the sofa. She knelt down at her daughter-in-law's side and said 'I have come to express my sorrow for your position.'

At first Harriett said nothing, she in her turn feeling overwhelmed to discover that yet another person had been let into the secret. After a while, she said 'Sit down, darling', and for a moment or two the Dowager believed that she might be on the point of unburdening herself. 'I want to tell you . . . ' she began and then stopped. Her mother-in-law asked her if she often saw the baby, and she replied, 'Sometimes.' The Dowager's advice was that she should make an effort to see her child more often. 'Baby belongs to you' she reminded her daughter-in-law 'and I hope you will take care of it.'

After the Dowager had gone, Harriett was left alone with her thoughts. She was now, perhaps more than ever before, in a state of shock as she faced the fact that what had been intended only for Charlie's ears was rapidly becoming common knowledge. She had 'coloured up' with anger and embarrassment when Mrs Hancox had said that morning, just as the clergyman's wife arrived, 'Lady Mordaunt, Mrs Cadogan knows all.' She had been so sure that she would be able to persuade Charlie to bury the past before anybody else got to hear about it. Now she did her best to limit the damage already done by asking Mrs Hancox to make sure that the story went no farther, particularly forbidding her to confide in Mrs Caborn.

Mrs Hancox went off to tell the housekeeper, no doubt with some delight, that she was not to be let into the secret. Mrs Caborn, a busybody who liked to have a finger in every pie, was distinctly put out at being excluded.

'Why?' she said indignantly. 'I have always been very kind to Lady Mordaunt.'

'Yes, that is the reason you are not to know as you've been with Sir Charles so long', Mrs Hancox replied, obviously very happy to be in the know herself.

The servants, even those who had not witnessed Lady Mordaunt's distress at close quarters, must all by now have been aware of the deepening crisis in the house. For months, even years, they had seen and discussed their mistress's behaviour, having observed far more of her goings-on than their more trusting master. They had said nothing to him, however, knowing, as servants did in those days, that their jobs might be in jeopardy if they did not observe a discreet silence. Certainly, any servant labelled a tell-tale might well experience difficulty in obtaining a good reference and finding another place. But now, as they saw the approaching storm, they knew the time had come to tell all. When Sir Charles started to question them, they revealed their earlier suspicions; he heard about the presence of Captain Farquhar at the Palace Hotel, the afternoon visits of the Prince of Wales, the attentions of Sir Frederic Johnstone. Most important of all was the confirmation by Bird and others that Lord Cole had remained alone with Lady Mordaunt at Chesham Place on 27 June until late at night, which bore out Lady Mordaunt's insistence that he was the father of her child. The servants' testimony, coupled with Dr Orford's suspicions about the baby's eye condition, left Sir Charles totally crushed and, as he later put it himself, he spent a day and a night of unspeakable anguish going through 'worse than death'. Mrs Caborn described how he was so distracted that he could not rest and how Bird became so worried by his state that he slept in his room for several nights to keep an eye on him.

The next day Sir Charles had another conversation with his wife. He returned to the question of the guests who had visited the house, giving her the chance once again to clear them from any stain of dishonour. She exonerated them all with the exception of Captain Farquhar and Lord Newport. Sir Charles then told her what he now knew about events at the Palace Hotel and she did not deny that she had dined with the Captain there on the very evening when she had written him the letter saying how lonely she was. She was silent, however, when Newport's name was mentioned, refusing to say anything, but Charlie urged her to clear his name, pointing out that he would be strongly suspected in view of their close friendship. Sir Charles himself knew that his wife had been on terms of intimacy with her cousin, but had always felt that this was sanctioned by the fact that they were close relations. She still refused to divulge anything, but seemed very troubled and said 'I will say nothing about him one way or the other.' He was struck at this interview, as he had been on previous occasions, by the lack of contrition in her attitude. She continued to insist that what she had done was quite commonplace in London society, with people always ready to tell her there was 'no harm' in it.

Later that day Mr Cadogan delivered a message to Sir Charles's brother at Staple Hill asking him to come at once. Johnny had not been over to the Hall since the confinement – he had been busy and his wife had given birth to a daughter a week after Harriett. Osbert was also sent for. Neither brother had any idea of the drama that had been unfolding at Walton, but they were not as surprised by the revelations as Charlie himself since they had been uneasy for some time about their sister-in-law's behaviour and had speculated as to whether she might have committed adultery with one or more of her many admirers. They could only corroborate the testimony of the servants; all the same it came as a shock to learn that their brother was beginning to talk in terms of a divorce.

14

The London Scene

The birth of Lady Mordaunt's baby had as yet caused little comment in London society, the qualifying 'prematurely' in the newspaper announcement adequately explaining the situation. The news had, it is true, caused some alarm at Compton Verney, prompting young Lady Willoughby to pack her bags in a hurry for fear of having to give birth to her baby in the country. 'It startled her so much' Louisa Scott told Harriett 'that she was for once roused into action by your fate and at once rushed off to London, so old Lady W wrote to Bunchey.'[76]

Apart from this there was little of interest to report. 'I've nothing in prospect except the theatre' Louisa told Harriett. She had seen their mutual friend Mrs Dicky Oswald, 'she looking oh! such a duck, but I can't say the same for him, but I know you like him . . .' Louisa herself was for some reason being persecuted by the 'fearful old D[uchess] of Montrose' whom she was doing her best to avoid. 'I swear and I make my family swear that I've a cough and can't leave the house!! So she comes to luncheon to judge for herself!!! She's furious at the bare idea of the Mary alliance but confesses that "Graham" [her son] has a will of his own.'[77] There were small items of news, for example that Bunchey, Harriett's sister Blanche, had arrived back in London from Torquay with a rampant cold and was in bed, 'poor soul', but the scandal of the moment was the elopement of their friend Mrs Vivian, who had gone off with the young Lord Waterford. 'Isn't it awful about Mrs Johnny Vivian?' Louisa wrote, 'quite too dreadful and too astonishing, it never appeared to me that she could care sufficiently for any one to take the trouble of running away with them, did you? Oh Law, I can't get over it!'

Alice Miles, in Paris, had also heard the news and was equally amazed, finding it hard to imagine such folly.

Fancy Mrs Johnny Vivian having crowned her exploits by carrying that fool of a Waterford off to Barcelona in triumph after the abortive poisoning attempt here. The husband has returned to England to try and get a divorce, which he is very unlikely to succeed in. I'm sure I trust he won't, for Waterford is quite sufficiently imbecile to marry her, which has been her aim all through: I think that scene in the Hotel must have been rich, the lover begging the injured husband to take her back, she rushing off to take chloroform, Waterford breaking open the door only to plunge head first into an *armoire à glace* to the utter detriment of the dresses he had probably paid for, and Johnny Vivian's refusal to fight on the grounds that she wasn't worth it! Altogether anything so fertile in comic incidents I never came across.[78]

Louisa did manage to spare some sympathy for the friend who was languishing in Warwickshire and missing all the fun. 'I went to enquire about you at Mrs Forbes yesterday and was enchanted to hear you're both going on well, but you must be getting rather tired of bed, I should think.'

One of Harriett's old friends, Lord Berkeley Paget, had also remembered her. Lunching 'in great force' at the Scotts prior to leaving on a trip to America, he had sent Harriett his love and asked for her address, unaware, like everyone else, of the crisis at Walton – in fact he seemed to think that all was well as he sent a message to say 'he was so awfully glad to hear it's all right'.

Louisa concluded her letter by saying 'Mother wants me to write for her so I must stop, you dearest of individuals – Thine ever, L. SCOTT' and she added a P.S. 'Do you want books – can I do anything about them for you?'

Meanwhile, many families were converging on the capital for the first drawing-room of the season, among them Lord and Lady Warwick and their children. The cold and rather disagreeable weather was not enough to deter the crowds waiting to admire the exquisite *toilettes* and fine gowns of the belles attending the event. Observers of fashion noted that the prevailing colours that year were violet and grey and flowers were being used in place of feathers by all the fashionable ladies. The latest fad was for 'curious paniers' worn by very lean and very stout women alike, and providing 'an unnatural protuberance in what appears to be a most inconvenient position'. For a woman of from twelve to eighteen stone to assume the Grecian bend was to do 'a palpable injustice to her charms', as the *Warwick Advertiser* put it. The vogue for decorating gowns with fresh flowers now verged on the absurd, as demonstrated by the outfit chosen by

Lady Holmesdale for a royal ball.[79] 'My dear, I can't help writing to describe to you the dress' Louisa told Harriett. The skirt, she wrote, was in a pale canary silk 'trimmed all over with streamers going up it of all coloured flowers and yellow and white laburnum'. In addition, the train in sky blue satin was adorned like the skirt with 'loads' of the same flowers and, Louisa wrote, 'Wonderful to say, it was *lovely*.'

As well as Louisa's letter, Harriett received one from Dr Priestley who told her that he had received several reports of her 'well doing' although he had heard that the baby was somewhat sickly. 'I cannot tell you' he wrote 'how sorry I was that you were not under my care for your trial.' He was also concerned about the practicalities of the cancelled arrangements

> It is the usual thing when a nurse had been engaged and a confinement comes prematurely to pay her whether she is required or not for of course she had been thrown out by the event and she has by her engagement to you been prevented taking [on] somebody else. I believe in case of dispute a nurse could claim board wages as well but this is not commonly demanded. I hope your little baby will live and do well.

This was probably the last letter addressed to herself that Harriett was to receive. The doctor had written to her as a responsible person who would be capable of dealing with such matters as the board wages of her employees. But from now on nobody was to treat her in this way. That week her mother and sister were to join her, but they would bring her little comfort, talking to each other endlessly about her future and engaging in discussions with Sir Charles and his brothers about herself and her baby's future without any reference to her. Such was the fate reserved for young women who had disgraced themselves and their family by getting into trouble.

15

Family Discussions

Charlie had already told Helen Forbes that the doctors felt it would be beneficial if she could spend some time with her sister, and now he wrote a note asking her to come immediately. She arrived on the Monday when Charlie, still prostrate after his latest interview with Harriett, felt quite unable to talk to her. He therefore wrote a note to Mrs Cadogan asking her to come down to Walton Hall and break the news. She took Helen aside immediately she arrived and told her what had happened, saying that there was more than one gentleman involved.

'Tell me' Helen said immediately 'is there one name mentioned? I mean the Prince.'

'Yes' said Mrs Cadogan.

'Oh,' said Helen, 'he has ruined the happiness of many families.' She went on to say that she hoped it would be kept a secret as nobody knew about it as yet.

Horrified to learn that Charlie had by now started to question the servants, Helen immediately telegraphed her mother who came at once. Charlie had recovered himself enough to give his mother-in-law a brief summary of the confession, without mentioning any names. He told her that although he had at first been incredulous, Harriett's continued insistence, coupled with his recent inquiries and discoveries, had convinced him that she was telling the truth.

Lady Louisa went straight up to see Harriett who remained quite calm and rational and confided fully in her mother, telling her the names of those involved, and on this occasion implicating Captain Farquhar, speaking of him as a brute who had ill used her and saying that the Prince too had bullied her into doing wrong. Sir Charles had the impression that Lady Louisa did not question the truth of what her daughter had to say, and naturally both she and Helen Forbes were dismayed by her revelations. It was one thing to have given her favours to the heir to the throne, but quite another to have misbehaved with a number of lesser men; and in any case how could she have been so idiotic as to have told her husband all about it when there was no need for him to know anything?

When Lady Louisa told Charlie that the Prince and others had bullied Harriett into misbehaving, this only served to fuel his bitterness against the men who had led her astray. Mother and daughter appeared to share his disgust at the behaviour of the men involved, saying that they would cut Captain Farquhar if they met him and would tell the butler not to let him visit the house which he normally did very frequently. Lady Louisa also said that she would not attend the Prince of Wales's drawing-room after what she had heard. Harriett had told her mother that Lord Cole was Violet's father and she agreed that this did seem likely, although she told Sir Charles that she thought it would be difficult to prove that the child was illegitimate. Helen expressed particular horror at Lord Cole's behaviour, knowing that even as he had been seducing Harriett, he had still been making her sister believe that he intended to marry her.

What was most upsetting, of course, was the effect that the scandal would have on the whole family, and particularly on the morals and the marriage prospects of the younger sisters. In addition, Lady Louisa was anxious about its impact on Lord Newport who was so closely related to them. She told Charlie that when questioned on the subject, Harriett had said 'Anything I said to Charlie about Newport meant nothing.' Charlie replied immediately 'Then she has deceived one or other of us.' Lady Louisa thought that Charlie had perhaps read too much into Harriett's remarks about her cousin. It was true that Harriett had been very fond of George Newport before her marriage, but that did not mean he had been guilty of misconduct at a later date.

Sir Charles remained unconvinced. He was aware that Newport had been one of the party during Harriett's convalescence at Hastings where he would have found plenty of opportunities to be alone with her, and Charlie was by now of the opinion that all the men his wife had consorted with were totally depraved. Nor could he forget that Harriett had refused to deny Newport's guilt.

Having spoken to her daughter, Lady Louisa went on to have conversations with Mrs Cadogan, Mrs Hancox and Jessie Clarke, none of whom doubted that Lady Mordaunt's confessions were true. Mrs Cadogan thought that Lady Louisa herself had no hesitation in accepting her daughter's guilt. All she could hope for, she told Mrs Cadogan, was that Sir Charles would allow her enough money to keep her out of wickedness, as she could not possibly take her back among the unmarried daughters at Moncreiffe.

When asked whether she had known about the troubles from the start, Mrs Hancox replied that Lady Mordaunt had begun trying to confide in her from the very first night, so that she had soon become convinced that something was wrong. She said that like Mrs Cadogan she had been astounded by Lady Mordaunt's insistence that adultery was something quite common among her acquaintances. Lady Louisa then spoke to Jessie begging her to stay with her daughter if she had to go away, and to look out the wedding presents given to her by her husband so that she could take them with her – 'but of course only if Sir Charles entirely approved'. Jessie promised that she would do so.

At first Charlie felt that Lady Louisa was as sympathetic and friendly towards him as she had always been. It seemed that she and Helen could well understand his bitterness towards those who had wronged him. Naturally though, their first preoccupation was that the whole affair should be kept as secret as possible in order to hide Harriett's shame and to avoid the inevitable slur that any scandal would cast on the rest of the family. Lady Louisa told Charlie that she had already written to Major Arbuthnot offering to release him from his engagement to Selina if he felt he could not ally himself with a family in disgrace. But she still hoped that Charlie would see his way to arriving at some kind of private settlement out of the public eye, and she was, of course, particularly anxious that the question of 'the disease' should not come out into the open.

Lady Louisa's desire to hush everything up conflicted with Charlie's growing conviction that there would have to be a divorce with no holds barred. He was determined to carry out his revenge against the men who had humiliated him. His annoyance boiled over when he thought of the expenses he had incurred, with the house in London, the extra footman, the ponies, only to find that others had been exploiting all the things that he had been paying for. In addition, and perhaps most important of all, how could he be expected to take back into his bed a woman who on her own admission had risked infection with a man she believed to be suffering from 'the disease'?

Faced with this argument, Lady Louisa reluctantly agreed that there was only one course for Charlie to pursue with honour, namely a divorce, but at the same time she begged him to obtain it as privately as possible using only one of the guilty men's names in order to avoid 'exposure'. She said that she was sure Sir Thomas would agree with her once he knew the facts.

Each day, as Harriett lay on the sofa up in her boudoir, wondering what was going on, her mother and sister would be closeted with Charlie, and sometimes with Johnny and Osbert as well, as they went over and over their worries about where Harriett would live and whether she would have to change her name after the divorce. Osbert later recalled asking Lady Louisa whether there was any prospect of Harriett marrying one of the guilty men once the divorce was through, but Lady Louisa pointed out that marriage with the Prince was obviously out of the question, that Captain Farquhar and Lord Cole had no money, and that this left the not altogether desirable alternative of Sir Frederic Johnstone. Since the possibility of re-marriage seemed doubtful, Lady Louisa expressed the hope that Sir Charles would make Harriett a liberal allowance so that she could live abroad with a female companion, thus perhaps avoiding the temptations she had yielded to previously.

Lady Louisa told the brothers that it would be necessary for her to be kept under strict charge and out of the reach of men, because otherwise she might return to the sins she had committed. It was doubly necessary for her to receive a good allowance so that she would not be tempted to 'make money this way'. Evidently Lady Louisa and Helen Forbes had no illusions at this stage about Harriett's fickle tendencies. In fact when Charlie told Lady Louisa that his sufferings were daily added to because his wife showed so little repentance, the mother replied 'A woman who has been as wicked as she has cannot have any conscience left.'

If there were innumerable question marks concerning Harriett's future, there was also the fate of the unfortunate child to be settled. One day, Mrs Hancox recalled, she was in the room when Lady Louisa and Helen Forbes started discussing the matter. 'She won't be able to take it home, your father won't have it there, and Lady Mordaunt can't have it dragging about with her' Lady Louisa said, adding 'Sir Charles is not likely to have it here and we can't expect him to, feeling as he does that it is not his own. We must put it out to a nurse, if we can find a place for it, but the difficulty is that we know nobody about here.' Mrs Hancox then offered to take the child herself, and Lady Louisa said 'I wish you would, it would be the very best thing to be done under the circumstances and it would save lots of bother.' Mrs Hancox told them she was prepared to bring the child up as her own, teaching her to work and depend on nobody. As soon as she was old enough, she would be told that she was illegitimate. Mrs Hancox stressed, however, that she would require suitable payment.

'What would you do it for?' Lady Louisa asked. Mrs Hancox said she would want 'a good round sum', mentioning thirty pounds, which horrified Lady Louisa, who said it would have to be paid in two instalments as they could not possibly afford to put down such a large sum all at one time. Mrs Hancox thought that the best thing would be to invest a sum under a trustee so that she herelf could have the interest and the principal could go to the child when she was older. Lady Louisa then drew up a memorandum of terms.

Mrs Hancox had pointed out that the baby clothes ordered by Lady Mordaunt were far too grand for a child who was to be brought up in a small cottage. The clothes were therefore packed up and Helen Forbes agreed to take them back to the shop when she returned to London, with a view to getting a refund. Sir Charles was in agreement with this plan as he had been shocked by the bill he was expected to pay amounting to £130 for baby linen and a cradle. He found the sum of £90 for body vests particularly extravagant. Was he to clothe another man's child in the most exclusive layette that money could buy?

Lady Louisa and Helen Forbes had become increasingly concerned about Charlie's determination to 'rake up' any evidence that would serve to substantiate Harriett's confessions. Their attempts at persuading him to arrive at some kind of private settlement had come to nothing; he had contacted his lawyer, Mr Haynes of Leamington Spa,[80] and it really did seem that nothing would divert him from his chosen course of pursuing a divorce with all the horror of its attendant publicity.

For years the 'criminal conversation' action for damages from a wife's seducer had favoured the wronged husband, and although under the new Act of 1857 the damages were to be distributed between the wife, children and husband at the discretion of the judge, there was still a considerable advantage for the injured husband if he could obtain indisputable evidence of 'criminal conversation', or to put it more bluntly, adultery, on the part of his wife. In Charlie's case, it seemed likely that he might be able to claim damages from all the men named by Harriett in her confession. It was therefore vital that as many servants as possible should be interviewed and that those who had left should be contacted as a matter of urgency before there was time for the Moncreiffes or any of the supposedly guilty men to bribe them into silence. The footman Frederick Johnson, a key witness, had already been approached and he had been able to give many details about Lady Mordaunt's activities during the time of his employment. His diary, which he probably did not release without demanding a generous financial inducement, was to provide valuable evidence and to corroborate many of the details which he and the other servants had already provided.

Lady Louisa's worst fear was that others would be instructed to question Harriett herself and that she would artlessly make her confession of guilt to people who would not scruple to use what she said in evidence against her. Most dangerous, in Lady Louisa's eyes, were Charlie's brothers Johnny and Osbert. She was sure that they would do everything they could to stiffen Charlie's resolve.

When Harriett asked if Osbert would come and see her, Lady Louisa made sure that she was in the room when he arrived. Harriett, however, refused to say anything as long as her mother was there. Osbert believed that Harriett had sent for him because she wanted to confide in him, and Lady Louisa probably had the same fear as she told Osbert that nothing should be said that might later be used against her daughter. Of course, Osbert said, he would not expect Harriett to divulge any secrets, but he added that if she wished to clear her husband, she would have to make her full confession to somebody. He then asked Lady Mordaunt if she wanted her mother to remain with her or not, and she said that she wished Lady Louisa to leave. Once her mother had gone out of the room, Harriett's reserve vanished, and she begged Osbert to advise her, pressing him to tell her what he thought she ought to do. He then gave her a lecture on the subject of repentance, telling her that if she would make up her mind to repent, she might even now be forgiven, that is, in a spiritual sense. Admittedly, he said, her sin was very great, but there was no limit to God's love and he added that she should be very thankful that she had been prevented from committing suicide as she now had the opportunity for repentance which would have been denied her if she had succeeded in her designs. Not surprisingly, this silenced her completely, and she certainly did not deny her guilt. Meeting with little response, Osbert did not pursue the subject. He later felt indignant when he heard that Lady Louisa had complained to Dr Orford accusing him of using his position as a clergyman to try to extract a full confession of her guilt.

Mrs Cadogan had not visited the Hall for several days, not wishing to intrude now that Lady Louisa and Mrs Forbes were there. She did go down, however, on Friday 19 March, after they had been at Walton for several days, and she found Harriett as usual lying on the sofa in her boudoir. Lady Louisa was also in the room. Mrs Cadogan was rather later than usual, and Lady Mordaunt asked her where she had been. She replied that she had been visiting a poor woman in the village, a great favourite of Lady Mordaunt's, who was seriously ill. Mrs Cadogan said that if she should die, what a sorrow and loss it would be, at which Lady Mordaunt said 'That is not sorrow.' Her mother then intervened, saying that Harriett was obviously thinking of herself and the troubles she was going through. Harriett responded by peremptorily asking her mother to leave the room. Mrs Cadogan, embarrassed, suggested that it would be better if she stayed, but Harriett was insistent and very reluctantly Lady Louisa agreed to go.

'I hope you won't take advantage' she said to Mrs Cadogan. Not quite sure what it was all about, Mrs Cadogan promised that she would pass on anything that was said, but as it turned out Harriett did not make any revelations to Mrs Cadogan at all. She simply put her arms round her and cried bitterly.

This made Mrs Cadogan realise that the confidence Harriett had displayed at the beginning of the week, after she had finally persuaded Charlie of the truth of her confessions, was now completely eroded. A kind of despair had settled on her as all around her the talking went on. When she had wanted to confide in somebody, like Osbert or Mrs Cadogan, her mother had done her best to stay in the room, treating her as if she were a child who could not look after herself. The worst of it was nobody seemed to understand when she told them that the members of her set in London had regarded a little illicit intercourse as a form of light-hearted amusement rather than as a deadly sin. In addition, she had been so confident of Charlie's love, of the power she had always been able to exercise over him, that she had never for a moment entertained the idea that he would want to divorce her. And now her mother and sister were warning her that he intended to start proceedings, and that she must say nothing to anybody, as anything she said would be used in evidence against her. They even suggested that she should write to Lord Cole, warning him that he was likely to be cited in divorce proceedings, so that nobody should 'pounce' on him when he was unprepared. Helen said she would take the letter and post it in London. According to Mrs Hancox, Harriett tried to write the letter, but tore it up and asked her to put it on the fire. This happened twice and she eventually said 'It won't do, I can't do it.'

Harriett felt by now that all the servants were suspect and that she could not feel at ease with them as she once had done. Her mother told her that Charlie's lawyer Mr Haynes was intending to question them all. It seemed in fact that there was nobody she could confide in, nobody who would come to her aid. And where were they all now, the men who had flirted with her, tempted her, written her letters, told her there was no harm in what she was doing? Where was her cousin Newport who had once assured her that if she ever needed a friend she could call on him? From all her friends there was nothing but silence.

Later that day, the 19th, Mrs Hancox was concerned when Lady Mordaunt asked if she could have a cold bath. 'I would do anything rather than be exposed to the world, a cold bath or anything' Lady Mordaunt said. Having also seen her patient lurking rather suspiciously near the cupboard where the medicines were now kept, Mrs Hancox feared that the spectre of divorce proceedings might reawaken Lady Mordaunt's suicidal tendencies and so she exercised even stricter vigilance in locking the laudanum away, with the additional precaution of handing the key to Bird for safe-keeping.

16

Sir Thomas Arrives

Helen had by now written to her father telling him about the revelations and about Charlie's determination to pursue a divorce. Sir Thomas was under no illusions about the seriousness of the situation, particularly in view of the fact that the Prince had been named. He was disturbed to learn that his wife and daughter had been openly, and most unwisely, discussing the matter with Charlie and his brothers, and he knew that urgent action would have to be taken to limit the damage already done. On Saturday 20 March he arrived at Walton and Charlie saw him briefly, asking him to discuss matters with Osbert who would put him in possession of the facts. Sir Thomas agreed to see Osbert but told him at once that he refused to hear anything except through his own lawyer. Although he had not yet seen his daughter he expressed the opinion very strongly that she was insane. He later said in evidence that he saw his daughter for a few minutes, but there was some doubt in the minds of those in the house as to whether he actually did or not.

Sir Thomas then heard what Charlie had to say, but did not mention to him his theory that Harriett was out of her mind. After talking to his wife and daughter about their conversations with Charlie, he made a point of seeing Mrs Hancox, and told her that on no account was she to take the child away with her unless it was at Sir Charles's request and on the understanding that he would pay all the expenses. Sir Thomas told her that nobody could compel his family to keep the child, as it had been born in wedlock and there was a great difference between feeling sure in one's own mind that a child was illegitimate and proving it by law. Since it was in any case impossible to know within three weeks when the child was conceived, Sir Charles's view was just a matter of opinion which did not go far in court. Sir Thomas accepted that Lady Mordaunt had talked to Mrs Hancox about her relationship with other men, but he could only think that she must have been 'insensible' at the time.

'Poor thing,' said Sir Thomas, 'I can see by her eyes she is not quite right now.'

Mrs Hancox stuck to her belief that Lady Mordaunt had always been 'sensible' enough to know and understand everything, at least when she had been alone with her; if she had behaved strangely, it had only been in front of others. According to Mrs Hancox, Sir Thomas then said 'Oh, ah, even a lunatic will know his keeper' and put an end to the conversation. Mrs Hancox was sure she had made it clear to Sir Thomas then and there that she did not think it was a question of madness.

Osbert managed to waylay Sir Thomas again before he left, but he repeated curtly that he preferred to hear things only through the lawyers, and was not prepared to listen to any stories about his daughter's guilt. He reiterated that he was convinced she was mad. Johnny afterwards saw him for about a quarter of an hour, and Sir Thomas said to him that even if the case were true, he really could not see what Charlie would gain by dragging it all out into the open. Johnny replied that it would depend on whether his brother decided to sue for damages from the various men involved. He finished by saying, 'Sir Thomas, you don't know the facts but I do, and therefore it's of no use my holding any private conversation with you as I understand from my brother Osbert that you have elected to be put in the possession of the facts through your solicitor.'

After a short meeting with Mr Haynes who had come over to Walton, Sir Thomas returned to London. Helen accompanied him.

That evening, and for several days afterwards, Mrs Hancox noticed that Lady Mordaunt seemed more upset than she had ever been before, now apparently realising that she would have no sympathy from her father. She had always hoped that he would be able to sort everything out with Charlie. She now felt utterly alone and abandoned by her family and by everyone else as well.

On the Monday after her return from Walton, Helen wrote to her brother-in-law, the Duke of Atholl, to bring him up to date with the situation. She had by now, of course, had time to talk things over with her father who had convinced her that Harriett must have been out of her mind when she made her confession to Charlie.

My dearest Iain

I have not been able to write to you before as I have been almost worried to death. I arrived at Walton last Monday and I am grieved to say that I found matters in a most unsatisfactory state. It seems that some days before I was sent for, Harriett had been to a certain extent quite out of her mind at times, and had said things in these sort of ravings which Sir C has chosen to take advantage of; he sent for his brother and they have never ceased trying to rake up every scrap of evidence they could gather in every quarter, and threaten to make a very serious affair of this, in spite of all we could do to prevent him. I sent for Mama, and Papa came directly afterwards. The latter is now staying with us, and has seen a first rate lawyer, who says that from all Papa tells him, of the sort of statements that C. M. has to bring forward, that whatever the world may think of them, they would go for nothing in law and therefore he thinks we have nothing to fear in that respect but of course our great object is to prevent anything being brought before the public which would be dreadful for us all. I hope and trust it may be avoided and Papa and indeed all of us here are doing all in our power to stop the Mordaunts who seem determined to push the matter as far as they can. Papa says if the worst comes to the worst he has several things to bring forward against Sir C. M. which you will understand, also about his leaving her alone so much at Walton.

Helen told her brother-in-law that if he wished to come up to London to give Sir Thomas some help and support, she would be glad to put him up. She had written to him in the first place because she did not wish to worry Louisa who was expecting another baby in August, but she asked the Duke to tell his wife as much as he thought necessary in order to prepare her in case the worst happened and they all had to experience the ultimate nightmare of a divorce.

Think what I have gone through dearest Iain. Of course we must all be careful not to mention a word of the subject to anyone at present.
    Goodbye dear,
                          from your affectionate sister
                                  HELEN FORBES[81]

On the same day that Helen wrote to Iain, Sir Thomas made one last attempt to make Charlie relent.

My dear Charlie,
    Upon serious consideration I have come to the conclusion that nothing I have heard incriminates Harriett in the very least. My honest belief is that although she may have been imprudent, she

has been blameless of infidelity to you. Her incoherent talk while suffering from the shock of a first confinement and from being told that she had presented you with a blind baby, I cannot credit anyone believing. I for one do not, and I cannot imagine your doing so. Anyone in her state of mind would jumble things together as one jumbles things together in a dream as happening to oneself or to others without even the remotest reason why one should do so. I should have gone down to Walton tonight but as Mr Haynes does not wish me to bring an adviser with me to Walton I shall await his statement here to save time and it entirely depends upon what that is what course I may adopt. In the meantime I have done and till then I shall do nothing so let me have it as soon as possible to Queen's Gate Terrace.

Sir Charles immediately showed this letter to Mr Haynes, who was incensed by its tone and wrote angrily in the margin 'Nothing of the kind, the fullest investigation was invited but no one has attended from Sir Thomas either individually or professionally'. Mr Haynes wrote to Sir Thomas affirming that no compromise was possible, and adding 'Sir Charles desires me to say that after investigation he has no doubts whatsoever of Lady Mordaunt's guilt and he hopes that you as her parent and natural protector will take immediate steps for removing her from his house.'

On the Monday, Johnny had moved in to the Hall and made it plain that he was there to stay, acting on behalf of the brother who was too upset to deal with matters himself. Lady Louisa had not returned to London with her husband and daughter, and throughout the weekend and on the Monday and Tuesday the discussions about Harriett's future were gone over yet again. Harriett herself was of course excluded from these conversations and there was little communication between mother and daughter, Harriett on the whole remaining silent in her mother's presence. By now plans were well under way to remove her from Walton and to set her up in a house in Norwood at Charlie's expense. By the Tuesday it seemed as if everything was settled. However on the Wednesday morning Mr Haynes told Lady Louisa that if she took her daughter away it would be at her own risk, and in doing so she would tacitly acknowledge her daughter's guilt. After this Lady Louisa left immediately on her own.

Harriett did not appear to be unduly upset when the last of her family departed from Walton. She remained frustrated, however, by the fact that she was distanced from Charlie, always feeling that if she could talk to him she would be able to explain things and persuade him to forgive her. The arrival of Johnny was not a good omen and he already seemed to have assumed the character of a warder. The thought that Charlie was still bent on divorcing her left her in low spirits, and when Mr Cadogan visited her on the Wednesday evening, and the conversation went round, as it always did, to the subject of her confessions, and to what she had said about her child, she once again broke down completely, sobbing and crying, and unable to speak.

The next day Harriett appeared to be far more cheerful. After her emotional outburst with Mr Cadogan, she pulled herself together and started making arrangements for herself and for her little girl. The plan to take her away to Norwood having been shelved, and her mother and sister being removed, she evidently felt that she was once again in control of her own destiny. Although the agreement drawn up by Lady Louisa with Mrs Hancox had been torn up after Sir Thomas's visit, Harriett now decided to ask Mrs Hancox herself if she would take the child and bring it up as her own. She said that whatever settlement was made, she would make sure that at least half of the allowance she would receive from Sir Charles, however small it turned out to be, would go towards the child's upbringing. 'I know you will care for it more than anyone else I know' she said, adding 'I hope they will not go and make ever such a fuss about it.' She herself could not see the need for lawyers; she felt that the whole thing could be sorted out quietly and cheaply and without the expense of a law suit which she knew her father could not afford. 'I am sure he has no money to spend in law, he had better by half be quiet' she told Mrs Hancox. She then asked Mrs Hancox whether she thought there was anything she could do to stop the case. Mrs Hancox said 'There is nothing now but to let the law take its course.' Mrs Hancox was impressed by how rational and composed Lady Mordaunt seemed during this conversation.

Lady Mordaunt's health had by now so far improved that she was able to walk through to her boudoir rather than being wheeled, and she began to take her 'carriage airing' every day with Jessie Clarke, who reported that on these outings she appeared to be 'calm and comfortable' if rather reserved and disinclined to enter into conversation.

17

Easter Weekend

On Good Friday, 26 March, Lady Mordaunt asked Mrs Hancox to go out for a drive with her. When the coach had been called, she ordered the coachman to drive to Mrs Hancox's cottage at Tysoe, as she wanted to know where her baby was going to be brought up. On the way she asked many questions about the cottage and about Mrs Hancox's family. She gave the impression that if she had to be separated from her baby she would rather it went to Tysoe with Mrs Hancox than anywhere else, but she did say that she hoped Mrs Hancox would try and persuade Sir Charles to let her as the child's mother take the baby with her if she had to leave Walton.

Although Charlie had no doubts about Harriett's guilt and Mr Haynes remained confident that her own confessions and the testimony of the servants would provide enough grounds for a divorce, it was obviously advisable to collect any material evidence that could be used in court, since the servants, particularly the old retainers, might be considered suspect on account of their loyalty to Sir Charles. The serious decision was therefore taken, with Mr Haynes's approbation, to search Lady Mordaunt's private papers. The key to her desk was obtained from Jessie Clarke and the desk was opened by Sir Charles in the presence of his two brothers who had been summoned to act as witnesses.

The results were dramatic. Secreted in some of the drawers and in a special box, they found Harriett's cache of at least eighteen letters from the Prince of Wales, a pocket handkerchief decorated with the royal plumes and the initials A.E., the pressed flowers with the note in Harriett's own handwriting saying that they were taken from the bouquet given her by the Prince for the Dudley House ball, as well as a lock of hair and a Valentine with a memorandum in Harriett's own handwriting which showed that this had been sent to her sometime before her marriage. It contained a poem headed 'Sincere Love' which ran:

> The truest wishes of my heart
> These lines convey to thee

They fond love's sentiment impart
In pure sincerity.

To find these treasured relics was enough of a shock for the sadly unsuspecting Charlie, but he also had to face up to the discovery of the affectionate letters written to his wife by Lord Newport, with their familiar tone and terms of endearment – for example, 'It really is too duckish of you asking me again to Walton . . . Goodbye darling, I shall be so glad to see your nice old face again . . . ' There was also George Forbes's letter written ten days after the wedding discussing whether he should accept her invitation to come to Walton in the near future and referring to Charlie as 'he' – 'you might change your mind or he mightn't like me to come so soon.'

It must be remembered that Charlie had been unaware of any correspondence with the Prince until told about the interchange of letters by the footman Frederick Johnson. There was therefore no doubt that it had been carried on in a sly and clandestine spirit. The Prince's letters, it is true, did not give any evidence of criminality, and were not at all passionate in tone, Harriett being referred to throughout, very properly, as 'Lady Mordaunt'. All the same, in view of the fact that they had been written to a married woman without the knowledge of her husband, they 'far exceeded the bounds of propriety', in the opinion of Sir Charles and his brothers. Coupled with the information supplied by the servants about the Prince's visits to Chesham Place, and remembering the warnings he had given his wife against encouraging any intimacy with the Prince, Sir Charles could only feel that he had been deeply wronged. Lord Newport's letters, more openly affectionate than the Prince's, could perhaps be pardoned on the grounds that, as a cousin, he had an excuse for using her Christian name and other endearments. All the same, he had called her 'darling', even after her marriage, and it had to be admitted that the letters suggested a deeper love than a simple family friendship.

When Harriett returned from Tysoe, she went upstairs to her room as usual. Normally, when she entered the hall after her drive, Bird would hand her the newspaper, but it is unlikely that on this occasion he gave her the *Birmingham Post*, which had given full coverage to the story that was soon to become known as 'The Warwickshire Scandal'. Its report ran:

The subject is seriously mentioned and deeply deplored in the highest class of society in the neighbourhood of Warwick, and among those who admit the story to be undeniable are many personal friends of the unfortunate husband. In the absence of names, we may mention that the family upon whom this heavy misfortune has fallen, is well known in South Warwickshire on account of its highly distinguished ancestry, its territorial possessions and prolonged public service. The lady's family and connections are equally illustrious as those of her husband, and by marriage she stands connected with some of the proudest branches of the English aristocracy. It is a female infant, the paternity of which is denied. It is stated that the lady has already left the house, and that the husband threatens to sell the establishment and go abroad. The occurrence has created a profound sensation throughout the district where the husband resides, and unbounded sympathy for him is expressed by all classes.

Unaware that her story had already broken in the press, or that her private papers had been disturbed, Harriett remained in good spirits, although she felt disappointed that Charlie did not come up to see her when she returned home. Instead, Dr Jones and Dr Orford arrived unexpectedly. They sat with her for a while, and Dr Jones asked her a few questions which she answered. She then asked Dr Jones where Sir Charles was and when he replied that he did not know, she burst into tears.

Dr Orford was still certain that the baby's eye condition was of gonorrhoeal origin. Dr Jones felt inclined to agree with him after seeing the baby that Friday and being told by Dr Orford about the prescriptions for certain lotions which he had discovered on opening the medicine cabinet. All the same he knew that these lotions were frequently prescribed for 'innocent' as well as for 'guilty' secretions, which weakened the case, as did the fact that when Dr Orford had examined Sir Charles to see whether he had become infected he reported that he had 'never found a man in a more pure state'.

Sir Charles had asked Dr Orford whether he had at any time noticed anything that might confirm the theory that his wife was mad. Dr Orford replied that he would certainly have noticed had there been the slightest sign of the post-natal mania which would have been accompanied by easily recognisable symptoms such as a feverish pulse, a hot head and dry tongue. Naturally he had realised that Lady Mordaunt was upset by the situation she was in, but he had never thought it was anything more than that. All the same he had decided that it would once again be wise to have a second opinion which was why he had asked Dr Jones to come in on that Good Friday afternoon. After the meeting Dr Orford reported to Sir Charles that Lady Mordaunt had answered the questions put to her 'rationally and afflictedly' without, in his view, displaying the slightest sign of being insane.

The next day saw the departure of Mrs Hancox, her term as 'monthly nurse' now being complete. Jessie resumed her duties in the bedroom and the boudoir, and a nurse arrived to take charge of Violet. It was probably after Mrs Hancox had gone, and when Harriett was out for her morning drive, that Sir Charles searched his wife's travelling bag and a private drawer in her desk, this time in Bird's presence, and discovered hotel bills from the Palace and Alexandra Hotels made out to Lady Mordaunt and endorsed by her. The first of these detailed her expenditure during her stay at the Palace Hotel from 7 to 9 November in 1867 – twenty-six shillings for the apartment, three shillings and sixpence for breakfast, with Jessie's costing half that amount, a penny stamp, presumably for the letter she wrote to Sir Charles, and three shillings and sixpence for the fire each day. Most revealing, however, was the fact that two dinners at fifteen shillings had been charged for on the first evening, which was the evening on which Jessie had seen Captain Farquhar on the landing, as well as claret for twelve shillings. At the Alexandra Hotel on 30 December 1868, she had paid eighteen shillings for dinners, as well as eight shillings and sixpence for champagne, and on the 31st she had paid six shillings for dinners and two shillings and sixpence for claret. An almanack, or diary, was also found. Looking through it, Sir Charles found a revealing entry for 3 April. In Harriett's handwriting he saw the words '280 days from 27 June'. At that date, of course, Sir Charles had still been in Norway, and Lord Cole had been with Lady Mordaunt alone at Chesham Place. Two hundred and eighty days equals nine months. This was perhaps the most powerful corroborative evidence Sir Charles had yet discovered and the diary was immediately shown to Mr Haynes, who agreed that it was of great value.

Dr Orford was now given the unenviable task of subjecting Lady Mordaunt to a physical examination in an attempt to establish whether or not she was suffering from 'the disease'. He went to see her on the Saturday afternoon, having previously talked to Jessie Clarke who was able to fill in some of the dates. Before examining

Lady Mordaunt, he said 'I don't see why you should continue this reserve with me. I know what's the matter with you and what made the child's eyes bad. I know when you got it – you first had it in about October 1867 and Captain Farquhar gave it to you, then you got better of it and Sir Frederic Johnstone gave it you again, is it not so ?' At first Lady Mordaunt did not answer and he said, 'You don't answer me. I shall still hold my opinion. If you say yes, I shall know I am right. If you say no, then I am bound to believe you.' Later he said that he was ready to testify that her answer was 'Yes'.

At Sir Charles's request, Mr Cadogan went to see Lady Mordaunt on Easter Day. He assured her that he had come purely in his ministerial capacity, as he would visit any other parishioner who was sick and unable to attend church. He told Sir Charles that as a parish priest he must be absolutely neutral and not take sides or be asked to give evidence. Mr Cadogan later told Helen Forbes about this pastoral visit as a proof of his own sincerity and Sir Charles's 'loyalty of purpose'.

Harriett still clung to the belief that she could explain everything to Charlie if only she could find an opportunity to talk to him. She formulated a plan for them to go away together, so that they could sort things out on their own, well away from both their families. She had settled her daughter's future and now wanted to do the same for herself. When her husband came up to her boudoir on Easter Monday, she asked him if he would take her away to the seaside so that they would have a chance to 'forget all about this'. His response was somewhat disappointing. Instead of agreeing and looking forward to the prospect of being alone with her as he had always done in the old days, he replied stiffly that he had no course in honour but to obtain a separation from her. This did not mean that he would be unable to forgive her provided she showed some sorrow for having dishonoured his name, rendered his home desolate and destroyed his happiness.

Harriett made no answer to this speech, and later, when Mrs Cadogan saw her, she seemed overpowered with grief and cried unrestrainedly several times during the visit.

On the Tuesday morning Lady Louisa came down to Walton without warning. When she arrived, as she told the Duchess of Atholl in a letter, she was refused entry by the servants, who eventually agreed to fetch the brothers Johnny and Osbert. It was they, Lady Louisa told the Duchess, who had been told to 'keep guard'. After some talk they relented and allowed her to see Harriett but 'only in the presence of that brother of his [Osbert] who has been at the bottom of nearly all the mischief' as Helen put it to her sister. As a result of Osbert's presence, the meeting was somewhat strained, and neither Harriett nor Lady Louisa made any attempt to draw him into the conversation. Lady Louisa thought that Harriett was if anything a little better, although still unable 'to collect her thoughts'. Osbert, however, later describing this episode when, as he put it, 'Lady Louisa came from London to see her without giving previous intimation', said that Harriett spoke for about ten minutes 'perfectly rationally and collectedly', asking several questions about her sister Lady Dudley and her family. There then came a moment when she seemed to change her demeanour entirely. According to Osbert, she 'fixed her eyes', put her hand to her forehead and gave some very vague replies to the questions put to her. After that she went very silent, and when her mother said she must leave, she burst into tears and begged to be taken away with her. Lady Louisa replied that it was not possible that day. Harriett then wept, evidently more unhappy at her mother's departure than she had ever been before.

18

New Tactics

There had been no suggestion in the newspaper reports that the rumours circulating in the county were in any way false, and much public sympathy was expressed for Sir Charles. From now on, however, the Moncreiffes were intent on reversing that situation. Certainly, any pity Lady Louisa might once have felt for her son-in-law had by now evaporated, and she was ready to join the rest of her family in blaming the Mordaunts for everything. As she put it to the Duchess of Atholl,

> I think they all seem to have tried in a very shameful way to drag things out of her while she was in this state which they now choose to say was not madness. She jumbled up a lot of names saying the child was not C.M.'s and naming in particular Arthur Farquhar, Lord Cole, Sir Frederic Johnstone and the Prince, but I suspect they will have difficulty in finding evidence against any, *specially* the latter. Lord C. is the one they wish to put the child upon and whose she said it was. These names you must take care you let go no further but you will both like to know all we can tell you.
>
> Goodbye dear, either Helen or I will write again.
>
> Ever your affectionate Mother

Both Lady Louisa and Helen settled down to write lengthy letters to Duchess Louisa describing the nightmare events of the previous week. First of all, Lady Louisa explained that she had left Walton

> *not willingly* but having been requested through the lawyers to do so. I had been there all the week before and hope not to have many such weeks to go through again. I don't think Harriet minded my leaving as her mind was too weak to care whether I was with her or not. She is very feeble in health, though otherwise well, but her mind now is quite vacant, at least she can't put two ideas together. It was all settled on Tuesday that I was to bring her to London Wednesday night as she was to go

to Norwood under Mrs Hemming's care and as Charlie Mordaunt's wife and he to maintain her at any rate for the present,
the doctor saying that every hour and every day she stayed there
was at the risk of her mind and body. However on Wednesday
morning the lawyer sent for me requesting I would take her
away on my own responsibility, acknowledging she was guilty
and in short removing her from his responsibility altogether. I *of
course* refused on those terms so he then said she must remain
there till Sir C turned her out for which he had sufficient proofs
and that I was to leave the house at once, so what could I do?
The lawyer gave me a letter to Papa requesting as her protector
he would remove her at once. This was answered yesterday by
our lawyer saying on those terms we could not, but on any
others we would gladly and so the matter rests till we hear
further. I shall remain here a few days longer till something is
settled as to what is to be done with her. In the meantime there
is no fear of them being *unkind* to her at Walton or I could not
have [left] her without one of ourselves. Charlie is very good to
her. You shall hear from me as soon as I know anything more.

Lady Louisa's insistence that Charlie continued to treat Harriett
well was balanced by her disgust at the way in which the brothers
and the lawyer were determined to make the most of her indiscretions. 'So much for the present' she wrote, and went on

> ... as for the rest, you know that while she was delirious the
> week after I left (which I only did because neither she or the
> nurse ever liked my being with her) she said all sorts of things
> which they took up and made every sort of enquiries. There is
> no doubt she has been *very very* foolish to say the *least* of it but
> as far as we can make out, there are no *proofs* by which he can
> divorce her or prove the child not to be his, both of which he
> wants to do and thinks he can get damages from 4 or 5 men!!
> and that no one will speak to them.

Lady Louisa confessed that it had of course been a great wrench
leaving Harriett on her own, even though she appeared to be
'tolerably happy' and apart from the brothers, all those at Walton
and particularly Jessie Clarke, were treating her with kindness. Lady
Louisa would dearly have liked to take Harriett away with her,
feeling that a change of air would do her a great deal of good, but

that was impossible for the time being. The worst of it was that the brothers had told her before she left Walton that on no account were any of Harriett's own family to visit her. She went on hoping that this ban might soon be lifted, and for this reason felt that she could not return to Scotland just yet. 'Here I must stay' she told the Duchess. 'The great discussion now' she went on

> is whether or not we should go with a doctor and lawyer and insist on taking her away. It seems a most touchy point as regards the law and her future. It is too dreadful leaving her there as she is not knowing what they may do to her next, but our interfering or not seemed a most difficult question but I hope it may end in our bringing her home.

So far, at any rate, Sir Charles remained under an obligation to acknowledge Harriett as his wife and to pay for her keep, which, as Lady Louisa wrote 'goes a long way with him, CM I mean, you have no idea to what extent'.

In her letter to the Duchess, Helen Forbes put the situation even more forcibly:

> The dreadful thing is [she wrote] that the Mordaunts do not seem to think anything bad enough to make out against her, and actually *try to* spread all the worst reports they can. One good thing is, that if they go on in the way they are doing, they *must* get themselves into a scrape sooner or later. I cannot tell you how dreadful it was when I first went down there, for they dinned into my ears all these horrrible things about Harriett, saying that she had confessed them all herself and swore she wasn't the least out of her mind, but that she knew perfectly well what she was saying. So of course I believed it all at first, until I had been there for some days, when I found out that there was no doubt whatever that she was still *quite* out of her mind at times. Of course one's first impulse, was that it should all be hushed up and arranged as quietly as possible, but now that we have found out that all these things that they have fished up about her, and what they call proofs are no proofs at all in law, and that what she says (sane or insane) goes for nothing, then of course it is one's duty to fight it out, at the risk of any exposure as although of course they will make out a very disagreeable story and the world may believe the worst of her, yet it will be a great thing to

prevent the divorce, as then he will be obliged to support her,
which for one thing would be a great saving to Papa and Mama,
who would otherwise be *obliged* to keep her, as I don't believe
Charlie will give her a penny if she is divorced, as he thinks
about nothing but money, and actually talks about sueing these
men for damages, isn't it disgusting . . .

Helen assured her sister that their father was sure Charlie would
not succeed in shedding his responsibilities. 'Papa has taken this case
up most tremendously, and declares he doesn't believe a word against
her' Helen wrote, adding 'I only hope that he and the lawyer are not
too sanguine.'

By now the family ranks were closing. The Moncreiffes were showing solidarity as they ranged themselves against the Mordaunts. 'Lord
D. has I believe been very nice about it' Helen wrote, 'and tries to
help him [Papa] as much as he can. Major Arbuthnot is also behaving very well.' The Mordaunts, on the other hand were, Helen considered, acting with great vindictiveness.

What the Mordaunts want is to try and force Papa and Mama
to take her away altogether and maintain her, thereby acknowledging that she has forfeited her right to be his wife. This of
course they can't do, and therefore Papa has refused, for as long
as she is C's wife, he *must* support her as such. Of course it is
dreadful to have to leave her there, in the weak state she is in
surrounded by torments, but the lawyer says this is a most
particular point, and that we must not take her away. . . . The
Mordaunts have certainly behaved throughout in the most
abominable disgraceful manner, altho' I must say that C. himself has been a mere tool in the hands of his brothers, and even
the words he spoke were always dictated to him by them. But
supposing she had been ever so bad, only think of the mean way
in which they treated her, not only trying to force her to say
things when she was in that weak state of mind, but making such
a commotion in the house, and proclaiming the whole thing to
everybody before she had hardly been confined a fortnight, and
when she was unable to say a word in her own defence . . .
Altogether there are certainly great hopes that C. will not be able
to get a divorce, but even if that is the case, one cannot see
anything but a miserable future for H. as she will never regain her
former position, and if she is only separated from him, she will

always be in his power, and the scandal and exposure in the meantime, and if there is a trial, will be most horrible for all of us. This is my feeling about it, but Papa doesn't seem to be the least uncomfortable about it. I mean, not as one would expect, and even poor Mama takes it wonderfully well, although she sees it quite in the same light as I do. You would be astonished to see how well and cheerful she is. Of course excitement and being busy keeps her up, and then she is never alone, and of course I try to cheer her up as much as possible. We do nothing but talk, talk, talk it over all day long, and think of all *sorts* of plans, which seem never to come to much. Of course one can think of nothing else. I think Mama is going back home as soon as anything is at all settled about what is to be done with H in the meantime. . . . I must leave off now darling, I think I have told you as much as I can remember about all this worry. I hope you won't make yourself ill bothering too much about it, from your affectionate sister,

HELEN FORBES

The best news that Lady Louisa was able to impart was that the baby was so much better. Her eyes in fact seemed to be quite all right, a beautiful grey colour, just like Harriett's. 'Mama says the baby looked as well and as nice as possible, and its eyes are all right now and look very pretty' Helen told her sister. 'This is a *great thing*, as it is almost impossible for them now to prove it was anything else but ophthalmia, as if it had been any other disease it would have lasted much longer Dr Priestley says.'

But all the other worries outweighed this one blessing, and Helen had to admit that she and her mother found it impossible to think of anything except Harriett and the dreadful situation that faced them all. Helen was naturally worried about her mother who was by now more than six months pregnant and had felt very tired after travelling to Walton and back in the day.

Mama is not quite so well today, as she was rather knocked up with her journey yesterday [Helen wrote]. I tried to persuade her to let me go, but she would go herself and came back the same day. The whole thing is really too dreadful and complicated and however much of truth there may be in C.M.'s story or not, I am afraid it cannot be anything but a most abominable opportunity for people to make the most of it, and it is already the talk of all London, and everywhere else.[81]

Both Helen and her mother feared that there was little hope of keeping the matter quiet. They realised that there had already been several paragraphs in the papers, mostly with nothing more specific than, 'a family in Warwickshire', although they believed that one account had mentioned names. Certainly at the weekend the *Warwick Advertiser*, copying from the *Birmingham Post*, reported that 'very painful rumours' had prevailed the previous week affecting the peace and honour of an influential county family and pointing to proceedings in the Divorce Court against 'persons of exalted rank'. In view of the alleged involvement of such people the writer of the report hoped that from a national point of view these rumours would turn out to be false.

The improvement in the baby's eye condition may have caused relief in the Moncreiffe camp, but for the Mordaunt doctors it brought an element of doubt. On 30 March, the day of Lady Louisa's visit, Dr Solomon came down from Birmingham and after examining the child told Dr Orford that he felt disinclined to alter his original diagnosis of purulent ophthalmia. He said that the previous conduct of the mother had to be taken into account in such cases, as it was hard to make a diagnosis on the basis of the current symptoms – which was why he placed so much importance on the prescriptions, particularly the Scottish one provided by Dr Irvine. These prescriptions, in his view, did not provide evidence of venereal infection, rather the contrary. Nevertheless, he could not rule out the possibility that the child was suffering from gonorrhoeal ophthalmia as a result of inoculation during its birth.

The next day Dr Orford and Dr Jones carried out a further examination of Lady Mordaunt's condition and they thought she seemed worse. She did then tell them that she had neglected to use her lotions since she had last seen them. Dr Orford, in spite of Dr Jones's more cautious approach, remained convinced that he was right in his diagnosis. Taking into account her own physical state and the condition of the baby's eyes, it all added up, in his opinion, to a venereal infection. Even he had to admit, however, that there was marked improvement in the condition of the baby's eyes.

Violet's eyes apart, everything in the situation had worsened, although Sir Thomas still seemed to hope he could force a private settlement drawn up out of public view. He had been encouraged by his lawyer's assurance that nothing Sir Charles had produced so far in the way of evidence would be likely to stand up in court. Through his lawyer he sent Mr Haynes a letter summoning him to a meeting at Walton with the Moncreiffes' legal adviser. Mr Haynes replied at once that he felt this was unnecessary as there was no intention of having any 'intercourse' which might lead to a compromise. Mr Haynes reiterated what he had said to Sir Thomas during their earlier meeting to the effect that there was no medium course in such cases. 'Sir Charles has a certain position to maintain' he wrote. 'At the same time, as I also mentioned to you, he has no desire to cause unnecessary publicity or needlessly to involve parties in the investigation. You would learn from your solicitor the usual course in these cases and that cannot be departed from.'

Sir Thomas replied that Mr Haynes should send any statement he had to make to Mr J. H. Benbow of Benbow and Saltwell, 1 Stone Buildings, Lincoln's Inn as soon as he conveniently could or alternatively come up to London himself, as it would not be possible for Mr Benbow to leave town at this time. Sir Thomas added that he would remain with his daughter Helen Forbes at 28 Queen's Gate Terrace, South Kensington, until Mr Haynes decided to send or come.

Worst of all was the growing publicity about the situation. Rumour was rampant, not only in London, but in Paris as well where by 1 April Alice Miles had already heard more than a few whispers. She wrote at once to her cousin in London, begging her to send full and particular accounts of Lady Mordaunt's 'awful row, by the side of which the Waterford affaire sinks into comparative respectability and decorum. Wales, Sir Fred Johnstone, Downe, Cole, Newport and Co, all to be had up in the Divorce Court: can't I imagine their faces and Lady Louisa Moncreiffe's!!!'[82]

Meanwhile, Sir Thomas was doing all he could to prove that the stories were unfounded. 'I believe Papa is going to contradict them to a certain extent' Helen Forbes told Duchess Louisa. Certainly on 2 April the *Birmingham Post* expressed some reservations about its earlier account, this time mentioning the Mordaunts by name.

A few days ago we stated that a report, seriously affecting a family of note in South Warwickshire, was current in Leamington and the neighbourhood. The family referred to was that of Sir Charles Mordaunt and the report seriously affected the character of his lady. Since we noticed the affair, we have thought it our duty to ascertain how much of the report is founded on fact, and we find that the whole story with regard to the threatened break up of one of the great Warwickshire families has arisen from the incoherent expressions of Lady Mordaunt herself, when suffering from the immediate effects of her confinement, and that all else that has been based upon this statement is at present unsupported by any corroborative evidence. The lady has not, as was reported, left her home; and as this is so it is probable that the threatened legal proceedings will not proceed beyond the stage of enquiry.

By now, at Walton, everybody had begun to realise that there had been a dramatic change as a result of Sir Thomas's visit, and the general impression was that Lady Louisa and Mrs Forbes had been 'hushed up'. It seemed that the Moncreiffe ladies had been forbidden to discuss Harriett's transgressions and would from now on subscribe to Sir Thomas's theory that she had been out of her mind ever since the confinement. In spite of this the lawyers continued to write to each other, and it was evident that Sir Charles still intended to take legal action.

In her letter to the Duke of Atholl, Helen had indicated that Sir Thomas would be looking for mitigating circumstances to excuse Harriett's behaviour. It might be possible, for example, to say that Charlie had neglected her, leaving her alone too much, or to allege that he had been incapable of fathering a child. It was not easy, however, to make such allegations convincing. As far as leaving her alone was concerned, it could be argued that Charlie had only behaved as a typical husband in his position was expected to behave, attending to his duties in Parliament and pursuing the sporting activities which were an accepted part of country life. He himself was willing to swear that the only time he had abandoned his wife for more than a few days was when he had gone to Norway, and she had decided at the last minute not to accompany him while strongly encouraging him to go away on his own. If he were to be accused of unreasonable behaviour in expecting his wife to travel to such an outlandish place, he was more than ready to point out that the accommodation for ladies on the trip had been exceptionally good. There had been six ladies on board the steamboat going out, and two others, his friends' wives, stayed in 'an excellent house on the river', where his wife would also have been put up had she accompanied him. He had even expressed his willingness to charter a special vessel for their trip.

As for the question of impotence, this was something which might well have rebounded on Harriett, involving the dragging up in court of sordid details concerning her own physical condition and the truth of prevalent rumours that she had herself been advised to undergo a minor operation to facilitate conception. When Mrs Hancox had heard the argument concerning Sir Charles's potency, she had said that she thought that it would fall down because they should have started divorce proceedings at a much earlier date if they had really thought that Sir Charles was incapable. If it could be proved, then it would simply confirm that the child was not his. Lady Louisa wondered whether, if Charlie was not prepared to 'be still' and keep everything quiet, then perhaps he could be forced into the dilemma of either proving his inability or of owning the child. This course was not adopted, probably being considered too dangerous.

The discovery of the letters and hotel bill obviously strengthened Charlie's case, but even so the Moncreiffes knew that provided Harriett could be persuaded to keep quiet from now on, the case might break down, as there was no absolute proof of adultery, nobody having ever 'caught her in the act'. Even the hotel bills did no more than prove that she had entertained a visitor to dinner. Charlie had weakened his own position by his initial reluctance to accept the truth of his wife's revelations, telling her mother and others that he thought she must have been feverish or unbalanced and only later 'choosing to say' that she was not mad after all and must be believed. On the other hand, as Sir Thomas well knew, Lady Louisa and Helen had undermined the madness theory by at first believing Harriett's story themselves. Mr Haynes told Sir Charles that they would find it hard to deny under cross-examination that they had at the outset accepted Harriett's guilt and entered into many discussions concerning her future on the assumption that her confessions were true. But since Harriett had only in fact made a full disclosure to the nurse, to Sir Charles himself and to her mother, the chances were that if she could now be persuaded to deny her guilt, or better still to keep her mouth shut altogether, Sir Charles's case would collapse and he would be forced to maintain her as well as her child for the rest of his life.

Johnny and Osbert, afraid that Harriett could still exercise her power over their brother, lost no opportunity of bolstering his resolve and reminding him of the wrongs that Harriett had committed, of her long and studied course of deceit towards the man who had loved and trusted her too well. They were worried when they realised that Charlie still treated his wife with tenderness and compassion, reserving his anger for the men who had wronged her. They did not overestimate the danger, for it seems that more than anything else Harriett now longed to return to life as it had once been, to go to Charlie as if nothing had happened, to be reinstated as his wife. She probably knew as well as the brothers that a reconciliation was not impossible. It was just a question of finding out the best way of going about it. Her earlier idea of pretending to be 'poorly' to gain her husband's sympathy had not been a success, and now that she was feeling better the most obvious way to re-establish her position was to gain an entry into her husband's bed, something which in normal circumstances would have happened anyway. Since Sir Charles showed as yet no inclination to cohabit, she would have to take the initiative herself at some time in the darkness of the night when all the servants were asleep and the house was quiet. Johnny, however, was taking no chances, and after his move to the Hall, he kept watch, diligently preventing his brother from falling once again under the spell of his bewitching wife.

It was one thing to thwart Harriett in any effort she might make to enter her husband's bed, but it was quite another to ensure that she did not tell him in any casual meeting in the house that all she had confessed to him was in fact untrue. Johnny and Osbert felt sure that this was what Lady Louisa would have advised her to do had she succeeded in speaking to her alone on her recent visit. For this reason it was decided that Charlie must leave the house at once, depriving Harriett of any opportunity to take back her original story.

On 3 April Mr Haynes wrote to Mr Benbow saying that since Sir Thomas had declined to assume responsibility for Lady Mordaunt as requested in his letter of 24 March, Sir Charles would, according to counsel's advice which had by now been taken, provide suitable accommodation for her pending proceedings. It had been decided that Lady Mordaunt should stay at Walton for the time being, while Sir Charles himself made plans to leave for Kingussie in Scotland on 5 April. Bird was to go with him.

The day before Sir Charles left, the Dowager attempted to make Harriett see that it was in her power to put a stop to all the publicity which was by now gaining momentum. As they sat on the sofa together in the boudoir she tried to reason with her daughter-in-law, pointing out how wise it would be if she could come to an agreement with Charlie thus avoiding the dreaded 'exposure' in court. And Charlie too, before he left for Scotland, wrote to his lawyers saying that provided Sir Thomas would listen to the evidence he could produce against several men, he himself would be willing to avoid a trial provided that others would make no opposition. He hastened to add that he did not view this as a compromise, but rather as a measure to expedite matters, without having to bring any of the evidence out into the open. He reminded Sir Thomas that Lady Louisa and Helen Forbes had at first accepted his wife's guilt and had tried to make him agree to a compromise. They had allowed that as a 'man of honour' he had no other course but to divorce her, but had begged him to do it as quietly as possible and this he was prepared to do.

Just before he left for Scotland on the 5th, Sir Charles sent a note up to the Parsonage telling Mr Cadogan that he was going away and adding that he was in a state of great grief. He expressed the hope that Lady Mordaunt would think a little of him, and that, as she had done him such injury, she would do him the justice of owning her wrong. Sir Charles also told Jessie before he left that he trusted she would wait on Lady Mordaunt and make sure that she had everything necessary for her comfort.

The next day, writing from Edinburgh, Sir Charles sent a four-page letter to Mr Haynes, giving as his future address the Spean Bridge Hotel at Fort William. 'My dear Haynes,' he wrote, 'it will not be possible for me to tell you all that I wish in one letter, but I will write at various times as the past occurs to me.' For the time being he dwelt on his own bitter realisation that his wife had been all too sane when telling him about her trangressions, and he stressed the fact that Lady Louisa and Mrs Forbes had been quite satisfied of her guilt until Sir Thomas arrived and planted the madness idea. He also told Mr Haynes that he was prepared to accept the theory that the 'precautions' Lady Mordaunt had taken had prevented her from passing on 'the disease' to him.

Mr Haynes received the letter next day and immediately sent it on to Mr Hunt, of the firm of lawyers chosen to be his agents in London, asking them to pass it on to Mr Inderwick who had agreed to act as Sir Charles's counsel. Mr Haynes was of the opinion that no time should be lost in taking the deposition of the landlord and waiter at the Alexandra Hotel where the assignation with Sir Frederic Johnstone had taken place. This was important, because once Sir Frederic had been served with a citation, he would obviously deny that he had ever been at the hotel and would try to suppress the evidence. Fortunately, the dinner bill for two dinners on 30 December 1868 would help to establish that Sir Frederic had been there alone with Lady Mordaunt that night.

The Moncreiffes now realised that as Sir Charles had left for Scotland there would be no chance of Harriett managing to regain his affection. All hopes of a private settlement were rapidly receding as Sir Charles continued to insist that whatever happened, the guilt of the men involved would have to be acknowledged. This meant that Harriett's confessions would have to be nullified, and the only way to do this was somehow to prove that she had been out of her mind when she made them. And if she could be proved permanently insane, then she would in any case be unfit to plead, and it would then be impossible to call her into the witness box. As a result, all the men who had been quaking at the thought of what she might publicly reveal, those she had already named or perhaps others she had not as yet implicated, would be able to rest a lot easier. At the same time Lady Louisa and Helen Forbes would be spared the ordeal of a court appearance, their somewhat indiscreet behaviour in discussing Harriett's future during their stay at Walton, based on the assumption that she was guilty, being acknowledged by both sides to be a vital factor in the case. As for Sir Thomas, he seemed resigned to the fact that his daughter would have to be dubbed a lunatic rather than labelled an adulteress.

On 5 April the Moncreiffes' lawyer wrote to give warning that Lady Louisa would be arriving in Leamington the next Wednesday on the train from Paddington due in at 12.35. What the lawyer did not say was that Sir Thomas would be with her. They spent a few hours at Walton and returned to London the same day. Sir Thomas said little to anybody, except to insist that Lady Mordaunt was insane. He made sure that he and his wife saw their daughter alone.

That evening, after Lady Mordaunt's parents had gone, Jessie Clarke found a letter in the pocket of a dress she was putting away. Evidently intended for Mrs Hancox, it was in Lady Mordaunt's handwriting

My dear Nurse, Pray say nothing more about the nonsense I talked when you were here.

Yours truly,
H. MORDAUNT

Jessie Clarke had been given instructions to intercept any letters written by Lady Mordaunt other than those directed to her closest relations. She therefore kept the note and it was later handed to the lawyers. When it was shown to Dr Orford he said that in his opinion it could only have emanated from a perfectly sane and coherent mind.

19

The Doctors

Before he left for Scotland, Sir Charles had charged Mrs Caborn with the task of retrieving the expensive baby clothes which Helen Forbes had taken back to London. Helen had promised to return them to the shop but had so far failed to do so, much to Sir Charles's chagrin. When the redoubtable Mrs Caborn arrived at 28 Queen's Gate, she was invited in by Mrs Forbes who chatted to her and asked after Lady Mordaunt. Helen Forbes refused, however, to surrender the baby clothes, and Mrs Caborn returned to Walton without having accomplished her mission.

Helen Forbes had told Mrs Caborn that her father intended to visit Walton again, this time accompanied by Dr Priestley. Sir Thomas had told the doctor about the delusions his daughter was supposed to be suffering from, among them the fear that the Mordaunts were trying to poison her. As a result Dr Priestley agreed to see Lady Mordaunt and to give his opinion about her state of mind, but after he had talked to her for a while in front of her father, he left the room and asked Jessie Clarke if he could have a word.

'Tell the Dowager Lady Mordaunt' he said 'that I came here at the request of the Moncreiffe family to see Lady Mordaunt but I fear I cannot help them much as I find Lady Mordaunt perfectly rational. They wish me to recommend a change of air for her but I do not think it would do much good.'

After talking to Jessie Clarke, Dr Priestley had a meeting with Dr Orford in the billiard room and told him that he did not think Lady Mordaunt was suffering under any delusions at the present time because when he had asked her if she still thought Lord Cole or Sir Frederic Johnstone had anything to do with the child she had answered 'No'. Dr Orford said that having seen Lady Mordaunt constantly since the confinement, he had never thought she suffered from delusions anyway. It was true that Dr Jones had talked of cataleptic hysteria, but he himself did not think she was suffering from anything of this nature, which would necessitate 'a perfect trance of apparent stupefaction'. He himself had never found her in that kind of state. He was also convinced that if she did show any signs of mania, these were 'simulated'. He recounted how when he and Dr Jones were giving her some stimulants to rouse her and a small portion trickled down her chin, it had startled her, which would not have occurred had she been in 'a dormant way'. Dr Priestley did not counter this, but when Dr Orford brought up the question of gonorrheal infection, Dr Priestley told him emphatically not to 'go and put *that* idea into the lawyers' heads'.

The Dowager Lady Mordaunt bore out Jessie Clarke's description of the message left for her by Dr Priestley. She said she was not at all surprised that he found Harriett to be quite rational and 'collected' as this was her own impression.

Having had little help from Dr Priestley, and meeting a wall of disbelief at Walton when he expressed the view that his daughter was insane, Sir Thomas decided to call in another medical man of his own choice, Sir James Simpson, an eminent gynaecologist who practised in Edinburgh, entertaining a wide circle of friends where he lived at 52 Queen Street. Well known for his achievements in the field of obstetrics, he had pioneered the use of chloroform in childbirth, although it had to be admitted that his first experiment in inhaling it had ended with himself and his assistant simultaneously falling insensible under the table. He was popular with his patients on account of his sympathetic bedside manner and his forceful personality, and along with Dr Priestley, who had been one of his pupils, he had been a valued adviser to the Moncreiffe family for many years.[83]

Sir Thomas and Sir James went down to Walton together on Wednesday 14 April. Jessie Clarke, who recalled that Lady Mordaunt had been in rather low spirits that day, was not in the room when Sir James saw Lady Mordaunt, but he did speak to Jessie and told her that if he were asked he would say that Lady Mordaunt was not in her right mind.

Mrs Caborn was out walking with the baby when Sir James arrived but she made sure that she was back before he left. She found him in the nursery arranging some scales and he then weighed and measured the baby. He very wisely did not say a word about Lady Mordaunt in Mrs Caborn's presence.

On his way back to the station, Sir James called at Dr Orford's house, The Cottage in Wellesbourne, and after some introductory remarks asked him whether he had weighed and measured the child. Dr Orford replied that he had not.

'They will ask you in a court of law if you did' said Sir James.

'I can't help that' said Dr Orford. 'I have not done so now nor am I going to do so'.

After one or two other remarks, Sir James said 'You know that Sir Thomas is going to bring an action for conspiracy.'

Dr Orford, realising that Sir James was trying to intimidate him, refused to say anything more, and after that Sir James went away.

On his return to London, Sir James advised Sir Thomas to have Lady Mordaunt examined by a doctor who was expert in cases of insanity. He personally recommended Dr Tuke, in his view the greatest living authority in the field.[84]

Helen Forbes took Dr Tuke down to Walton on 15 April. In the train she explained to him that her sister was still suffering from delusions. She said that Harriett had told her that there were dead bodies in the room and that she was convinced that she was being poisoned or pursued.

On their arrival at Walton, Mrs Forbes and Dr Tuke had luncheon with Lady Mordaunt. Afterwards Dr Tuke told Jessie Clarke that Lady Mordaunt had suffered a fit of hysteria at the end of the meal, during which time she seemed to be perfectly incapable of thinking. Dr Tuke and Mrs Forbes then went with Lady Mordaunt to her sitting-room, Jessie Clarke waiting in the room next door. Dr Tuke concentrated his questions on the delusions which Mrs Forbes had told him about, and at first Lady Mordaunt refused to answer, proving just as uncooperative as she had been with Sir James Simpson and Dr Priestley. Eventually, when questioned about the dead bodies, she said 'But there were dead bodies there.' Dr Tuke then went next door and questioned Jessie Clarke, asking her whether Lady Mordaunt was capable of ordering her own carriage, and whether she noticed things when they were out driving. Jessie Clarke replied that Lady Mordaunt's wishes were always consulted, that the carriage was ordered when she asked for it, and, yes, she *did* notice things when they were out.

After that Dr Tuke went back into the sitting-room and Mrs Forbes came out, talking about the baby to Jessie Clarke and generally keeping the conversation going. After a few minutes Dr Tuke called Jessie into the sitting-room, where she saw Lady Mordaunt standing on a rug in front of the fire with her hands clenched and her eyes fixed. Jessie was sure that she had never seen her mistress in that kind of state before, and it was her belief that the manner was assumed in order to get rid of the doctor who seemed to be irritating her. Jessie gave her some water to drink, asking her what was wrong, and she then sat down, apparently in some kind of nervous state. Dr Tuke felt troubled by her lack of response, and he said to Jessie 'Do you say she is thinking now because in my opinion she is totally incapable of thinking?' As Lady Mordaunt continued staring vacantly in front of her, Dr Tuke himself seemed to become agitated by her attitude and her lack of response to his questioning. Clasping his hands he went down on one knee and begged her to tell him if there was anything he could do for her. 'My dear lady,' he cried, 'you do not wish to be sent to a lunatic asylum do you?'

Dr Tuke then went away, and after he had gone Helen Forbes took Lady Mordaunt out into the garden where they walked about together for about half an hour. That evening, Lady Mordaunt said nothing when she was being dressed and Jessie thought that she had been very unsettled by Dr Tuke's visit. She continued in this state for the next few days. Jessie herself felt angered by the doctor's visit, and it seemed to her that the unexpected arrival of strangers was having a very bad effect on Lady Mordaunt.

Mrs Caborn agreed that it was the presence of the doctor that had caused Lady Mordaunt's strange behaviour. The housekeeper had once again contrived to appear at the right moment, taking the baby in to its mother when the doctor was there. She agreed with Jessie that Lady Mordaunt was standing absolutely motionless, and added that she appeared 'much heated', so much so that Mrs Forbes suggested opening the window, although this was not done because of the baby. Dr Tuke had afterwards asked Mrs Caborn if she had ever seen Lady Mordaunt in that state before, and whether she often had similar attacks. Mrs Caborn said 'What attacks?', adding that she did not see Lady Mordaunt often enough to know.

Helen Forbes went back to London with Dr Tuke that evening, Sir Charles having left instructions that friends and family could visit his wife but not stay overnight. After they had gone, Mrs Cadogan went down to the Hall and found Lady Mordaunt looking well enough physically even though she seemed very depressed. She asked after the Cadogan children, and then inquired where Sir Charles was. Mrs Cadogan replied that he was in Scotland and said 'Why don't you write to him and tell him you are sorry?'

'I am not sorry' she said.

Mrs Cadogan remonstrated with her for adopting this attitude, but she did not retract her remark.

After his visit to Walton, Dr Tuke told Sir James Simpson that as a result of seeing Lady Mordaunt and going into the history of her case with great care, he felt confident that she had suffered under puerperal mania with delusions since the fifth or sixth day after the birth of her child, that she was of unsound mind and would need careful watching and special medical treatment. This was in spite of the fact that he had made no attempt to see Dr Orford. He said that he had questioned Lady Mordaunt about the delusions reported to him by Helen Forbes, but he had not brought up the question of her original allegations as they seemed to him so unlikely that they must have been delusions, which were quite common in a patient suffering from puerperal mania. Sir James told Sir Thomas Moncreiffe that he thought Dr Tuke's diagnosis was sound, agreeing that delusions were quite common in such cases. He then wrote to Sir Charles.

> 52 Queen Street,
> Edinburgh
> 18 April 1869

Sir,

I have no right whatever to address you upon the case of Lady Mordaunt and in venturing to write you I do so without the knowledge of Sir Thomas Moncreiffe or his family.

3 days ago I saw Lady Mordaunt and had no doubt that she was insane. I advised a physician more intimately acquainted with lunacy than I am to visit her. Dr Tuke, perhaps the greatest living authority on insanity in London has in consequence gone down and has sent me his opinion to the effect that she has suffered under puerperal mania with delusions ever since the 5th or 6th day after the birth of her child or earlier, that she is at present of unsound mind, requires careful watching and special medical treatment and in consequence he advises her instant removal as the *only* possible chance of recovery.

This view of the certainty of which I feel perfectly assured, gives quite a new complexion to the whole case. Besides I know and feel that all the medical opinions about the existence of gonorrhea to be so unfounded that they will not bear any examination in a Court of Law while the idea mentioned to me by

Dr Jones of her dating the day of delivery from the last monthly illness (27th June) is exactly the way of counting the duration of pregnancy followed by almost every *Scottish* woman.

The child is now (some six weeks after its birth) only of the length and weight of a child at the full time. I weighed it and measured it. I would greatly wish to see you that I might explain these matters more fully to you *viva voce*. If the case is not arrested Lady Mordaunt will, I fear, be driven into a state of fixed and permanent insanity. I feel sure that no one and above all a husband would willingly and deliberately inflict so dreadful a result upon a fellow being and above all on his own wife. The world at large would revolt at such conduct as you well know. On Wednesday I shall I believe be obliged to be a witness before a committee of the House, but I shall be back again by Thursday or Friday.

I have the honour to be

Your obedient servant
J. F. SIMPSON M.D.

Dr Tuke's report, and Sir James's acceptance of his findings, brought a new element into the case. Dr Orford and Dr Jones had both been insistent that Lady Mordaunt had never showed the slightest sign of puerperal fever or mania, the conditions which were related to childbirth. It seemed extraordinary that two eminent doctors were prepared to accept this new diagnosis which was based on such a superficial examination of the patient and without any reference to those who had treated her in the days after she had given birth. Sir Charles, who was in any case extremely displeased that the Moncreiffes had arranged for their doctors, and particularly the 'mad doctor', Dr Tuke, to examine his wife without his permission, felt far more ready to accept the local men's opinion. He certainly had no intention of meeting Sir James and discussing the matter with him. He did, however, ask Dr Orford and Dr Jones to examine his wife yet again.

As a result, the two doctors went to see her on 18 and 23 April and they agreed that her manner and conversation appeared to be 'perfectly coherent and natural'. Dr Orford remained convinced that there was and never had been any sign of hysteria, catalepsy, puerperal mania or any other form of madness. In fact, the country doctor laughed at the whole idea of insanity.

Jessie Clarke was later to describe how on the 23rd Lady Mordaunt when dressing in the morning had again seemed depressed and had cried, saying she was sick to death and in great trouble, and she spoke of her grief at the position she was in. Later, however, after Dr Orford and Dr Jones had been to see her she appeared to be more 'composed and comfortable'. Jessie observed that the local doctors did not upset her as much as the others did.

Over the next few days those at Walton Hall saw increasing signs of what they believed to be Lady Mordaunt's attempts to 'simulate madness'. As they began to realise what line the Moncreiffes were to take, they felt increasingly scandalised and incredulous. They were sure that Harriett's mother and sister had never mentioned the question of madness before Sir Thomas appeared, 'their great desire being to hide her shame as privately as possible'. Mr and Mrs Cadogan, Mrs Hancox, Jessie Clarke, Dr Orford, Sir Charles and his brothers, all those in fact who had been in almost daily contact with her, were all prepared to swear that there was no question of insanity. That Harriett was in some sense disturbed by the events of the last weeks was undeniable and Dr Orford was sure that although she naturally seemed at times to be almost prostrate with weakness and excitement, this was no more than he would have expected from someone in her situation. He was prepared to admit that when he had visited Lady Mordaunt over the Easter weekend, she had refused to say a word to him, except on the third visit when he had asked her if he should see her again, and she had said 'Come again tomorrow.' He had attributed this silence to the fact that he had been giving her a not very pleasant medical examination. He refused to believe that her mind was in any way affected nor did he ever have any evidence that she suffered from delusions. As for the question of puerperal mania, he resented the fact that his professional competence was being questioned. He himself had never observed the slightest signs of the fever and delirium which would accompany this condition.

It seemed to Dr Jones that Lady Mordaunt was revealing the normal symptoms suffered by somebody who had a weight on their mind even though her strange silences were, to say the least, unusual. Both Dr Jones and Dr Orford were so sure there was no question of madness that they were prepared to testify to that effect, telling the lawyers that they could see no reason to call in any other medical men to confirm their opinion. Both the doctors were convinced that the patient would not be eating and sleeping so well if she had been in any sense of the word mad, and they were equally sure that she would not be able to recover from her anxious state until she had fully removed the weight from her conscience with a complete confession.

Mrs Cadogan agreed with everybody else. She said that although at times Lady Mordaunt would lie on the sofa without speaking, with a fixed look on her face as if deep in thought, it had never occurred to her that she could be insane. It was true that at times she would cry and fling her arms round Mrs Cadogan's neck but this was more a sign of unhappiness than of insanity.

The argument was now well under way as to whether Lady Mordaunt's original 'light-headedness' as well as the more peculiar behaviour which was now beginning to emerge could be real or feigned. In the days following the visits of Dr Priestley, Sir James Simpson and Dr Tuke, Dr Orford did sometimes notice that his patient behaved somewhat strangely, but she soon returned to normality if he spoke to her firmly, telling her if she went on like that he would send for a doctor to treat her for madness. As an indication of her peculiarities, Dr Orford described how she took to shaking hands with her left hand, and when he remonstrated with her and said 'Lady Mordaunt I don't like your left hand, I would rather you would give me your right hand', she laughed and did so. On another occasion, when she was still in her dressing-gown and Jessie Clarke told Dr Orford that this morning she had refused to get dressed, he sat down and waited to see what would happen. After a while she put her hands over her face and appeared to laugh. He remonstrated with her again, and she then got up and said 'I think I'll go to London today', afterwards crossing the room to the bell and saying 'Will you send my maid Jessie Clarke to me' by way of ending the interview.

Another time, when she was silent and refused to say anything, Dr Orford spoke to her very forcibly about her conduct, and Jessie Clarke told him that she had cried a great deal after this visit but next day had seemed much more cheerful and more her normal self. When pressed to diagnose her condition, the doctor said it was really very difficult to say what was the matter with her; her strange trances when she would stand like a statue in the middle of the room, her refusal to answer questions, and the vacant expression she would sometimes adopt, seemed to him to indicate that she was a good actress rather than a maniac.

20

The Evidence

Reassured by Dr Orford's insistence that Lady Mordaunt's oddities were assumed, Mr Haynes pressed on with his inquiries, diligently taking statements and as far as possible leaving no stone unturned. He knew the importance of interviewing possible witnesses before they could be persuaded to give testimony for the opposing side. This was the stage when servants could make capital out of what they had observed, when footmen might be offered sums for either handing over or withholding their diaries, and lady's maids could be manipulated with substantial sums of money either to keep quiet or reveal all. Mr Haynes had wisely taken statements from several of the servants before the Moncreiffes found time to muster their forces, and the swift enrolment of the footman Frederick Johnson, who was only too ready to testify against the demanding and pleasure-seeking employer he had come to dislike, was an astute move on the part of the provincial lawyer. Among the local witnesses there was considerable loyalty, and Dr Orford, even when faced by a barrage of letters and visits from eminent colleagues, remained steadfast in his belief that Lady Mordaunt had always been free from anything approaching mania or insanity. He also stuck to his diagnosis of the child's gonorrhoeal ophthalmia which in his opinion had been caused by unhealthy secretions from the mother, even though this was something that the other doctors had seized on as a way of proving his unreliability as a practitioner and possible witness.

When questioned by the lawyer all the servants stuck closely to the story as they had originally told it to Sir Charles. All their accounts tallied in every detail. With their help Mr Haynes was able to piece together a convincing account of the first two years of Lady Mordaunt's married life, the secret embraces, the afternoon visits, the interludes in hotels.

Mrs Hancox described how she was visited by 'a professional' as she put it, after she had returned to her cottage in Tysoe, who asked her about Lady Mordaunt's mental state. She said that she told him 'in a firm decided manner that Lady Mordaunt was quite in her right mind, and that she was simply pretending to be mad to get herself out of the scrape she had got into'. She was more than ready to give a detailed description of her month's stay at Walton Hall and had no scruples about revealing all Lady Mordaunt's confidences, how, for example, Lady Mordaunt had told her about the time she had consulted Dr Priestley about 'the disease' and he had 'pooh-poohed' the idea and said it would get better after the confinement. She said that Dr Priestley had given her remedies up to a fortnight before the birth of her child. Lady Mordaunt had also revealed that she felt sick a fortnight after the time she had counted from the last week in June — eight months exactly, and she had always been able to name the very date and the very hour of conception. Mrs Hancox herself had never felt any doubt, from what she had heard, that it would come to a divorce, and when Lady Mordaunt had been drawing up a memorandum concerning the care of the child, she had recommended that it be made in Lady Louisa's name, as Lady Mordaunt would no longer be Lady Mordaunt after the divorce went through. When she was told about the letter Lady Mordaunt had written to her asking her to forget all that had been said, Mrs Hancox recalled that Lady Louisa had already asked her before she left to say nothing about what she had heard.

Mr Haynes had interviewed Jessie Clarke after the departure of Mrs Hancox and before Sir Charles left for Scotland. She told him all that she knew, from the time when she had accompanied Lady Mordaunt to Scotland and had noticed her intimacy with Captain Farquhar. She also told him about the Prince of Wales, mentioning that Lady Mordaunt had read her the letter which the Prince had written to congratulate her on her engagement. She now added that she had noticed stains on Lady Mordaunt's linen during those times when she was seeing Captain Farquhar, although she had not realised their significance at the time. As for Lady Mordaunt's condition following the birth, she knew that she was distressed, but it had never occurred to her that she was mad, even if she often seemed sad and uncertain what to do.

The only details Jessie Clarke omitted in talking to Mr Haynes were connected with the letter from Captain Farquhar which she had found on Lady Mordaunt's dressing-table and had afterwards shown to Bird. She had not told Lady Louisa about this either. Lady Louisa had, however, confirmed that Captain Farquhar was stationed at the Tower at that time. Jessie had also persuaded Bird to say nothing about the letter out of sympathy for Lady Mordaunt, not wishing, perhaps, to be the person who provided the most incriminating evidence, or giving herself the reputation of being the kind of maidservant who would read her mistress's letters.

The footman Frederick Johnson, like Jessie, was able to tell Mr Haynes a great deal about Captain Farquhar – about the visit to the Alhambra and the Captain's many appearances at Walton Hall. He recalled the episode in the autumn of 1867 when he had taken a note from Mrs Cadogan up to Lady Mordaunt's boudoir and found Captain Farquhar there with Lady Mordaunt and carving tools between them, and he described how Lady Mordaunt had reprimanded him for walking in without knocking. Important, too, was his testimony concerning the letters he had delivered or posted to Captain Farquhar and the Prince.

Before his departure for Scotland, Bird had told Mr Haynes all that he could remember about Lady Mordaunt's behaviour before her confinement. He had not, of course, seen much of her following the birth of the baby, although once she felt well enough to go for her daily drive he had handed her in or out of the carriage each time she went out, finding her quite normal in her behaviour and as courteous and charming as she had always been towards him. He had never noticed any 'aberration of mind' on these occasions. She always spoke rationally and appeared to understand everything that was said to her. One day when he told her that he had given the coachman instructions to take her for a nice drive, she said 'Oh, thanks' and another time when she came in from driving, she asked if she would be able to catch any perch in the brook. He had taken her fishing once or twice in previous times, but he said he was afraid it was too cold as yet and she answered, 'Oh I suppose it is.' On another occasion when he gave her the newspaper before she went upstairs after coming in from driving, she took it and thanked him just as she used to do in the days before her confinement.

Sir Charles now added to his original statement a defence of his actions subsequent to the birth, refuting the charge that he had set everything in motion before he had fully alerted Harriett's relations to the situation. He recalled how he had begged Mrs Forbes to come, and how both she and her mother had been put in possession of the facts as he saw them before he had sent for his brothers. As for the spectre of madness, he admitted that he had at first wondered whether Harriett's revelations could have resulted from 'light headedness', but the two doctors, as well as Mrs Cadogan, had soon persuaded him that her state stemmed from the fact that she had something overwhelming on her mind. And surely any woman who such a short while after a confinement had been clear-headed enough to insist that the word 'prematurely' should be included in the newspaper announcement must have been in full command of her senses. As far as he was concerned, the only abnormal thing about her was her promiscuity. 'My opinion now is' Sir Charles wrote 'that what *she sought was perpetual admiration from many men* and the same idea led to prostitution with many, and I do not think that she cared for any particular man more than another, otherwise she would have left me entirely for some one of them.'

He realised that the Moncreiffes would try, in Harriett's defence, to make out that he had treated her badly, and he thought that evidence should be given on this point by impartial guests to the house. In any case, he was sure that she had no possible cause for

the long and studied course of deceit practised towards me who loved and trusted her only too well, and to whom she has left *an illegitimate child which cannot be proved to be such, a desolate home, and a name dishonoured which never before was tarnished*. With such opportunities as she had of fulfilling and doing justice to her home and to what should have been a good and honourable position I will only add that I believe such a case as hers never has occurred or is ever likely to occur again in all time.

The Moncreiffe lawyers meanwhile were doing all they could to foil Mr Haynes's investigation. Mr Haynes soon realised that Dr Priestley had been brought into line. He had gone up to interview the doctor in London, having been told about the message he had left for the Dowager saying that he could find no sign of madness. It was disappointing to discover that Dr Priestley was now lining up with the other Moncreiffe doctors and seemed quite prepared to accept the diagnosis of puerperal mania.

When Mr Haynes went to the Palace Hotel to collect statements from the staff there, it looked suspiciously as if his rivals had got there first. Nobody seemed to remember very much about anything. James Dempsey, the manager, and two waiters, Frederick Hodgkinson and John Trice, all declared that they did not know either Captain Farquhar or Captain Farmer, although the manager remembered seeing Captain Farmer's name in the visitor's book for 7 November struck out and Captain Farquhar entered on the same line. But he did not know if Captain Farmer had been there and in any case would not know him if he saw him. He produced the large ledger known as the day book which contained entries concerning visitors' accounts and bills. The entry on 7 November for two dinners at 15/- for Lady Mordaunt, and Captain Farmer/Farquhar's payment for a room on the third floor for three nights were found, although the Captain did not appear to have paid for any refreshments. The manager said that the hall porters wrote the visitors' names in their book and the manager did the same in his book. They did not send names in to the paper unless the visitors wanted them to do so. 'I generally ask them if they desire it and I suppose I asked them in this case' said the manager. The manager left the room at one time to see what he could find out, but he was unable to discover who had waited on Lady Mordaunt. Each waiter kept a memorandum but all those who might have been involved seemed to have destroyed all their records for 1867, and they could not be expected to remember at that distance of time who had been on duty. John Trice was prepared to say that he could remember Lady Mordaunt coming to the hotel, but that he did not recall waiting on her, could not remember who did, and did not recollect the name of either Captain Farmer or Captain Farquhar. The other waiter interviewed said that he did not even know Lady Mordaunt by sight. Two porters, Alfred Brett and George Jeffreys did, however, recall the name Farmer being scratched out in the arrivals book and the name Farquhar being substituted when the mistake was recognised.

These were small setbacks, however, when balanced against the mass of material that had already been collected, and Mr Haynes felt confident enough to dismiss the question of madness as an irrelevance, pressing on with setting the divorce proceedings in motion as soon as possible. Nobody he had interviewed at Walton Hall had retracted what they had first said to Sir Charles, rather they added to it. Mr Haynes felt sure that he had sufficient evidence to pursue the divorce and that the testimony of Dr Orford and Dr Jones, who had been in attendance on Lady Mordaunt in the weeks after her confinement, would count for far more than the evidence of the London doctors, which was based on the evidence of somewhat fleeting visits. Sir Charles backed him up, being prepared to put in writing that he conscientiously believed his wife was feigning insanity under the influence of her family, and particularly her father, to evade the present proceedings and to avoid publicity both for herself and for those she had incriminated.

After studying all the evidence produced by Mr Haynes, Sir Charles's counsel, Mr Inderwick, wrote that in his opinion Lady Mordaunt's own confessions, together with the statements of the witnesses, provided a case against Lord Cole and Sir Frederic Johnstone. On the other hand, although there was a strong suspicion surrounding the Prince of Wales and Captain Farquhar he believed that there was not enough firm proof to proceed against them. It was true that the Prince had continually visited Lady Mordaunt at times when he knew that Sir Charles was not at home, but nobody had actually caught him 'in the act'. It was said that 'actual evidence of impropriety' might have been obtained had it not been that at a house where it happened, every member of the staff had been changed before Sir Charles's agents had been able to get there. As to Lord Newport there was nothing more substantial than his letters which alone were not sufficient. 'The case against Lord Cole and Sir Frederic Johnstone' Mr Inderwick wrote 'depends solely upon the evidence of the witnesses, as Lady Mordaunt's statements, although strong enough against herself, are not evidence against either of these gentlemen, and divested of these confessions the case is very weak against them both.'

Mr Inderwick thought that the question of Sir Charles's incompetency could be dismissed, as it obviously had not occurred to him or to his family to question whether or not Lady Mordaunt was carrying his child during the time of her pregnancy. Other points, such as the claiming of damages against the guilty men, would, he thought, be dealt with at the time of the trial. Meanwhile his first task was to advise on the final draft of the petition for divorce which would have to be served on Lady Mordaunt and the citation which would be delivered to the two co-respondents, Lord Cole and Sir Frederic Johnstone.

Sir Charles assured Mr Haynes that there would not be any difficulty in tracing the whereabouts of the two men when it came to presenting them with the citation. Sir Frederic Johnstone was always to be found at Coventry House, Melton Mowbray, during the hunting season, but he would by now be in London when not attending whatever race meeting happened to be taking place. Lord Cole could be contacted at his father Lord Enniskillen's place, Florence Court, Enniskillen; there would be no need for Bird to be called back from Scotland to identify him, as the groom Stevenson would be quite capable of doing that. As to Captain Farquhar, if it was decided after all that he should be called on, he could be found wherever the Coldstream Guards were quartered.

Sir Charles himself disagreed with Mr Inderwick on the subject of Captain Farquhar, believing strongly that it would strengthen his case to proceed against him as well as the two others, the evidence against him being even more important in his case than Lady Mordaunt's confession. Since Jessie Clarke was now ready to testify that there had been stains on Lady Mordaunt's linen consistent with adultery, this, coupled with the evidence of the meeting at the Palace Hotel, would surely be enough to incriminate him. Lady Mordaunt's insistence that her husband would only have been in the way if he had accompanied her on her shopping trip could also be used to good effect. Bird had testified that Lady Mordaunt had continually corresponded with Farquhar, and in addition Lady Louisa and Helen Forbes had been very ready to believe his guilt, saying that Harriett had spoken of him as a brute who had ill-treated her.

> If Farquhar was put in as a co-respondent I think he would not attempt a defence himself as he has long since been ruined, his father having refused to pay his debts which have twice been paid by his brother who alone has saved him from prison and he has been trying for several months to exchange from his regiment and get an appointment in India. This I knew previously but I have heard lately that which I did not know before, that he has long ago by report been notorious as an adulterer and the worst of characters and I think we can ascertain perhaps that this is not the first crime he has committed.

Sir Charles left it to counsel to decide whether or not the evidence was sufficient to avoid the danger of a libel action. His uppermost feeling was that the proceedings should start as soon as possible. Already the expenses were mounting; there were retainers to pay and bills to deal with, a guinea here, five guineas there. Sir Charles wanted all the formalities to be over as soon as possible so that he could be rid of the wife he had loved not wisely but too well.

21

The Petition, 30 April 1869

In London rumours proliferated, and those involved were all too aware that if Lady Mordaunt could not be proved insane Sir Charles would press on with a divorce, even though it was by no means clear as yet whom he would name, or what evidence he had managed to collect. It began to look as if the 'dreadful crash' which Queen Victoria had prophesied as an inevitable result of high-born behaviour was about to take place. Arthur Farquhar, among others, was distinctly uneasy and had been for some time. As far back as February he had started trying to get himself transferred to a staff appointment in India. When she had seen him in March Louisa Scott had thought there was something odd about him, in fact she had told Harriett that she was very puzzled by his attitude: 'A. Farquhar has taken offence at me now, why goodness knows, but he's never been here once and hardly speaks when I meet him.'

The Prince was still abroad, but he too must have been feeling apprehensive, although he was putting a brave face on it. On 10 April, the *Warwick Advertiser* had published a report under the headline WHY?, quoting the London correspondent of the *Manchester Guardian* who reported that the Prince of Wales had recently received a communication from home which would cause him to 'shorten his sojourn in the Levant' as it was 'the especial desire' of the Queen that he should return to London by the second week in May. As a result, his visit to the King of Italy, for which arrangements had already been made, was to be postponed until another occasion. The reasons for this change of plan were easily explained, but the Prince himself showed no signs of anxiety. He was said to be in good form, taking a lively interest in everything.

On their way home the royal couple stayed for a few days in Paris, where they were greeted by letters from the Queen in which among other things she warned Alix against being tempted to spend too much on dress. She told Bertie that there was a very strong feeling against the luxuriousness, the extravagance and the frivolity current in society, not to mention the many scandalous stories now circulating. The Prince, however, was reassuring. He told his mother that he had only ordered two very simple but exquisitely made items for Alix. 'If there is anything I dislike,' he wrote, 'it is extravagant or outré dresses – at any rate on my wife.' He went on to say that sad stories of scandals in high life had indeed reached his ears, which was to be deplored, in particular, he added pointedly, the way in which people 'wash their dirty linen in public.'[85]

Particularly serious for the Prince and his set was the suggestion that Lady Mordaunt could have caught the 'disease' from one of those she had named. Although Dr Priestley had tried to stifle any such idea when it was brought up by Dr Orford, he now realised that the rumours were already rife, and that the prescriptions he had himself prescribed were likely to be used as evidence. He therefore decided to write to Sir Charles.

17 Hertford Street,
Mayfair,
London W
April 25/69

Dear Sir Charles

I have had a conversation today with our mutual friend Mr Duff of Fetteresso, and from him I gather that some importance is attached to prescriptions of mine as incriminating Lady Mordaunt, notwithstanding my explicit statement to your solicitor that I was in possession of no information which could in the least degree affect her Ladyship's character. I think it therefore best to write to you directly and assure you that Lady Mordaunt never consulted me for any venereal affection, nor was such an ailment ever mentioned in her consultations with me. Further I believe she could not have been suffering from any venereal ailment during my attendance upon her, for I several times examined her in such a way that any such symptoms could not have escaped me.

I declined to furnish particulars of my attendance upon Lady Mordaunt to your solicitor because it is well understood among physicians that all communications made to them by patients are strictly confidential and an attorney making a preliminary enquiry has no more right to expect a physician to furnish him with information which may have come to him in the exercise of his professional duties than to expect a Father Confessor to reveal the secrets of confession. I was very particular to explain to your solicitors that I did not wish to place myself in opposition to any investigation you desired to make in reference to Lady Mordaunt's character, that in my professional capacity I knew nothing whatsoever which could be used against her, but that in consonance with the general rule observed by my professional brethren I must decline to go into details. I trust this was fully explained to you, for I desired to act in no unfriendly spirit. You will I dare say readily understand that endless mischief might arise unless medical men were most particular in these matters, and that to furnish details in matters of delicacy concerning the wife to the husband, or concerning the husband to the wife without the consent of both, would be mischievous in the last degree.

I may however without any breach of confidence inform you that any *prescriptions* I wrote for Lady Mordaunt were for such ailments as the most chaste woman may suffer from, and if you have been advised to the contrary you have been misled into grievous error. Lady M had very sensitive mucous membranes and I can well understand that during her pregnancy she may for this reason have suffered great discomfort and indeed have had some symptoms simulating a venereal affection, without being in any degree tainted by a more specific ailment. I dare say you know I went to Walton a fortnight ago to see Lady Mordaunt with her father and the result of my investigation then, was to convince me that she had not been in her right mind after her confinement, nor had she fully recovered her reason at the time of my visit. Women often enough after delivering have accused themselves and others of faults never committed, while under the effect of mental aberration and I do not see how it can be proved that Lady M was in her right mind *at any time* after her confinement. It is true that Mr Orford is of the opinion that Lady Mordaunt's mind never has been deranged but to state this positively is to assume a very *grave* responsibility, and when Dr Orford still insists that Lady M is perfectly well when it is perfectly obvious to others skilled in puerperal and mental ailments that she is of unsound mind, it necessarily throws doubts on the soundness of his opinion concerning the earlier period, [on] other matters such as the premature confinement [and] the ophthalmia or eye complaint of the child. The entry found in

Lady Mordaunt's Pocket Book, in my opinion admits of explanations in consonance with her innocence. Of course I know
not what other evidence there may be and wish that I have
nothing to do, but I think it right, as I trust you will think it
friendly, to put these matters before you, and show you that
they admit of a different interpretation to that which has been
put upon them.

　　With kind regards, believe me

Yours very truly

WM A. PRIESTLEY

On the day that this letter was written, expressing as it did the
conviction that Lady Mordaunt had not been in her right mind ever
since her confinement, Mr Cadogan received a message from her
asking him to go and see her at the Hall as she had apparently expressed a wish to be 'churched' in order that she could give thanks for
the safe delivery of her child.

　　Remembering how deeply distressed Lady Mordaunt had seemed
when he had last been down at the Hall, Mr Cadogan was surprised
to find her on this occasion looking extremely well and cheerful. She
appeared to be slightly annoyed when he remarked on this fact, and
said quite briskly that although she had been a little 'seedy' she was
now 'quite well, thank you'. At first they discussed everyday topics
such as the weather, and where she had been for her carriage drives.
Lady Mordaunt then asked after Mrs Cadogan and was told that she
was at present in Leamington visiting her father. Mr Cadogan added
that his wife was planning to go away first of all to London and
then to visit friends in the west of England. Harriett said she hoped
Mrs Cadogan would come to see her before she left and told him
how 'dull' she felt as a result of seeing so few people. After these
preliminaries, Mr Cadogan turned the conversation to the business
he had come about, and told her that it would be very 'inexpedient'
for her to attend a churching service in her present circumstances,
when 'a gross and notorious scandal' was hanging over her. As they
had already discussed the position she was in, he felt sure she would
understand what he meant. He said that if she persevered he would
have to ask the Bishop's advice. At that she 'beat the carpet with her
foot in apparent anger' and then suddenly remarked 'Charlie is much
mistaken if he thinks he will be able to prove the nonsense I talked is
true', and added 'If I could see him I would set it all right with him in

a few minutes.' Mr Cadogan, somewhat perplexed, did not pursue the matter, and Harriett herself changed the subject, suggesting that they should go out into the garden to see the flowers, but this he declined to do, and she walked with him to the door of her boudoir, shook hands with him and said goodbye.

The next day, 26 April, Helen Forbes arrived, giving as the reason for her visit the need to break the news to her sister of the death of their grandmother, the Dowager Countess of Bradford. Jessie had already noticed the announcement of the death in the newspaper the day before, and had shown it to Lady Mordaunt who had said 'Poor thing! We will be required to go into mourning', which Jessie thought was a totally sane reaction. In fact Lady Mordaunt adopted a very practical attitude, saying that two mourning dresses would be enough and herself selecting proper mourning jewellery to go with them.

As soon as Helen Forbes arrived, she asked Jessie how her sister seemed, and Jessie replied 'Very well.' After lunch the two sisters strolled together in the garden for a while.

Jessie was sure that Mrs Forbes was putting pressure on Lady Mordaunt to take back what she had said earlier. For example, at dinner Lady Mordaunt asked Jessie, who was waiting, to come up to her chair saying she wanted to tell her something. 'You know, Clarke,' she said, 'it is all very well them making this enquiry. I just want to ask you a few questions in regard to what you have heard me say as to my statements.' She said that only part of what Jessie had told the lawyer was true.

'My lady,' said Jessie, 'whatever I have said regarding you is perfectly true. I am only sorry that I should have anything to say at all.'

'I don't want to enter into these things with you' said Lady Mordaunt. 'We all have our faults.'

Helen Forbes then came in and the conversation ended.

Before she left, Helen told Jessie she thought there must be something the matter with Lady Mordaunt's mind, but Jessie replied emphatically that she had not noticed anything wrong. Two days later Helen Forbes returned. She told Harriett that she would be there until 1 May as Charlie had now relaxed his rule that none of the family should be allowed to stay overnight. Helen expressed surprise that Lady Mordaunt looked so well and Jessie agreed that her mistress really seemed to have recovered her health and was now looking much better than she had done ever since her confinement. The sisters drove out together in the carriage every day, talking to each other naturally and easily. During the course of one of their conversations Harriett raised the question of Violet being christened in church and Mr Cadogan came down from the Parsonage on the morning of Friday 30 April to discuss the matter with her. Before speaking to Harriett, he told Helen that his position was purely a 'neutral' one, and that he had only ever visited Lady Mordaunt to give her the normal pastoral care. He did not in any way wish to become involved in the legal side of the situation. Helen accepted this and said she felt it would be in order if she joined in the discussion about arrangements for the christening, particularly as her sister had already asked her to be a godmother. She told Mr Cadogan that she would be leaving for London the following evening on the 7.57 train from Warwick, but could come back for the christening if her sister wished and provided that the plan proved to be agreeable to everybody.

On 27 April Sir Charles travelled down to Edinburgh from Kingussie and met his lawyer there in order to put his signature to the petition for the dissolution of his marriage. This was presented to the Judge Ordinary of the Court for Divorce and Matrimonial Causes the next day. He petitioned on the grounds that during the months of May, June and July 1868 Lady Mordaunt had been frequently visited at 6 Chesham Place by Lowry Egerton Cole, commonly called Viscount Cole, and that 'on divers of such occasions, and particularly during the last week of June 1868, and from that time to the 7th day of July 1868, inclusive, the said Lady Mordaunt committed adultery with the said Viscount Cole'. It was also alleged that adultery had been committed during Cole's stay at Walton Hall from 10 to 14 July 1868 and in January 1869. Sir Frederic Johnstone was said to have committed adultery sometime in November 1868, and between the 14 and 28 December 1868 at Walton Hall, and on or about 30 December 1868 at the Alexandra Hotel, Knightsbridge. There was one final clause:

That on one or more occasions, which your petitioner is unable more particularly to specify, between the 25th day of June 1868 and the 28th February 1869, the said Lady Mordaunt committed adultery with some person other than the petitioner.[86]
Wherefore your petitioner prays –
That your Lordship will be pleased to decree that his marriage with the said Harriett Sarah Lady Mordaunt be dissolved by reason of the adultery, and that your Petitioner may have such

further and other relief in the premises as to your Lordship may
seem meet.

C. MORDAUNT

There had been some suggestion that it would not be in order to
deliver the citation to the co-respondents in view of the supposed
lunacy of Lady Mordaunt, but Sir Charles's lawyers thought that this
argument was absurd, people in the past having in any case been
convicted upon the evidence of a lunatic. Ignoring the madness issue,
they saw to it that the citation was delivered to Sir Frederic Johnstone
at his house in Arlington Street and he was commanded to appear in
court in order to make an answer. If he failed to do this, he was
warned, the court would proceed to hear the charge and pronounce
sentence, his absence notwithstanding. He was told that he or his
solicitor should attend at the Registry of the Court in Doctors' Commons, to enter an appearance in a book provided for that purpose,
without which he would not be allowed to address the court. A
similar citation was served on Lord Cole a few days later at his house
in South Street, Grosvenor Square.

Mr Haynes now had to carry out the distasteful task of delivering
the petition to Lady Mordaunt and he went over to Walton on the
afternoon of 30 April accompanied by Osbert Mordaunt and Dr Orford. On his arrival he was surprised to see a smart carriage standing
in the stable yard and when he asked whose it was the servants
told him that it belonged to Lord Dudley who had driven over for
luncheon. They said that after the meal his lordship had walked out
into the garden with both sisters, although Lady Mordaunt had subsequently come indoors on her own.

It was Mrs Caborn's job to vet all visitors and so Mr Haynes and
Osbert went straight to the housekeeper's room. Mr Haynes said
that he wished to see Lady Mordaunt, adding, as an inducement,
that he had come at Sir Charles's request. A discussion ensued as to
whether he should wait before going up to Lady Mordaunt's room
until Lord Dudley and Mrs Forbes came in from the garden, but
Mr Haynes said that as he was on a professional visit which had
nothing to do with Lord Dudley he would go up to see Lady Mordaunt straightaway. Mrs Caborn then took Mr Haynes upstairs to
the boudoir. He found Lady Mordaunt sitting on the sofa with her
back to the window. As she had just come in from the garden she still
had her hat on.

Seeing her for the first time, as she raised her eyes to him with such an earnest and pitiable look on her lovely face, the lawyer felt so overcome with emotion himself that he asked her whether he might take a chair. She made a slight inclination with her hand, and he sat down, trying to avoid her eyes which seemed to him to be full of grief and shame. Hastily he began to tackle the matter in hand. He apologised for the suspense caused her in the last few weeks.

'Your good husband has been most anxious to get at the whole truth' he told her 'and I very much regret to say the result is that he feels compelled to appeal to the divorce court and I have the unpleasant duty to serve your Ladyship with the petition and what is called the citation, from the court.' At this she looked down at her hands which were folded in her lap. He then produced an envelope containing copies of the two documents and gave them to her. She took the envelope and held it for the rest of the interview, which lasted for about a quarter of an hour, during which time she remained, as Mr Haynes put it, 'mute'.

Mr Haynes thought he detected a faint smile cross Lady Mordaunt's face when her sister entered the room.

'Please do not retire, Mrs Forbes,' said Mr Haynes, adding, 'there are no secrets; mine is a purely professional, though a very unpleasant visit'. He told the sisters that he would advise Sir Charles to comply with any reasonable request they might make, and he said hoped that Mrs Forbes would find it convenient to stay at Walton for a few days. He felt that no one could be so proper a companion to Lady Mordaunt at this time.

When Lord Dudley came into the room, Mr Haynes rose and introduced himself. Lord Dudley said, 'Mr Haynes I presume.' The lawyer then produced the original petition, saying that he had given Lady Mordaunt a copy. Lord Dudley read it:

Victoria, by the Grace of God, of the United Kingdom of Great Britain and Ireland, Queen Defender of the Faith, to Dame Harriett Sarah Mordaunt, of Walton Hall, in the County of Warwick: Whereas Sir Charles Mordaunt, Baronet, of Walton Hall, in the County of Warwick, claiming to have been lawfully married to you, has filed his Petition against you in our said Court, praying for a dissolution of his marriage, wherein he alleges that you have been guilty of adultery: Now this is to command you that within eight days after service hereof on you, inclusive of the day of such service, you do appear in our said Court, then and there to make answer to the said Petition, a copy whereof, sealed with seal of our said Court, is herewith served upon you. And take notice, that in default of your so doing, our said Court will proceed to hear the said charge proved in due course of law, and to take further notice that, for the purpose aforesaid, you are to attend in person, or by your proctor, solicitor, or attorney, at the Registry of our said Court, in Doctors Commons, London, and there to enter an appearance in a book provided for that purpose, without which you will not be allowed to address the Court, either in person or by counsel, at any stage of the proceedings in the cause. Dated at London, the twenty-eighth day of April, one thousand eight hundred and sixty-nine, in the thirty-second year of our Reign.

CHAS. J. MIDDLETON
Registrar

While Lord Dudley read the document, Mr Haynes spoke again to Lady Mordaunt, asking her whether she had any special request for him to pass on to Sir Charles. But she remained silent, as if stunned.

As soon as he had finished reading the petition, Lord Dudley handed it back to Mr Haynes, and asked if he could speak to him alone. He then accused the lawyer of trying to draw Lady Mordaunt into conversation which he had no right to do, adding that he himself believed Lady Mordaunt to be 'perfectly insane'. Mr Haynes replied that he had not gained the remotest idea from his conversation that he was talking to an insane person. The two men then went out into the garden and continued their conversation walking on the gravel path outside the house. Lord Dudley asked if the documents had to be delivered personally and Mr Haynes replied that they did.

'Supposing you cannot do this?' Lord Dudley inquired.

'If there is any attempt at evasion the law would provide a remedy' replied Mr Haynes, adding that nothing was ever gained in that way.

'What is your principal evidence?' Lord Dudley asked.

'My lord, you must excuse me entering into detail, your own solicitor Mr Benbow would tell you that it was contrary to all practice, and as I have said, names and dates are on the copy.'

'It is a most serious thing for both families,' said Lord Dudley, 'but Lady Mordaunt is perfectly out of her mind at the present moment.'

Mr Haynes begged to differ. Lord Dudley then asked if counsel had been consulted, and Mr Haynes replied that in a case which was of such importance to both families he would never have taken on the responsibility of encouraging Sir Charles to take active measures without counsel's advice. Lord Dudley said that although his sister-in-law might have been imprudent, flirting and so on, both before and after her marriage, he was sure that it had never been anything more.

'I fear it is far beyond that' said Mr Haynes.

Lord Dudley also referred to the possibility of Lady Mordaunt being taken away from Walton, and Mr Haynes said that he had suggested this course of action earlier but that Sir Thomas had not pursued it. He himself still felt that it could be beneficial for Lady Mordaunt, and if it was wished for as adding to her comfort, he knew that nobody would object and the question of alimony could readily be settled between Mr Benbow and himself. He insisted that Sir Charles was the last man to make it a matter of pounds, shillings and pence.

They continued to walk up and down the gravel path for about a quarter of an hour, during which time Lord Dudley bluntly asked Mr Haynes if he thought Lady Mordaunt was guilty. Mr Haynes replied that he had not the least doubt about it from the evidence taken by himself and that if it had been his own sister he would not have been able to complain about Sir Charles's action. Lord Dudley said once again that Lady Mordaunt was quite insane and Mr Haynes once again dissented.

Afterwards, thinking over his interview with Lady Mordaunt, Mr Haynes came to the conclusion that her reception of him, her look of remorse, her changed attitude when Mrs Forbes entered the room, could not possibly be described as lunacy; it was more like a state of deep distress. As to her silence, that was obviously assumed on the advice of her family to prevent her from saying something that could be used against her. The question of whether or not she had been capable on this day of comprehending the documents handed to her was later to become of vital importance, but there was little doubt in Mr Haynes's mind on that day that she had a good idea of what they contained.

Before Lord Dudley left at about seven o'clock that evening he made a point of telling Jessie that he did not think Lady Mordaunt was guilty, although he was prepared to admit that at times she might have been imprudent. He asked Jessie whether her mistress had acted on this occasion as she normally did, and Jessie replied that she had been more reserved than usual.

Mr Cadogan called the next morning, 1 May, as he had promised, and saw Mrs Forbes who told him that her sister had chosen the sponsors for the christening. Mr Cadogan said that he could arrange for the ceremony to take place on 6 May, which was Ascension Day. He then spoke to Lady Mordaunt herself and thought that she seemed very pleased to see him. He said he understood that she wished arrangements to be made about the baby being received openly in the church. She said at once, 'Yes, yes; I should like baby to be received in church', adding that her sister had agreed to be a godmother and Lord Dudley the godfather. She hoped that Mrs Cadogan would consent to be the second godmother. All these suggestions were made without any prompting from him and throughout the interview he thought she seemed perfectly 'sensible'. But from that time onwards he heard nothing more about the christening, and as it turned out, he was never to see Lady Mordaunt again.

22

The Last Days at Walton

Mrs Forbes returned to London in the evening, leaving her sister alone at Walton, without family or friends at this time of crisis, and surrounded by the servants who had agreed to testify against her.

Now, in the great house, the annual spring cleaning had already begun under the able supervision of Mrs Caborn. The carpets were coming up in every room in turn. The blinds were down in the deserted rooms, many of which were now locked. Lady Mordaunt, anxious maybe to establish her position as mistress in her own house, tried to assert herself by gaining access to one of the locked rooms. She therefore approached Mrs Caborn, saying she wished to go to the library. Mrs Caborn gave her a bunch of keys and she unlocked the door into the library, which was in darkness. Mrs Caborn opened one of the shutters to let in some light, and asked Lady Mordaunt whether she needed assistance in finding anything. The carpets were all up, but Lady Mordaunt, without answering Mrs Caborn's question, sat down on one of the chairs. Mrs Caborn hovered around, fussing about her and advising her not to stay in such a cold room. But Lady Mordaunt ordered her to go back to her dinner. A little while later, Jessie Clarke was sent to find her and she persuaded her to go back to her room.

As soon as Lord Dudley was able to communicate with Sir Thomas, telling him about the contents of the petition, evasive action was set in motion. Every possible use was to be made of Harriett's stunned and shocked appearance on receiving the petition and the doctors were marshalled to visit her and make a further appraisal of her state of mind.

On 5 May, Helen Forbes turned up quite unexpectedly at the Hall. The first thing that Mrs Caborn knew about it was when she came upon her washing her hands in Lady Mordaunt's room. Lady Mordaunt asked if Mrs Caborn had got a room ready for her sister and Mrs Caborn said she had not, but she would give directions to the housemaid that this should be done. Mrs Forbes then told Mrs Caborn that she had come down at her father's request and the next day she announced that Dr Priestley would be arriving that morning accompanied by Dr James Alderson, who was President of the College of Physicians and one of the most distinguished doctors in the country,[87] and by Dr Tuke, the 'mad doctor'. Helen Forbes gave Mrs Caborn instructions to say nothing to Lady Mordaunt about their imminent visit.

In the morning, before the doctors arrived, Lady Mordaunt was seen 'about the house' as usual, and she appeared to the servants to be perfectly sane. At about twelve o'clock Jessie Clarke took some soup to Lady Mordaunt and Mrs Forbes in the lunch room, otherwise known as the ante-room. Mrs Forbes asked if she could have some brandy and soda as she was feeling poorly. When it was brought, Harriett laughed and said 'Helen, if you drink all that I am sure you will be tipsy.' A little later, while Jessie and other members of the 'establishment', including Mrs Forbes's servant, were at dinner, Lady Mordaunt came to the door and called Mrs Caborn out to tell her that lunch for the visitors who were expected should be laid in the breakfast room rather than the ante-room. Mrs Caborn said that she was very sorry but the carpet was up in the breakfast room, and Lady Mordaunt said 'Oh well, it does not signify.' Giving the excuse that she wished to move a sofa to make more room for the guests, Mrs Caborn went in and saw Lady Mordaunt sitting at her writing table with a basin of soup beside her, Mrs Forbes near her on a low chair. Lunch was laid in the ante-room for five.

Dr Alderson and Dr Tuke were the first to arrive and Dr Priestley appeared soon afterwards. They found Lady Mordaunt in the luncheon room, still seated at her work table and apparently writing a letter to Sir Charles. She talked to the doctors at first, but soon lapsed into what they described as 'taciturnity', naturally somewhat overwhelmed by this formidable trio of illustrious men. Dr Alderson started asking her some questions, but urbane and pleasant though he was, he was unable to elicit anything except some monosyllabic replies. Finally, she refused to answer him at all. She joined the doctors at luncheon, but left the room with her sister before the meal was over, standing for a few moments at the door quite motionless, as if unconscious, or playing at 'statues'. Mrs Caborn was then called to the ante-room and found one of the doctors sitting at the desk. She suspected that they were preparing to write down what she said, but she refused to answer any questions about Lady Mordaunt. They told her that they merely wanted to know how far Lady Mordaunt gave the orders in her own house, but she said 'I am very sorry, you will excuse me in answering any questions, I have had nothing to do with it', and at that she left the room.

The doctors later went up to Lady Mordaunt's sitting-room and found her greatly 'perturbed, distressed and afraid', but in spite of this they stayed for an hour and tried to talk to her. She still refused to answer any questions. By this time Jessie Clarke was back in her own day-room and she now no longer sat in Sir Charles's dressing-room during the day time as she had after the confinement to be near Lady Mordaunt, although she still slept in the dressing-room at night. The doctors had rung the bell in the dressing-room and she found them there. Dr Priestley asked her if Lady Mordaunt was often in this state. 'What state?' she asked, and Dr Priestley then said that Lady Mordaunt had seemed very queer indeed. Dr Alderson remarked on the fact that she had eaten so little at lunch and wondered whether their presence had influenced her. Jessie pointed out that she had already eaten something at twelve o'clock and both the doctors agreed that she had told them this herself. When Dr Tuke emerged from Lady Mordaunt's sitting-room, he said she had suffered from a similar attack when he was there before, but Jessie said she hadn't noticed her behaving at all oddly since then. The doctors asked Jessie if Lady Mordaunt was having any kind of medicine and she told them that Dr Orford had prescribed a tonic for her. The doctors were at the house for about four hours in all. Dr Tuke still stuck to his opinion that Lady Mordaunt was suffering from puerperal insanity and catalepsy, although on this occasion he had the impression that the latter was less severe than before.

After the doctors left, Lady Mordaunt seemed reserved and did not join Mrs Forbes at dinner. She was the same next day, not getting up till lunch time. When Mrs Forbes left to go back to London, she remarked to Jessie that her sister was not as well as usual. However, in the afternoon Jessie saw her reading the papers quite normally.

On their return to London, Dr Tuke and Dr Alderson filed their affidavits concerning the mental state of Lady Mordaunt as it had appeared to them in the course of their visit to Walton. They admitted that the hysterical catalepsy seemed less severe than it had been previously, and that they had been informed by those around her that Lady Mordaunt often seemed better than she was on the occasion of their visit, but nevertheless they felt sure that any improvement was likely to be no more than temporary. They insisted that Lady Mordaunt had been suffering all along from puerperal insanity accompanied by delusions, some of which still existed. They described her present state as one of extreme weakness, with an incapacity for sustained thought, accompanied by a failure of memory and an inability to understand or answer any but the most simple questions, with 'an entire unconsciousness of her present position, duties and responsibilities'. Any mental exertion or excitement forced on her, even during her more lucid intervals, would be attended with great danger and would in their opinion seriously imperil her recovery. They all agreed that she was in no fit state to appear in court.

On 7 May, the day after the doctors' visit to Walton, a summons was taken out on behalf of Harriet Sarah Dame Mordaunt, the respondent to the petition, calling upon the petitioner, Sir Charles, to attend the Right Honourable James Plaisted, Baron Penzance, the Judge Ordinary of Her Majesty's Court for Divorce and Matrimonial Causes, at Westminster, on the following Tuesday 11 May to show cause why the proceedings should not be stayed and the time for filing an answer to the petition extended until Lady Mordaunt was in a sound state of mind. This summons was issued by Sir Thomas's solicitors, Benbow and Saltwell, who also entered an appearance for Lady Mordaunt 'by consent'.

At a conference hastily called between Sir Charles's lawyers, Mr Hunt and Mr Inderwick, this summons was discussed, and Mr Inderwick stated his opinion that it should be opposed on Sir Charles's behalf, without any affidavits or other evidence being procured for the time being. He said that the other side would have to produce affidavits and appropriate time would be given to peruse these.

At the summons the doctors' evidence was read, and the Judge left the matter open until the next summons day which was to be on 25 May. In the meantime, Sir Charles's lawyers were required to prepare the affidavits which would explain why he did not think it necessary to stay proceedings.

It was still hard for those who had been in close contact with Lady Mordaunt over the weeks to believe that the question of her sanity could really prove to be a serious issue. When Mrs Cadogan called at the Hall at about six o'clock on the day the doctors filed their affidavits, she found Harriett in the boudoir, looking perfectly normal. Mrs Cadogan had come to say that she was going away the following day, and Jessie Clarke, who was in the dressing-room, heard them conversing quite naturally, Lady Mordaunt laughing and talking in her usual vivacious way. Mrs Cadogan explained that she was going down to see the clergyman on the Mordaunt estate at Berkley in Somerset. She would also be seeing the Dickinsons who rented one of the houses there. 'Oh, you are going to stay at Four Oaks I suppose' Harriett said, and Mrs Cadogan replied that she would indeed be going there. Mrs Cadogan then made some reference to the position that Harriett was in, and as always when this happened, she appeared to listen, and then changed the subject abruptly. On this occasion she said that she had been reading *The Moonstone* by Wilkie Collins which she was enjoying very much. She asked whether Mrs Cadogan could recommend anything else like it, but Mrs Cadogan said she thought it was rather a frightening sort of book and that she would be better reading something a little more cheerful. Harriett told Mrs Cadogan that she had been doing some plaiting work and illuminating, but not a lot of either. The conversation then went on to the subject of her sister, the Duchess of Atholl. After this Harriett rang for Jessie Clarke and asked her to fetch a photograph of herself which she gave to Mrs Cadogan, saying that she would be going away soon. This did not surprise Mrs Cadogan, who knew that there had been several plans for Lady Mordaunt to go away with her mother to Weymouth for a change of air. Recalling her visit later, Mrs Cadogan said she could not remember anything strange in Lady Mordaunt's behaviour. She had found her rational and 'sensible' throughout.

When the Dowager Lady Mordaunt went to Walton on Sunday 9 May for the afternoon service she arrived early and drove round to the stable yard, leaving the carriage there. She walked through the stone archway, across the servants' quadrangle where the game larder was situated, to the housekeeper's room, in order to inquire about her daughter-in-law's health. While she was chatting to Mrs Caborn, Lady Mordaunt suddenly opened the door and said assertively, 'Mrs Caborn, will you bring me some bread and butter.' She looked surprised to see the Dowager there, and she immediately turned back into the passage without saying anything. It cannot have been pleasant for her to feel that her mother-in-law had come to the house to talk to the housekeeper rather than to herself. However she returned a few moments later and told Mrs Caborn that she wished to see Bird, which was strange, as Bird was miles away in Scotland, a fact she must have known. The Dowager then said, 'How do you do, Harriett?', kissed her, and added 'I have not been to see you lately,

because you have not asked me to call.' Harriett took the bread and
butter and left the room, and when the Dowager went out into the
passage, she found her daughter-in-law just outside, sitting on a large
box which was used for storing coal. She went up to her and said
'Harriett, we have had enough of this; we quite understand what it all
means; you had better get up and go', obviously thinking she was
play-acting again. The Dowager gently touched her arm, Mrs Caborn
appeared and the two went upstairs together. The Dowager then
went to church and returned home immediately afterwards, musing
on the fact that her daughter-in-law was acting strangely in order to
deceive everybody and make them think she was mad.

The next day, 10 May, Jessie Clarke thought that Lady Mordaunt
seemed particularly well. She gave orders for her carriage to be
brought round and for the baby to be got ready to go with her.
Accompanied by the new nurse, who had recently arrived, Lady
Mordaunt and the baby went out in the carriage for about an hour.
At about two o'clock that afternoon Sir Thomas arrived unexpectedly. Mrs Caborn was out when he arrived and he told Jessie Clarke
that he intended to stay the night. Jessie said she had no authority to
sanction this in the absence of Mrs Caborn. Sir Thomas ignored her
and sent his carriage away, asking that his luggage be taken upstairs.
Lady Mordaunt greeted him quite naturally and appeared pleased to
see him. They spent the afternoon together, but he later testified that
he was unable to converse with her. When he asked her whether she
would like him to return another day, and whether she would like to
see her mother and sisters, she did say 'Yes'. All the same, he had the
impression she just did not really care either way.

At about two o'clock next day Lady Kinnoull arrived, apparently
without warning. Harriett spent the afternoon with her father and
her sociable grandmother. Before they left that evening around half
past four, Lady Kinnoull drew Jessie Clarke aside and told her that
during the visit Lady Mordaunt had acted strangely, putting her
handkerchief and a card case into the grate. Sir Thomas had managed
to retrieve them before they became too badly burnt. She had also, it
seemed, asked for some arrowroot and when this was brought to her
she immediately left the room and poured it away. She had then gone
downstairs and when she came back up, the front of her dress was
open in a rather improper way. Jessie Clarke told Lady Kinnoull that
she herself had never seen any behaviour of that kind. Afterwards,
Lady Mordaunt talked to Jessie about the dress her grandmother had

been wearing, which, she said was 'a very nice dress, but not very nice for her', meaning, Jessie thought, that her grandmother was rather too old to wear such a short 'walking' outfit. 'What a larky old thing she is!' Lady Mordaunt said to Jessie.

That evening, at about eight o'clock, Jessie answered a call from Lady Mordaunt, who said she did not feel very well. Jessie asked her if she would like a little brandy and hot water, and she said she would. Jessie went down to get some sugar, and on her return she observed a towel blazing in the fire. Jessie took the towel out with the tongs and extinguished the fire. This seemed to annoy Lady Mordaunt, as she peremptorily told Jessie to leave. Mrs Caborn attended her for the rest of the evening.

The servants were naturally disturbed by this turn of events, never having observed such behaviour before, and suspecting that it had been assumed on the orders of her father. It was in any case an alarming development which was reported to Sir Charles in a letter, his mother in all probability also being informed since she arrived next morning to see the situation for herself. As usual a message was sent up by Mrs Caborn, and the reply came back that Lady Mordaunt would be delighted to see her mother-in-law. Perhaps as a result of what had happened the previous day, the fire had not been lit in the boudoir, a fact which the Dowager commented on as soon as she entered the room. She kissed her daughter-in-law and said 'Harriett, you are cold, why don't you light a fire?' She replied 'I don't mind it much, I am not very well today.' Harriett then suggested that they went out for a walk and she disappeared into her bedroom to put on her things, the Dowager following her. While they were chatting, Mrs Caborn appeared offering to help put on Lady Mordaunt's boots. At the same time she remarked that the boots were not thick enough for walking. Lady Mordaunt resisted the housekeeper's attempts to help her, saying that nobody could put on the boots as well as herself.

The two ladies then went out and walked in the garden for about half an hour. Harriett asked about the Dowager's daughters, Eleanor and Constance, inquiring whether the governess Miss Acton was still with them. The Dowager explained that the rest of the family had gone away, but she had stayed at home to look after her ailing son Arthur. Harriett seemed genuinely concerned about Arthur's health and asked if it was the same illness that he had suffered from the previous year. 'Oh no,' the Dowager replied 'it is a bad attack of nettle rash, diarrhoea and rheumatism.' She then went on to talk about the death of Harriett's grandmother, the Dowager Lady Bradford, asking whether it would make any difference to the family finances, perhaps providing a bit of extra income, and Harriett replied that it would help a little. The Dowager also inquired whether 'the pretty villa at Cannes' owned by Lady Bradford would be left to one of Sir Thomas's sisters, but Harriett said she thought it would go to his brother who lived in Australia. The Dowager was pleased with this reply, since it showed that Harriett's family had discussed the matter with her, which they would never have done if they had really thought that she was mad.

The subject then changed to Major Arbuthnot and his engagement to Selina. The Dowager asked Harriett whether she knew him and she said 'No, but I hear he is a very nice man.'

As they walked up the garden Lady Mordaunt remarked on the beauty of the cowslips in the fields beyond the ha-ha. When they reached the top of the pleasure grounds she started to pick some honeysuckle, and the Dowager asked if she might have some for Arthur. Harriett replied, 'Oh yes certainly', and then said that she would get Broadbridge to gather some flowers for her. They went into the kitchen garden, but could not find Broadbridge at first. They opened the hothouse door but he was not there, nor was he in the peach house. Meanwhile they discussed the question of the christening, which had not taken place on the date suggested by Mr Cadogan. Harriett wanted to know whether her mother-in-law thought that the baby should be taken to church. The Dowager said that it was necessary, explaining the difference between private baptism and reception in the church. She appeared to understand.

They found the gardener near the hotbeds and Harriett asked him to provide some flowers for Arthur. Broadbridge later recalled how he gathered a quantity of blooms and gave them to the Dowager. The two ladies then went back into the house through the conservatory and the Dowager asked Harriett if she was taking her tonic medicine. She replied that she was. Although she was asked to go upstairs, the Dowager then said she must leave as Mr Smith was waiting for her in the carriage. Holding the swing door open for her mother-in-law, Harriett said she would like to see Mr Smith, but felt she had perhaps walked far enough, adding that she would be glad to see him on another day. 'I kissed her,' the Dowager later recalled, 'we parted, and I have never seen her since.'

Throughout this interview the Dowager never felt that Harriet's mind was impaired. There had been times, of course, especially after the confinement, when she had found her daughter-in-law disinclined to converse, but on the whole she had not experienced any difficulty in communicating with her. There had just been the one occasion when she had really seemed ready to confide in her, saying 'I want to tell you . . . ' but stopping quite short as if remembering she must not say anything. The Dowager, like the servants, felt that Harriett's apparent strangeness during her grandmother's visit had been engineered by her father, and that she had been told to set fire to the towel to show to Jessie how mad she was.

Reports of the strange events on the day of Sir Thomas's visit with Lady Kinnoull had by now reached Mr Haynes. The lawyer, too, was sure that Lady Mordaunt's eccentric conduct on the day of Lady Kinnoull's visit had been stage-managed by her father. He felt that by his action Sir Thomas had now forfeited his right to visit his daughter.

Excuse me [wrote Mr Haynes] as the legal adviser of Sir Charles Mordaunt in requesting that you will abstain from repeating your visits at Walton Hall as from a report I received this morning from Walton I have reason to believe that your visits are not with that legitimate object which induced Sir Charles to throw his doors open pending the present unhappy proceedings to all Lady Mordaunt's immediate relations. This request must equally apply to the attendance of any further medical advisers who without limit you have had the liberty to introduce at Walton up to the present time, except by mutual consent or by order of the court. I on the part of Sir Charles deeply regret this step but which I feel fully justified in taking from the scene that occurred at Walton yesterday the 11th instant during your temporary presence and which on no former occasion had occurred nor had there been the slightest indication of on any former occasion.

A similar letter was written to Lady Kinnoull. These letters provoked an equally stiff reply from Mr Benbow, expressing disbelief that Sir Charles would expect Lady Mordaunt to remain at Walton Hall in the care of servants and without any contact with her own family.

I have therefore to inform you that Sir Thomas proposes to remove her from Walton forthwith and he will go there for that purpose on Saturday next the 15th instant. Lady Mordaunt will be brought to London and I will inform you by tomorrow's post whose house she will be staying in.

Although Mr Haynes wrote back protesting that there had never been any intention of putting a general restriction on visits from Lady Mordaunt's family, Mrs Forbes having been continually 'backwards and forwards', Mr Benbow insisted that Lady Mordaunt would be removed from Walton. Her father would go down to collect her from Walton the following Saturday, and she would to start with be staying with her grandmother Lady Kinnoull at 14 Belgrave Square.

Harriett herself probably knew nothing of all this and she appeared to Jessie Clarke to behave quite normally once her father and grandmother had left. On 12 May, when Jessie went into the bedroom as usual to dress her, she seemed 'very composed and comfortable'. She asked the time and said she would like some medicine. They chatted about clothes, and Jessie mentioned a particular dress which Mrs Forbes had remarked on during one of her visits, believing it to be a new one and saying how pretty it was. Lady Mordaunt had said she was surprised that her sister did not remember it as she had often worn it at her house in Newe. This exchange suggested that Lady Mordaunt, far from being mad, had a rather better memory than her sister. That same day she also sent for Mrs Caborn and asked her to cash a cheque, but Mrs Caborn said that she would not be able to cash it until the Saturday. Lady Mordaunt said that would not matter, and although Mrs Caborn offered to lend her twenty pounds in notes and coins she refused the offer. Mrs Caborn then gave the cheque to her brother, Mr Cobb, thinking that he would be able to cash it earlier than the Saturday, but although he said that he would, he was unable to do so. Mrs Caborn afterwards handed the cheque to Osbert. She felt that as Sir Thomas was coming to fetch his daughter on the Saturday, Lady Mordaunt should have some cash to go away with.

On 13 May Dr Jones paid a visit to Walton, no doubt alerted by Mr Haynes as to Jessie Clarke's discovery of the towel on the fire. He gave as the reason for his visit the fact that Dr Orford had told him that the child had a 'mother's mark' on her skin and wanted to consult him as to its removal. This gave him an opportunity to observe Lady Mordaunt in the light of what had happened during Sir Thomas's visit. On the doctor's arrival, Lady Mordaunt was coming

downstairs in her walking costume, and she greeted him kindly. He
went back upstairs with her to her boudoir and entered into a general
conversation which she kept up very well, 'every now and then' as he
put it 'evincing emotional embarrassment'. Among other things, the
doctor remarked on a beautiful fern which was on the table, expressing his admiration for it and asking if the neighbourhood was rich in
similar specimens. He carried on the conversation by talking about
flowers in general, and he also asked if there was any other conservatory except the one adjoining the house and she said there was one
in the garden and asked if he wanted to see it. He replied that he
would like to take a walk with her very much and she then accompanied him downstairs. They went through the conservatory and out
onto the broad walk, conversing generally until they returned to the
house.

Osbert arrived just as they entered the hall. Harriett said 'How
do you do' and asked him when he had returned from Scotland,
to which he replied that he had come back the night before. Mrs
Caborn had said that the usual five o'clock tea was ready in the
ante-room and Lady Mordaunt asked Dr Jones if he would like to
join her. Osbert went up with her to her sitting-room, Dr Jones
remaining in the hall. She talked to Osbert quite naturally about
various subjects such as Scotland, the weather and fishing. He asked
about Sir Thomas's visit, and then proceeded to lecture her, telling
her he thought it was foolish of her to sham illness in front of her
relations. 'You are perfectly sane', he told her, 'and everyone here
knows it.' He added that he said this for her own sake because he had
heard the 'tricks' she had played when Lady Kinnoull was there. 'If
you contrive to behave thus before your own relations' he said 'and
they succeed in showing that you are not in your right mind, you will
probably be treated as a mad woman for the rest of your life – you
shammed before Lady Kinnoull and yet you are perfectly rational
with me.'

'Oh,' she replied, 'I am very much better than I was then.'

He said it was not a question of her health but that everybody
knew she put on an act in front of her relations. She flushed and did
not reply. According to Osbert she then said in quite a different
drawling tone, 'Oh Osbert, are you going back to Crick?' This was
the parish he had left eighteen months before and he replied sternly,
'You know I am not at Crick now and it is of no use your trying to
humbug me. I am going back to Birmingham tonight probably. You

know perfectly well I am at Handsworth.' She replied 'Oh yes, I know' and immediately turned the conversation back to Scotland, assuming her original tone, without drawling or faltering any more. He remarked on her mourning dress, and Harriett explained to him how her grandmother had married Lord Bradford after her first husband, Sir David Moncreiffe, had died. Osbert felt that anybody who could explain such a complicated relationship had to be sane.

After this exchange, Harriett said she would rather have her tea brought upstairs to the boudoir, but Osbert persuaded her to join Mr Jones in the ante-room. They found when they went downstairs that Dr Orford had also arrived. Dr Jones poured her out a cup of tea but she did not drink it. She told Dr Orford that she had hurt her finger and she asked if he had any court plaster to put on it. Dr Jones said he would like to see her finger but her glove fitted so tightly that she could not take it off. She said that she would go upstairs to see if she could find any plaster there.

Before leaving the Hall, Mr Jones went up to see Lady Mordaunt. 'I could not be so uncourteous as to leave the house without saying goodbye' he told her. At that she took his hand and, as he put it, expressed in warm terms her thanks for his kindness and her hopes of repaying him. Dr Jones went away feeling that his conversation with Lady Mordaunt had been entirely normal. He was still prepared to swear that there was nothing unusual in her mental state beyond what a great weight of affliction on her mind could hardly fail to produce. Dr Orford too remained sure that there was nothing in the slightest degree wrong with her mind.

When Osbert went to say goodbye, he promised to come again the following week and he told her once more to follow his advice and stop shamming. To this she made no reply.

Jessie recorded how that evening Lady Mordaunt 'temporarily assumed silence'.

'My lady,' said Jessie, 'it is no use your trying to deceive me.'

According to Jessie, Lady Mordaunt broke her silence after that, saying 'Well, Clarke, you know it is very hard to know what to do.'

On Saturday 15 May the day started as usual with Lady Mordaunt reading books and looking at the newspapers. When Osbert arrived in the morning he went upstairs and found her finishing her breakfast. He told her that she was to leave Walton. After hearing this news she was silent for some time, but at last she said, 'I would like to go away.'

'I will render you any assistance in packing that I am able to give you' said Osbert. 'I have told Clarke to pack what is necessary for the present and if there is anything left behind which you may want, you can write for it.' Harriett walked up and down the room until Clarke came and went with her into the bedroom to see to the packing. She selected what she wanted to take and gave Jessie directions as to how it should be packed. After a few minutes she came back to the sitting-room and sent for Mrs Caborn, telling her to find a railway rug which was kept in the hall, specifying the colour. She then conversed with Osbert about various subjects in a way that seemed to him quite rational. He told her that Sir Thomas was coming to fetch her, but she made no comment. When he picked up the paper, the *Post*, and looked at it, she asked what news there was and he said not much. She asked whether her friends the Armstrongs were leaving Kineton, and when he questioned her as to where they lived, she replied correctly, 'The North House.' She said, 'The last time you were in London was when you were in Chesham Street, wasn't it?' and he replied that he had been once since and pointed out that it was actually Chesham Place. She said 'Yes' and asked if there had been any pigeon-shooting. He said he had read some accounts of it in the papers.

'Ah but I forget, you never cared much about it' she said.

'No, not much' he replied.

A note was then delivered from the Dowager, saying that Arthur Smith was worse, and Harriett expressed sorrow at this news. After that she appeared to become confused, assuming what Osbert described as 'strange conduct' and saying something about his mother being weak. At this he launched out into one of his perorations, telling her that he did not want any nonsense; she must talk to him sensibly, otherwise he was not prepared to listen to her. She relapsed into silence and to break the tension he suggested she should come for a walk. Although she was reluctant at first she finally decided to go out with him and put on her hat. They wandered around the garden for half an hour and she remained very silent, although she again expressed sorrow about Arthur's condition. After they had gone indoors, Osbert remained either in the ante-room or the hall, but Harriett went up and down the stairs several times. At one-thirty she rang the bell and ordered lunch and asked if the brougham would be ready at two o'clock. Osbert counter-ordered this, as he knew she would not have to go until twenty to three. While they were at lunch,

Osbert gave her what he described as 'a severe lecture' about her behaviour and told her that he and his family had no doubt about her
guilt and had ample proofs of it, so she had better not 'sham' any more
otherwise she might 'get up' more scenes in London as she had done
during Lady Kinnoull's visit to Walton. He warned her that she would
not gain anything by trying to delay the trial. Osbert recorded how
she then went very red and jumped up from her chair and said 'You
haven't any proofs, if you have got proofs why don't you bring them
here?' He then said 'We have ample proof as you will see at the proper
time and the proper place and it is useless denying your guilt now.'

'The best course to pursue is silence under such circumstances' she
said.

'Very well, don't sham madness any more as you will do yourself no
good in the end and possibly much harm.' He referred to her adultery
and then she broke out angrily, 'Osbert, you shall not talk like this, if
you do I shall quarrel with you. Please go up and fetch my work.'

'No' he replied, 'your father will be here directly; it's not worth it.
You'd better finish your lunch.'

Soon after this Sir Thomas was announced and Osbert said, 'Now
once more take my advice and behave sensibly both now and after you
get to London. I understand how difficult it is for you to know what to
do if your relations have encouraged your shamming, but depend upon
it you will get no good by it.' Osbert then left her and found Sir
Thomas, Helen and Major Arbuthnot in the hall. They went into
the ante-room with him to have lunch. According to Osbert, Harriett
talked rationally, asking Major Arbuthnot how her sister Lina was.
When Major Arbuthnot was later left alone with Osbert, he said by
way of conversation that he had never seen Lady Mordaunt before.

'Well, you have seen her under rather painful circumstances' said
Osbert.

While Sir Thomas and Mrs Forbes went upstairs to prepare for the
departure, Osbert showed Major Arbuthnot round the house. He then
handed Harriett's cheque to Sir Thomas and suggested they could cash
it as they went through Warwick. Sir Thomas said she would not want
any money, so Osbert went upstairs and gave the cheque back to
Harriett. Sir Thomas told her to tear it up and she said 'Well, whose
orders am I to obey today?' She eventually did as her father told her.

Osbert said goodbye to his sister-in-law in the porch. She pressed his
hand slightly before going out to the brougham where Helen Forbes
was waiting for her. Before entering the fly with Major Arbuthnot, Sir

Thomas said 'Osbert, do try and get Charlie to look at both sides of the question.' Osbert replied 'I have, and he has done and you may depend upon it, Sir Thomas, that that woman has been shamming for the last month or so.' Sir Thomas ignored this parting shot. He simply said 'Goodbye' and they drove off. For the first time since her marriage, apart from Jessie's brief holiday in Scotland, Harriett did not have her own lady's maid with her.

Sir Thomas later said that his daughter did not seem to understand that she was leaving, nor did she care about it. She had not asked to say goodbye to her baby, and there was certainly no question of her taking the child away with her. Nobody had really explained to her what was happening. As the train neared London, however, she became agitated, wondering perhaps what her future was going to be. Sir Thomas showed little sympathy. With his large complement of daughters, he was used to crying fits, and he was not too worried when, as they reached the station, Harriett grew hysterical. He put this down to the fact that there were a number of roughs at the station who were noisy and menacing.

23
Interlude in London

As soon as she arrived at her grandmother's house in Belgrave Square, Harriett became more like her old self, taking an interest in what was going on around her, making plans for her baby, thinking about going shopping and talking about the social season that was getting under way. It was all just like the old days; soon her sisters would be arriving and already Jane Laing, the Moncreiffe governess, had come down from Scotland to get things ready for the rest of the family. Harriett had been told that Jessie would not be coming up to London to join her as it seemed better to have a clean break from the retainers who had all been so ready to tell tales about her.

Jane Laing was the daughter of the local doctor and had been employed as a governess at Moncreiffe House. Harriett seemed delighted to see her. In the absence of Jessie Clarke the governess did her best to dress her hair, and they talked freely to each other, exchanging reminiscences about the schoolroom days. Lady Moncreiffe had explained the situation to Miss Laing, priming her 'to do all she could to help'.

The day after she arrived in London, Harriett wrote a chatty letter to Charlie, which he received at Kingussie where he was still staying.

My dearest Charlie
I think you will be rather surprised to see me writing from here but I came yesterday with Papa and Helen as I was not very sure about Orford's advice and I wanted to see some of them for a little bit. I am better than I was but still rather uncomfortable. I hope that you have been getting on pretty well with your fishing. I saw Osbert yesterday before I came away. He lunched at home with me. Your mother is very anxious about Arthur as he is still very delicate. Major Arbuthnot came with them yesterday too, he is here seeing Grandmama today. He seems a nice sort of creature, very much altogether the sort of thing for Lina. I have not asked them yet what sort of presents she has got most of but I think I will choose something tomorrow to give her

myself or perhaps wait till you get back to decide upon it. I have got such a jumble in my head as I have got Flamberie [Lady Kinoull's parrot] behind me so you may imagine what it is like. Miss Laing is here as some of them have come up but Mamma has not come yet as she brings the girls here tomorrow. Will you write me a line and tell me what you think about a present for Lina and if I had better get it now or wait until I see you about it.

Believe me ever your loving wife

H. MORDAUNT

Lina's wedding is to be here as I think you have heard before, only of course on account of G.M. [Grandmama] Bradford's death there will not be much going out for us this year. I am going to part with Clarke as I don't care much about her. I have seen another maid who I think will perhaps do but I have not had time to try her yet. I think we had better leave baby with Maria at Walton and let the servants come up to Chesham Place at once.

When he received the letter, Charlie read it through carefully, impressed by its normality. It certainly was not the kind of missive you would expect to get from a mad woman. He then examined the envelope which had a London postmark showing that it had been posted on 17 May and he came to the conclusion it had originally had a stamp on it which had been removed, probably before it was dry. He suspected that the family had taken the stamp off in the hope that the letter would not be sent, realising that it could provide him with a useful piece of evidence concerning her sanity. It was possible that Harriett might have then managed to post the letter herself. Another theory was that the letter could have been a 'design by the family' to draw him into a correspondence, which his advisers told him he must on no account do. In any case he did not reply.

The only strangeness the letter revealed was Harriett's belief that she could take up her life in London again as if nothing had happened. She seemed to be blocking out all her recent troubles, wishing only to 'return to the world'. This attitude could have been worrying for her family. They had at this stage no right to restrain her and there was nothing to stop her going out to visit her friends, or even contacting the Prince.

The Prince and Princess had arrived back in England a few days before. They both looked relaxed and well. The Prince, to his mother's delight, was on his best behaviour. He was so loving and attentive to his wife, now pregnant with her fifth child, that people were putting their recent trip into the category of a second honeymoon. The Queen had, it is true, found something to grumble about, complaining that the companions the Prince had summoned for the Nile trip had added to the expense and were in any case a very odd selection of people. And yet here Bertie was, back in England, as debonair as ever, and so innocently charming that it was difficult to believe anything bad about him.

Although the Prince was reassuring to his mother about the rumours of a scandal, he knew that he had to put an end to the whispers before the situation threatened the peace and accord which he had built up with his wife. It was perhaps no coincidence that when two doctors were sent to Belgrave Square to assess Lady Mordaunt's mental condition, one of them was the Prince's own physician, Dr Gull.[88] They were given the task of acquiring the medical evidence which would justify her removal from London and allow some restraint on her freedom.

Dr Gull and Dr Priestley arrived at Belgrave Square and were introduced to Lady Mordaunt, who had not been warned that they were coming. Dr Gull was a formidable man, with a dark complexion and a strong look of the Emperor Napoleon. It was said that he could exercise some sort of power over his patients. When he talked to Lady Mordaunt he had little response, and as a result he reported that she seemed totally incapable of stringing two sentences together, let alone of managing her own affairs. Dr Priestley reported that in his opinion the expression on Lady Mordaunt's face indicated a state of great mental weakness. Both doctors agreed that her pulse was very feeble and that she was altogether in very bad health. They concluded that she was of unsound mind, and that she should be placed in a house where she could be watched over by experienced attendants used to looking after mental patients.

A day or two later Helen Forbes wrote to Jessie asking her to send Lady Mordaunt's photograph book, some music, her needlework and her black gown to Lady Kinnoull's house. The album was the one which contained the photographs of the Prince of Wales, Lord Cole and others. It was probable that the family thought this would be better in their hands rather than Sir Charles's in the weeks to come.

24

Further Evidence

After Harriett had left Walton, Osbert, on his brother's instructions, took away her private box for examination. In it he discovered the letter written by the Prince of Wales on 16 November 1868 prior to his departure for Europe and the Middle East. On 17 May he went over to Walton again to search for more letters. He had seen one addressed to Lady Louisa on Harriett's table before she left Walton but it had subsequently disappeared and he now found it unposted among other papers in a small box. He opened and read the letter:

> I haven't heard from you so long that I don't know whether you have gone back home or if you are with Helen. I am writing this by myself after dinner as Charlie has not come back yet. I should be thankful if you could send me a little more of that nice sticking plaster you gave me when I married as I want it very much and I cannot get it in Leamington. The sooner you can send it me the better as I have got such a sore finger. If Lina wants a maid and if I could persuade her to go do you think Clarke would suit her and I would take Louisa if she has not already left you? I must say good night now as it is getting late and with love
>
> believe me ever your loving child
>
> H. MORDAUNT

The box included several cheque book counterfoils which Osbert examined with care, discovering that the cheque for thirty pounds which Harriett had written just prior to her departure was the first in a new book and was numbered 'No 121'. Osbert referred to the previous book and found that the last number was 120, which made him conclude that his sister-in-law had been sufficiently capable of managing her affairs to carry on the numbers from one book to another. He also discovered a cheque made out to Captain Farquhar on 16 June 1868, the day after Sir Charles had left for Norway, and another cheque for ten pounds to the Prince of Wales. Other finds were three pots of ointment for 'scalding' which agreed with the prescription from Dr Irvine already discovered. In addition there was a lock of hair, which definitely was not Sir Charles's although Osbert was unable to say whose it was. It was pressed into a pocket book.

On Wednesday 26 May, again at Sir Charles's direction, Mr Haynes made a further search at Walton Hall and in the drawer of the writing table in Lady Mordaunt's sitting-room found five of the letters addressed to her by Lord Newport, some of them before her marriage. He also discovered a Valentine in an envelope and another lock of hair. The Valentine was probably the one which Harriett had received the previous February. The sentiment expressed suggests that it had been sent by an admirer who had known her from his earliest youth, perhaps Lord Newport.

> I love thee still, I love thee still
> As truly as when first we met
> E'er grief o'er life had breathed its chill
> Or sorrow's tear my cheek had wet
> I love thee still, I love thee still
> Thy changeless constancy and truth
> Thy name yet wakens pleasure's thrill
> Star of my bright and joyous youth.

In the same drawer Mr Haynes discovered an envelope endorsed in Lady Mordaunt's handwriting, 'Odds and ends of former days'. In it he found a letter written by Lord Newport on 1 January 1866 from the Cavalry Barracks Windsor and endorsed in her handwriting 'Harriett from N. Xmas 1865'. There were two newspaper cuttings which ran: 'We hear the lovely and youthful Miss Harriett Moncreiffe is on the eve of being married to Sir -- Macpherson'; and 'Three affectionate friends are requested to prove their affection by coming forward and applying their remedy themselves.' All these finds were added to the evidence already collected.

Since it had now become clear that the Moncreiffes intended to stay divorce proceedings with the plea that Lady Mordaunt was out of her mind, Mr Haynes started to take further statements from members of the family and the servants who had seen her in the weeks before she left Walton. Mr and Mrs Cadogan, out of loyalty to Sir Charles and with considerable reluctance, also agreed to testify. They were all prepared to state that Lady Mordaunt was sane. If she had acted strangely at times, they agreed, this was 'put on'. Since family members might be considered biased, and the servants could always be open to bribery, it was important to find other witnesses of impeccable integrity, and it was for this reason that Mr Cadogan and his wife had been persuaded to talk to Mr Haynes. Mr Cadogan continued to insist that he had only visited Lady Mordaunt in the course of his pastoral duties, and had treated her as he would any other parishioner who was in some kind of distress.

Sir Charles told Mr Haynes how everything had changed after Sir Thomas Moncreiffe's visit to Walton. It was his belief that Sir Thomas had encouraged his daughter to feign madness and had instructed the rest of his family to say that she suffered from delusions. He quoted Jessie Clarke's testimony concerning the visit of Lady Kinnoull who had 'aided' Sir Thomas in trying to set Harriett up.

Recalling that his wife had on several occasions referred to her father's financial difficulties, Sir Charles suspected that Sir Thomas would want to delay proceedings in order to benefit for as long as possible from the allowance that Sir Charles was paying into his hands. The worst that could be imagined was that if Lady Mordaunt were really in the end to be proved insane, then he could not 'in justice to his character' proceed further against her, and would have to withdraw his petition. Sir Charles now realised that as a result of this new tactic his whole case might be jeopardised and it seemed to him that the latest line taken by the Moncreiffes was 'unchristianlike' to the last degree 'by having I believe urged her to simulate insanity and to deny her guilt they are causing her to add sin to sin when she had previously confessed her guilt and perhaps might have been led to repentance'.

Sir Charles carefully went over his conversations with Lady Louisa and Mrs Forbes, with all the indications there had been in these that they fully believed in Lady Mordaunt's guilt, Lady Louisa even going so far as to say that 'a woman who has been as wicked as she has cannot have any conscience left'. He highlighted the fact that Lady Louisa had passed on Harriett's description of Captain Farquhar as a brute who had ill-treated her, and of the Prince of Wales as a man who had bullied her into doing wrong. In this connection he noted the warning given to him by Lord Dudley when he had first become engaged, after which he had always warned his wife against any intimacy with the Prince in view of his bad reputation. As evidence of the degree to which his wife had been corrupted by those she consorted with, he mentioned how she had repeatedly asked him to tell her something 'naughty'.

Mr Haynes was now able to take further evidence from Mrs Hancox who had been away on a monthly engagement. She too described her conversations with Lady Louisa and Mrs Forbes, stressing how ready they had been to agree that in the circumstances a divorce was inevitable. She maintained that they had made no mention whatsoever of madness except to say that Lady Mordaunt had been mad to tell Sir Charles what she had done and ought to have let him find out for himself.

The letter written by Georgie Forbes in answer to Lady Mordaunt's invitation to visit her at Walton soon after her marriage was also handed over. Sir Charles explained to Mr Haynes that George Forbes's brother was married to Lady Mordaunt's sister Helen whom he described as 'a highly improper character'.

It was at this time that Bird told Mr Haynes about the letter written by Captain Farquhar from the Tower of London which Jessie Clarke had found on Lady Mordaunt's dressing table. He said that he had not mentioned it before because Jessie had persuaded him not to, but seeing the way things were going he had changed his mind.

This new revelation made Sir Charles more sure than ever that Farquhar's name should be included among the co-respondents. His brother John backed him up, writing to Mr Haynes from Spean Bridge on 23 May, suggesting that the letter from Farquhar described by Bird and Clarke should be used, even though it could not actually be produced. In addition he thought the fact that Harriett had said 'Yes' to Farquhar's name among others when Orford had listed those who might have given her the disease was reason good enough to include him. 'It must also be borne in mind that Captain Farquhar has not a shilling to defend himself with and more risk may be run with him without any fear of a counter action than has apparently been run in Sir F. Johnstone's case already.'

John Mordaunt added that Lady Louisa had constantly referred to Captain Farquhar as one of the names mentioned by her daughter. She would find it difficult in the witness box, without perjuring herself, to deny that both the Prince and Captain Farquhar had been named. As a result, John Mordaunt thought, it would be advisable to serve both Lady Louisa and Helen Forbes with a subpoena to appear in court at the earliest possible moment.

Sir Charles's counsel, Mr Inderwick, had by now perused the whole collection of papers relating to the case which were already being described as 'voluminous'. Mr Inderwick was to appear for Sir Charles at the summons on 25 May. Mr Haynes had been informed that Lady Mordaunt was to appear 'without prejudice' at the hearing and that Mr Benbow would represent her.

A summons was also issued for Sir Charles, his solicitor or agent, to appear on the same day to show cause why the co-respondents should not have a month's further time to file their answers to the petition.

25

The Forsaken Victim

Much as Harriett would have liked to stay in London, it had become increasingly apparent to her family that she must be sent away as soon as possible, and certainly before the summons on 25 May. What was needed was a quiet place where she would be observed by people who could be relied upon to come to the right conclusions. Young ladies who had misbehaved themselves could surely look for nothing better than to be shut away without the right of appeal, so that those she had wronged by dragging their names out into the open could be put well out of range of her testimony. The mechanism for achieving such a result was familiar to those who were experienced in caring for the insane. Knowledge of what tended to happen in such cases had probably caused Dr Tuke's strange outburst when, at Walton, he had gone down on his knees, crying out 'My dear lady, you do not wish to be sent to a lunatic asylum do you?'

Although Dr Gull had expressed some uneasiness about the legality of the course they were undertaking, Dr Tuke for his part was prepared to accept the inevitable. He therefore contacted a widow, Mrs Carruthers, a 'lunatic nurse' who was known to him, and engaged her to look after Lady Mordaunt at Clifton House in Worthing which had been rented for the purpose. Worthing was considered to be suitably secluded and less dangerous than fashionable resorts such as Weymouth or Hastings where Lady Mordaunt might have encountered some of her friends. Mrs Carruthers, who was used to attending 'persons whose minds were deranged', knew exactly what was expected of her. An approach from Dr Tuke spoke for itself.

The house at Worthing was staffed by servants hired by Sir Thomas, and a local surgeon, Dr Harris, had been appointed to attend Lady Mordaunt on a regular basis. Miss Laing took her down to her new home and for the first few days she seemed to enjoy going out for walks and drives. Soon, however, her interest began to wane, and she started saying she wanted to go back to Walton to be with her husband and her child. Her frustration grew with each day that brought no news from home. She said that she could not understand why Sir Charles did not come to see her or communicate with her in any way. When she asked to go to London and was told that she could not, she became very angry.

It soon dawned on her that she had lost her freedom. She could not leave the house unattended and was not allowed to go shopping although she frequently expressed a wish to do so. In fact the formidable Carruthers put all the shops out of bounds, saying that she did not think her charge was capable of making any purchases. The carriage drives began to pall, the suburban streets being a poor substitute for the Warwickshire lanes Lady Mordaunt had once bowled along in her own pony carriage. Conversation, too, seemed pointless. Each day stretched out interminably, empty and dull. She tried to read, but found it hard to concentrate. When she got up in the morning, there was nothing to look forward to so that sometimes, after she had had her bath, she would go back to bed again. Miss Laing's efforts to dress her hair were far from satisfactory and she longed for the days when Jessie Clarke had arranged it with such skill. She would try to dress, choosing her clothes, and then changing her mind and trying others, but it was a useless exercise since nobody would see her and there was nobody, and nothing, to dress up for. Her wardrobe was limited; most of her best dresses remained at Walton, and she grew tired of the ones she had, and at times so frustrated that she tore them to pieces, perhaps hoping that somebody would buy her something new. On one occasion she put her hat down the water closet. She showed her dislike of the clothes she had by going down one evening to the drawing room dressed only in a muff, an opera cloak and some stockings, greatly shocking her former governess who came to the conclusion that she had no shame.

Since she was not allowed any cash, Lady Mordaunt helped herself to some coppers belonging to Mrs Carruthers, and she gave a penny to the butler, asking him to buy her some tooth powder. With the rest she bought some postage stamps, but although she would sometimes start to write a letter, she never finished it. What was the point? She knew that anything she wrote would be intercepted so that there was not the slightest hope of ever receiving an answer. Nor was there any possibility that she would be able to creep out to the post box. Miss Laing and Mrs Carruthers watched her far too carefully for that. During the day she was never left alone and at night Miss Laing slept in her room. All the time the eyes of Miss Laing and Mrs Carruthers were upon her. 'I shall go mad if I am watched like this' she told them.

As the weeks went by Miss Laing started to report a deterioration in Lady Mordaunt's mental state as she became more apathetic, less inclined to get up in the mornings. She wandered around the small house like a lost soul, going into the bedrooms so that the servants were ordered to keep their doors locked. This made Lady Mordaunt more frustrated and angry than ever and she demanded a hammer to open them, saying that she was afraid Sir Charles might be locked up inside. She became obsessed with the idea that she must see her husband again. As she grew increasingly upset and disturbed, she lost interest in her food, at times eating practically nothing, and at others altogether lacking the energy to lift the spoon so that Miss Laing felt she had to feed her to prevent her from starving. On the other hand she would sometimes help herself to the food ravenously with her fingers, stuffing it into her mouth.

Then, when she had finally lost all hope of going back to Warwickshire, she started asking repeatedly that her baby should be brought to her. Her pleas fell on deaf ears.

During the first two weeks in June, Harriett's family visited her quite frequently. Her mother had returned to Scotland ready for the birth of her baby which was due at the end of June, but Helen travelled down to Worthing several times, and Blanche went and stayed for a week. Sir Thomas also appeared on several occasions, but at the beginning of June he was called away to Scotland and did not reappear. Dr Harris, according to instructions, visited the house frequently to observe the patient, but apart from that she received no callers of any kind and was totally cut off from the world she had once known.

Meanwhile, in London, the season was getting under way, with the usual glittering round of parties. The fashion of the moment, particularly for the more daring, was to visit the St James's Theatre, where Offenbach's *Orpheus in the Underworld* was playing to enthusiastic audiences, *The Times* reporting that 'the most outrageous can-can that ever desecrated the London stage' had been 'rapturously encored'.

The Waleses, in a gesture of solidarity, had given everyone a lead by holding a ball at Marlborough House, the prelude to a full programme of events which were to be more extravagant than ever. This year the ladies' dresses were altogether overladen with fresh flowers, and the hair styles and chignons were even more contrived than they had been the year before.[89]

The weather grew gradually hotter until in July it became almost unbearable, and Alice Miles found that it was 'a great deal too hot to do anything but lay on the sofa in an artistically darkened room' with one of her admirers to amuse her. Alice, unlike the unfortunate Harriett, was free to enjoy all the delights of town. Among her admirers was Harriett's cousin 'Baby Dupplin', who was making himself singularly useful handing her into her carriage and generally escorting her. On 10 July she reported in her diary that she spent 'the most charming day at Hurlingham surrounded by all my ancient adorers, with Lord Dupplin the new favourite at their head'. On 11 July, which was a Sunday, Alice spent a 'delicious' day at Hampton Court with another beau 'laying lazily under the trees, watching the goldfish swim in and out among the water lilies, talking or being still just as the spirit moved us'.[90]

But sadly for the lovely Lady Mordaunt, who had been the brightest star in the social firmament just a year ago, there were to be no enviable invitations, no outings on the river, no bright gowns garlanded with hothouse blooms. The pressed flowers from the bouquet given her by the Prince had been snatched from their hiding place and were now lodged in a lawyer's office, joining other cold, labelled exhibits. The cache of letters from the Prince would also soon be on display, with Bird the butler and Jessie Clarke the lady's maid ready to swear that the handwriting was his. Lady Mordaunt's honesty in confessing to her transgressions had robbed her of her wealth and of her freedom. She was a prisoner, sitting in dim rooms where the blinds were always drawn, unable to communicate, to write or receive letters from her friends, forbidden to see anybody, sitting alone, but always observed.

By now there were strong rumours that the Mordaunt case had been abandoned and would never be brought to court. This could only have been a relief to Lord Cole who had naturally been alarmed to hear about the affidavits filed by the servants at Walton Hall. His lawyers had been trying to extract copies of their testimony from Mr Hunt who had firmly refused the request. Any delay was a relief to Lord Cole, who on 12 July managed to marry his heiress. As usual Alice Miles summed the situation up succinctly:

Lord Cole, in mortal terror of perhaps in the event of a divorce taking place, being dragged into becoming the fair delinquent's [Lady Mordaunt's] happy number 2, hardened his heart to the extent necessary to lead the ugliest Miss Baird to the altar. Having raised her to the rank of Viscountess though, there I suppose he considered his obligations ended, since three days after his marriage he was seen wandering disconsolately in the Park with the expression of a man who has arrived at l'été de St Martin's dreariest days, instead of being still in the first rosy flush of la lune de miel. As for Waterford and Vivian, that has quite faded into a thing of the past, and scarcely provokes now a blush from some over-hypocritical ingénue, or a warning 'hush! hush! my dear, don't you see the girls!' from the Dowager in command.[91]

A few days after Lowry Cole's wedding, Selina Moncreiffe married William Arbuthnot and that evening at the Moncreiffe Arms at Bridge of Earn, Dr Laing, the family doctor and Jane Laing's father, proposed a toast to 'the other married members of the Moncreiffe family', including Lady Mordaunt. He was not surprised, he said, that the Moncreiffe sisters had reached such high positions in life, and he referred in glowing terms to their personal beauty as well as to their high moral worth. In fact he felt that there were no other ladies to equal them in the whole of Scotland, and with the home training they had received they 'could not but turn out good wives'. The doctor was sure that the cloud at present hanging over Lady Mordaunt would soon pass away. He had known her for many years as a happy, light-hearted girl, of the kind most likely to have their actions and words misconstrued. The fact was that in a state of temporary insanity she had given utterance to statements that had been 'taken advantage of'.

In spite of the marriage, and the local doctor's welcome support, the Moncreiffe family on the whole had little to celebrate. On 20 June Lady Louisa had given birth to a sickly child, a seventh son, Claude, whose health was giving much cause for concern, and it was not until after Selina's wedding that she was able to visit Harriett at Worthing. Even then she was only able to stay for a few hours, going out with her daughter for a short drive, and then returning to London.

For the rest of the world, Lady Mordaunt seemed to have vanished from sight. Few people knew where she was or what had become of her, although some said she had been sent to an asylum and would remain locked up so that she could not incriminate the Prince of Wales. Remembering the stories that had circulated the previous summer about the Prince and the ponies, many found it easy to believe that Wales was guilty and should be brought to book. The *Warwick Advertiser* reported that contrary to all the rumours the case was in fact proceeding and there was no probability of it being withdrawn.

Meanwhile, whatever was going on in his mind and whatever he really knew or believed about Lady Mordaunt's case, the Prince continued to appear unworried, relaxed, urbane and affable. He was perhaps more attentive to his wife than he had ever been, and they were frequently seen together in public. The Princess looked rather thin and ill and seemed at times to be in pain, but the Prince was in splendid health, more robust than ever, although it had to be admitted that he had put on rather too much weight.

The Queen herself had agreed to come down from Balmoral for the two state balls which were to be held at Buckingham Palace in July. They proved to be magnificent occasions, with 1,500 invitations issued for the first and 1,800 for the second. The Prince and Princess appeared together at both, and at the second the Princess wore a particularly lovely dress in blue tulle, with forget-me-nots and diamonds in her hair. The Queen seemed to be in good heart, apparently suffering less than usual from the giddiness which afflicted her whenever she went into crowded places. Her son's efforts to be exceptionally charming and dutiful had certainly paid off, and when he accompanied his mother on a visit to Aldershot, the Queen told Vicky that he was 'as affectionate and simple and unassuming as ever'. She was sure that 'no Heir Apparent ever was so nice and unpretending as dear Bertie'.[92]

The Prince had carried out a number of worthy public engagements, among them the laying of a foundation stone for the new wing being added to the Earlswood Asylum for Idiots at Reigate. Then, after the second state ball, he and Alix set off for Manchester to attend the Royal Agricultural Show and to watch the hunter trials at a 'leaping ground' nearby. They were greeted with much *éclat* wherever they went, and at a ball given by the Earl of Ellesmere at Worsley Hall, the Prince surprised and delighted his fellow guests when he set himself up as 'a sort of dancing free rover, requesting a *tour de valse* from the fair visitors all over the ball room, whether he had made their acquaintance or not. Moreover he gracefully avoided any appearance of being guided in his selection, on the score of beauty alone.'[93]

Giving Goodwood a miss, the Prince and Princess went on to Hull where Bertie opened a dry dock to be called after his father, and they then travelled straight on to Wildbad where it was hoped the waters would benefit the Princess's health.

26

Lawyers and Doctors

While Lady Mordaunt remained shut up at Worthing, with little or nothing by way of an occupation, the lawyers, by contrast, were feverishly active as they struggled to get all the necessary documents together. 'You have indeed given us plenty to do' Mr Haynes wrote to Mr Hunt, pleading for extra time to prepare all the affidavits. 'The witnesses be so wide' he complained 'and I should like to see and go through the drafts with as many as I can so as to require as little alteration as possible.'

In accordance with Mr Haynes's instructions, Mr Inderwick had now engaged as Sir Charles's leading counsel one of the most eminent lawyers of the time, Mr Serjeant Ballantine,[94] who also had to examine all the drafts. His fees were high in accordance with his status. For a start he charged twenty guineas for looking through the affidavits as well as four guineas for a double consultation.

To save time, Arthur Haynes's son had been despatched to Scotland with the drafts for Sir Charles to peruse, but when he arrived at Banavie near Fort William where Sir Charles was now staying, he encountered an unexpected setback. For some reason Sir Charles was having second thoughts as to whether his wife had mentioned Lord Cole's name in her original confession. Mr Haynes said this change of heart was 'perfectly unnecessary', especially as the nurse had confirmed that Lady Mordaunt had mentioned Lord Cole's name – she had overheard it as she left the room. 'My son' Mr Haynes told Mr Hunt 'strongly urged him not to strike it out, but he will have his own way.' To get round the difficulty, Mr Haynes suggested that it should be said that on swearing the affidavit Sir Charles had suffered 'a small degree of doubt'. Also awkward was the fact that Mr Jones was in his turn having some reservations about his original testimony. He was, Mr Haynes explained, 'very willing but very cautious' and now wanted to base his opinion on the prescriptions alone, which Mr Haynes thought 'would at once be cut from under us by Priestley swearing what the prescriptions really were'. This involved another lengthy conference with Jones in order to sort the matter out.

By 19 June all the affidavits had been looked over by Mr Inderwick and 'shaped' into their final form ready to be filed. In addition the exhibits, including letters from the Prince and others, had all been listed. With such an impressive array of paper work, Mr Haynes was sure that he had a good case, and it still seemed to him unlikely that the issue of madness would stand up in court.

Now that the main preparation for the hearing had been completed, Mr Haynes was able to take a short break at Great Glenn in Leicestershire. He could not, however, escape altogether from what he described as 'this unprecedented case' and he continued his correspondence although somewhat hampered by the fact that he was away from the office and could not consult the relevant papers. He wrote to Mr Inderwick on 21 June asking whether, if the judge thought that Lady Mordaunt had been sane when her father took her away from Walton on 15 May, this would still allow Sir Thomas to 'trump up' a case for insanity at the present time? There were doubtless numerous medical men in London quite willing to make affidavits to suit the case. 'If we do not now succeed,' wrote Mr Haynes, 'her insanity will never cease and it will be a perfect denial of justice to Sir Charles who would be saddled with a quasi insane wife and her father (who has not a penny) living with his family upon Sir Charles's allowance.'

From every point of view it was essential to press on with divorce proceedings. 'Only get the judge to proceed and all insanity and defence will at once vanish' wrote Mr Haynes.

The encouraging news was that Lord Penzance had finally directed the co-respondents to file their answer to the petition within the next week. This made Mr Haynes feel confident that the case would go ahead. Nothing had been heard from Worthing, and it looked as if Sir Thomas would find it hard to prove his daughter's insanity. In any case, Haynes had thought all along that the three doctors consulted by Sir Thomas who had spoken of puerperal insanity had produced a very weak case since it was acknowledged that this condition was always preceded by fever, and yet there had never been the slightest suggestion that Lady Mordaunt was feverish at any time following the birth. As for Sir Thomas, Mr Haynes was convinced that he had 'made arrangements' with his daughter to act out 'all her subsequent scenes with the strange doctors'. The introduction of Major Arbuthnot on the day she had left Walton was in his opinion another indication of Sir Thomas's deviousness. After all, no 'military force' had been required to remove her. It was only the presence of Osbert Mordaunt that had frustrated Sir Thomas's 'wicked design' to get an affidavit from the Major, who would have been treated to a prearranged 'scene'. As it was, Lady Mordaunt had been given no chance to act strangely, and indeed she had laughed quite naturally 'in apparent friendship' when Osbert had said goodbye and given her some 'wholesome advice'.

Dr Priestley, for his part, had in Mr Haynes's opinion behaved disgracefully. First of all he had undertaken to help Lady Mordaunt 'hide her shame' in London. Then, after the birth, in spite of his original belief that there was no madness to be seen, he had blatantly changed his mind and had subsequently tried 'in every shape and form to pull Lady Mordaunt through it'. In a P.S. to his letter, Mr Haynes wrote: 'If it had not been for the providential accident of a premature confinement, Priestley would have taken care that there was no disease either with the child or mother beyond what is usual, and perhaps the child would have turned out a boy instead of a girl and all Sir Charles's estates centred in a bastard.' Worse still, the adulterous liaisons would have continued and there would have been 'an annual production amongst these wolves in sheep's clothing'.

Not only was the doctors' case for madness distinctly shaky, there was also considerable support for Sir Charles among the public, who believed that Lady Mordaunt was guilty, even if she was bearing the brunt of the punishment that should have been meted out to all the gentlemen involved, and, most particularly, to the Prince. This view was forcibly expressed in a leading article which appeared on 26 June, conveniently timed to appear just before the hearing, in the *Royal Leamington Chronicle*. It was entitled 'The Late Scandal – Public Morality in 1778 and 1869'. The article quoted a conversation recorded by Boswell in his *Life of Johnson*. Boswell's conviction that in Scotland a man's career could be unfavourably affected as a result of destroying the peace of a noble family was contrasted with Johnson's cynical pronouncement that an Englishman suffered little as a result of wanton behaviour. The leader writer feared that if the Mordaunt case were to be dropped as some thought it would be, then it would be possible to conclude that the contemporary Englishman was just as likely now to err without suffering any punishment to his career or reputation as he would have been in the days of Dr Johnson. And although the guilty man could carry on his life as if nothing was wrong, the woman in the case was likely to receive more than her full measure of disapproval and rejection.

The scandal which has been circulating in Warwickshire during the last few weeks is said to have 'terminated' in the consignment of *one* of the parties concerned to a lunatic asylum; a terrible punishment truly, which might satisfy the demands of the severest social code. The scandal-devouring public and the rigidly righteous in our social life will probably be silenced and contented; but that truer and higher morality, if it really exist, which will not be satisfied by the knowledge that vengeance has been visited upon a prostrate and forsaken victim, and will at least desire that equal retribution should be done to both, what has it to say of that *other*, who, report avers, is too high in social position for justice ever to reach!

The question was whether the other person, who had been equally guilty, would be allowed, just because he was a member of the *stronger* sex, to avoid 'that chastisement which has visited the weaker one in such terrible form'.

Is the term 'weaker' really to be used in the horribly satirical sense of implying that if there is participation in guilt there is no share in the immunity from the just punishment of social transgression? Or can it mean weaker in the sense that in the dreadful hour of shame and exposure, so far from the world casting the same lenient eye upon the offender and successfully shielding her from the degradation which she has incurred, it will not scruple to assume towards her an air of virtuous abhorrence – her own nearest and dearest will desert her, or will torture her with reproaches, till in the anguish of despair which is worse than death, the unhappy victim, bereft of reason, commits self-destruction, or is consigned for the rest of her days to an asylum for lunatics? And that other who is stronger, and therefore is so shielded! – where is he? He peradventure will still be found reposing in the shelter of that household which he quitted in disguise, like a very felon, for the set purpose (so runs the report) of destroying the happiness of another, – and which he may leave again and again for all 'society' cares or dares, upon the same errand of iniquity, and to the terrible undoing of another, whom the world refuses to screen or excuse because

she is weaker than he! 'The court, the camp, the field' will still
be free to him – perchance the throne itself, – but alas, however
lofty and powerful may be his position, he cannot again raise
her to that from which *she* has fallen, and where she will ever
lie –

'so low,
And none so poor to do her reverence.'

The only redeeming feature, in the opinion of the *Leamington
Chronicle* writer, was that a great deal of indignation was felt by
many people, and much had been expressed in Warwickshire at the
conduct of a person in high position in this domestic tragedy. It was
generally thought that the Prince should have been subjected to a
strict investigation in order that his guilt or innocence might be
demonstrated, since the longer such an inquiry was delayed, the
deeper would be the suspicion. With all this in mind the article
concluded on a resonant moral note.

> This case has been known through the length and breadth of the
> kingdom as 'the Warwickshire Scandal' and indeed it would be
> a grave scandal to this Christian country if it could be said with
> truth by the moralist of our own day that rank or social status
> could screen a man, any more than a woman, from the just
> penalty of his misdoing.

Certainly on the face of it, the writer went on, the heavy hand of
disapproval lay on the young lady's head; her act had apparently
brought shame onto everybody connected with her, while the five or
six men who had tempted her (or whom she had seduced, according
to which way you looked at it) were able to emerge from the scandal
unscathed. 'A boy as is bad aint never so bad as a girl' George Brattle
declared in Trollope's *The Vicar of Bullhampton*, and even the clergy
felt that the sin of adultery, unlike any other, must be deemed unfor-
givable as far as the young lady was concerned. It was believed that
rigidly moral attitudes and fears of social ostracism were vital factors
in discouraging women from going astray.[95] Many people were ready
to believe, however, that the carefree morals of the Prince and his set
were to blame for the unfortunate Lady Mordaunt's promiscuity. She
had been led to believe that there was 'no harm' in doing what she
had done because 'everybody did it'. And now it was she who was
suffering and not the Prince.

With all the affidavits assembled, between them giving what seemed to him incontestable evidence that Lady Mordaunt had been sane right up to the time of her departure from Walton, Sir Charles felt sure that the judge would rate the evidence of the London doctors as patently inadequate. How could he fail to see that the madness issue was simply a ruse to protect the men Harriett had incriminated?

Sir Charles's confidence was ill founded. The outcome of the hearing was as unexpected as it was disturbing. On 1 July a letter from Mr Haynes reached him at Banavies breaking the news that far from dismissing the madness question, the judge had allowed counsel on Lady Mordaunt's behalf to let two medical men visit her at Worthing with a view to reporting on her present state. They were Dr Gull, the Prince's doctor who had visited her in Belgrave Square, and Dr Alderson who had gone down to visit Lady Mordaunt at Walton with Dr Tuke.

Sir Charles was enraged. Now it seemed that even the judge was conspiring to help Lady Mordaunt evade justice. He was so 'partial' that he had apparently treated with contempt the seventeen carefully prepared affidavits from the Mordaunt side. Sir Charles believed that he should at least have insisted that the Moncreiffe doctors read the affidavits before going down to Worthing. As it was, they would be fully primed by Sir Thomas, while Harriett herself would be given enough warning to prepare her madness act before they arrived.

Having read Mr Haynes's letter, Sir Charles made immediate arrangements to travel south for consultations. In the meantime, he agreed to send Dr Jones and Dr Orford down to Worthing to make their own assessment. They were to be accompanied by an eminent 'accoucheur' or by an insanity doctor who would be particularly asked to look into the puerperal mania theory which had been 'set up' so shamefully. The choice of such a doctor was not straightforward; Sir Charles had originally thought of Sir William Jenner, but as he was a Court doctor, this could prove unwise as there was a danger that 'the Prince of Wales might influence him'.[96]

Mr Haynes, on receiving Sir Charles's letter, immediately wrote off to Mr Hunt telling him that his client was not surprisingly 'sadly displeased and disappointed at the last hearing and the result'. He keenly felt that his very clear case was being answered by 'fraud, stratagem and imposition upon the Court'. Sir Charles was due to visit Mr Haynes with his brothers the next day, and although the lawyer expressed his intention of doing all he could 'to reconcile them to the present crisis' he knew they were all convinced that the hearing had been a complete farce and that a visit from the London doctors should never have been sanctioned. It was John Mordaunt's belief that Dr Alderson, in support of his own madness theory, would do his best to 'gull' Dr Gull.

Believing as he did that the situation was now critical, Sir Charles agreed to accompany Mr Haynes to London next day, 5 July. Mr Haynes hoped that Mr Inderwick would be prepared 'to advise some decisive course'. There had meanwhile been a further delay as Dr Alderson and Dr Gull had only just submitted their reports of the visit to Worthing, and these could not be verified in time for the summons which had been fixed for 6 July. Mr Benbow therefore requested an adjournment of the summons until the following Tuesday, the 13th. Mr Hunt wrote back at once to say that he could not agree to an adjournment.

On 6 July at four o'clock in the afternoon, Mr Hunt and Mr Inderwick had a consultation with Serjeant Ballantine and Mr Haynes. On the same day an order was issued stating that Sir Charles should be at liberty to send down any medical witnesses he liked, but that Dr Harris, the Worthing doctor, could be present at the interview if he so desired.

When the affidavits of Sir Thomas's doctors were filed next day it became clear that they stood by their diagnosis of puerperal insanity, taking it for granted that Lady Mordaunt had suffered the usual early indications of the disease soon after her confinement – the hot and painful head, the 'muttering' delirium, the feverish pulse. They reported that after taking her pulse, examining her tongue which was 'stained' and observing that her hand was cold and clammy, they had proceeded to ask her questions, receiving nothing but monosyllabic replies. They came away with some scraps of paper she had written on. One was directed simply to 'Ireland' asking for some port to be sent as she was so badly off. The doctors dwelt on her fears of being poisoned, on her screams in the night and her attempts to get through locked doors. They did not question the reports made by Mrs Carruthers that she had become incontinent, on one occasion 'performing the offices of nature' on the drawing room carpet and 'laughing immoderately' as she did so.

Dr Alderson was of the opinion that Lady Mordaunt's symptoms had become 'aggravated' since he had last seen her on 6 May at Walton and felt he could now provide conclusive evidence of 'cerebral disturbance'. Dr Gull described how he had plied Lady

Mordaunt with questions, receiving some rather odd answers. For example, when he had asked her whether she thought any steps could be taken to correct the reports that had been spread about respecting her, she had replied that a dose of castor oil would put it all right. Dr Harris for his part was prepared to state that from the very first time he had seen Lady Mordaunt he had been sure that she was suffering from puerperal mania. Since then he had visited her frequently and she had showned no signs of improvement whatsoever.

Jane Laing and Dorothy Carruthers now added their reports. Both women described how Lady Mordaunt would stand upright in her carriage when it was in motion, not, they thought, because she was intent on 'self destruction', but simply because she had no idea what she was doing or where she was at the time. They swore that she was suffering from delusions, thinking that her husband Sir Charles was in the house, or that her clothes were in some way connected with the devil. According to Mrs Carruthers she insisted on wearing her hat 'to save her mother and father', whom she regarded with great antipathy. She was depressed, hysterical, apathetic, restless and dreamy in turns and in addition she became 'dreadfully excited' when asked to take wine or the tonics ordered by the medical men. Miss Laing described her lack of personal cleanliness and modesty, her desire to besmear herself with her evacuations, her unwillingness to take a bath, her tendency to pick up anything dirty, such as horse dung. Altogether, the two ladies and Dr Harris agreed that her memory was non-existent, that she was incapable of giving any information about the charges brought against her. Mrs Carruthers summed it all up by declaring: 'I have had great experience in the care of insane persons and say that I am convinced that the said Lady Mordaunt is utterly unable to exercise her judgment or memory upon any subject whatever.'

Sir Charles felt incredulous when he was told about the doctors' reports. He mistrusted even more the evidence of the 'lunatic' nurse. And if his wife was behaving at all strangely this was entirely due, he believed, to the treatment being meted out to her by her attendants.

On 10 July Dr Orford and Dr Jones made their visit to Worthing accompanied by two eminent London medical men, Dr Reynolds, a Professor of Medicine at University College, and Dr Burrowes,[97] neither of whom had ever seen Lady Mordaunt before. Dr Orford travelled down alone to Brighton, meeting the other doctors there and travelling on with them to Worthing. They were met at the station by Dr Harris who took them to the house. Sir Thomas had been there the day before, staying overnight, but he left before the impressive array of doctors put in an appearance.

The visitors first of all received an account of Lady Mordaunt's state from Miss Laing and Mrs Carruthers, interviewing them separately, the normal procedure in cases of insanity being to inquire first from people in the house what the condition was like. Carruthers gave a dramatic picture of Lady Mordaunt as a complete lunatic, describing all kinds of strange actions, while Miss Laing told the doctors that she had watched Lady Mordaunt's mental state deteriorate during the two months she had been at Worthing so that she was by now unable to carry on a conversation, and was very restless. Miss Laing said that she frequently heard her giggling in a silly manner. At meal times she often behaved in an 'unladylike' manner, helping herself from the dish with her own fork and spoon, or even using her fingers.

After they had spoken to the two lady attendants, the doctors talked to Dr Harris, who discussed some medical details and told them that he thought Lady Mordaunt had become quite childish in her behaviour.

It was decided that Dr Orford should talk to Lady Mordaunt first as he knew her well and the other doctors thought this would give her confidence. Orford found her reclining on a sofa, neatly dressed, with her hair well arranged. Later, the doctors were told that as she found both Miss Laing and Miss Carruthers quite incapable of doing her hair the way she liked, she had taken to arranging it herself.

To his annoyance Dr Orford found that Dr Harris and Miss Laing were both present and when he queried this, they said they were under instructions to stay. He decided to ignore them.

'Well, my lady, how do you do?' he said to Lady Mordaunt.

'How do *you* do, Mr Orford?' she replied, obviously recognising him at once.

When he asked to see her tongue she said she thought it was rather a nasty one, but she obediently stuck it out and he kindly said 'I think it is a very nice one.' When he said he was going to feel her pulse, she raised her hand to meet his. He then asked after her eyes and she said they were 'not very good, I think the stuff I have been taking has affected them'. Dr Harris explained that she had been prescribed a little steel. Later Dr Orford asked to look at her eyes but did not see anything peculiar about them. He then went out and waited in the garden while the other doctors went in to see her.

Lady Mordaunt received Dr Jones 'kindly' and shook hands. To put her at her ease he began with ordinary topics of conversation, such as the weather, and how she liked Worthing, contrasting the small garden there with the magnificent grounds at Walton. As he later put it in his report:

I then alluded to the cricket match going on at Lord's between the two schools of Eton and Harrow, wearing at the same time in the button hole of my coat the blue ribband of Harrow. To these various observations she only occasionally replied and then almost monosyllabically but her several replies were always rational answers to my questions.

After a time Dr Orford was asked to come back in and he returned to the drawing room by way of the conservatory. He too remarked on the fact that there was a nice garden at the back of the house, and a croquet ground. All the same, he said 'It is very poor after Walton is it not?' She did not reply.

Dr Reynolds and Dr Burrowes then joined the other doctors, and when they were introduced to Lady Mordaunt, she bowed slightly, looking at them intently before putting her head back on the couch and gazing into space. Dr Jones asked her some more questions, but she simply answered 'Yes' or 'No' or 'I don't know'. Dr Reynolds, having heard that she had suffered from toothache recently, asked her whether her wisdom teeth were troubling her, and whether she had in fact cut them yet. She replied that she did not know.

'Let me see' he said.

She sat up, leaned towards him and opened her lips but kept her teeth clenched so that he was unable to see inside her mouth. He then tried another tack, saying that if her wisdom teeth were the cause of her trouble, there would be some swelling beneath her ear. As he put his hand out towards the angle of her jaw, she pulled away sharply, saying 'There is no occasion for that, thank you'.

Before he left, Dr Orford asked if he should take any message to Walton.

'Yes thank you' she said.

'Well, what message shall I take?'

'You can ask Sir Charles to come and fetch me'.

After this crisp interchange, it was not surprising that Dr Orford remained firm in his belief that Lady Mordaunt was perfectly sane.

After they returned from Worthing, the doctors had a meeting with the object of producing a common report, but after a lengthy discussion, they found it quite impossible to reach any degree of unanimity about Lady Mordaunt's present state of mind. Mr Hunt begged them to send in their reports as soon as possible. 'On account of the near approach of the Long Vacation every day is of importance and I shall be much obliged by receiving as soon as possible your reply to the above preliminary to your formal report' he wrote to Dr Burrowes on 12 July. The reports had to be ready by the 24 July but even so Mr Hunt felt that he would be 'much driven to prepare and get the affidavit on the file by the time limited'.

Dr Orford and Mr Jones both wrote agreeing that Lady Mordaunt was perfectly capable of understanding the painful circumstances she found herself in and of answering the charges brought forward against her. Dr Orford was prepared to admit that as a result of his visit to Worthing he could vouch for the fact that Lady Mordaunt's brain had become lethargic through lack of its accustomed healthy stimulus of a varied life, but he believed that this would soon be shaken off if she could return to a more normal existence. He pointed out that since leaving Walton she had never been left for a single day without a dependent of the Moncreiffe family with her. She was constantly watched and since this was the case, was it surprising that she sometimes behaved strangely and, being denied the company of her husband, had got to the pitch where she sometimes imagined he was with her? Since she was not allowed to purchase a single garment for herself, it was equally understandable that she had developed some odd 'fancies' as to dress.

Dr Jones for his part reported that it was impossible not to be struck by Lady Mordaunt's apparent indifference to everything. He felt that her vacant look, or to put it more technically her 'cataleptic stare', was probably not assumed, and had in fact become something permanent. He thought that this had been caused by the terrible situation she was in and by the behaviour of her medical attendants towards her. As he put it: 'It is difficult to conceive that a Lady so young and so accustomed to the giddy vortex of London Society could so completely command her feelings as to put [an attitude] on and retain [it] for so long a period as she now has done.' He also pointed out that the situation Lady Mordaunt had been in at Walton was diametrically opposed to her present one. There she had been surrounded by the comforts of home and by people who were sincerely convinced that she was sane. At Worthing by contrast her attendants were all too ready to see her peculiarities as 'so many confirmations of . . . the reasons for their being engaged to attend her'. In addition it was inevitable that she should be affected by her unfamiliar surroundings. Dr Jones summed the matter up emphatically: 'For these reasons I consider Lady Mordaunt's removal from Walton and her residence at Worthing powerfully calculated to aggravate her symptoms and to be extremely prejudicial to her recovery.'

He also complained about the poor facilities offered to him and his colleagues compared to the opportunities afforded to Sir Thomas's chosen doctors when they paid their professional visit. They had been allowed to interview her without Dr Harris in the room, and had even been invited to luncheon. And yet in spite of their advantages, 'these three gentlemen' had in his opinion failed to give a correct diagnosis. What Dr Jones in his heart believed was that Lady Mordaunt would immediately regain 'consciousness' and become her natural self were anyone to say to her 'I have the gratifying duty to perform of telling you that your husband Sir Charles Mordaunt has forgiven you, that the past is forgotten, that you may return to Walton and your house in Chesham Place as soon as you like and resume your former position in society.' It seemed to him that by assuming a peculiarity of conduct for so long, much encouraged by those around her, she had now become the victim of her own attempts to deceive.

When Dr Reynolds sent his report to Mr Hunt, he apologised about its length, saying that he had found it almost impossible to put it into a smaller compass or to come to any firm conclusion. The few facts gleaned in his interview were not really enough to enable him to answer the question as to whether Lady Mordaunt was insane or not. As far as her physical state was concerned, Dr Reynolds thought that she was in good health, her complexion ruddy, even at times 'dusky', and her eyes were bright. He could not see any lack of 'symmetry' in her features, or any inequality in the pupils or any absence of power in her limbs. When he later watched her from the window as she walked in the garden, he observed that her step was firm and steady. This led him to believe that she would be capable of attending to business affairs. 'It is not in accordance with my experience' he wrote 'that a lady of twenty-one years of age should be in such a state of mental fatuity that she could give no directions as to her affairs, she being at the same time in good bodily health, free from the slightest trace of paralysis of either trunk, limb, feature or voice.' The lethargy that Lady Mordaunt evidently suffered from to an increasing degree could easily have been the aftermath of 'strong and exhausting emotions'. On balance, believing it was inconsistent with his experience that the one act of uncleanliness described by Carruthers should necessarily be due to disease of the mind, Dr Reynolds came down on the side of those who felt that Lady Mordaunt was sane enough to deal with her own affairs.

Dr Burrowes took a contrary view. On 12 July he wrote Mr Hunt a short note saying that after observing Lady Mordaunt and listening to her conversation, he had come to the conclusion that she was at that time 'quite incapable of instructing a professional man to conduct her defence in the impending trial'. He did not give any reasons, nor could he precisely define the nature of her unsoundness of mind, and when Mr Hunt asked him to be more specific, he said that he found it hard to form an opinion on the basis of the short interview he had been allowed. He concluded that 'If all the extraneous information is to be excluded and treated as untrustworthy I have not sufficient data upon which to form an opinion.'

Mr Hunt, worried by this reaction, told Dr Burrowes that as there was no need for unanimity among the doctors, he should send in a separate report giving his own opinion 'at the earliest practicable moment'. To help him in his task, Mr Hunt provided him with copies of all the affidavits prepared by the medical observers of 'the other side', as well as those filed on behalf of Sir Charles, pointing out how important the latter were. Dr Burrowes devoted an evening to reading them through and putting into 'connected form' the rough notes he had made after his visit to Worthing. He found the task very perplexing and wrote to Mr Hunt saying that he wished he had been furnished with more information before going down to Worthing. On 21 July Mr Hunt wrote him a letter marked 'Immediate' begging him to send in his report without waiting for any more information. He said that Mr Serjeant Ballantine had impressed on him the need to pass all the relevant reports to the judge by that Saturday at the latest. Burrowes wrote back at once saying that as he had to go out on public business that evening and was embarking on a professional journey the next day, he really had no time to 'write out afresh' the details he had jotted down.

Exasperated by this prevarication, Sir Charles then persuaded his cousin Herbert Murray and his friend Sir John Packington to visit Dr Burrowes in the hope of persuading him to come into line. To their dismay he told them that he intended to say that Lady Mordaunt was insane and unlikely to recover. They then told him that he had far better not put in a report at all. Mr Hunt finally went round to his house and collected the rough notes he had made after his visit to Worthing, and left it at that.

When he read the reports, Lord Penzance could not fail to be struck by the differences of opinion revealed by the various doctors. Whereas Sir Thomas's medical advisers were prepared to accept that Lady Mordaunt had been suffering for months from puerperal mania, Sir Charles's were, with a varying degree of certainty, ready to believe that she had all along been perfectly sane. Most puzzling for the judge was the fact that those who had been present in the weeks following the birth resolutely refused to accept that there had ever been any signs of puerperal fever or mania at that time.

At the hearing before the judge in chambers on 21 July, there was a further postponement due to the fact that there were still a few more affidavits to come. Mr Serjeant Ballantine opened by explaining that certain allegations had been made blaming Sir Charles for causing the many delays. This, he said, was far from being the case. In fact Serjeant Ballantine blamed the delays on the 'voluminous' nature of the affidavits and the time required to read them. The judge finally ordered that the documents should be brought down to his chambers so that he could spend an hour reading them the following Tuesday before dealing with the ordinary summons business.

The special hearing in the judge's private room took place on 27 July, with an imposing array of lawyers, including, on the Moncreiffe side, the Solicitor-General, Sir John Coleridge. The judge, in view of the intense public interest in the case caused as a result of the position held in the fashionable world by the parties involved, not to mention 'the association, according to rumour, of high rank in the suit', had allowed representatives of the press to be present including a reporter from the *Leamington Chronicle*. The judge reminded 'the gentlemen of the press' that in reporting the case they should respect the feelings of the great families involved.

Serjeant Ballantine opened by saying how anxious he was to bring the matter to a conclusion as soon as possible. He quoted the case brought before the late Sir C. Creswell when that judge had refused to continue proceedings because a person involved was obviously insane. On the other hand it had to be said that a judge could continue a trial even if somebody decided to remain obstinately mute.

Yet the Mordaunt case was of such 'peculiarity' that it differed in many ways from anything that had yet been presented in a court of justice. If Lady Mordaunt had really been mad when she made her confessions, then even if she were now sane she would be unable to answer any questions on that subject. Then there was the suggestion that she had been feigning, which made the whole matter far more difficult to fathom.

Serjeant Ballantine pointed out that the judge had no actual power to try the question of madness in chambers and Lord Penzance agreed. It had become increasingly plain that nothing could be done on the basis of the affidavits alone, but that the witnesses would have to be cross-examined in open court before a jury. This could not be done before the start of the next term in three or four months' time. Meanwhile, the health of the lady in question might well improve so much that she would be able to stand up in court herself, exercising her right not only to deny her adultery but to make any counter-charge such as cruelty or neglect on the part of her husband.

This being agreed, the question remained as to what would become of Lady Mordaunt in the intervening time. It was decreed that as the husband still had right of custody, it would be better for Sir Charles to take her into his care. Serjeant Ballantine assured the court that Sir Charles was willing to assume responsibility until the trial, although he would certainly 'like to have one person removed from her to whom much that had occurred was attributed'. This person was Mrs Carruthers.

Sir Thomas was now ordered to answer at once, appearing as 'best friend' for the purpose of setting up that Lady Mordaunt was not in a fit state of mind. His answer was filed on 30 July.

Sir Thomas Moncreiffe, Baronet, appearing herein as guardian ad litem for the Respondent Harriett Sarah Dame Mordaunt, by John Henry Benbow, his solicitor, saith that at the time when the citation in this suit was served upon the said respondent, to wit, on the thirtieth day of April, in the year of our Lord one thousand eight hundred and sixty nine, the said Respondent was not of sound mind, and that she has never since been and she is not now of sound mind.

The next day Benjamin Hunt filed Sir Charles's answer, taking issue on the setting up of his wife's insanity. On 1 August Sir Thomas went down to Worthing and spent the night there. On 3 August the judge, having read the statement and heard counsel on behalf of the Petitioner, directed that the issue be tried before the court by a special jury.

The news that the Mordaunt case had been adjourned until the autumn had soon become common knowledge. Alice Miles described the adjournment as 'a master stroke of Lady Louisa's', adding 'We shall be well into the shooting season then, and even scandal recedes baffled into the background, when weighed in the scales of the masculine mind with partridges, grouse, pheasants and woodcock.'[98]

Already the summer season was drawing to a close and by now London had virtually emptied. Goodwood, Alice Miles observed, had 'cleared out everybody', which made for a dearth of gossip, the few disconsolate Guardsmen left in the metropolis 'reviling their hard fate' as they stared out of the window wondering 'why the deuce a fellah should be put upon in such a way', and pondering whether their friends had backed the right horse for them at the races. Sir Charles, who would normally by now have been heading for the Highlands, was forced to spend his days in London closeted with his lawyers.

27

The Move to Bickley

The judge had now made it clear that on 5 August he would issue an order laying down the conditions on which Sir Charles would reassume the care of his wife. The lawyers would have liked Sir Charles to leave all the arrangements to them, but this he refused to do, as Mr Haynes ruefully explained in a letter to Mr Hunt on 30 July: 'We have had a long conference with Sir Charles today, but have been unable to prevail upon him to leave the matter generally to counsel, as he feels most strongly, and certainly he has ground for so doing from the course which has been pursued by Sir Thomas Moncreiffe.'

Far from allowing unlimited access as Sir Thomas would have liked, Sir Charles had altered the proposed conditions even more stringently, crossing out some of the original recommendations in red ink, and insisting that his letters should actually be read out to the judge in order to make sure they were not overlooked. Always at the back of his mind was the fear that the lawyers would act too leniently on his behalf. For this reason he was determined to see Serjeant Ballantine himself to make sure there was no wavering. Mr Haynes gave directions to Mr Hunt to this effect.

> Please therefore to make an appointment with Serjeant Ballantine for Monday next with such fee as you think right, at which you had better attend, and write tomorrow direct to Sir Charles at Walton Hall and he will be with you on Monday at 11 a.m. Sir Charles will then state his views fully and we must leave it to him and Counsel to settle matters in their own way.

Sir Charles was insistent that all the present staff were to be discontinued, particularly the lunatic nurse Carruthers who, it was believed, had during her stay at Worthing been giving his wife 'daily tuition' in the art of feigning madness. He wanted to reserve for himself the power to choose her lady companion and lady's maid, and to decide where she should live. Her immediate relations, as well as her legal and medical advisers, would be granted right of access on the understanding that they gave two days' notice.

Many details had to be sorted out as quickly as possible. The allocation of costs was of great concern to Sir Charles. Although he was quite prepared to pay all reasonable charges, as well as to continue his wife's pin money, he told Mr Haynes that he was resolutely opposed to making any payments on account, particularly to his father-in-law. He was not keen, either, on the medical advisers being allowed unlimited access, as he was sure that would lead to ruinous expense for somebody, most probably himself.

It had been suggested by the judge that a female relation from each family should be named to stay with Lady Mordaunt, and Blanche Moncreiffe had already been chosen for Sir Thomas. Sir Charles was enraged, however, when it was recommended that his unmarried sister Mary should be put in the position of visiting an immoral woman, and he was equally certain that his married sister's husband 'would not permit such a thing'. Since his mother was excluded and he had no other female relative, he wanted the judge to allow a friend's name to be substituted.

As far as the choice of medical advisers was concerned, the judge, having noted the complaints of unfairness made by Sir Charles's medical men, insisted that two doctors should be appointed, one to be nominated by each party. They would be given equal opportunities for access. Various suggestions were made, and it was then agreed that Dr Reynolds, the more cooperative of the doctors who had visited Lady Mordaunt at Worthing on Sir Charles's behalf, should be his nomination, while Sir Thomas would appoint Dr Gull. Lord Penzance chose as referee, to hold the balance between the other two, Dr Wood, who practised at St Luke's Hospital in Kensington and was experienced in the care of mental patients.

Both doctors were out of town until 4 August, but as soon as they returned, Mr Haynes approached Dr Reynolds, who agreed to take on the task. Mr Haynes then called on Dr Gull at his house in Brook Street, announcing to the servant who greeted him that he had come on urgent business. He was peremptorily told that the doctor was too busy to see him until the following morning. Mr Haynes then sat down to write a note, but before he had finished, the servant came to say that the doctor would see him after all. Mr Haynes was shown into his room and he explained the object of his call. As they stood together, Dr Gull tapped him good-naturedly on the shoulder and said 'Mr Haynes, Lady Mordaunt is certainly ailing, but there is no disguise about it.'

'You will excuse me, doctor' said Mr Haynes 'but we, that is Sir Charles, thinks otherwise.'

Mr Haynes was later told that Dr Gull had 'declined to act unless he had a certificate under the Lunacy Act, as he considered Lady Mordaunt was given in his charge'. Thoroughly exasperated by what he considered to be an unnecessary delay, Mr Haynes wrote a note to Dr Gull pointing out the need for urgency due to the fact that the lease on the Worthing house was just about to run out. As to the certificate, Mr Haynes considered this quite unnecessary as the doctors were not being asked to take charge, simply to visit Lady Mordaunt and make their reports.

Dr Gull replied by saying that he thought a certificate of Lady Mordaunt's mental unsoundness should be made out, otherwise it would be illegal to go on 'restraining' her, as indeed, in his opinion it had been all along. 'I shall be quite willing to act' the doctor promised Mr Haynes 'but I must be assured that I am doing so according to the terms of the law in respect of insane persons.'

The judge now made a custody order which placed much responsibility in the hands of Dr Gull and Dr Reynolds, who were to approve the choice of Lady Mordaunt's lady companion, as well as her servants and visitors. Although Sir Charles and Sir Thomas were to have access at all reasonable times, this too was subject to the control and restrictions thought necessary by the two doctors. As for the money side of things, Sir Charles was required to pay Mr Benbow £300 on account of costs and maintenance up to 10 August and he would thereafter bear the expense of the necessary establishment, as well as footing the medical bills. Lady Mordaunt's pin money would be paid as usual into her bank account at Messrs Greenway and Smith in Warwick. This arrangement was to continue until further order.

Sir Charles was far from pleased by this outcome. Not for the first time the suspicion entered his mind that the judge could be 'partial'. However, to look on the positive side there was now a chance that, given the proper treatment and surrounded by the right people, his wife would regain the equilibrium which had to some extent been upset by the restraints of her life at Worthing.

The place of residence had not been decided by the time the judge issued his order, and the debate continued for some days as to where Lady Mordaunt should go. At first Sir Charles had thought of sending her to Ramsgate, but the doctors favoured somewhere nearer

London in order to make visiting easier. Eventually the Bromley area was suggested as a suitable location, and Sir Charles found a house called Page Heath at Bickley, not far from Chislehurst, where his uncle Francis Murray was the rector. It was a pleasant house, large, light and cheerful, although somewhat expensive to rent, as Sir Charles did not hesitate to point out. It was not too far from the railway station at Bickley.

In spite of the order having been issued, Dr Gull still hesitated, refusing to act without the certificate. Unknown to Sir Charles, he arranged for Lady Mordaunt to come to his house for further assessment, but after seeing her he ended up by being as unsure as everybody else as to whether what he called the 'monotony' of her behaviour was really a symptom of insanity or not. He evidently did not feel able to press for a certificate after that encounter as he agreed to act without it. This was a relief to Sir Charles and his lawyers because they felt that the issue of a certificate would have prejudiced the case from the start.

Sir Charles had a long conference with Dr Haynes on 9 August when he pressed the lawyer to make arrangements for his wife's removal to Bickley. He felt that he had a right to do so, as the order had only specified the place of residence, and not the companions she should have on her journey. He was much exercised as to the choice of 'proper parties' to effect the removal, hoping to find friends rather than mere domestics, although always bearing in mind the danger that any conversations held at this stage could affect their evidence at a later date.

Sir Charles was determined to do all he could to put his wife at her ease during the journey, and with this in view, he expressed himself happy to allow Blanche Moncreiffe to accompany her sister and to stay with her until such time as the doctors had managed to appoint a lady companion. He persuaded Mrs Cadogan 'as an intimate friend' to go too, accompanied by Bird and Dr Orford. Mr Benbow, Sir Thomas's solicitor, was also asked to join the party 'in a friendly but professional way' but he declined, saying that he 'did not know Lady Mordaunt'.

Mrs Cadogan, accompanied by Bird and Mrs Caborn, left London on the morning of 16 August and arrived in Worthing at about midday. They hired a fly from the station, and when they arrived at the house they found Sir Thomas walking in the garden with Dr Harris. He asked them why they had come.

'To fetch Lady Mordaunt' Dr Orford replied.

'On what authority?' Sir Thomas asked.

'On the authority of the order of court' said Dr Orford, adding that he also had written authority from Sir Charles.

Sir Thomas then said that would not be sufficient without an order from Drs Gull and Reynolds for removal. Not of course, that he wished to prevent or forbid them from taking her away. Dr Orford said, if that was the case, why had he bothered to come down to Worthing?

'Merely to point out the difficulty' said Sir Thomas.

Throughout this altercation, Mrs Cadogan and Mrs Caborn had remained in the fly, and when it was suggested that they should come inside to see Lady Mordaunt, they declined and stayed where they were. Dr Orford went into the house with Bird, and Blanche went upstairs to tell her sister they were there. Lady Mordaunt came down and shook hands with Dr Orford, and they talked about the weather for a while, but it seemed that what she really wanted was to hear the latest Walton news. She asked Bird whether the laundry maid Elizabeth had sent all the things back from the Laundry House?

'Oh yes, long ago' Bird replied.

Lady Mordaunt then brought up the subject of Arthur Smith, the Dowager's son, as she had read about his death in the paper. She spoke about the boy very sympathetically, saying how much Mr Smith and Lady Mordaunt must miss him and how sorry Mr Smith in particular must be as Arthur was his only son.

During Bird's conversation, Sir Thomas, Miss Laing and Blanche waited in the small conservatory, making sure they could hear what was being said.

Sir Thomas went out and spoke to Mrs Cadogan, telling her that he would not under any circumstances agree to her accompanying his daughter to Bickley. Mrs Cadogan felt very upset, as she had made the journey at Sir Charles's insistence and at considerable inconvenience to herself. Dr Orford, for his part, had decided that he was not prepared to take the responsibility of removing Lady Mordaunt against her father's wishes, and so there was nothing for it but for the whole party to turn round and go home.

The authority of Dr Gull and Dr Reynolds was then sought and on Friday 20 August Bird went down to Worthing for the second time. Mr Hunt, the London lawyer, accompanied him but did not go to the house, staying in a nearby hotel in case of trouble. This time, however, everything went smoothly. Lady Mordaunt was waiting in the hall, dressed up and ready to go, obviously extremely glad to be leaving the gloomy house at Worthing. Sir Thomas, Blanche and Miss Carruthers were to attend her on the journey. Bird thought that she stood up to the journey very well, joining in the conversation along the way, and seeming cheerful and at ease.

Everyone, including Lady Mordaunt herself, seemed to be impressed by Page Heath, which was described as a 'most delightful and cheerful house'. It was quiet and secluded, surrounded as it was by a pleasant garden, and it had several bedrooms, as well as servants' quarters, a nursery, cellars and stabling.

Sir Thomas went off to London before dinner, but this did not worry his daughter who seemed to enjoy the meal. Bird had brought grapes from the vinery at Walton and Lady Mordaunt pronounced them 'very fine'. He had also brought some beans but she seemed disappointed that there was no fish, and she asked Bird if he had caught any lately, harking back as always to the times when they had caught perch together, sitting by the brook. Although nobody had mentioned the baby, she proposed that they should drink Violet's health.

After dinner Bird noticed that Lady Mordaunt suddenly became what he described as 'absent'. He could not tell whether her vacant stare was assumed or not, but he thought it could be accounted for by the fact that she had not quite settled in yet at the new house. Later that evening he heard her laughing in a strange, uncanny way.

The next morning Lady Mordaunt asked whether any books had come from Bubbs's Library. She also asked for *Punch*, but Blanche explained that the last number had accidentally been left at Worthing. In the ensuing days she often harked back to Walton, questioning Bird about what was going on there, apparently pleased to find somebody who would talk to her about the people she had known on the estate. She surprised Bird with her good memory for people and facts. One day she asked him if the toasting cheese was now all finished. He replied that it had gone discoloured and could not be kept and she then talked about the woman who had made it. Bird had forgotten her name, but Lady Mordaunt had not. When they had cheese for lunch she asked whether it came from Sir Charles's estate in Somerset, which in fact it did. She also asked after the Padburys, the bakers at Wellesbourne, and wanted to know if they were getting on better. Bird was impressed by what she could remember, which was strange in view of the fact that Dr Priestley and Dr Gull had declared that her memory was 'annihilated'.

On their first Sunday at Page Heath the sisters went out for a drive in a hired carriage with Bird in attendance, enjoying and remarking on the beauty of the countryside.

When Sir Thomas came down for an hour that evening, he agreed with Bird that his daughter was better. Bird recorded that she behaved well in front of her father. Sir Thomas sat with the sisters while they ate, but did not dine himself. The next day Lady Mordaunt seemed very quiet, neither talking nor laughing. She went out for a drive at seven in the evening, drank some whisky and water and went to bed.

On 25 August Dr Reynolds, acting for Sir Charles, reported on the current situation at Bickley, having visited Lady Mordaunt that day in the company of Dr Gull, who was acting for Sir Thomas, and Dr Hughes, a local doctor from Bromley who had been nominated by Dr Reynolds to look after her on a day-to-day basis. Dr Reynolds had known Dr Hughes for several years, and felt that he was everything that could be desired for the purpose. He was to take his duties seriously, calling at least twice a week, making fifty-one visits in all during Lady Mordaunt's stay at Page Heath, and often staying with her for hours at a time, all at Sir Charles's expense.

The next choice that had to be made was a replacement for Mrs Carruthers. It was again Dr Reynolds who made a recommendation, suggesting that one Sarah Barker, who had been employed for five years by a friend of his as a parlour maid, should fit the bill. Dr Gull agreed and Sarah Barker was appointed. She was to combine the duties of parlour maid, lady's maid and nurse, sleeping in Lady Mordaunt's room and spending much of the day with her as well. She and all the other attendants had been told to keep a diary, and it seems that Lady Louisa also instructed her to write regular letters about Lady Mordaunt's behaviour.

Some difficulty was experienced in finding a lady companion to replace Jane Laing, as Dr Reynolds explained to Mr Haynes:

The peculiar position in which Lady Mordaunt is placed renders some ladies a little reluctant to take upon themselves the office and one whom I nominated and who was approved by Dr Gull was obliged to withdraw at the instance of her mother, however I have found another lady, the daughter of a medical man whom

I have known for some considerable time and who will I believe undertake the duty.

Dr Reynolds wrote again on 29 August to say that this lady, a Miss Keddell, had accepted the post. The only drawback was that she would not be able to start for at least a month, so provided Sir Charles did not object he had agreed that Blanche should stay on at Bickley for the time being to fill the gap. This was agreed. It was also agreed that if Bird should be called away to join Sir Charles in Scotland, his place should be taken by another Mordaunt retainer, Leon, or Lewin, Cotterill, the footman at Walton, who was known to be steady and 'clean in appearance'. Dr Reynolds thought it desirable that there should always be a man in the house.

The doctors did not leave Lady Mordaunt alone for long, and Bird soon realised that she dreaded their visits. He described how she began to get fidgety and cross as soon as the telegram arrived announcing that Dr Gull and Dr Reynolds would visit her on Wednesday 23 August. It seemed that day as if nothing was right. She began to act really strangely, going up the steep back stairs to the maidservant's room, and then to Mrs Caborn's room, which, being over the kitchen, was very hot. Bird advised her to return to her own room where it was cooler. She also went to Bird's room and sat on the bed for a while.

As soon as they arrived the doctors started telling Lady Mordaunt what a grave position she was in. At the same time Dr Reynolds held her pulse to see what effect this would have on her, and was perhaps disappointed to find that it had none. When they said they wanted to do everything they could for her, and asked if there was anything she would like, she thought for a bit and then said that she would like a Newfoundland dog. She also asked for some toothpicks, which Bird knew she was not normally in the habit of using.

That evening, after the doctors had gone and she had been out for a drive she asked Bird if he could remember the name of the man who had brought her the paper at Walton; he realised later that she was referring to the petition served on her by Mr Haynes. Later in the evening she had one of her laughing fits, standing in the passage, and when Bird asked her what made her laugh, she made no answer, but stared at him vacantly. When she was going upstairs to bed, she said 'Bird, you need not sit up; Sir Charles will put the gas out.' Bird realised that she said this because at Walton Sir Charles had always waited until everyone else had gone up to bed before making sure that all the gas lights had been put out. There was, however, no gas at Page Heath.

Noticing how upset the doctors had made Lady Mordaunt, Mrs Caborn asked her whether she liked any of them. She replied that of all the doctors she had seen, she thought Dr Priestley was the most sensible, and when Mrs Caborn asked if she liked Dr Gull and Dr Reynolds, she replied 'I like Dr Reynolds, but Dr Gull always frightens me.'

The next morning Bird asked her if Mr Haynes was the person she had meant when she had talked of him bringing the paper to Walton, and she said, yes, that was the name. From this Bird deduced that the doctors had been talking to her about the petition. She asked him twice for Osbert's address, and also wanted to know whether Sir Charles had paid Jessie Clarke's wages.

On Saturday 28 August Lady Mordaunt asked Bird what time the train went to Warwick, as she intended going to Walton. He said he would look it up and let her know. At dinner she asked where Sir Charles was and Bird told her that he was now at Corrour, shooting grouse. She inquired whether his letters and papers were being properly sent on. Bird told her they were, but she made no comment. On the Sunday she inquired if Bird had found out the times of the trains and added that she would like her things packed for her journey to Walton. Bird told her 'in a very quiet way' that he was afraid it was useless to think of going as Sir Charles would not meet her there and, he added, 'I doubt whether he would allow your ladyship to go till something was done with regard to getting yourself out of the very serious position you have put yourself in.'

Bird reminded her that the doctors had done their best to assist her and that many eminent lawyers would be glad to help.

'Yes, to get me through the divorce court I suppose' she said with some bitterness.

It was part of Bird's mission to persuade Lady Mordaunt that she should confide in somebody, in order to get all her troubles off her mind. It was hoped that if she really started talking to someone sympathetic, she could be brought to see the value of pushing ahead with the divorce. Bird suggested that she might like to see the Dowager Lady Mordaunt, or her sister-in-law Miss Mary, or Mr Osbert. She replied that she would like to see Miss Mordaunt very much, but not Mr Osbert as he had not behaved very well towards her before she left. Bird said, on the contrary, he had been very kind to her.

'No,' she said, 'he made me look so very small.'

She added that she did not like to be treated like that, but, Bird wrote in his diary,

I said I was afraid, my Lady, it was your own fault. What did you tell Sir Charles, he was not the father of the child but Lord Cole was? You could hardly expect Sir Charles to take your Ladyship and child again after that. She said there was a great deal more made of her confession at her confinement than there ought to have been.

Lady Mordaunt then said that Sir Charles had married her to take care of her, and now he had sent her away from Walton.

'My lady, pardon me, what have you been sent away for, and could Sir Charles do otherwise?' Bird asked.

She still thought she could go back if she promised that 'she would not do it again'.

Bird asked her sharply what she meant, but she would not answer, and later that day her behaviour became eccentric; she was found going down to the cellar, saying that she wanted to see something, and Bird told her there was nothing to see, except a great many bottles. Later, they found her hat in the garden, full of stones. At breakfast next morning, she inquired why Sir Charles did not send any grouse, but Bird explained that the weather being so hot, they would not keep.

Lady Mordaunt was obviously unhappy. Her first pleasure at moving to Page Heath had already begun to wear off. Although the old retainers from Walton were kindly and attentive, she was still virtually a prisoner. And above all, life was extremely dull. Bickley in September was not a lively place. There was nothing to look forward to, and little to do except to go for walks or drive about in the surrounding countryside. At first she went out in a hired cab, a degrading form of transport for somebody who was used to travelling in her own carriage. Probably thinking of the days when she had driven the two grey ponies along the Warwickshire lanes, she now asked hopefully whether there was a pony carriage available. Later a close carriage was sent down from Walton for her use. She did not like that particularly either and so Bird asked the groom Stevenson to send Sir Charles's open carriage and pair. This arrived with the two chestnut horses, providing her with a stylish equipage. Soon after their arrival, Lady Mordaunt asked the coachman, Charles Sandford, whether he would let her drive them, but he refused. She took an interest in the horses, going round to the stables to feed them with carrots as she had done at Walton, and she often asked questions about them, inquiring whether the mare was lame, as she had the habit of knocking her legs.

The new maid, Sarah Barker, arrived on 7 September. Lady Mordaunt at first appeared to take to her, as she was less obtrusive than Carruthers and she did at least allow her to go shopping on occasions. But as time went on she began to find her too domineering like all the others.

'You had better change places and be Lady Mordaunt and sit in the drawing room and dine in the dining room' she told the maid.

Although at first Lady Mordaunt had appeared to be remarkably amenable, as the days went monotonously by she grew more restless, running up and down stairs and wandering through the rooms. She began to show a strange tendency to spit when out in the carriage, or even, on one occasion, in the drawing room. In her frustration she would open the carriage door when it was in motion, and once, as if in a desperate bid for freedom, she jumped out of the carriage and made off on her own so that Barker had been obliged to run after her along the road to Chislehurst. The lady's maid, obeying instructions, wrote to Lady Louisa on several occasions, giving full weight to Lady Mordaunt's peculiarities.

Bird, however, thought that all in all, apart from the hysterical laughter and the vacant look which he noticed from time to time, Lady Mordaunt had settled reasonably well. She seemed to him to be quite 'sensible' on the whole, and he thought she was definitely capable of carrying on a coherent conversation. All the same, those around her found her at times extremely trying. Barker wondered at first how long she would be able to stand her restlessness and oddness. Lady Mordaunt, for her part, often complained to Bird about those around her, saying that she wanted to get rid of them because 'they did not keep their place'. Bird thought she did not like them because they were too firm, which they were obliged to be in order to 'keep her anywhere near right'. What seemed to upset her most of all was her loss of status. No longer in charge of her own destiny, she was unable to leave the house without permission, or to go out of her room at night. Bird was in charge of her money and she worried about whether or not the servants had been paid. She hated the way she was told what to do, as this made her feel 'small'. Equally, she disliked the way doctors were sent to see her, observing her and asking her endless questions. It was not surprising that she often seemed listless and apathetic. She developed a worrying tendency to hide things; a letter from Mrs Hancox was found behind a fire brick in the drawing-room grate, and one of the maids discovered her wedding ring in the fireplace.

One day when she had been in a disturbed state, laughing and crying by turns, she deliberately cut her hand at dinner with a knife. Bird mopped up the blood with some bread and got a rag to tie it up. She began to cry.

Sometimes she seemed better than others, asking quite normally about the household accounts or playing backgammon. One day she addressed a letter to Miss Bowen, Ironmonger, London Bazaar, Parade, Leamington, requesting that a good child's rattle should be sent to Walton. This letter Bird did not send, but one that she wrote to Sir Charles was duly despatched and delivered.

Dear Charlie,

If you are in the way of shooting any good stags at Crewe [Corrour] will you try and bring home a head to put up in the nursery at home. I am getting on better and hope to see you soon.

Yours affectionately,

H. MORDAUNT

The next day she was in what Bird described as a 'peculiar' state. She wanted hot beer for breakfast instead of tea. Bird told her it would give her a headache. She was much wilder about the eyes than Bird had ever seen her. At dinner she slid off her chair under the table and had to be lifted up by Blanche and Bird, whereupon she spat on the carpet. She also stood in the dark passage for a while. That evening, when Bird was at the writing desk in his bedroom, she came in wearing her nightgown and stood there laughing; she had got out of bed while her maid was undressing in the next room. Bird asked her what she wanted at that time of night and then Barker came and took her away. Next morning when he asked her if she recalled the incident, she said, yes, it was a mistake. But Barker always locked her into the bedroom after that.

When Mr Hughes came she seemed to be more normal, even though the doctor asked her what Bird described as 'silly questions'.

She looked better about the eyes, but still behaved eccentrically at times, and she was frequently seen standing by herself with her hand on her head.

The reports sent through to Sir Charles made it plain that all attempts had so far failed to gain his wife's confidence and it was hard to know what should now be done. The trouble was that as soon as anybody got anywhere near a renewed confession, she would take refuge in silence and then start to act oddly. Bird could not make it out at all; sometimes she would behave quite normally, and he would have hopes that she was on the mend, and then she would have a relapse and do something strange, like asking if there was any pastry for breakfast. To this Bird replied 'Certainly not', it was not used at breakfast. He suspected that she was being deliberately difficult. One evening at dinner she asked if the men were going out that night and could get her some blue cotton, and Bird had to remind her that by now the shops would be shut. Another time she would be quite rational, playing the piano and singing, much as she had done at Walton, and asking sensible questions, such as whether the croquet set that he had sent for from Walton had arrived or not.

Lady Mordaunt had begun to show some interest in her own family and when she heard that her sister, the Duchess of Atholl, had given birth to her first son, she expressed pleasure, and said that she would buy some toys for the baby. The news later came through that the baby had only lived for a day.

It soon became clear that Lady Mordaunt resented the fact that her younger sister had been given the task of watching over her. Whenever Blanche was around, she would become more assertive with the servants, giving orders, and showing signs of being put out if she was not obeyed. For example she asked Bird to rearrange the fire, although there seemed to be nothing wrong with it. She altered the bill of fare in the cook's book, and moved the furniture in the drawing room rather pointlessly, saying that it would keep the glass door from slamming, Bird's comment being that it would have been all very well if there had been any wind. One day at lunch she told her long-suffering sister that she wished she would go away.

'For I hate you,' she said.

By now both sisters were reaching the end of their tether, but it was still some time before Miss Keddell would be free to take over the job and a temporary replacement had to be found. Meanwhile Mrs Herbert Murray, the wife of Sir Charles's uncle, expressed a willingness to move in for a couple of weeks even though it meant leaving her own young family in London. Sir Charles accepted her offer with gratitude. The approval of Dr Wood, the 'referee', had to be sought, but he was altogether in agreement. In his opinion it was imperative that Lady Mordaunt should not be left altogether in the hands of servants and he felt that Mrs Murray was a very suitable person to fill the gap. When Bird asked Lady Mordaunt what she thought of the idea she seemed pleased, remarking that her old friend Captain Vivian was Mrs Murray's uncle. She told Bird she was glad that it would give Blanche a chance to go home. After all, she added, she would be going home herself shortly. Bird told her once again that this was not possible, and he pressed her to consult her friends, and to get the whole thing settled without further delay. He pointed out that if there were a divorce, both she and Sir Charles would be free to marry again, whereas if she remained in the state she was, what would become of her? She would, as Bird put it, 'very likely be shut up in some place where she would not be able to do as she liked'. She replied by saying that she wished her friends would come and take her away, or why not Sir Charles who, after all had 'legs, feet and boots'.

Sometimes Lady Mordaunt seemed to have forgotten about her baby, and when Mrs Hancox wrote enclosing the latest photograph of Violet, she did not seem in the least interested. At other times she had her little daughter very much on her mind, and one evening at dinner she called Bird in and asked him 'to write to the Dow [the Dowager Lady Mordaunt] to send baby'. She said she would like to see her child, but not Mrs Hancox, and she asked whether Maria could bring her. Bird had to point out that Maria had left Walton some time before and had found another place somewhere. He would have liked to arrange for the baby to come, but he thought it would be impossible to do anything as Dr Reynolds and Dr Gull were both away and nothing could be arranged without their sanction.

Bird frequently overheard Lady Mordaunt talking to Blanche about Sir Charles, asking why he did not come and take her away. One day, when she was out in the carriage with her sister, she seemed very upset.

'Oh Blanche, you do not know what it is to be without one's husband and baby' she said in a tone of great sadness.

It had been decided that Mrs Caborn should return to Walton for a few days, and Florence Stephens the cook at Walton was sent in her place. Lady Mordaunt seemed delighted by this turn of events, as she had always liked Stephens, who was far less domineering than Mrs

Caborn. She brought the croquet set as well as some flowers and fruit. When she went into the drawing room on her arrival, Lady Mordaunt greeted her warmly.

'Stephens, how are you – are you quite well?' she asked. She immediately began asking about all the people she had left behind at Walton. When Stephens told her about the flowers she had brought, Lady Mordaunt said 'Yes, I have seen them. They are rather too much blown', which in fact they were.

Lady Mordaunt was concerned about the smallness of the kitchen, and hoped that Stephens would not find it inconvenient and would not miss having a scullery maid. She began to talk freely about old times, asking Bird, somewhat out of the blue, what was the name of Sir Frederic Johnstone's valet. Next morning Lady Mordaunt called Stephens into the dining room asking her to bring the bill of fare, and then proceeded to order lunch and dinner, just as she had done at Walton, remembering things that she had particularly liked on the menu in the past. After breakfast she picked up *The Times* and began reading the births and deaths as she had always done at home. Bird asked her if she had heard the thunder and lightning the night before and she replied 'I should think I did.'

For lunch they had some bass which Lady Mordaunt said was not quite so good as it had been at Walton. Both Bird and Blanche noticed how much better she seemed and how sensible her conversation was. She was in fact quite herself again, and 'very good company', as Bird put it. In the evening, however, there was a minor crisis. The maid came to warn Bird that Lady Mordaunt had put on her hat and gone out. Bird found her wandering along the road in a leisurely kind of way. When he asked what she was doing, walking in the dark, she replied that she thought it would help clear the headache which had come on during the afternoon. She agreed to return without any difficulty and still seemed to be in a good mood, drinking champagne that evening at dinner.

Probably the reason why Lady Mordaunt liked Stephens was that she came in and took orders, rather than giving them. This encouraged her to take a more intelligent interest in the running of the household, and she was soon to be heard discussing the different ways of cooking the grouse that had been sent by Sir Charles and Mrs Forbes, or asking if the maids had made the beds, or whether there were any fly papers as there were so many flies about. Sometimes Lady Mordaunt would alter what was put down on the menu slate, and sometimes she would assent to it. She had her own ideas, too, for example suggesting that Mrs Stephens should cook some plaice with 'a little water souchet', and follow it with toasted cheese. She had very definite likes and dislikes: she was very fond of pigeon pie and potted grouse, as well as the scones Mrs Stephens made for breakfast, and she particularly approved of her soup.

'When baby comes,' Lady Mordaunt said, 'I should like you to make some white soup, the same as you have made before for me. I shall have the baby here bye and bye' she added. Bird suggested that she should ask the doctors about this, but she said she could not see the use of the doctors as they all seemed to have the same opinion. Bird told her he thought doctors usually formed opinions of their own.

The only time Lady Mordaunt seemed annoyed with Stephens was when she sent a message via Bird asking her to come in without her slate and Stephens turned up with the slate in her hand in apparent defiance of orders. One day she mentioned about the ducks that had been sent from the farm as all Taylor's had been taken by the foxes. 'Poor Taylor' she said, laughing as she always did when the gamekeeper's name was mentioned. Sometimes she confided in the cook a little, telling her how much she hated inquisitive people.

When Blanche decided to go away for two days, she asked Bird to accompany her to Waterloo. He had expected to get back in time for dinner, but returned later than he had intended. Barker took over the waiting that evening, and when she went in with the dinner, Lady Mordaunt asked her where Bird had got to. He arrived when she was half way through her soup, and she was angry with him and told him that he ought to have asked permission to accompany Miss Moncreiffe. The fact that he had not, she said, 'made her look so little'. Bird understood what she meant, in fact he thought it was a sensible comment, and he admitted that he ought to have let her know. But she told him that he had treated her unkindly. 'I said I was very sorry to hear her say so' Bird wrote in his diary, adding that he tried to assure her that he had not the remotest idea of

> hurting her, her family or any member of it with the slightest disrespect and I thought she ought to know me better than think so and I felt much hurt at it. I left the room and came back in about ten minutes with sweets. She was standing by the fire place. She came towards me and took my hand in both of hers

and said, 'Bird, forget and forgive. I am very cross tonight.'
I said 'Very well my Lady, think nothing more of it.' I then
told her we had some grouse from Corrour. She enquired if Sir
Charles had shot any deer. I said I thought not.

For the rest of the evening, Bird reported, Lady Mordaunt seemed
quite good-tempered and pleasant, talking as always about the past.

Bird never ceased to be amazed by what Lady Mordaunt could
remember. Mrs Caborn agreed with him and thought that Dr
Hughes, Barker and the other doctors were quite wrong when they
said that she had no memory at all. In fact Mrs Caborn thought that
Lady Mordaunt could remember things better than she could herself.
Bird described how one day when they were out driving, she asked
him if he recollected the time when they had come home from
Virginia Water in Captain Chaplin's drag, missing the train and
getting home very late. He also recalled how she had talked about her
sister-in-law Alice Portman, and had asked whether Alice's little
daughter Ethel would be with her when she went to stay at Goldicote
with the Dow. Bird thought this was remarkable, as he himself would
have been quite unable to remember the child's name. He said, surely
Ethel was a boy's name but she insisted it was a girl's name, which
once again proved to Bird how good her memory was.

Lady Mordaunt could also at times be remarkably observant, and
Bird was impressed when she remarked on the pin that he was wearing in his scarf, which she said was very like the one that Sir Charles
had given her to fasten her shawl.

'Why, Bird, you are wearing one of Sir Charles's pins' she said.

'No, my lady, but it is certainly very like one of his.'

'Yes, one he gave me to wear in my shawl' she told him firmly.

Any reminder of Sir Charles would immediately start her wondering why he did not come to take her away 'from this dull place' where
there was nothing to see and nothing to do. On Sunday 12 September,
when she was alone with Bird, Lady Mordaunt asked him if he knew
when Sir Charles would be coming. Bird told her that he was afraid
Sir Charles would not come to Bickley, nor give permission for her to
go to Walton, until the case was either settled in the Divorce Court or
by some other means, and the matter of Sir Frederic Johnstone and
Lord Cole was cleared up.

'You know your ladyship told him he was not the father but Lord
Cole was' said Bird.

'Mrs Cadogan should never have been put in possession of the facts of my confession' was Lady Mordaunt's reply.

'It was your ladyship that told Mrs Cadogan – not only her but several others' said Bird.

Bird told her that she would be wise to seek advice from her friends and relations and from Dr Gull and Dr Reynolds, who would be only too glad to help her. He thought that she should ask for guidance when they came to see her later in the week.

'What use would one woman be against twenty men?' she asked.

Bird ignored her question and reminded her about the 'awful exposure' that would result if the case were to be tried in open court, with all the evidence being published in the newspapers. She asked what would become of the evidence if it was not opposed in court, and Bird told her he thought it would be suppressed, but of course that was only his opinion. He reminded her that a divorce would leave her free to marry again, instead of ending up confined in 'some place'.

'My lady, perhaps I am talking too much for you, stop me at once if I am' said Bird.

'No, Bird, I like you to talk about it for no one else will' she replied.

After that she changed the subject and talked about Walton, about the honey that Taylor had given her, and the mare Armchair which had been so good at jumping ditches out hunting. She told Bird that she had preferred Armchair to her other horse, Dandy, which had always struck her as being more like a pack-horse. Even so somebody had once offered her £300 for him and she had never ceased to regret the fact that she had refused the offer. Her mind went continually back to Walton and she evidently enjoyed having someone to reminisce with. She asked Bird if he remembered herself and Miss Scott making toffee in the nursery kitchen and burning two saucepans.

She also said I ought to be pensioned off and have a farm (most sensible idea I thought) for I knew too much about the family matters. I said I hoped she did not think I abused that knowledge. 'Oh no' she answered 'only you know too much for those just coming into the family' . . . She also spoke about the Hermitage getting blown [up] at Dunkeld, what a wicked thing to do and the Duke had not money to spare in that way etc. She put out candles in the drawing-room, first lighting her flat one to light her upstairs.

Blanche returned next morning, and at lunch Lady Mordaunt hid her plate of pigeon pie in the sideboard drawer. 'Miss Blanche asked me to go in and see if she would not eat something' Bird recounted. 'I did so but she told me that if she had wanted any lunch she would not have come in here.' Believing that she might be ill, Bird thought it better if the carriage did not come round that afternoon, but she contradicted him, telling him that she thought it was a hard thing that she could not do as she liked about lunch without people dictating, 'meaning doubtless Miss Blanche and self' wrote Bird.

At dinner, after the drive, Lady Mordaunt was very talkative, remembering the tenant farmers at Walton – Gibbs, Hitchcox and Biddle, saying how she thought the first was rather good looking but delicate, and the second was rather more 'durable', perhaps because he had such a good wife.

The night before Blanche left for Scotland, the sisters drank wine at dinner and finished with sherry and water before going up to bed. The next morning Lady Mordaunt seemed a little on edge, but Bird thought this was due to the fact that she had drunk more wine than she was used to, and not because Miss Blanche was going away. In fact Lady Mordaunt did not seem at all put out by her sister's departure. She was much more upset when she heard that Stephens was leaving, especially as this meant that Mrs Caborn was due to return. She asked Bird why Stephens had to go. She said it seemed a pity as Stephens made things so very nice.

The day before Stephens left, Lady Mordaunt asked when Mrs Caborn was coming, complaining that she had not heard from her at all. 'In fact I never get letters now from any one' she said, adding that she often thought the postman must be dead. Before Mrs Stephens left, Lady Mordaunt asked her to make up her account. Stephens said that she had already made it up, and that Bird had paid it.

Mrs Herbert Murray arrived on 17 September, her visit sanctioned by Dr Wood, as Dr Gull and Dr Reynolds were both still away. Lady Mordaunt received her well, but she seemed rather unsettled as she always did when there was any change in her circumstances. Bird hoped that Mrs Murray would be able to discuss matters with her frankly, telling her the facts about her present situation, which he believed her sister had not been able to do. Bird even suspected that

Miss Blanche had never been told the facts herself, her parents not wishing to corrupt her.

On her first night at Page Heath, Mrs Murray had told Harriett that she wanted to be her friend and to help her as much as possible.

'I know everything, and all the sad trouble you have been in' said Mrs Murray.

At that Harriett flushed and said 'I know I have been very wicked but I did not know it at the time.'

Shocked as she was by Harriett's circumstances, and believing that it was quite wrong for a young girl to be shut away from the world and deprived of her freedom, Mrs Murray felt that Harriett should be taken away from Page Heath as soon as possible.

'I wish you could be in London when the winter comes, then I could often see you' Mrs Murray said at dinner, explaining that she thought Page Heath would be far too 'dull' when the cold weather came.

'I should like that,' Harriett replied, 'but I should like the baby to be there too.' She told Mrs Murray that she did not want the baby 'to be looked down upon'.

Mrs Murray also brought up the subject of Mrs Cadogan, believing that she might perhaps be able to act as a confidante.

'Was she not a great friend of yours?' Mrs Murray asked, but Harriett replied that she was only 'rather' a friend, adding after a silence that 'people had no business to talk'.

'But it was you that talked yourself and told Charlie everything' said Mrs Murray in some amazement.

Harriett, who had felt betrayed by Mrs Hancox and Mrs Cadogan for abusing her confidence, broke out angrily 'And what business had Charlie to go jabbering about it to other ladies?' She paused for a moment and then said to Mrs Murray 'Do you call yourself a lady?'

'I hope so' Mrs Murray replied.

'Then what do you come ferreting about here for?' she asked.

Mrs Murray said that she had not come to ferret, as in any case she knew everything already. 'I have only come to stay with you when no one else would' she added.

After a long pause Harriett said 'Don't you ever make your daughter marry a man she does not care for.'

Mrs Murray was taken aback by this remark. 'But did you not then care for Charles?' she asked. 'Surely you did!'

'I did not when I married him, but I did afterwards' was Harriett's reply.

'What could make you do such foolish things – surely you could not care for all those men?'

'No I did not,' said Harriett, 'only one.' But she did not say who that one was.

Mrs Murray then asked her whether if she went back to Charles she would still care for him and she said 'Oh yes.'

On the following day Harriett once again reiterated how she did not want the baby to be looked down on, and in the course of a conversation after dinner she asked Mrs Murray if she knew what it was 'to have a husband and yet not to have a husband – one who cares only for fishing, hunting and shooting, and thinks you only a pretty stupid little fool'.

When they were discussing the Marquess of Waterford's divorce case which was at that time in the public eye, Mrs Murray remarked that she had no patience with men behaving as they did and getting away with it. Harriett agreed.

'Yes, we have to bear all the ignominy' she said.

Conversations like this took place between them every day, and although they proved to Mrs Murray that Harriett was in some anguish, she never thought of her as an insane person, or treated her as such. Mrs Caborn noticed how kind Mrs Murray always was to Lady Mordaunt, who responded by behaving well and naturally, always making sure that she was on time for breakfast, and calling for Mrs Murray on the way downstairs. Sometimes Mrs Murray read to her, and she seemed to enjoy the reading in a natural and happy way. Like everybody else, however, Mrs Murray noticed the change that came over her whenever any of the doctors were announced. She would become 'mute and still' and hardly say a word.

On Mrs Murray's second day at Bickley, Dr Wood, 'the referee', paid his first visit to Page Heath, accompanied by Dr Hughes. When he arrived Lady Mordaunt was upstairs getting dressed for a walk and she appeared in the drawing-room with her hat and gloves on. Mr Hughes introduced her to Dr Wood and she said rather defensively 'I am very well.' Dr Wood said that he was glad to hear it, and suggested that they should sit down and have a chat. He settled himself beside her on the sofa, and asked her various questions which she answered without too much delay. When he asked her how long she had been at Page Heath she did not reply, and he repeated the question several times before she said that she did not know exactly. When he repeated the question yet again, she gave various replies, laughing 'as if there were some joke involved'. He then tried to impress on her that it was a very serious matter and that he could see nothing in it to laugh about. He told her that he was appointed by the judge, that he did not come as a partisan and that any attempt at acting a part would create a most unfavourable impression. He told her that he was very experienced in such matters, and that she must not try to deceive him. She then looked him straight in the eyes and said 'What do they blame me for?' He told her that she knew perfectly well, that it was unnecessary for him to go into any details, and he begged her to be candid with him. In return he promised to answer any question she might put to him. She remained silent after that, and he then asked to feel her pulse. Still saying nothing, she held out her tightly gloved hand, and when he asked her to remove her glove, she pulled it about half off and then gave up 'almost as if drowsiness had overtaken her'. The doctor noted that her pulse was slow and her hand cold and clammy. After this he asked her whether she was wearing boots or shoes, to which she replied, 'Boots', which was the correct answer. He then asked her to remove them and she obediently did so. He felt her feet and found that they too were cold, which led him to the rather obvious conclusion that her circulation was bad. When he asked permission to look into her eyes, she meekly went to the window as instructed, but couldn't resist smiling as if she found the whole situation rather amusing.

After this she sat down near the piano which gave Dr Wood the idea of asking her to play. He asked her if she was fond of music, and she said 'Yes', and inquired whether he was. He replied in the affirmative, and asked if she would sing for them. She made 'a movement of acquiescence' at once and went to the piano. As he looked through her pile of music, Dr Wood's attention was caught by a song of Lord Houghton's called 'Strangers Yet' and he asked her to sing it, placing the music in front of her when she agreed. 'It was evident' Dr Wood rather unkindly wrote 'that she was not a very efficient performer', but after some hesitancy, a few wrong notes which she at once corrected, and some rather shaky timing, she started to sing in a voice which Dr Wood described as weak and uncertain:

> Strangers yet, after many years of life together
> After fair and stormy weather;
> After travel in fair lands;
> After touch of wedded hands.

Why thus joined? Why ever met,
If they must be strangers yet,
After childhood's winning ways,
After care and blame and praise?[99]

About half way through the verse, the similarity of the words to
her own position seemed to overcome her and she burst into tears.
After a while, Dr Wood asked her to sing again, which she did,
the tears still rolling down her face. This struck him as showing a
somewhat unnatural docility. When she eventually broke down completely Dr Wood asked her what it was that was distressing her. 'It's
very foolish, it's only hysterical' she told him. He asked her if she
used to sing the song at home and when she said 'Yes', the tears
started to flow again.

Dr Wood then started to talk about the baby, and Lady Mordaunt
repeatedly expressed a wish to see her child. Just before he left he
looked round the room to see 'what purposeless act' he could ask her
to perform 'for the purpose of still further testing her docility'. He
took a porcelain vase off the mantelpiece and asked her to hold it in a
certain position and then requested her to turn it upside down, which
she did without question, and then put it back on the shelf when he
told her to. She could have been forgiven for questioning the doctor's
sanity herself in asking her to do such a pointless thing, but she did
not. When Dr Wood was about to go, she once again expressed a
wish to see the baby, which he promised to try and arrange.

After the he had gone, Lady Mordaunt found Bird looking at Lord
Houghton's song.

'What beautiful words' he said.

Lady Mordaunt sat down at the piano and began to play and sing
the song again. She did not finish it, and when after lunch the maid
brought her things for going out she was found burning the song
sheet. After that Bird reported that she seemed 'very peculiar' and she
started laughing a great deal.

The next day, 19 September, she was better and Bird took the
liberty of suggesting that she might write some letters before going
out for her walk. She replied sadly that she had none to write. Bird
was then bold enough to suggest that Sir Charles might come to see
her and talk about the affair, which would give her an opportunity to
apologise for the injury she had done by her infidelity. Bird spoke out
plainly about how she stood and what the consequences would be,

mentioning the names of the four she had 'done wrong with'. She then spoke for the first time and said 'Sir Charles had no business to take away my letters.'

'Just put yourself in the same place as Sir Charles' said Bird. 'He tells you he has been familiar and done wrong with other ladies. Would you not if you could find any and take them away and use them against him as he will undoubtedly use yours against you at the trial?'

She thought a little, and said 'I suppose so.' But she added that she thought there was 'no business to be a trial about it'.

'How can it be avoided, your ladyship, if you will not do anything to try and prevent it?' Bird asked her. 'Imagine to yourself the exposure and disgrace it will bring on many families.'

By this time Lady Mordaunt's mind seemed to have switched away from the subject and later, after the conversation had ended, she seemed to be very disturbed. Mrs Caborn found her burning the book in which the meals were recorded, and on the afternoon walk she behaved strangely; she sat down in the road and asked for a fly to take her home.

28

The Murrays

Although Mrs Murray felt that she got on well with Harriett, she became increasingly worried by the situation at Bickley. She had come down to Page Heath sincerely hoping that if she treated Harriett with kindness she would behave more normally, and might in the end confide in her. The strain of trying to deal with her was beginning to tell on her own health and one day she had such a bad headache that she was unable to accompany Harriett on the afternoon drive. On her return Harriett found Mrs Murray lying down in her room. She seemed rather put out and asked what had caused her headache.

'Partly thinking and worrying about you' said Mrs Murray.

'Why do you worry?' she asked.

'Because I know so well what is before you if you persist in the foolish manner you often have, now you know you must be taken away from us all and can never go back to Walton.'

'If that is so' she asked, 'why does not Charlie come and tell me so?'

Mrs Murray then asked whether Harriett would like to seek help from somebody in the family, suggesting that her husband, Mr Herbert Murray, might be able to give her some advice. Harriett said that she would like to confide in him, and she then kissed Mrs Murray and for a few minutes seemed lost in thought, eventually putting her hands behind her head and saying 'What shall I do, what shall I do?' Mrs Murray advised her to try and help herself along the lines she had suggested, but she changed the subject. On subsequent occasions, when they started to talk things over, Harriett would always break off in the middle with the same anguished cry, 'What shall I do?' Mrs Murray thought that if only she had felt able to press her harder, Harriett would have talked more freely and really told her everything that was troubling her.

Mrs Murray still believed that the 'dullness' of her present existence was the cause of Harriett's frustration. She therefore decided to organise a trip to the Crystal Palace, which was not too far away, hoping that a change might cheer her up.[100] They went up in the carriage on 21 September with Bird in attendance. When they arrived they walked through the gardens leading up to the Palace, and they then went into a theatre where there was an opera in progress. Bird thought that Lady Mordaunt enjoyed it, although at one point her vacant expression came on and she seemed to be looking at the audience rather than the performers as if she was trying to see if there was anyone there that she knew. As she seemed tired they did not stay long, and they went out by the refreshment department. Bird noticed that as they left the transept, three ladies walking by seemed to recognise Lady Mordaunt. Bird did not know who they were. Going back through the gardens, when they had nearly got as far as the boats on the lake, Lady Mordaunt suddenly became so overcome with fatigue that she said she must sit down, and to the embarrassment of her companions, she subsided onto the weighing chair. When Mrs Murray remonstrated with her, she promptly sat down on the gravel path instead. To minimise the embarrassment, Bird knelt down beside her and pretended to pick some pebbles out of her boot before gently lifting her up. He felt thankful that there was nobody around to witness her eccentric behaviour except a man passing by on a velocipede, who registered a certain amount of amazement at the seat she had chosen.

Although in Bird's view Lady Mordaunt had not shown much interest in what went on, the outing was on the whole considered to be a success, and Mrs Murray felt that Harriett had behaved sensibly enough, except perhaps for the incident with the weighing chair, which could be excused simply as tiredness. That evening at dinner, Harriett asked Mrs Murray about her husband.

'Is he very particular?' she inquired.

'No, he lets me do pretty much as I like' replied Mrs Murray, who then asked whether Charlie had been 'particular'.

'No, he was very kind, he let me do all I wished' said Harriett.

'Would you rather that he had been more particular?' Mrs Murray asked.

'Yes, much rather' said Harriett. Mrs Murray took this to mean that if Charlie had been firmer, she would never have got into the mess she was now in.

The next day Harriett did seem better and she behaved in a sensible way, without once bursting out laughing. She reported to Bird that one of the lamps in the passage was smoking and asked him to turn it down, which he felt was a rational suggestion. In the afternoon she seemed inclined to talk, so Bird immediately tried once again to make her see more clearly what opportunities were open to her. He told her that she had just two options – either to go through the divorce courts and to be free thereafter, or if she persisted in 'not trying', she would end up by finding herself 'shut away from the world'. When she asked what she should do to obtain a divorce, he advised her to confide in some of her friends and put her case in their hands. He suggested that she should consult Lord Dudley but she said she did not care for him, nor for her sister Lady Dudley either. She still felt that Sir Charles should come himself and tell her what to do, and she thought it was not Bird's place to direct her – 'which I admit was a most sensible expression,' Bird added in parenthesis.

So long as Bird treated her with friendly respect and did not try to lecture her, Lady Mordaunt appeared to get on with him well, and at times she even became a little flirtatious with him, treating him like one of her gentlemen friends in times past. When they were out one day, they got down from the carriage in order to walk up a hill called Shirley Common. Lady Mordaunt then asked Bird to hold up her dress as it was too long. While driving home she got the umbrella and gave him a push with it on the back and laughed when he looked surprised. The same day when she was sitting at dinner she rather strangely requested him to make her elbows meet behind her back. He did his best but was unable to make them meet. She seemed pleased that he had tried.

On 23 September Dr Wood and Dr Hughes paid Lady Mordaunt another visit. Dr Wood thought that on the whole she was more cheerful than she had been before, although still remarkably 'docile'. When the doctors first arrived she behaved somewhat oddly, standing quite motionless like a statue, apparently unconscious of their presence. It was quite a long time before she took Dr Wood's proffered hand, but when he asked her to sit down, she 'came to' and did so. Then began the usual succession of questions which she answered after shorter or longer intervals of silence or abstraction, always, when roused, smiling as if waking from a reverie.

Dr Wood's brief on this occasion was to ascertain whether Lady Mordaunt was capable of dealing with her own money. He started off with a simple test, handing her various coins and asking her to say what they were. She replied correctly, but seemed unable to do a simple sum when he asked her what two half crowns and two florins came to altogether. She never got it right in spite of his repeated questions, although he suspected that she would have done if he had given her a little more help. It then seemed to occur to her that she would really rather like some money of her own, and she playfully closed her hand on some of the coins the doctor had given her to hold. He told her she had better write a cheque which she seemed more than willing to do, taking up her pen but then going into one of her apparent trances, sitting silent, passive and statue-like before rousing herself and writing on a piece of paper directed to Greenway & Co of Warwick the sum of £500 and signing her name. At Dr Wood's suggestion she wrote a memo on the back of the paper asking that the order should be posted to her at Page Heath 'by return or as directed'. Dr Wood asked what he should do with the money to which she replied laughing 'Give it to me.' When he said he would give her £5 out of the £500, she readily agreed and when he was leaving she reminded him of the arrangement and said 'You will give me the five pounds.' Dr Wood went away that day still wondering whether, if he had taken a blank cheque and filled in a large amount of money, she would have happily signed it without for a moment realising that she was doing anything imprudent.

As usual the interview with Dr Wood left Harriett upset and angry. Mrs Murray noticed that her charge became increasingly irritable and difficult while she herself was beginning to find her task more and more distasteful. It was after all very annoying when she was doing her utmost to be kind and helpful, to be accused of 'ferreting'.

Sarah Barker also noticed how disturbed Lady Mordaunt seemed to be after the doctors had been to see her. When they walked in to Bromley to do some shopping she went into a shop to make 'some trifling purchase' and without saying anything sat gazing fixedly at one of the shop men in a most embarrassing way. That same night she became 'very wild and hysterical', and when Barker begged her to compose herself, she said 'I think I am crazy or mad. I will pretend to be mad for a bit. It would do Sir Charles good, for he deserves to be beat.' The next day they went out for a walk and nothing un-toward happened except that Lady Mordaunt suddenly sat down in the middle of the footpath.

Harriett was in a particularly defiant mood on the Sunday follow-ing Dr Wood's visit. Bird thought this was because she had invited Dr Hughes to come and play cards the evening before and he had not turned up. When Mrs Murray mentioned this fact to her, she said

angrily that she did not want any doctors. She asked Bird if he had
sent for them, and he replied 'No, certainly not.' He told her he
thought they were sent by the Judge, Lord Penzance, and she reiterated that she wished they would stay away.

'I know what I have done', she broke out, 'I know what they want
and I know what you all want, coming spying here, but I will not be
treated as if I was nobody.'

Mrs Murray assured her that she only wished to treat her with
kindness, adding that in any case she would soon be leaving. Bird
said that he for his part would before long be returning to Walton as
Sir Charles was due back from Scotland in the near future. He told
her that this would be a good thing, as she appeared to be getting
very tired of all those around her.

'No, I don't wish you to go but I wish Sir Charles would come and
tell me all about these things himself' she said. What she was really
complaining about, she added, was that Caborn and the other servants were acting as if they were Lady Mordaunt and she was nothing.

On the Sunday evening, after having asked Dr Wood's permission,
Herbert Murray came down from London. His wife had told him
that she wanted to return home because she and Harriett had been
quarrelling. When he arrived, he found Harriett waiting at the door
to greet him. She did not ask him in but took him into the garden
where they walked together for a while. Dr Wood had in any case
given him instructions that he was not to enter the house. Harriett
talked to him very freely and, it seemed to him, quite rationally. She
began by asking him to give her the latest London news. He said
there was none to tell, as it was a dull time of year and there was not
a soul in town. The only information he could give her was that they
had found the body of an unfortunate judge called Mr Patten, one of
the leading Scottish lawyers, with his throat cut. Harriett said she had
never heard of him but she thought it would be a good thing if more
lawyers were to cut their own throats as there were too many of them
in the world. She added that Charlie had turned lawyer lately but that
he had not done himself much good by it.

Harriett then talked very naturally for several minutes, asking
whether there were any good plays on in London and answering all
the questions Murray put to her. She reminded him of the time when
he had arrived at Moncreiffe and had found her with her younger
sisters playing croquet on the lawn. She spoke to him about servants,

asking him whether he did not find old retainers rather troublesome, as they would not always let people have their own way, citing Cobb, the bailiff at Walton, although Murray had a suspicion she was really referring to Bird.

Herbert Murray then told Harriett that his wife would not be able to stay much longer and asked what she would like to do. She suggested that Blanche should come back as she believed she was still staying with their sister Helen in London. Herbert Murray said this was not the case; he knew that Blanche had gone back to Scotland. Harriett said that it really did not matter as she herself was in any case going back to Walton shortly.

'You know perfectly well that you cannot do so' he said.

'Why does not Charlie come and tell me so?' she as always replied.

After this Herbert Murray went straight back to London without entering the house. He felt that he had got on well with Harriett and had begun to gain her confidence. She had behaved on the whole quite normally, only breaking into hysterical laughter from time to time. She had also turned to him and shaken hands for no particular reason.

The following Sunday Herbert Murray made a second visit. It had been arranged that he should take Harriett to church at Hayes in the afternoon, but when they got there Harriett said she would rather not go in. They drove straight back to Page Heath and walked to Bickley Church. Herbert Murray asked if Harriett would like to go in for the end of the service. She said that she would very much and followed him in. They were there for about half an hour and they sat through the sermon, Harriett behaving very well, only laughing three times 'in a kind of smothered way'. Herbert Murray pretended not to notice and when on the way home she apologised for her bad behaviour, he told her he was quite satisfied as he knew she had tried to check it. She told him it was the first time she had been to church since her baby was born.

When they got back to Page Heath they sat in the garden for more than an hour, and she answered all the questions he put to her, though sometimes after a considerable pause. She also asked him inconsequential questions, about dogs, horses, cats or the shooting. He had the impression that her memory was very good, although she did rather hark back to his visit to Moncreiffe, bringing up the subject time after time. Herbert Murray thought she was not so much weak in mind as a bit odd at times, what with the hysterical laugh and the fixed look. He spoke to her quite openly about her 'absent' moods, which became known between them as the 'brown study'. She told him that she did not answer his questions straightaway because she was thinking.

Harriett complained openly to Herbert Murray about the tediousness of her present life, and of how she longed to go up to London again. She then asked him, as she asked everybody, why Charlie did not come himself to discuss things with her, to which he replied that he had done so by letter. She then asked her recurrent question, 'What shall I do?'

Herbert Murray said that he found it hard to give her any advice, as she would suspect him, because he was Charlie's uncle.

'You do suspect me a little, don't you?' he asked.

'Yes, I do' she replied, laughing.

He then suggested that she might ask her uncle Johnny Fiennes to help her. He was married to Lady Louisa Moncreiffe's youngest sister, Augusta, and was one of the few relations on her side who lived in the south of England.[101] Harriett responded very well to the idea and Herbert Murray suggested that she should write a letter herself, asking for a meeting. She ended by thanking him, saying that nobody had given her such good advice before.

After that they went back into the house, and dined with Dr Wood who had by this time arrived. Herbert Murray was surprised by the marked change in Harriett's behaviour when she was in the doctor's company. She had talked with him so freely and naturally, but now by contrast she refused to speak to the doctor, or to answer even the simplest question – such as, how many brothers did she have. When she first saw Dr Wood, she went into her statuesque pose and then suddenly looked up at him and smiled. During dinner she remained silent, but appeared to follow the conversation. Both Dr Wood and Herbert Murray told stories and anecdotes, and Harriett laughed heartily in all the right places. Dr Wood came to the conclusion that although at times she seemed preoccupied with her thoughts, yet she never had the appearance of anything like depression, and he described her manner and conduct as of the kind expected of 'a silly and weak-minded child' rather than that of an insane person.

Herbert Murray, meditating on his meeting with Harriett and on her changed behaviour with the doctor, felt convinced that she was playing a part, in fact he thought that her manner was 'decidedly put on'. Like his wife, Herbert Murray felt upset about Harriett's unnatural isolation at Bickley. He confided his worries to Bird who received the impression that he was 'much grieved for the poor thing'. Bird himself was prepared to admit that 'her case was a most sad one, enough to make anyone sorry for her'. However he felt obliged to add that it had been entirely brought on by her own indiscretion. At the same time, in fairness, it had to be said that she had been 'to a certain extent misled by men who were older and ought to have known better'.

Before he went away, Herbert Murray asked Harriett whether she would like him to return the next day to take her to the Crystal Palace where Blondin was due to perform. She said that she would very much like to go. Mrs Murray was to return to London that evening to see her children and would shortly be leaving for good. Herbert Murray had told Dr Wood that he must find a substitute without delay to fill the gap until Miss Keddell arrived. Since Dr Reynolds and Dr Gull were both still away, Dr Wood shouldered the responsibility of finding somebody else. He at once sent a telegram to Mr Haynes asking whether his cousin Miss Elizabeth Parsons would be available on a temporary basis.

Back in July Miss Parsons had been staying with Mr Haynes in Leamington when he had asked her whether she knew of anyone suitable to look after Lady Mordaunt. She had, without any prompting from Mr Haynes, offered to help, 'as a friend', but had subsequently been told that she had been objected to by the 'other side'. Now, when Mr Haynes showed her the telegram, she agreed to go down on the Monday. Apart from the fear of partiality voiced by the opposition, she was in every other way a suitable choice. At the age of sixty, she was too old to risk being corrupted by the errant Lady Mordaunt, and in addition her background was impeccable. Her father had been rector of Goathurst in Somerset and prebendary of Wells Cathedral for over fifty years, and she now lived at the Rectory with her brother who had taken over the living from their father.

After the Murrays had gone, Bird found Lady Mordaunt alone in the drawing-room and launched into an accusation, telling her that he was perfectly satisfied she was as sane now as she had been twelve months before, and that by her present conduct she was only deceiving her husband and friends, in fact everybody, by putting on and 'shamming all those silly things'. He felt that it was high time she 'roused' herself.

'What, Bird, in my own house?' she said and asked him what right he had to talk to her in that way. He said he was sorry to tell her that he was perfectly convinced that she had been 'shamming' and trying to 'gull' everybody and he warned her that if she continued to act in this way he would tell people and expose her. He then left the room.

The next day, probably as a result of this conversation, Lady Mordaunt seemed very disturbed. She rang the drawing-room bell and asked Bird to move the chiffonier which stood against the wall into the middle of the room in place of the round table. He pointed out how curious that would look and advised her to leave it where it was. She also altered the cook's slate, and hid it in the book cupboard in the drawing-room.

Before going down to Page Heath, Miss Parsons called at Dr Wood's house in Harley Street. Although the doctor himself had been unexpectedly called away to Wiltshire, Miss Parsons lunched with his wife who gave her a letter of introduction to Lady Mordaunt and assured her that she would have a cordial reception.

The Murrays arrived at Page Heath in the morning, Mrs Murray staying to help Miss Parsons settle in, and Herbert Murray taking Harriett to the Crystal Palace by train. The trip went well and Harriett behaved 'sensibly' the whole time with hardly a single 'brown study' or fit of hysterical laughter to mar the occasion. She seemed to take more of an interest in things than she had done on the previous occasion, particularly enjoying the velocipedes which were a complete novelty to her. During the months when she had been virtually imprisoned, velocipede mania had spread from France, where, it was reported, every French boy had his velocipede as every English boy had his cricket bat. But by virtue of her isolation she had missed out on all the reports about them and she now watched with amazement as the cumbersome machines raced round the paths and fountains. When she had seen enough of that, they wandered round the glass and china courts, Harriett taking an apparent interest in all the goods on show and buying some eau de cologne and some sugar plums.

As for Blondin, she seemed disappointed by his performance. When she had seen him at the Alhambra, it had been much more exciting as he had balanced high up on a thin rope. The whole occasion, she said, had been much 'prettier' in that more daring location. Here the rope was thick and very near the ground, and the music was far too loud. Music of all kinds, Herbert Murray noticed, seemed to upset her, reminding her as it did of earlier, happier times. She seemed to get very hot and faint and Herbert Murray took her out before the performance had finished.

Before they had gone inside, Herbert Murray had suggested that Harriett should loop her dress up to keep it off the ground, and he thought it strange that she forgot to put it down when they went inside as the average young woman would have done. That she did care about her clothes, however, was proved by the fact that she was upset when she realised that she was the only lady in the theatre wearing a hat. Herbert Murray did not think this mattered too much, especially as there were very few ladies there anyway.

On the journey home Harriett told her uncle that she had toothache, but in spite of this she sat in the carriage eating sugar plums. She was very silent, which she explained by telling him that she had 'a fit of the blues'. Herbert Murray did not find this surprising; after all, the thought of going back to isolation in Bickley after a day out was enough to make anyone feel depressed, let alone a young woman in Harriett's situation.

As they got closer to home, Herbert Murray reminded Harriett that the new companion would be there when she got back. She seemed apprehensive, asking nervously whether Miss Parsons was a governess and obviously fearing the worst.

Miss Parsons had arrived about five o'clock, having by mistake got out of the train at Bromley rather than going on to Bickley. When she finally arrived at Page Heath in a fly, the servants gave her some tea. Harriett arrived some time later and went into the drawing-room where she stood stock still, staring at Miss Parsons and not saying a word. Miss Parsons handed over the letter of introduction from Mrs Wood which Harriett read but made no comment. She then turned and went out of the room. Herbert Murray noticed that with him she had been quite forthcoming and had conversed in an easy manner which made her silence on confronting Miss Parsons all the more of a contrast.

After she had finished dressing for dinner, Miss Parsons was startled when she came out of her room to find Lady Mordaunt standing right outside her door. She hid her surprise and made some comments about the gloomy weather and asked about Blondin's performance. That evening Lady Mordaunt watched Miss Parsons intently all through dinner out of the corner of her eye, saying nothing. She did not eat any of the food that was put in front of her until they came to the cheese straws at the end. These became a topic of conversation, and Miss Parsons said they ought to have a better name and would be called *pailles de fromage* in Paris. Everybody, including Lady Mordaunt, laughed at this, and when the dish was passed to her, she took it and ate all the cheese straws that remained. After dinner Herbert Murray played a rubber of whist with her, but the game was never finished as she was still complaining of toothache and it was thought advisable for her to go to bed early. She played quite well, with the exception of a revoke.

Mrs Murray asked her husband, rashly as it turned out, to take 'a soothing mixture' up to Harriett's room. He sat on her bed while she drank the medicine, and then quite suddenly she threw herself into his arms saying 'Shut the door, shut the door.' He remonstrated with her, saying that 'this would not do between relations'. Then she said 'I suppose I had better go to bed quietly.' He hastily rang the bell for her maid and left the room.

Herbert Murray had told Harriett that she ought to visit the dentist, but she could not decide whether to go or not. They tossed for it and he lost, but because her toothache suddenly became very bad she decided that something would have to be done. Rather than arranging for her to see a local dentist, he took her up to London to see Mr Rogers of Hanover Square. The tooth was stopped, which was very painful, but Herbert Murray reported that she behaved 'admirably' throughout the treatment. Afterwards they went for a short walk down Regent Street, Conduit Street and Bond Street and after looking at one or two jewellers' shops, Harriett noticed and commented on two very pretty dresses, one of them with spots on it, which were displayed in a window of the large shop called Redman's.

The emptiness of London at this time was certainly not lost on Harriett. Herbert Murray had told her that she ought to come and stay with them once they had settled back in town, but he had pointed out that for the present she might well be better off at Page Heath. She laughed and said she really thought she was. As they drove down Piccadilly she recognised and bowed to somebody who was passing by, but when Murray asked her if she would like to sit in the Park for a while she said she would rather not, as there would be nothing to see there.

When they were in the train going home, Harriett talked a good deal and Herbert Murray told her how well she looked. This led him on to say how sorry he would be to have to say anything which might lead to her being shut up as insane. He was sure that she was no more mad than he was himself, even if she did sometimes ask some silly questions.

'What shall I say when they ask me how I found you?' he wanted to know.

'Tell them I am quite well.'

'Yes,' he said, 'that is all very well, but suppose I do say so, what will the doctors say? You behave so foolishly with them that they won't say you are all right unless you alter your behaviour with them.'

When he asked her why she behaved in such a silly way with the doctors, her answer was that she did not want them, they bored her and did her no good. She would like to pay them their bills and be done with them.

At the next station somebody else got into the carriage and that was the end of the conversation.

On her return, Harriet said she would like to go out for a drive, but Herbert Murray told her that she must lie down and rest for a while. She went upstairs to her room, lit some matches and set fire to the curtains. Mrs Caborn happened to go in soon afterwards and she quickly put the fire out. When Mrs Caborn asked Lady Mordaunt what she thought she was doing, she remained silent; the usual vacant look came over her face and she burst into tears. Later they all went out for a drive, and in the evening Herbert Murray played three games of écarté with her. Later she played the piano and sang with a great deal of feeling.

The next morning Mrs Murray went away, travelling back to London with her husband. When she had gone, Miss Parsons and Harriett walked over to the Rectory at Chislehurst to see Herbert Murray's elder brother, the Revd Francis Murray, another of Sir Charles's uncles. Mrs Francis Murray greeted Harriett most affectionately and sent her and Miss Parsons home laden with flowers. It was a long walk and they did not get back until two o'clock, but all the same they went out for a drive later, to Greenwich and Blackheath. That evening Harriett said that she felt rather sick and she seemed disinclined to eat.

On the same evening there was a curious incident. Just before dinner Lady Mordaunt told Bird that she wanted to do up a parcel and asked for some brown paper and string. She did up the parcel

herself but did not seal it. She then asked for a stamp. The parcel was
addressed to

> H.R.H. The Prince of Wales,
> Marlborough House,
> High Street,
> Warwick

and she asked Bird to post it. However after dinner he and Miss
Parsons looked at it and found inside it a sheet of notepaper addressed to the Prince at Walton à Ville,[102] Warwick. The emerald and
diamond horseshoe ring which the Prince had given her for a wedding present was enclosed, but there was no message in the parcel. Later Lady Mordaunt seemed unsettled, and she was seen walking about upstairs undressed, although she hastily went back to bed
when her maid appeared. It was difficult to make out whether she
was genuinely disturbed or simply play-acting. When they asked her
next day where her ring was, she said she did not know and appeared
to have forgotten all about the parcel.

During the first few days of her stay Miss Parsons worked very
hard to gain Lady Mordaunt's confidence. To start with Lady Mordaunt was, as Miss Parsons put it, 'restless beyond description', never
sitting still for very long. She continued to act oddly at meals, speaking very little and, when she did, talking in a low, quick sort of way
mainly in monosyllables. After a few days, however, Miss Parsons
noticed an improvement and she wrote with satisfaction that her
charge seemed to be taking to her. Miss Parsons tried to interest her
in reading, but there never seemed to be much time, what with all the
walks and carriage drives Lady Mordaunt insisted on taking, and
then she tended to go off to bed rather early. Mrs Murray had tried
all kinds of things, but had come to the conclusion that Harriett had
'no mind for occupation of any kind'.

Miss Parsons soon noticed the look that Bird had described as
'absent' and that Herbert Murray had called the 'brown study'. Miss
Parsons would often say 'A penny for your thoughts', but got little
response. If Harriett did reply it tended to be in a childish voice, and
all in all Miss Parsons thought she was not mad at all, just rather silly
and childish, for example picking up a handful of pebbles off the road
and throwing them away one by one. The Revd and Mrs Francis
Murray had taken Miss Parsons aside during the visit to Chislehurst
and said how very strange Lady Mordaunt's manner really was and

they had asked 'Poor thing, is she always like this?' Francis Murray was inclined to think that she really was an imbecile as he did not think she was clever enough to sham. But husband and wife both agreed that Miss Parsons seemed the ideal person to look after Harriett, and if anybody could restore her mind, which was certainly 'overbalanced' at the moment, then Miss Parsons was the person to do it.

After a few days with Lady Mordaunt, Miss Parsons did not feel too hopeful that there would be any 'amendment', especially after Mrs Caborn told her about the episode when Lady Mordaunt had lit a Lucifer match and set fire to the curtains. She gave orders from then on that all dangerous things must be kept out of Lady Mordaunt's reach.

All the same, Miss Parsons did not despair. She felt that in spite of all her oddities, there was something very appealing about Lady Mordaunt. In fact at times she was so openly affectionate that it was impossible not to get quite fond of her. Even when she was doing something really stupid there was often a mischievous glint in her eye. Miss Parsons certainly felt very sorry for her especially as she seemed at times so forlorn and helpless, and she could not share the Revd Francis Murray's rather harsh opinion of her. She agreed that in all probability Harriett would never have been over-intelligent, more likely a delightful but rather weak character, who became 'an easy prey to wicked men and the great indulgence of too kind and too confiding a husband'. But this did not mean that she was 'unredeemable' and Miss Parsons was determined to do what she could to save her soul. On her return from church on Sunday 3 October, Miss Parsons told Harriett that they had read the story of the burning fiery furnace and asked her if she knew about it. She said that she had never been taught it, so Miss Parsons told her the story, and then read the collect for the day and said it would be a nice little prayer for her to use. She responded very well, and indeed began to talk more rationally than Miss Parsons had ever known her to do, in the end saying, 'I know I am very silly.' Miss Parsons did not deny this, and suggested that she should pray to God to forgive her daily shortcomings. If she did, God would surely hear her and answer her prayers. 'Extraordinary to say' wrote Miss Parsons

she not only took this in but remembered it for in the night when she thought her maid was asleep, she crept out of bed, quiet as a mouse, knelt down and appeared to be praying for a few minutes. She then got back into bed very quietly and had a good night. All this was rational and this morning she is better than I have seen her.

There certainly had been a noticeable improvement in Lady Mordaunt's behaviour since Miss Parsons had been at Page Heath and in the last two days she had been 'quite talkative (for her)'. Encouraged by this, Miss Parsons discussed with Mrs Caborn the possibility of allowing Lady Mordaunt to have her baby with her. Both women were in favour of the idea, and Mrs Francis Murray agreed with them. Miss Parsons had often heard her mention the baby, and she would play the line from a song 'Yes, my child, I'll live for thee' over and over again. When Dr Wood paid his next visit, Miss Parsons broached the subject with him and he said he had always thought that was the one thing likely to 'rouse' Lady Mordaunt. He promised to do all he could to make it possible.

He was in any case not too happy about Lady Mordaunt's condition and since there seemed to be little likelihood of any permanent improvement, both he and Dr Hughes felt that the Miss Keddell should be pressed to come as soon as possible, so that Miss Parsons could help her to settle in before she left. They would in fact have liked Miss Parsons to stay on as well, but she did not want to make any promises. Both Bird and Mrs Caborn thought that she was having such a good effect on Lady Mordaunt that they too hoped she would stay.

Dr Wood had decided that he must make a more serious attempt to find out whether Lady Mordaunt was capable of writing a cheque. He first questioned her about her visit to London, but she seemed vague as to dates, and got impatient with his persistent questioning, saying quite crossly 'I told you that before.' He asked her if she would now write him a cheque, and when she agreed he rang the bell and asked Bird to bring her cheque book. She was as before completely 'docile' and Dr Wood believed that she would have written anything he asked. She seemed bewildered by the whole situation and he had to keep prompting her, but when the cheque book was placed in front of her, she wrote a cheque for £30, signing her name 'fluently' and without hesitation. With a little help and encouragement she added the date almost correctly, only putting 1868 instead of 1869. Dr Wood asked her what money she wanted out of it, and she replied

'Two and sixpence', which he gave her, and she put it on the table telling him that she would use it to buy some wool. When he left he asked her if she was satisfied that she had got full value for the cheque and she replied that she had. Afterwards he drew a line through the cheque to cancel it.

Hearing that Mrs Caborn was going to London the next day, Lady Mordaunt asked her to cash a cheque for £30. She had written the wrong date, which perhaps was not surprising in view of her isolated state, and although the writing was rather blotted, the cheque was otherwise all right. In the afternoon Francis Murray looked in to see her, but it seems that he did not have a very significant conversation with her. She probably sensed that he was unsympathetic.

On Bird's last day he went in to say goodbye to Lady Mordaunt and asked her whether she had any message for Sir Charles.

'Tell him I am getting on' she replied, adding that she supposed Sir Charles would be 'buying some more horses for hunting', which showed that she was well aware what time of year it was. She wished Bird goodbye, shook hands with him and said that she hoped Sir Charles would come to fetch her soon.

Bird left next morning before she was up and she did not seem to miss him; indeed when Miss Parsons returned that evening from a visit to London, she found Lady Mordaunt 'wonderfully well' and very keen to hear all about her day in town. She behaved very well at dinner and aftwerwards settled down in the drawing-room and wrote a letter to her mother.

Just before Bird's departure, Lady Mordaunt had written a letter to Lady Louisa which made no sense at all, but now, perhaps because there was nobody looking over her shoulder, or perhaps because she was feeling better, she managed to be quite coherent. She checked the date from the newspaper before starting. 'My dear Mother,' she wrote,

I am at last able to write a line to tell you that I am at liberty to write to you and say I am quite well. Bird has taken a journey home to-day; he has become very cockey of late. I hope Bunchey was not any the worse for her visit. She seemed in good spirits, but did not divulge much home news. I should be much surprised at a frost if it came. Goodbye.

Yours affectionately,

H. MORDAUNT

Thinking that it would give Lady Louisa some pleasure to read this sensible letter from her daughter, Miss Parsons decided to post it, but not before she had made a copy which she sent to Sir Charles.

Another letter, written at almost the same time, was not sent, as it was written in a 'silly' hand, with a great many blots. It was addressed to 'Dr P', asking him to buy her a box of things at 'Cremems' and telling him in confidence how much she had improved since her change of air.

The departure of Bird seemed to lift a weight off Lady Mordaunt's mind and for a few days, without his watchful presence, she was seen to be happier. At breakfast she poured out the tea and coffee, talked rather more than usual 'and behaved so nicely that you would not have said there was anything the matter'.

Things improved even further after the arrival of Miss Keddell, who first saw Lady Mordaunt on the sofa pretending to be asleep. After a while she opened her eyes and began to join in the conversation and asked Miss Keddell whether she enjoyed riding and music. She then suggested that they played draughts together. She added that she hoped Miss Keddell would not find Page Heath too dull.

Although Miss Keddell was a rather quiet and reserved sort of person, she and Miss Parsons got on well and Lady Mordaunt appeared to enjoy listening to their conversation. Miss Parsons found it a relief having two people there as this did away with the terrible awkward silences which occurred when Lady Mordaunt was in one of her silent moods. Lady Mordaunt also seemed happy with the arrangement as it saved her from having to talk to people with whom she had little in common.

Although she had not received an answer to her previous letter to Charlie, Harriett now sat down to write another.

> My own darling Charlie – I began an epistle to you last night but I had no time to finish it. There are two ladies visiting here at present who I am sure you would be glad to see. I wish you would make haste and come back. I want the wages paid dreadfully, but I shouldn't kneel to you to ask about them.
> Yours affectionately,
HARRIET MORDAUNT

The maid Sarah Barker thought that at this time Lady Mordaunt really believed Sir Charles would come and see her, discussing where he would sleep and saying that she herself would have to go under the bed or in one of the drawers.

Miss Parsons was delighted by the change that seemed to be coming over Lady Mordaunt. The strangeness she had noticed at the beginning of her stay was gradually becoming less noticeable, and she had hopes that her charge was returning to normal. Miss Parsons was in fact growing increasingly fond of Lady Mordaunt in spite of all her peculiarities, even finding her odd tricks quite amusing at times. It seemed that her policy of treating Lady Mordaunt with respect and kindness was beginning to bear fruit. Mrs Caborn, however, was more sceptical, and she warned Miss Parsons that Lady Mordaunt varied from day to day and might well relapse back into her old ways. All the same, Miss Parsons nursed the hope that if she could be left alone for a good long stretch with companions she liked, and 'with no doctors or anyone to excite her', she might eventually become 'perfectly herself again'.

Dr Wood agreed. Whatever the Moncreiffe doctors might say, it was his mission, as a doctor, to do his best to find a cure for his patient's disorder. Now, to speed up the recovery, he promised Miss Parsons that he would write to Mrs Hancox and ask her to make arrangements for Violet to be reunited with her mother.

29

Mother and Daughter

After receiving her summons from Dr Wood, Mrs Hancox packed up at once and took the baby down to Page Heath on Saturday 9 October. As soon as she arrived, Mrs Caborn immediately rushed forward, seized the baby and carried her into the drawing-room, Lady Mordaunt following. When she reached the drawing-room door, Lady Mordaunt turned and looked at Mrs Hancox 'honestly in the face'. She then shook hands and said 'Well, nurse, how do you do.' Mrs Hancox was struck by how well she was looking. She told the nurse that she must have done 'a good part by that child, it does look well' and Mrs Hancox replied 'I am very glad your Ladyship is satisfied with it.' Lady Mordaunt did not take the child or kiss her, but she did offer to write Mrs Hancox a cheque to cover her expenses.

The nursery had been prepared for Violet and the nurse, and that evening Lady Mordaunt went up to visit them. She shut the door in a conspiratorial way, saying 'Don't let us be overheard.' She asked whether Violet had been a trouble to her, and whether her husband and her daughters Jennie and Polly had minded having her in the house. At first Lady Mordaunt behaved in a way that seemed to Mrs Hancox perfectly normal, until, quite suddenly, she went and sat down on the floor in a corner of the room.

'Are you in the habit of doing such silly things as that?' Mrs Hancox asked, looking her straight in the eyes.

'Sometimes' she replied.

Mrs Hancox told her not to trouble herself to behave like that in front of her, as there was no misunderstanding between them. 'You'll never get well if you give in to nonsense like that' said Mrs Hancox in a matter of fact kind of way.

After that Lady Mordaunt came and sat down in a chair and behaved quite sensibly, talking for about half an hour. When she went out she told Mrs Hancox to make sure to ask for anything she wanted.

The next day was Sunday. Lady Mordaunt went into the nursery several times, looking, Mrs Hancox thought, a little absent. She did not take too much notice of the baby, but in the afternoon Mrs Hancox took Violet into Lady Mordaunt's room. The child sat for a while on the nurse's lap, staring at her mother.

Then, quite suddenly, Lady Mordaunt covered her face with her hands.

'Oh, baby, you must not look at me like that. I cannot stand that gaze. Those eyes are just like your father's. Take her away, Nurse.'

Mrs Hancox hastily left the room.

Although for the rest of the day Lady Mordaunt seemed to be all right, the next morning the scene was repeated. Lady Mordaunt had come into the nursery where Violet was asleep and had asked normal questions, like whether the baby had slept well. Then she asked if she could see Violet's eyes again, as she had not had much chance to do so the day before. As soon as the baby woke Mrs Hancox carried her through to the bedroom, but once again Lady Mordaunt put her hands over her face, saying that she could not bear to see the staring eyes which reminded her so much of the father's. She seemed at times almost to resent the child, harking back to the time of her birth and saying how unfortunate it was that she had been born early at Walton. 'If I could have got up to London' she said 'this child would never have been allowed to come forward.' Mrs Hancox understood her meaning too well. The child would have died at birth and no questions would have been asked. 'You may call it by what name you like' said Mrs Hancox 'but I would say that the baby would have been murdered then.'

That afternoon Miss Parsons and Miss Keddell came up and told Mrs Hancox that Lady Mordaunt seemed to be a in a rather poor way. Mrs Hancox went straight to her bedroom and found her lying on the maid's bed crying.

'My lady, don't you feel well?' asked Mrs Hancox.

'No, not very, but there is nothing the matter really' she replied. She put up her hand beckoning Mrs Hancox to come nearer and then said, 'You know I can't help this sort of thing sometimes.'

Mrs Hancox took her hand and asked her what brought it on. 'Oh my own thoughts' she said. 'When I begin to think, such lots of things begin to crowd upon me at once . . . at least . . . everything, you know' she went on, pressing Mrs Hancox's hand. 'When I begin to think' she repeated 'sometimes I laugh, sometimes I cry, sometimes I feel as if I could do anything and its very hard for me to be put here and to be governed by these people when I ought to govern them.'

'Well, my lady,' said Mrs Hancox 'if you really feel that, why don't you try to govern and show that you don't like being governed, giving up those silly tricks which make some think you are not able to govern yourself.' Mrs Hancox then asked her if she would be happier if the baby was not there, and she said she thought perhaps she would, referring again to the eyes. Mrs Hancox said that if she felt like that, it would be possible for Violet to be brought up at Tysoe until she felt able to care for her and see to her education. 'I will make a nice little scholar of her ready for you' Mrs Hancox promised, asking her whether that was what she really wanted. She replied that it was, and at once became more cheerful. Mrs Hancox advised her to confide in the next doctor who came to see her, and meanwhile she promised not to do anything to 'tease' her with the baby.

'I think I have too many people about me' Harriett then complained, referring to the two companions.

'You have a nice comfortable companion in Miss Parsons' Mrs Hancox reminded her. 'Why not make her a confidante?'

'I have not a person about me I can trust' was Lady Mordaunt's sad reply. She pressed Mrs Hancox's hand again, and then referred to the fact that the child had already started to call Mrs Hancox Mamma, and that she herself would do the same. Touched, Mrs Hancox then repeated the promise she had made at Walton, that if ever Lady Mordaunt wished to see her baby, she would bring her at once to anywhere in England that the mother might happen to be.

It seems that this conversation had gained Lady Mordaunt's confidence, because later that afternoon she went to Mrs Hancox's room with the obvious intention of having an intimate conversation. As she did to everybody, she began by talking about Sir Charles and expressing her intention of going back to Walton. As usual she was told that this would not be possible. Mrs Hancox said she thought it was a pity that she insisted on deluding herself as well as everybody round about her, playing tricks so that they thought she was insane.

'But I'm not insane' she said.

Mrs Hancox then asked why she behaved in such a strange way. 'I have nothing at all to do' Lady Mordaunt explained 'and it was not bad fun to play a few tricks. But stop,' she added, 'I don't want to put myself in your power although I know I can't deceive you.'

'Please yourself,' said Mrs Hancox, 'you can't deceive me nor the doctors either for long, and if you are not insane, why have three or four doctors to attend you?'

'I don't want any,' she said, 'I never asked them to come. I am as well in health as possible, and there is nothing for them to come for.'

Mrs Hancox told her that it was said by people in general that she was insane and that the case for madness would be tried in London shortly.

'Surely not,' she said, 'for I am no more so than you are at any time.'

'Thank God' said Mrs Hancox. 'I knew you were not and I felt quite thankful to see the expression on your face and to feel the natural pressure of your hand.'

Lady Mordaunt then asked how it would end and Mrs Hancox told her she was sure it would end in a divorce and the sooner the better for her sake.

'You know all about my friends' said Lady Mordaunt.

'Yes' said Mrs Hancox, and she advised her then to show some moral courage for once, which would mean telling her lawyer that she meant to do what was right. She should ask him to bring the divorce about as soon as possible so that she could get her liberty and be away out of England as quickly as she could.

She asked then who had been the first to describe her as insane. 'Was it that Osbert Mordaunt?' she asked.

'No, Sir Thomas your own father was the first I believe' replied Mrs Hancox.

She made no answer but seemed to accept that what Mrs Hancox had said was true.

This frank conversation struck Mrs Hancox as being the breakthrough they had all been waiting for. When she heard about it, Miss Parsons was fully in agreement. Lady Mordaunt indeed seemed to be a different person, quite normal in fact. For several weeks now, those about her, Bird, Mrs Caborn, the Murrays, and now Miss Parsons and Mrs Hancox, had been pointing out to her that her quickest way of escaping the tediousness of a life in virtual captivity, surrounded by prying and domineering people, was to push on with the divorce which would restore her freedom.

It had been difficult to accept any advice from the servants, but now that Miss Parsons and Mrs Hancox had put it to her the message was beginning to come home at last. They hoped that they had made her realise that she should no longer trust her father so implicitly, and would in future feel able to ignore the advice he gave her.

As usual Harriett had received no reply from Sir Charles to the letter she had written to him, but a letter had arrived from her uncle John Fiennes, who wrote from Trunkwell House, Reading.

> Dearest Harriett – Herbert Murray told me that you might like to hear from me. I can only say that I should be very glad to see you and take you about if you wished it as you must really be very dull all alone. We are coming or rather going up to the Queen's Gate Terrace for the winter on November 1 and after that I could run down to you. I can assure you that I can never forget your kindness to me when I had the fever five years ago and would do anything in the world as far as in my power lay to try and make you cheerful and happy. Aunt Gussy sends you her love and with mine,
>
> believe me,
>
> > your affectionate uncle,
> > JOHN FIENNES

This letter gave Harriett renewed hope that she might at last have found somebody in the family who would be willing to listen to her. And she still believed that Charlie would one day agree to see her and talk things over. And so she wrote to him once more.

> My dear Charlie – I wish you would not be so occupied with your fishing as to forget all about baby and me, as Bird has made a frightful mess about things here. We want you so very much to come and put things straight.
>
> > Yr affecte wife,
> > HARRIETT MORDAUNT
>
> I had a letter from Uncle John Fiennes asking me if you would like them to take me about a little for a change.

She addressed the letter to Walton Hall and sent it off.

After the conversation with Mrs Hancox, the companions and the nurse had been closeted together, trying to decide what they should do as a result of Lady Mordaunt's virtual admission that she had been feigning. They felt sure that somebody should be advised as soon as possible of her change of heart, and it was decided that Dr Reynolds should be told at once as he had always remained unconvinced that Lady Mordaunt was mad. The doctor had recently returned to London, and on 14 October Miss Parsons took the train to London and went to see him at his house in Harley Street. She told him that Lady Mordaunt had 'almost admitted to the Nurse that she has been acting a part to accomplish an end'. It did in fact seem that Lady Mordaunt had 'altered the manner' that had been the cause of Miss Parsons being engaged to look after her. Dr Reynolds listened to what Miss Parsons had to say and then made her sit down at once to write a note to Mr Haynes, stating that in these changed circumstances it would be very wise for Dr Wood to see Lady Mordaunt again, and asking him to write an order to this effect as soon as convenient.

Mr Haynes immediately informed Mr Hunt about this dramatic development, pointing out that if what Miss Parsons had told Dr Reynolds could be substantiated, it would be 'perfectly confirmatory of Dr Reynolds's opinion from the commencement'. It might even prove to be the finish of Sir Thomas's case.

In order to assess the latest situation, Sir Charles got in touch with yet another Murray uncle, Robert, the eldest, suggesting that he should call on Harriett as a friend, with the aim of finding out her present feelings. Since Robert Murray was shortly setting off for Italy with his four daughters he said he would go over to Page Heath at once to say goodbye. When he arrived, Mrs Caborn greeted him and said that Lady Mordaunt would be delighted to see him. He found her sitting in the drawing-room with Miss Parsons writing some letters, and she greeted him in a manner which he thought was pleasant and natural. She was neatly and plainly dressed, wearing no jewellery except her wedding ring. After a few minutes he asked her whether she would like to walk with him in the garden. She said that she would and sent for her hat and coat. When the maid brought these, she seemed to hesitate in a slightly strange way before putting them on. Robert Murray later told Charlie in a letter that at first she was rather constrained, but when he told her to 'unfreeze and be natural' she altered at once. They talked about all sorts of things and it seemed to him that she was 'as rational as possible'.

He then said, 'Harriett, I want to give you a bit of advice if you will let me.'

'Don't preach to me, I've had enough of that' she warned him.

'No, that is not in my line' he replied. 'I want to give you a bit of worldly advice and tell you what I think is best for you to do and you must not be angry with me.'

She promised him that she would not and he suggested to her that she must be getting very weary of the life she was leading.

'Yes, and I worry myself day and night not knowing what to do' she admitted.

His advice was to get the divorce over as soon as possible. Was there no one, he asked her, to whom she could turn for advice?

'I don't know' she said, adding that her father only wrote to her about the shooting and that sort of thing.

'Get him to let the divorce take place quietly' he suggested, warning her that if she allowed the trial to take place to prove whether she was well enough to go through the divorce, things would certainly be brought up against her which she would give the world to conceal.

'Yes,' she said, 'I know that and I do not know what to do.'

'Surely' he said 'you must have formed some plan in your own mind for your future life.'

'I want to go back to Walton and Charlie.'

'That, you may take my word for it, you may never do. He will never take you back and if you did go, no one would speak to you.'

'Why should I not go back?'

'Because you were not true to him'.

'Oh he was so tiresome and I wanted to make some alterations amongst the servants there and he would not let me,' she said.

'That is all nonsense. You had the house for yourself and friends, and did just as you pleased.'

'Yes,' she admitted, 'Charlie did let me do as I liked.'

'Well,' he said, trying to bring matters to a conclusion, 'what do you want to do now?'

There was a long silence and then, finally, she said 'I want to live for baby and him.'

Robert Murray said that she would not say who the 'him' was, although in view of what she had just said it was easy to believe that she was referring to her husband. But he ignored the remark and told her that for his part he would like her to get her divorce as soon as possible. 'With your pretty face you will soon get someone to marry and take care of you' he assured her.

'But who will marry me?' she said sadly, adding 'I shall have to ask someone myself.'

'You will find someone to love you.'

Robert Murray described how she 'fired up' at that and asked whether he wanted to insult her. 'Perhaps you want me to love you or your brother Francis' she said.

'Certainly not. I want you to love some man who will take care of you. You should not be angry, as I am telling you this for your own good.'

She calmed down then and took his hand, assuring him that she would not be cross again. It was only that she was so bothered about everything. She told him that the lanes where she went for her daily drives had become hateful to her. He then said that he was going away to Italy for some months with his family and wanted her to promise him that she would get the divorce as soon as possible, which would help her to escape from her present situation. He was sure that the longer things went on as they were, the worse it would be for her body and mind. She then promised him that she would no longer be at Page Heath when he returned home.

'I wish I could go abroad with you and the girls and that he could come with us. It would be so jolly' she said sadly.

She began to talk about the baby, and what a 'horrid bore' it had been that it had been born early. She then said she hoped it would not be ill-treated. Robert Murray asked who was it she was talking about.

'You must be deaf' she answered. 'People are always asking me the same question over again. I mean Violet. I hope that she will not be ill-treated.'

By this time they had nearly walked as far as Bromley and back. She seemed more relaxed now, the only sign of nervousness being the taking on and off of the wedding ring on her finger which she did continually. Once, when a carriage passed and raised a cloud of dust, she apologised and said she must spit the dust out of her mouth. He told her that he thought this was the best thing to do. When they had nearly reached the house, she said she did not want to go in. She took Robert's arm several times, walking more and more slowly, finally subsiding onto a paling in what he described as a rather unnatural manner, simply going down 'plump on a middle bar of a post and rail, crouching herself up'. He recalled how her mood had frequently changed; one moment there would be a pleasant smile on her face and then this would quickly be followed by a perplexed frown. Sometimes she was slow in answering so that she needed a sort of spur such as 'Come now Harriett, you know what you wish. Answer me', and this brought her back to the subject.

Robert Murray's brisk manner and kindly intent eventually

caused Harriett to speak more freely, and she began to confide in him, telling him again how she worried a great deal at night, thinking and thinking and always coming back to not knowing what she could do. She pointed out how thin she had become, particularly on her neck and shoulders, as a result of all the worry. There seemed to her to be no way out of her problems, as Charlie refused to see her or to answer her letters and she was frightened to ask her father for help.

The impression Robert Murray was left with was that Harriett was quite sensible enough to understand all that he had said when he spoke openly to her about the benefit of getting her divorce through as quickly as possible. He certainly did not notice any signs of madness, simply 'a curious observance and as it were lassitude of thought coming across her now and then which ceased the moment I recalled her to the subject in hand'.

After leaving Bickley, Robert Murray gave Sir Charles an account of his visit, telling him that Harriett was tired of her present life and wished to obtain her divorce. Charlie noted that his uncle had advised her to take steps in that direction and she said she intended to do so, promising that when he next saw her she would not be in her present position. Robert Murray was of the opinion, as a result of his visit, that Harriett was quite sane and capable of instructing her solicitor.

After receiving Harriett's two normal-sounding letters, as well as the copy made by Mrs Caborn of her letter to Lady Louisa, Sir Charles had fixed to see Dr Reynolds and Robert Murray in London the following day, 16 October. Mr Haynes had also intended to come up to London but, he explained, 'indisposition and engagements tie me sadly to my house'. However he saw Sir Charles and his brother John on 19 October in Leamington and reported that they were in an optimistic mood, believing that Robert Murray's testimony and the nurse's new evidence would dispose of the madness theory for good. They now hoped that the insanity issue and the main question of the adultery and divorce, 'the merits', could be consolidated into one. Better still, if the judge would now accept, on Lady Mordaunt's own admission, that she had been feigning all along, then he might 'try the main issue without bringing up the question of insanity'. So sure were the brothers about the whole affair having reached a momentous phase that they wanted an immediate and united opinion from all the lawyers about the next step to be taken. Mr Haynes felt this was hardly practicable as Serjeant Ballantine was out of town at that time, but he did write to Mr Inderwick in the hope that his opinion would be sufficient. 'Sir Charles wishes Mr Inderwick to know' wrote Mr Haynes

> that last Friday Oct 15th Lady Mordaunt told Robert Murray (brother of Herbert) that she was sick of the life she was leading and wished to obtain a divorce and evinced a determination that if she could see Sir Charles and knew he would not alter his determination she would at once admit her guilt. Sir Charles will see her if Mr Inderwick recommends.

Mr Inderwick's reply, written on 22 October, was hardly encouraging. Not for the first time, Sir Charles's ideas were given the legal veto. Mr Inderwick was of the opinion that the judge would not allow the two issues to be tried together and would not allow the 'merits' to be gone into at all until the insanity issue had been disposed of. 'And if Sir Charles withdraws from the proceedings as far as the insanity is concerned, the Judge will in my opinion stay the suit altogether' wrote Mr Inderwick.

As for the question of Sir Charles having a meeting with his wife, Mr Inderwick did not think that would be prudent at all, unless it were to be held in the presence of 'some third person who could be an independent witness of what took place'. He admitted that it might help to satisfy Sir Charles himself about his wife's state of mind and enable him to come to some determination as to the future course of the suit. 'I do not however advise Sir Charles to see her and I think Lady M might very well be made to understand Sir Charles's determination of the divorce through some other person' was Mr Inderwick's final word on the subject.

30

A Trip to London

After her conversation with Robert Murray, Harriett seemed for a few days to be in a highly nervous state as she waited for developments, always wondering whether now that she had said she would agree to a divorce, Charlie would at last come to see her. On the day after Robert Murray's visit, she woke early, feeling very hysterical, and soon after six o'clock she sent for Mrs Hancox who told Barker to give her some sal volatile. This soothed her down at once, but she remained subdued and she did not go near Mrs Hancox all day. She went out for a walk with Miss Keddell, 'taking several turnings', and when they came back she acted strangely, removing furniture, turning pictures to the wall and getting her paint-box out in order, she said, to paint the door-plate. Next day, although she nursed the baby for a while, she remained very restless and 'mischievous', in particular showing signs of wanting to 'cut things up'. On the Tuesday she complained of a headache and in fact for some hours seemed to be in real distress. There were occasional bursts of laughter, but otherwise she was very quiet. All through the following week she was inclined to be 'troublesome', constantly going up and down stairs, and finding it difficult to converse with anybody. In addition she did what Mrs Hancox described as 'the most ridiculous things'.

By the end of the week she began to settle down again and started to talk to those around her. This gave Mrs Hancox the opportunity to remind her that the time had come to make some decisions. She then asked what was likely to become of her, and Mrs Hancox told her that she would be put into a private asylum. At first she said that this could hardly be worse than what she was experiencing at the present time, particularly mentioning the fact that she was not allowed to see anyone 'without an order from somebody'. Mrs Hancox told her that she would soon notice the difference; she would have none of the comforts and luxuries that she was able to enjoy at Page Heath, and would be put in a 'private gentleman's house without servants of her own', and her life would be 'plain and quiet'. This prospect did not appeal to her at all and she asked Mrs Hancox what she should do to avoid it. 'Send for your solicitor' was once again the nurse's advice.

But Harriett was not sure whether she could do it. 'I don't think I can trust myself' she said. 'My head is sometimes very forgetful so that I shall have to leave it to my father to do and we won't talk about it any more.'

Dr Wood now felt that the time had come to ascertain how the reunion with her baby had affected Lady Mordaunt. After issuing instructions that she was not to be told about his visit in advance, he went to Page Heath on 25 October accompanied by Dr Hughes, introducing himself on his arrival to Miss Keddell whom he had not met before. Lady Mordaunt did not greet him with any enthusiasm, at first ignoring him and then offering him her left hand, as she had once done to Dr Orford, and telling him, in response to his inquiry, that she was 'quite well'. The way she said it seemed to imply that there was absolutely no necessity for his visit. She did however, appear to be much brighter than he had ever known her. When he said that he would like to see the baby, she volunteered to fetch her, and left the room. This gave Dr Wood a chance to have a quiet talk with Miss Keddell, who told him that Nurse Hancox would not trust Lady Mordaunt with the baby, as she would sit her on the floor and fail to support her back, or put her on the edge of a chair without appearing to see the need for any precaution.

Lady Mordaunt came back without the baby who was eventually brought in by Mrs Hancox. Dr Wood observed that she made no move to take the baby in her arms, and although she showed pleasure 'it was rather of the kind a child would manifest at the presence of some novelty which was curious rather than directly interesting or amusing'. Although she certainly did not shun the child, Dr Wood never saw any manifestation of normal maternal feeling or affection. She did, however, suggest to Violet that she should ask Dr Wood for half-a-crown, which impressed everybody as it showed she had not forgotten the episode on a previous visit when she had asked for that sum herself.

Dr Wood left the baby with Lady Mordaunt and Miss Keddell and went next door to talk to Mrs Hancox. He asked her whether she would have any hesitation in trusting Lady Mordaunt with the baby and she replied that she certainly would not leave it in her care as it would not be safe. Dr Wood then asked her if she thought that Lady Mordaunt would deliberately injure the child. She replied that she believed her ladyship would kill it.

Later, on thinking this over, Dr Wood came to the conclusion that there were certain inconsistencies in the nurse's description of Lady Mordaunt's behaviour. Her belief that the mother was capable of killing her baby hardly tallied with her expressed opinion that Lady Mordaunt knew perfectly well what she was about. The doctor thought her belief that Lady Mordaunt would kill her child was really based on the obvious fact that she did not understand the care needed in looking after such a young child. This in its turn could be explained by lack of experience in bringing up young children and also by the fact that she had hardly had any contact with her baby since the first days at Walton.

As the time was getting on, Lady Mordaunt invited Dr Wood to stay to dinner, as any normal lady of the house might have done. Although she did not usually make any effort to change for dinner, on this occasion she went upstairs and reappeared in full evening dress, though without any jewellery. When dinner was announced, she made an impressive entry into the dining-room, as if she really were mistress in her own house, taking her place at the head of the table and starting to serve the soup in the conventional way although she gave up half way through and had to be helped by the 'servant in waiting'. She herself ate little, taking a few mouthfuls and failing to finish anything. When Dr Wood remarked on this, she said she had made a very good luncheon. After dinner, when the servants had left, Dr Wood took the opportunity of asking her whether she wanted Mrs Hancox to stay or go. She apparently had difficulty in answering, and Dr Wood gained the impression that her feelings for Mrs Hancox were a mixture of 'kind feeling and dislike'. She then said, with some indignation, that Hancox had talked to her about a divorce, and asked what right she had to do so.

In the drawing-room it was agreed that they should have a game of whist and when the cards were brought they each drew one, and it was decided that Dr Wood and Lady Mordaunt should play together, Dr Hughes partnering Miss Keddell. Dr Wood was glad to see that Lady Mordaunt dealt and played the cards properly although every now and then she needed 'rousing' when it was her turn to play. She made some mistakes, but when these were pointed out, she corrected them, apologising in a natural manner. When the game was over, she said that she was tired and went up to bed. The doctors then questioned Miss Keddell, who said she thought that Nurse Hancox was a source of irritation. Barker was then summoned, Mrs

Caborn meanwhile looking after Lady Mordaunt. Barker was only too pleased to give the usual catalogue of Lady Mordaunt's 'irrational acts' which were not, in her view, assumed for the purpose of deception, but were quite involuntary.

Believing that this would be his last visit to Page Heath, since the case was soon to be heard, Dr Wood decided that he would like to see Lady Mordaunt before he left. He went up to the bedroom accompanied by Miss Keddell and Dr Hughes. By this time she was in bed, and she looked understandably annoyed and disconcerted by this intrusion. She made it clear that she thought it unnecessary. There was absolutely nothing wrong with her, she said, and she continued to insist that she had no need of doctors. However when Dr Wood said that he had simply come up to feel her pulse as he had forgotten to do it earlier, she became docile again and held out her arm.

Dr Wood came to the conclusion after this visit that Lady Mordaunt was in fact much improved, with a better ability to carry on a conversation and a greater manifestation of intelligence. He now felt there was a reasonable prospect of her recovery, but that this would depend on the avoidance of all possible sources of irritation, 'her mind being kept at perfect rest with only such diversion as was agreeable to her'. Bearing in mind Miss Keddell's opinion that Mrs Hancox was becoming a source of irritation, he thought that he would advise Dr Gull and Dr Reynolds to send her and the baby away without delay so that Lady Mordaunt's recovery could be consolidated.

News of Lady Mordaunt's improved condition soon began to spread, and there were reports in the newspapers that she might well prove capable after all of putting in an answer to the petition. The Mordaunts were certainly hoping that this would be so, and that the Prince's name would be included when the case came to court. Sir Charles's mother and brother had all along refused to accept the lawyer's advice that the Prince's name should be left out of it. The Dowager, convinced that the Prince was guilty, had asked Henry Mills, a Mordaunt cousin who lived at Pillerton Hersey a few miles from Walton, to examine all the affidavits and other papers and give his opinion as to whether or not the Prince should also be cited. Although probably none too anxious to become involved, Mr Mills had agreed to do what he could, and on 2 September Mr Cadogan had delivered the documents to him. Noting particularly the Prince's frequent calls at Chesham Place, Henry Mills thought that the documents contained 'such reflexions on the Prince of Wales and Captain Farquhar as appear to me out of place while they are not also made co-respondents'. He realised that Sir Charles himself would have liked to include the Prince and the Captain, but had been overruled by his counsel. After carefully studying all the papers, Henry Mills expressed himself ready to join those within the family circle and outside it who believed that justice would not be done unless both men were added to the list.

The *Birmingham Daily Post* agreed, being strongly of the opinion that it was imperative for the case to be heard at the first possible moment, since the affidavits already filed involved 'so many of high position, including one of the highest personages in the realm'. It was only fair to those involved that proof of the truth or falsity of the allegations should be established without delay.

Other newspapers followed and the reports were read with dismay in some quarters. For the Prince they came at a most inopportune moment. The Princess's baby was due at the end of November, and the news that Lady Mordaunt might after all be well enough to give evidence at the forthcoming trial was something he could have done without. Worse still was the threat that he himself might be added to the list of co-respondents. It was all the more provoking as the stay at Wildblad had been such a success, the Princess patently benefiting as a result of taking the waters there, and the whole family enjoying what was described as 'the salubrious air of this wild and high valley'. They had all played croquet on the lawns of their hotel and had been able to take walks in welcome privacy 'without being mobbed by inquisitive townsfolk'.

The Prince had returned to England to find that everything was not quite so straightforward as he had hoped. It was hardly proving easy to establish Lady Mordaunt's madness. The incarceration at Worthing had not driven her as insane as might have been expected, and after two months at Bickley there were still doubts even in the minds of some of the medical men who had been so carefully chosen. Particularly worrying was the fact that Dr Wood had turned out to be a waverer, especially as he had been appointed by the judge himself to act as a referee between the opposing teams. Lord Penzance, trusting him as an independent observer, would certainly attach great weight to his findings.

All this posed a threat to the Prince's improved relationship with his wife. The best he could do was to take her into his confidence, informing her of all the developments in what he described as 'this unfortunate case'. To the Queen he wrote 'Dear Alix has entirely taken the same view in the matter that I have and quite sees that it is an absolute necessity for me to appear in Court, should I be called.' But he still hoped this would not happen; the doctors would have to be brought into line and particularly Dr Wood with his aggravating tendency to talk of a cure when all that was required of him was to agree that Lady Mordaunt's condition was irreversible. It was unfortunate, too, that Dr Gull and Dr Reynolds had gone off on holiday at such a crucial time. Their absence had given Sir Charles the opportunity to introduce his own agents, notably the Murray brothers, who had grossly overstepped the mark in talking to Lady Mordaunt and trying to persuade her that she would like the divorce to go ahead.

When Herbert Murray next contacted Dr Wood to seek permission for another visit to Bickley, he sensed that there had been a change of policy. For the first time Dr Wood put obstacles in his way. Herbert Murray had said that he planned to take Lady Mordaunt to a fireworks display at the Crystal Palace, but Dr Wood had refused to sanction the outing. The reason he gave was that the fireworks would be too noisy. His theory was that the patient should be kept in a quiet environment for her own good.

Dr Wood had even shown signs of refusing to allow Herbert Murray to go down to Page Heath at all, but had relented at the last minute. When Murray told Harriett what had happened she exhibited some annoyance at what she termed the doctor's 'meddling', at the same time saying how pleased she was that he had at least managed to defy Dr Wood by coming down to see her. She thanked him over and over again, saying that she longed for visitors and was bored to death and sick of the place she was in and of the 'everlasting lanes' she had to walk in.

The doctors had also refused to let John Fiennes visit Harriett at Page Heath, but Herbert Murray believed that he could get round this by arranging a meeting in London.

Harriett seemed very pleased at the prospect of going to London to meet her uncle, and altogether Herbert Murray thought that she seemed far better than she had been when he had seen her last. He observed that she was laughing in her pointless way far less than before. Violet was brought down to the drawing-room for Herbert Murray to see, and Harriett amused the child by playing on the piano with what he described as 'great feeling', although she eventually became rather upset, as she always did when she heard music which reminded her of happier days. She asked whether Mrs Murray could come and stay with her again, but he said that Dr Wood and Dr Gull had forbidden it. She then begged him to take her to London that evening to see a play, but he told her that was not possible either without the doctors' sanction. However he promised he would ask their permission for another time. She herself agreed that it would not be wise to go to the theatre anyway, on account of the publicity it might arouse.

Herbert Murray went down to Bickley again on 27 October and told Harriett that he had arranged for her to meet John Fiennes in London the next day. At first she seemed hesitant about going, but then told Herbert Murray that she would see her uncle if he thought it was a good idea. He said he was sure it was, and promised he would come down next morning to take her up to London. She told him this would not be necessary.

Herbert Murray was very pleased with Harriett's behaviour on this visit, as she seemed to be perfectly natural and pleasant and able to converse quite easily. The weather had by now turned very cold and there was snow in the air but she seemed keen to go for a walk, and when they were out she never laughed at all, although this started up again to a certain extent once they were indoors. He also for the first time noticed the restlessness that other people had talked about. She kept going in and out of the room. At dinner she hardly ate or drank anything, but this was not, he thought, because she was having one of her fits of the 'blues'. After dinner they played at écarté, and she did not play at all badly, although her attention tended to wander. They then went on to dummy whist, Harriett playing the dummy hand, but this was not so successful as she evidently had 'no notion of the game'.

Next morning Lady Mordaunt called the coachman early and gave orders that he should drive her to London. He said this was not possible as there had been a heavy frost and the roads would as yet be too slippery for the horses. Undeterred, she called for Barker and told her that she must accompany her to London by train. Miss Keddell, rather worried about Lady Mordaunt's sudden show of independence, expressed the intention of coming too, and in the end they all travelled up together. When they reached Victoria Station, Harriett told Miss Keddell that she did not need her any more and that she could have a day in London on her own. Barker was to come with her in a hansom cab to the Murrays' house in Chester Square and after that she too would be free to do as she liked.

Mrs Murray was surprised when the doorbell rang and the maid ushered Harriett into the drawing-room.

'I thought you were to drive up; Herbert has gone to meet you' said Mrs Murray. Harriett explained about the slippery roads. 'Go and take your things off' said Mrs Murray. 'You know your way upstairs.' When Harriett came down again, they talked about various subjects until Herbert arrived back from his abortive journey to Page Heath. He suggested they should go out for a walk, Mrs Murray's maid helping Harriett to put on her things as Barker had already left. Harriett seemed disappointed that 'Uncle Johnny' had not yet arrived, so Herbert tried to pacify her by taking her shopping. They were on their way to Bubbs's Library when he said 'Now I will show you the same dress that you saw the last time you were in London.' Although they were on the opposite side of the road to the shop where the dress was displayed, Harriett immediately said that it was not the same one. Although almost identical, it had slightly larger spots. Herbert Murray had not noticed the difference himself and in his opinion the episode proved that Harriett was not nearly so stupid as some people liked to make out.

They were out for about an hour and a half and most of the time Harriett said very little, telling Herbert Murray that she preferred listening to talking. Then, when they got back to the house, she went straight upstairs to take off her hat and coat. Meanwhile Mrs Murray's father, General Arbuthnot, had arrived unexpectedly, to Mrs Murray's annoyance, as she said she had not wanted any of her relations to see Lady Mordaunt. She quickly told him that Lady Mordaunt was there, and as he went into the drawing-room Harriett appeared through another door at the end of the room. He, expecting to meet the Dowager, was amazed when he saw the young Lady Mordaunt coming towards him, looking very lovely indeed.

'I don't know if you know Lady Mordaunt' said Mrs Murray.

'No' said the General. They sat down on the sofa together and chatted for a while, Harriett telling him that she had just come up for the day and that she had enjoyed herself very much that morning at the Baker Street bazaar. General Arbuthnot was charmed. Mrs Murray left them together while she went to see to things, and a little while later she came back into the room with John Fiennes who had just arrived. Mrs Murray pressed her father to stay to luncheon but he said that he would rather not as he was leaving London shortly. As he was going, Harriett asked Mrs Murray why she had not introduced her to the General, but Mrs Murray said she thought she had done so. General Arbuthnot then bowed to Lady Mordaunt and left the room. After he had gone, Herbert Murray said 'Now let us have luncheon.' They all sat down, and although Lady Mordaunt ate her lunch 'comfortably', particularly enjoying the sweets, she did not say much. Afterwards it was suggested that she and John Fiennes should have a walk. When the maid was helping her to put on her coat and bonnet, she talked to her easily and naturally, asking about the current fashions, and how dresses were being worn these days.

After the walk, Harriett chatted for a few moments to Mrs Murray who was lying down in her bedroom. She then went downstairs, Barker having by now arrived. The maid met her on the stairs and asked her if she would like some tea, but she said no, it was time to go, and she asked Barker to fetch her muff. Herbert Murray accompanied her to the station. As far as the Murrays were concerned it had been a successful day, and Harriett had behaved remarkably well, only laughing a few times.

When she was later asked her impression of Lady Mordaunt, the Murrays' maid said that she had not noticed anything unusual except that she had occasionally stopped and stood in the 'thinking' position. Mary Hunt, the nursemaid to Mrs Murray's children, agreed that Lady Mordaunt, although quiet, had seemed perfectly normal. She had come into the nursery and said what a pleasant room it was. She then spoke to the eight-year-old Murray daughter, asking her whether she could have some bread, a remark which the child ignored. She also asked if she could wash her hands and was taken into the night nursery for the purpose.

Lady Mordaunt was very uncommunicative on the journey home. She did not confide in anybody about her meeting with John Fiennes and the Murrays could only guess at what had taken place.

31

Winter at Page Heath

The Prince had as usual spent his birthday at Sandringham with the Princess. Towards the end of November they returned to London and on 26 November the Princess gave birth at Marlborough House to a daughter, Princess Maud.

Soon after the Prince arrived back in London, Dr Gull paid a visit to Page Heath. He reported that Lady Mordaunt had behaved rather strangely, and although he found it hard to say whether or not she was truly insane, he did think that she would be incapable of giving evidence in court, and might well end up in an asylum.

Dr Reynolds went down to Bickley separately and he observed that Lady Mordaunt hardly ate anything at dinner. She referred to him as 'Lord Bradford' whenever she spoke to him. After dinner Mrs Hancox told him that she believed Lady Mordaunt to be perfectly sensible in 'everything she said and done before me' while she had been in the house. She had said much the same to Dr Gull.

After this it seems that the other doctors were hurriedly brought into line. On Monday 1 November, Doctors Wood, Hughes and Reynolds were all summoned to a meeting at Dr Gull's house with Mr Benbow, Sir Thomas's lawyer, in attendance. As a result a terse report on Lady Mordaunt's condition was drawn up. The doctors unanimously agreed that Lady Mordaunt was mentally incapable and incompetent to attend to the care of herself or her affairs. Dr Wood wrote to Mr Hunt on 5 November

As Drs Gull and Reynolds at our conference on Monday 1 November agreed with me as to Lady Mordaunt's state of mind I do not think that there can be any objection to my stating to you that in my judgment Lady Mordaunt is not in a fit state to give instructions which could be relied upon in any important matter of business. I am satisfied that the symptoms of a weak state of mind which she manifests are not assumed though I can understand some persons thinking they are because under some circumstances her conduct is much more rational than at others.

Dr Wood went on to say that although Lady Mordaunt could at times be 'roused' to some mental activity, yet she could never keep up a sustained conversation. If any confirmation of his current opinion was needed, he could quote a case recently admitted to St Luke's Hospital of another young woman in a very similar state following childbirth.

Dr Wood agreed to meet Mr Hunt to explain his reasons further, but not until late the following week, as he had to make 'a distant country journey' over the weekend, and would be at the hospital for the whole day on the Monday and Tuesday. The most suitable time for the meeting would be immediately after he had breakfasted at eight o'clock. Mr Hunt wrote back to say that he was not looking for a meeting; what he wanted was a report on Lady Mordaunt's state of mind. Dr Wood replied on 9 November questioning whether he was really at liberty to make a formal report without the approval of the judge. 'It seems to me that I should be in some danger of appearing as a partisan if I furnished a report to one side only when I must presume the object of the Court was to have a perfectly independent witness.' He wondered whether a way round the difficulty would be to furnish 'the other side' with a duplicate.

It was clear that none of the doctors wished to put pen to paper at this particular moment. Dr Hughes, when he in his turn was asked to send in his report in order to explain his reasons for declaring that Lady Mordaunt was mad, wrote back to ask whether Sir Charles would object to having a conversation with him, as he felt he could say more in half an hour than he could write in half a dozen letters. He had heard that Sir Charles was in town at this time and if he could go down to Bromley, Dr Hughes undertook to have a room placed at his disposal, so that he could report on his recent conversations with Miss Keddell, Mrs Caborn and Sarah Barker. This offer was not taken up – in fact it is doubtful whether the letter was ever answered by the lawyers, who treated it with contempt. It was evident, in any case, that all the doctors were playing for time.

Sir Charles, incredulous as he was about the doctors' verdict, wrote urgently to his uncle Robert Murray asking him for a full description of his visit to Page Heath when by all accounts he had gained a very different impression from the doctors. Robert Murray's reply, written on 8 November from Rome, was uncompromising. He gave full details of his conversation with Harriett, describing how, after her initial reserve, she had, when he had spoken to her firmly, confided in him freely, expressing her anxieties and her desire to escape from the situation she was in. Her momentary lapses of concentration and slowness to answer were the only unnatural things he had noticed about her.

By this time Miss Parsons had left Page Heath, but on Monday 1 November she dropped in 'casually' as she happened to be passing through. Lady Mordaunt welcomed her 'nicely' and asked if she would like to go upstairs to take off her bonnet, saying that she would bring her some eau-de-cologne. Miss Parsons felt that Lady Mordaunt was most pleased to see her, and chatted quite rationally. When Miss Keddell left the room, Lady Mordaunt hugged and kissed Miss Parsons several times. Although she did not eat any lunch she otherwise behaved well, which seemed strange as Miss Keddell said she had earlier behaved very foolishly. Lady Mordaunt, Nurse Hancox and Miss Keddell drove Miss Parsons to the station, but they had to go back to the house to fetch the cloak which Miss Parsons had left behind, and this made Lady Mordaunt laugh a great deal.

The doctors were probably by now more than ever convinced that Violet and Mrs Hancox should be sent away, since it was evident that, whatever Miss Keddell might say about the nurse's tendency to irritate Lady Mordaunt, her stay at Bickley had coincided with the obvious improvement in Lady Mordaunt's mental state. The more Mrs Hancox remained at Page Heath, the more evidence she would be able to furnish about the very normal conversations that had gone on between herself and Lady Mordaunt in the nursery. And so, on 2 November, the mother was parted from her child. Just before she left, Mrs Hancox took Violet in to say goodbye to Lady Mordaunt who was still in bed. Miss Keddell said that she did not seem to be unduly upset about her daughter's departure.

On the Friday of that week Lady Mordaunt's father arrived at Page Heath. She was having her luncheon when he arrived.

'My dear, how do you do?' he said.

She got up and kissed him. 'Well, Papa, how are you?' she asked.

'I think you are looking well, and plump' he said. It was a strange thing to say, since everybody else always remarked on how much weight she had lost.

'Your face has grown very thin' she countered.

Miss Keddell left the room so that father and daughter could talk in private at the dinner table. Afterwards Harriett seemed very upset. She left the dining-room, went upstairs and flung herself on her bed.

Her father remained downstairs, and after a while Miss Keddell went up to her room and with some difficulty persuaded her to go back downstairs. She finally agreed and went straight to the piano as if she did not want to talk to her father again. Sir Thomas waited for a while and then said it was time for him to go. He asked Harriett if she had any message for her mother and sisters and she said she had not. When he was leaving, she stood still, and laughed, as Miss Keddell put it, 'immoderately'.

In the evening she seemed very low and depressed and more 'absent' than ever.

On the Saturday following, Herbert Murray went down and took Harriett for a walk and a drive. He immediately noticed a difference in her. She seemed to have lost interest in everything, and at dinner she would neither eat nor talk. Her father's visit had apparently cast her into a gloom deeper than any she had known before. She had of course suffered from her bouts of depression, her fits of the 'blues', all along, but this was worse.

'Barker, I hate you' she said, adding 'I hate myself, I hate everybody about me. I want to die. Give me some poison and let me die.'

When they were out walking, Barker handed her a rose out of the hedge, remarking that there was no rose without thorns and no pleasure without pain.

'It is all pain and no pleasure now' said Lady Mordaunt.

Briefly Herbert Murray's efforts to take her out into the world and to persuade her that there was an alternative road had lifted her out of her melancholy. But since her father's visit she had sunk back into depression and all her oddities had begun again, as if at his instruction.

On the Monday after Sir Thomas's visit Miss Keddell asked Lady Mordaunt if she had heard from him. She said she had not, and when Miss Keddell wanted to know if he would come down again, she replied that she did not know. She seemed upset at the mention of her father and behaved in a 'most indelicate and improper' way for the rest of the day. At dinner she drank a whole tumbler of water, cut a very large piece of steak and put it into her mouth, but had to reject it as it was too big. The next day she became very hot and feverish. Dr Hughes was sent for and he prescribed a day's rest in bed. Miss Keddell sat with her on and off, but she refused to talk, and the only remark she made was 'Barker, bring a big knife.' Miss Keddell said that she also caught her trying to push a pin into her ear.

On the Thursday Dr Reynolds as well as Dr Hughes came to see her. She was still feverish, and had started muttering to herself. Miss Keddell could not catch what she said, but thought she heard her saying, 'Oh, God, oh God, oh God' in anguished tones. In a day or two her temperature went down, but she still seemed, in Miss Keddell's words, 'very lost'. She remained quiet, and Miss Keddell found it hard to have any kind of conversation with her.

A day or two later, on Barker's evening off, Mrs Caborn helped her get to bed. After talking about Sir Charles, and saying that she wondered what he was doing to amuse himself, Lady Mordaunt went silent for a while, eventually telling Mrs Caborn how worried she felt. She looked so tormented that Mrs Caborn felt sorry for her, and did her best to comfort her, advising her to 'quiet herself' and to get to sleep as soon as possible. Mrs Caborn's kindness seemed to help, for she slept well that night and in the morning was in an unusually amenable mood. When she was asked what she wanted for breakfast she answered 'What you like' and Mrs Caborn replied, 'My Lady, it is what *you* like.' In the end she settled for coffee in the drawing-room, after which she ate a good breakfast without causing any difficulties. At supper time she went into Mrs Caborn's room and asked for some bread and cheese which was brought to her together with some ale. While eating it she talked about Walton and asked after some of the tenants, and she also wanted to know what had happened to Mrs Cadogan. 'She has never written me a line since baby's birth' Lady Mordaunt complained.

To Miss Keddell's surprise Lady Mordaunt was quite talkative that evening, reminiscing about her visits to London with Herbert Murray, and remembering particularly the velocipedes.

By this time statements had been taken from those who had been able to observe Lady Mordaunt's behaviour at Page Heath, and the diaries written by Mrs Caborn and Bird had been copied, although Sarah Barker refused to send hers in, saying that she had written such unpleasant things down in it that she did not think it would be fair to Lady Mordaunt to put it on view. Mr Haynes became increasingly weary and irritable as he read the statements through, scrawling tetchy comments in the margin such as '?What!!' or '?Meaning?!' when any of the witnesses hinted that Lady Mordaunt was not altogether normal.

The most satisfactory testimony came from Florence Stephens who described how Lady Mordaunt had given orders and chatted just as she had done at Walton. At the other extreme were Sarah Barker's bizarre descriptions of Lady Mordaunt getting into the bath when there was no water in it or dressing up her bible as if it were a baby. Most of these things Mr Haynes dismissed as 'hearsay'. Nobody else had seen Lady Mordaunt, for example, put her hat down the W. C. or had heard her threaten to drink the oil in the night light or gabble the Lord's Prayer most irreverently, laughing wildly as she did so.

Not that the other, more reliable, witnesses could deny that Lady Mordaunt did act very oddly at times. But whereas Barker was sure that she would never have been able to keep up the feigning so consistently, Miss Parsons was fairly certain that she was play-acting whenever she went into one of her 'absent' fits or started laughing uncontrollably. Miss Parsons had heard her say herself that sometimes she 'put it on'. Asked why she did so she replied 'Oh I have an object, I think it will be better in the end.' When Miss Parsons had told her that nothing was gained by deceit, there was a long pause before Lady Mordaunt went on to say 'If I were to humble myself to Sir Charles, I could settle it all in two minutes.' Then, when Miss Parsons asked her why she did not do so, she replied 'Because I do not think it right for wives to humble themselves to their husbands.' On another occasion when she was childishly taking ribbons out of her work box and scattering them crazily about the room, she had said that if Sir Charles came to see her, she would do all that sort of thing 'tremendously'.

Miss Parsons in all honesty had to admit that there were times when Lady Mordaunt did the most extraordinary things, like hiding under her bed and refusing to come out, and she often acted in a very childlike way. 'I don't want my opinion known,' Miss Parsons wrote,

> but I will tell you in confidence that what my lady is suffering from is the worst form of hysteria. It is hysterical madness, I am sure of it, and no wonder when you think of the life of excitement she has had, *all stopped at once*. Restore her to what she has lost and she would be well in a few days, but how she is to get well, living as she does, I cannot say.

Herbert Murray agreed. In his opinion, the treatment meted out to the unfortunate girl had all been a 'grievous mistake'. Bearing in mind her history of hysteria and the complete change from a hectic life of frivolity and gossip to her present isolated existence, he thought it was little wonder that she had gone rather odd. She had after all no resources of her own to fall back on except music, since she was not given to reading and seemed to have lost all interest in her 'work'. The doctors only upset her, and how could they possibly pronounce on her condition on the basis of a few visits? Herbert Murray felt sure that a change of scene would be beneficial. If Harriett could be moved to some location where she would see more people and be out of range of the doctors, the improvement in her condition which had been noted after he had taken her out and about might well become more permanently established. As it was, however, he was by now having grave doubts about what would happen if she saw a solicitor, particularly as the arrival in the house of any stranger always made her go silent immediately.

In spite of the uncertainty as to whether Lady Mordaunt was feigning or not, Sir Charles's lawyers when they met were able to issue a statement to the effect that after reading all the papers, they could see no satisfactory ground on which to assume that Lady Mordaunt was of unsound mind and incapable of instructing a solicitor. All the same they advised Sir Charles to submit the question of his wife's sanity to a jury. They thought it essential for the matter to be properly cleared up for her sake as well as his, bearing in mind that she was at the moment being quite unfairly labelled insane. The lawyers believed that the question of Lady Mordaunt's sanity could not satisfactorily be tried without the whole of her circumstances 'attendant upon and consequent to her confinement being brought before the Court'. This meant that all the evidence so carefully collected by Mr Haynes would be used to prepare the ground for the subsequent divorce case.

Mr Hunt advised Sir Charles to discharge if possible the order made by the judge in August so that Lady Mordaunt could be moved to a more lively location out of reach of the doctors. It was decided that two new doctors, Dr Forbes Winslow and Dr Tyler Smith,[103] should be sent down, well briefed, to Bickley, in the hope that they would provide medical confirmation of Sir Charles's theory that Lady Mordaunt's condition would improve immediately if she were to live a more normal life in more cheerful surroundings. In spite of objections from Sir Thomas's lawyer, Lord Penzance gave his permission, stipulating that the doctors should arrive 'unexpectedly'.

Herbert Murray went down to see Harriett a few days later and they talked about her future. She told him that if she were to be moved anywhere, she would like to go to London. When he suggested that she should try to help herself and write to her father, all she said was 'I don't wish to be ordered about by him'.

Mrs Murray stayed at Page Heath for the weekend, but she sensed from the moment she arrived that things had changed for the worse. Harriett remained stubbornly silent and on the Sunday everything came to a head, as she started throwing things about, smashing a flower glass and flinging her 'illuminating box' onto the ground, laughing as she did so. She proceeded to rush out of the house and throw herself on the wet grass. 'I then took her out driving' Mrs Murray told Sir Charles

and during our walk on Hayes Common she quite frightened me by occasionally running off as hard as she could tear, laughing immoderately, throwing her muff about etc till at last I was thankful to get her into the carriage and bring her home when nothing particular occurred except her persistency in sitting down in all directions, several times on the oil cloth in the hall etc.

Mrs Murray was quite shocked by Harriett's behaviour at the table. She went into the dining-room and gnawed a piece of chicken, and then seized a piece of cheese which she devoured, rind and all, so quickly that Mrs Murray thought she would most certainly be sick. At luncheon, she took off her plate a slice of fat beef, which she threw into her mouth and after chewing it spat it all out. Then she mixed some gravy and jelly together, in short her behaviour was horrid.'

Mrs Murray told Sir Charles that she had come to the conclusion that there was little hope for the future. She had met Dr Hughes who had talked strongly about the unsoundness of Harriett's mind, and had asked her 'as a test' whether she would let Lady Mordaunt venture out alone in her present condition. She had to admit, that after what she had seen that weekend she certainly would not. 'I am indeed sorry to have such a tale to tell' wrote Mrs Murray.

Mrs Caborn wrote an equally depressing letter to Sir Charles on 1 December. She reported that Lady Mordaunt's mother had been down the previous afternoon and had spent about two hours with her daughter before catching the 4.30 train back to London. They had gone out for a drive together in the closed carriage, so that there had not been the slightest chance of anybody eavesdropping. As a result of this visit, Mrs Caborn believed, Lady Mordaunt had been behaving worse than ever, refusing to write cheques for outstanding bills and smashing ornaments in the drawing-room, burning books and anything she can get hold of. I told her she would have to pay for all she had destroyed; I have since removed every ornament. I am much grieved to be obliged to give you so sad an account of Lady Mordaunt's state of mind

    I am, Sir Charles,

Yours obediently,

S. A. CABORN

There was little doubt in Sir Charles's mind that the apparent deterioration in his wife's condition could be attributed to the fact that her parents were inciting her to act as madly as possible for the benefit of the two new doctors, who both visited her independently in mid December. By that time the weather had turned very cold and the Kent countryside, so pretty in summer and autumn, was bleak and windswept. The first thing that Dr Tyler Smith noticed was that Lady Mordaunt's red and swollen hands were covered in chilblains which were much in need of dressing. He was considerably shocked by her physical appearance, and he noted that her circulation was 'wretched' and that she was painfully thin. He could not, however, agree with Sir Thomas's doctors that there were any signs of puerperal mania, and as an eminent accoucheur he should have known what he was talking about. He had taken the trouble to have a meeting with Dr Orford and felt far more ready to accept the diagnosis of the man who had attended Lady Mordaunt at the birth than to embrace the theories offered by practitioners, however learned, who had not appeared on the scene until a later date.

Dr Forbes Winslow, the second doctor nominated by Sir Charles, visited Lady Mordaunt a few days later and both doctors expressed their intention of paying another visit in about ten days' time. Sir Charles felt very anxious when he heard that a few days before Christmas Sir Thomas and Lady Louisa, this time accompanied by Helen Forbes, had paid another unscheduled visit to Page Heath. He was sure that they were preparing Harriett for the doctors' visits and encouraging her to step up her act.

Sir Thomas, having made sure that his wife and daughter were able to gain admission, had left almost immediately, but Lady Louisa and Helen remained behind and spent a long time talking to Miss Keddell. Even before Mrs Caborn let Sir Charles know about this visit, which in his opinion had been carried out in direct opposition to the order of the court, Sir Charles had become convinced that it would be necessary to dismiss both Barker and Miss Keddell since he believed that both were being influenced by the Moncreiffes. He had known for a long time that Barker was corresponding with Lady Louisa and he had suspected that Miss Keddell could be in collusion with her as well. The reported conversation between Miss Keddell and the Moncreiffe ladies only confirmed his suspicions. Mrs Caborn had not, of course, been able to hear what was said, but it was not hard to guess. Sir Charles wrote to Mr Haynes on Boxing Day asking him to inform Serjeant Ballantine of what had happened, and to assure him that Jessie Clarke was holding herself in readiness to attend Lady Mordaunt, as was Mrs Hancox who was still refusing other engagements so that she could take the child to her mother as soon as Keddell and Barker had been given their notice.

On Christmas Eve Dr Tyler Smith carried out his second visit to Page Heath and Dr Forbes Winslow went down a few days later. They both interviewed Sarah Barker who gave them a lurid account of Lady Mordaunt's behaviour, talking of her being subject to 'sexual excitement', practising self-abuse and crying out on several occasions that she wanted a man. The doctors did not know how much of this they could believe, and from their own observations they found it impossible to say whether or not Lady Mordaunt was mad or simply feigning. As for her physical state, they felt certain that she was in need of treatment. Although her chilblains had healed, the scars they had left were still very visible. Both doctors made the point that Page Heath was far too cold for somebody in Lady Mordaunt's state of health, and they recommended that she should be removed to 'some warmer and more sheltered neighbourhood'. This was exactly what Sir Charles had hoped they would say.

In Dr Forbes Winslow Sir Charles had found a useful ally. He had been involved in a lawsuit with a relation over the ownership of the private asylum founded by his father, and had subsequently become disillusioned with private asylums in general, believing that it was too often in the interest of the owners to keep their patients permanently shut up rather than trying to cure them. In the same way the system could be abused by people who wanted their relations to be put away for good. In his opinion more could be done by treating the mentally unstable as normal human beings and preferably allowing them their freedom. He was able to quote the case of a man who had been taken to an asylum, 'drugged with chlorodyne', put into a cold bath and subsequently 'thrown into a padded room'. Dr Forbes Winslow had saved him by treating him 'in a proper and humane way', letting him dine at his table like one of the family, and taking him off drugs. As he himself put it,

> If you are asked to treat the poor insane
> To ease their anguish, pacify their brain . . .
> You must not give your patients chlorodyne,
> But if excited, ask them up to dine;
> And one safe medicine all the rest will beat –
> It's Winslow's soothing syrup given neat.[104]

He was therefore much more likely to recommend 'soothing' treatment for Lady Mordaunt and a return to a more normal life. For the time being, however, he felt unable, on the strength of two visits alone, to say whether or not Lady Mordaunt was insane.

By the middle of January it became known that the case of Mordaunt v. Cole was due to be heard in the Divorce Court within the next few weeks, along with a 171 others. In some of these cases, damages had been laid at £10,000 which was, as one newspaper commented, 'a good deal to get for the loss of an unchaste or drunken wife'.

There was to be no respite for the lawyers on either side as they worked with increasing urgency to collect all the necessary documents. On 8 January Mr Haynes went down to Bickley and spent two days interviewing Sir Charles's servants. They all said that apart from hearing her laugh rather strangely from time to time, they had not noticed anything unusual in her behaviour and they had certainly never seen her do anything improper, although Leon Cotterill the footman did recall that she would often race up and down stairs and he had to say that in general he found her 'peculiar'. Mrs Caborn, for her part, had to admit that now she had seen with her own eyes actions of the kind she had previously only heard about from Barker. If previously Lady Mordaunt had acted a little strangely, she was now doing things in a way that was plainly indecent. On one occasion Mrs Caborn had seen her sitting astride one of the dining-room chairs and rocking across the room on it, making lewd noises, and she had, according to the housekeeper, behaved 'most improperly' in front of a portrait of the Queen which was hanging in the drawing-room.

On 14 January Mr Hunt, for Sir Charles, issued what was described as 'A Service of Notice of Motion to appoint a day for the

Trial'. The decision concerning the date was to be taken on 18 January. A list of special jurors was drawn up and on 21 January Mr Inderwick was asked to decide who would be subpoenaed. He included all the servants employed by Sir Charles, with the exception of Broadbridge the gardener. All members of the family, with the exception of John Mordaunt, were to be included. The doctors Orford, Jones and Solomon would of course be called, but Mr Inderwick wrote 'no' alongside the names of Jane Laing, Jane Keddell, Sarah Barker and Dorothy Carruthers, who were all likely to be used as key witnesses by 'the other side'. Mr Haynes also omitted Dr Wood from his list after he eventually, after much procrastination, came out on the side of those who believed that Lady Mordaunt was not feigning and could not properly be held accountable for her words or actions.

Mr Haynes, whose health had been giving cause for concern for some time, had returned from his expedition to Bickley considerably worse and there were serious doubts as to whether he would be fit enough to appear in court. Mr Inderwick's advice was asked as to whether Mr Haynes's evidence could be dispensed with at the trial by reason of ill-health, and if so what course should be pursued. His answer was that if Mr Haynes was unable to attend at the hearing, an order should be obtained to take his evidence on commission as it was vital to have his description of Lady Mordaunt's state of mind on the day he had taken the petition to Walton.

As the date of the trial came nearer, Lady Mordaunt's eating habits became increasingly eccentric. When Mrs Stephens had been doing the cooking, serving the food that Lady Mordaunt had ordered in the way she liked, there had been little trouble, but when Mrs Caborn took over and failed to consult her about the menu, she became resentful; and her tendency to refuse food or to hide it could simply have been a protest at what she considered to be very bad cooking. Later she seemed to develop genuine eating disorders. On one occasion, having refused to eat anything, she devoured four tartlets in a row, followed by a lump of cream cheese, afterwards complaining of a headache and being very sick. In October after her father had been to see her, and when she realised that she was no longer going to be allowed out in London with Herbert Murray, she really went on a hunger strike, every visitor in turn reporting that she had sat through the meal eating nothing.

'You are looking well, and plump' her father had said. She must have thought he was mad. Didn't she know herself, and wasn't every-body saying, how thin she was getting? 'They fool me to the top of my bent' Hamlet had muttered to himself, and she might have said the same. It is possible that her refusal to take food was part of a regression to childhood, to the days when to throw the plate of food on the floor or to lie face down in the road is the child's own way of asserting authority. But nobody at Bickley knew what to make of it, especially when around Christmas time she had suddenly stopped starving herself and had begun to eat ravenously, gnawing at chicken bones and challenging Mrs Caborn to see if between them they could eat a whole plate of chicken breasts. She began to frighten Miss Keddell by bolting her food, drinking water and soup and then eating oranges and beef steaks in quick succession. After that she appeared to be choking and finally she was sick on the table. Mrs Caborn took her off to the drawing-room like a naughty child and she then tried to set fire to the housekeeper's cap with the candle.[105]

In the new year her behaviour in general had become increasingly outlandish. Once she asked Mrs Caborn to take up the carpet in the room where Mrs Murray had slept and move it to the nursery in an apparent hark back to the days at Walton when the carpets had been taken up for spring cleaning. She became more and more embarrass-ing when out walking, trying to snatch children's hats off, and fre-quently lying down in the road. She had gone up to a beggar lady and offered her a dead leaf, an Ophelia-like gesture. 'God bless thee, poor thing' she had said. She could no longer throw ornaments about as all these had been locked away, but for good measure she seized Barker by the hair and dragged her down the passage, laughing loudly as she did so. She blacked her face, set fire to a new packet of handkerchiefs, and 'took the broom' to Miss Keddell. 'If your ladyship goes on like this you will be locked up,' protested Miss Keddell.

'You will be locked up afterwards' Lady Mordaunt replied.

On 7 February a notice was delivered to Benbow and Saltwell, Sir Thomas's lawyers, stating that they were required to produce to the court at the trial of the sanity issue a certain letter written by Lady Mordaunt to her mother and sent through the post on the 8th day of October 1869. This was the letter written by Lady Mordaunt and copied by Miss Parsons, in which she had referred to Bird becoming rather 'cocky'.

Mr Inderwick advised that 'the other side' should also be required

to 'admit' the handwriting of various documents which included the
Prince of Wales's letters. A subpoena was therefore issued by Benjamin Hunt to the Prince, ordering him to appear on 12 February at
eleven o'clock in the forenoon in order to identify his own handwriting and to bring with him and produce all letters written to him by
Lady Mordaunt since her marriage. This naturally caused the Prince
some concern, showing as it did that his name would almost certainly
feature in the trial. He therefore told the Princess what had happened
and asked the Lord Chancellor, Lord Hatherley, for advice. Lord
Hatherley counselled him to avoid raising any question of privilege if
he should be subpoenaed to appear in court and meanwhile urged
him to inform his mother before she heard the news from anybody
else. The Prince then explained to the Queen that it was his painful
duty to tell her that he had been subpoenaed to appear as a witness by Sir Charles Mordaunt's counsel. She immediately telegraphed
him, pledging her support and wrote him an affectionate letter, urging him to be more careful in future.[106]

Since the Prince had so far only been subpoenaed to confirm his
handwriting, he was advised to send a representative who could testify on his behalf. As to Lady Mordaunt's letters to him, he should
simply say that he did not have any.

The hope was that the Moncreiffe doctors and attendants who
would be summoned during the first days of the trial would put the
case so strongly that the jury would have no option but to bring in a
madness verdict and that would be the end of the matter.

By this time Sir Charles's counsel had prepared their brief. In the
opening paragraph the lawyers claimed that the question of motive
was very important, Lady Mordaunt's motivation being very strong.
It was clear to them that she wished to hide her own disgrace, to save
the honour of her family at any cost, to retain her position and the
liberal fortune settled on her by her husband, as well as to shield
'someone in high authority' from being involved in a court case. In
addition, they pointed out, the pressure of parental influence had to
be taken into account.

All the evidence, the lawyers considered, now confirmed the truth
of Lady Mordaunt's confessions. These simply could not be regarded
as delusions. It was a well-known fact that cases of insanity were
never feigned until after the crime had been committed, and in this
case there had been no suggestion of insanity until after Lady Mordaunt's transgressions had been revealed to her husband.

Harriett Mordaunt (ABOVE, LEFT) and three of her sisters: Louisa, Duchess of Atholl (ABOVE, RIGHT); Helen, Mrs (later Lady) Forbes (BELOW, LEFT); Georgina, Countess of Dudley (BELOW, RIGHT).

The Prince of Wales, 1868

Lowry Cole, later 4th Earl of Enniskillen

Dr William Gull

Dr Maudsley

Mrs Florence Stephens, the cook

Henry Bird, the butler

ABOVE: Cartoons by Carlo Pellegrini. LEFT: The Prince of Wales with Francis Knollys (1870). RIGHT: William, 1st Earl of Dudley.

Walton Hall: the Entrance Hall

Sir Charles Mordaunt in shooting mode

Maimée, the second Lady Mordaunt

Sir Charles Mordaunt on horseback

Walton Hall in the 1860s

Violet Mordaunt, 5th Marchioness of Bath

The brief went on to say that in a real case of insanity an attack almost always came on gradually, but when it was simulated its onset would be far more sudden. This had certainly been so when Lady Mordaunt had begun to behave strangely after the visit of her father the previous March. Ever since then she had continued to 'improve upon' her act. The fact that Lady Mordaunt had never herself denied that she was insane in 'indignant terms' was another proof, as this was something really mad people always did. She had managed, in a way that no insane person would have been able to do, to maintain over a prolonged period a 'safe silence', resolutely refusing to discuss her confessions, or her transgressions. As for the 'filthy acts' reported by Carruthers and Barker, these, if true, were typical of the deeds done by prisoners who were feigning insanity in order to avoid punishment for their crimes.[107] Cases, the lawyers maintained, could be quoted to show how easily even the most eminent doctors had been taken in despite close observation of a such people over a long period of time. This all went to show, the brief continued, how absurd it was for doctors like Dr Alderson or Dr Gull to pronounce judgement after seeing Lady Mordaunt for a couple of times and then only briefly.

A careful analysis of all the medical reports had revealed to the lawyers that Dr Alderson had at first diagnosed 'defective action of the brain following puerperal insanity' and then had expressed a different opinion based on the observations of Miss Laing who, as the Moncreiffe governess, had no doubt been 'very well tutored' as to what line she should take. Dr Gull for his part never mentioned puerperal insanity, but based his conclusion that Lady Mordaunt was mad entirely on the statements made by Miss Laing and Mrs Carruthers. Dr Burrowes, after reading these statements, and seeing Lady Mordaunt just once, had come to the conclusion that her mind was 'shattered by remorse', and he agreed that she was insane even though he could see no indication of incoherence or of delusions. Dr Reynolds, for his part, said that he could not see any sign of 'fatuity' in Lady Mordaunt. In his opinion she simply looked bored – 'as well she might,' the lawyers added.

The inconsistencies in the doctors' opinions were thus apparent, and although Dr Gull on 9 November had written to say that he and Dr Wood, Dr Reynolds and Dr Hughes were unanimous in their belief that Lady Mordaunt was mentally incapable, yet they had declined to give their reasons. As for Dr Hughes, it was to be expected that he would 'follow in the wake of his superiors', but Dr Reynolds, it seemed, had undergone an extraordinary change in his opinion before deciding to agree with Dr Wood, and this he would have to explain if put into the witness box. As for Dr Tyler Smith, he was most emphatic that nothing could be more improper than the treatment that was now being meted out to this unfortunate lady and he was confident that she would immediately improve if moved to a warmer and more suitable location.

Much emphasis was placed on Sir Thomas's influence and his determination to keep his daughter, as the lawyers put it, 'under his insanity tuition'. He had always made sure that he visited his daughter, whether at Walton, Worthing or Bickley, in order to prime her before she was due to be visited by Sir Charles's doctors. It was shocking to think that in order to save the honour of the family in general, and her sisters in particular, he was prepared to sacrifice his daughter by sending her to a lunatic asylum. Why, it had to be asked, had Sir Thomas gone to the expense of taking medical men down to her at Walton when she was in fact being satisfactorily cared for by the local practitioners? The answer was simple.

'Oh,' says Sir Thomas, 'the expense will all come out of Sir Charles's pocket in the end, let the result be what it may', and accordingly Sir Charles has received the following little bill from Sir Thomas's solicitor of his medical attendants amounting to £402. 10s. 8d for one month.

The lawyers thought it likely that when he had gone down to Walton on 7 April the previous year, Sir Thomas had taught his daughter how to assume her 'extraordinary and unusual appearances, muteness, vacancy etc' and had then introduced his own medical men 'for the express purpose of establishing and not allaying the question of insanity'. Among the doctors, Dr Tuke appeared to have been 'the principal leader'. The whole affair was in fact

without exaggeration one of the most painful but at the same time most heartless and wicked cases that had been brought before the Court of Divorce since the establishment of that tribunal, both as regards the young respondent, for she is now only in her twenty-second year, and the co-respondents who were received and treated by Sir Charles as friends of her family, they being strangers to him prior to the marriage.

It had been reported, it was hoped falsely, that Lord Dudley had

declared that 'no gold should be wanted' to bring Sir Thomas
Moncreiffe 'safely through'. All the same, in view of the fact that Sir
Thomas's pecuniary means were so very 'narrow' and his family so
large, it did seem likely that the Moncreiffes would never have
embarked on legal proceedings unless they had some guarantee of
financial help from somebody in the event of the case going against
them.

The brief had been prepared on the basis that the period following
the confinement and up to Lady Mordaunt's removal by her father
from Walton would be dealt with first. After that it was thought
that they would trace as concisely as possible what had happened
prior to the birth, perhaps dealing first with Lady Mordaunt's flirtations with George Forbes and Lord Newport, which, to say the least
of it, 'called for great rebuke'. As for 'the other side' that is, the
Moncreiffes, it seemed that they were prepared to excuse everything
with the help of their flawed diagnosis of puerperal insanity. It was
pointed out in the brief that if such tactics were to set a pattern in
future for providing errant married ladies with an excuse for promiscuity, then their husbands were 'much to be pitied'.

It was noted that on 15 May the previous year seventeen affidavits
had been filed by Sir Charles's witnesses, all testifying that Lady
Mordaunt had been sane throughout. The lawyers found it strange
that none of this evidence had been challenged by Sir Thomas. His
answer had simply been to send his daughter away to Worthing in the
care of a 'lunatic' nurse appointed by Dr Tuke who himself kept a
mental asylum and who probably knew all too well how madness
could be induced. But having read all the evidence, Sir Charles's
counsel still felt sure that 'the other side' would find it very hard to
prove insanity.

On the Saturday before the trial was due to begin, Lady Louisa
took the most eminent of all the doctors, Sir James Simpson, down to
see Lady Mordaunt at Bickley. He had last visited her when she was
at Worthing and he was impressed by how much 'stouter' she had
become since then. She appeared to recognise him and conversed
quite sensibly at first. Lady Louisa then asked her if she would like to
see Blanche, but she firmly said no, the only person she wanted to see
was Charlie. After that she became less coherent, and wandered a
little, and when they left, she asked Sir James to be sure to send her
the book, the glass jar, and the new footman he had ordered for
her. This strange list of requests was enough to confirm Sir James's

opinion that she was even madder than she had been the previous summer.

Jane Laing was also sent down to see her former charge a few days before the trial. She was quite taken aback when she saw how much weight Lady Mordaunt had put on. Her attendants told her that she was now eating ravenously all the time and they were continually having to let out her clothes.

On her return to London, Miss Laing reported that when she had first seen Lady Mordaunt, she had behaved quite normally for about ten minutes, and had then thrown herself quite suddenly onto the floor, afterwards crawling about the house on her hands and knees. She had also tried to eat a piece of coal.

Disturbing though such reports were for Sir Charles and his advisers, they still believed that it would not be difficult to convince the jury of Lady Mordaunt's sanity at the time she had made her confessions and on the important date, 30 April 1869, when Mr Haynes had delivered the petition.

32
The Insanity Trial

As the date of the trial drew nearer, public excitement mounted. The case, as the *Warwick Advertiser* put it, was bound to 'excite deep and painful interest in Warwickshire', and the apparent involvement of the Prince ensured that it would arouse a nationwide concern. For weeks now the newspapers had carried references to the scandal, and in one of the most scurrilous the Prince had been pictured in coronet and ermine, holding a glass of champagne, and surrounded by images of the theatre and racing, as well as by a fine array of bottles and decanters. In addition there were some caricatures of a spindly man, undoubtedly Sir Charles, shooting pigeons, or hauling his wife up a Swiss mountain. Also depicted was a young woman in a pony carriage drawn by two grey ponies. Lewd use was made of umbrellas, lady's or otherwise. The public warmed to such revelations, scenting that the scandal was really about to break, whatever efforts were being made to suppress it.[108]

On 12 February it was announced in *The Globe* that after various delays the Mordaunt Case was due to to come on 'in serious earnest' the following Saturday, and the report stated that 'a number of learned mad doctors' had been subpoenaed to give evidence to the effect that the respondent, Lady Mordaunt, was of unsound mind and incapable of putting in an answer to the petition. On the other side it was said that Sir Charles Mordaunt's legal advisers were prepared with numerous witnesses to controvert this view. In any case, the newspaper reported, the fashionable world being as fond of sensation as it was, the case was likely to attract 'a far greater number of well-dressed spectators than the divorce court would accommodate'. As a result the proceedings would take place at a special court to be set up in Westminster Hall.

The Prince, meanwhile, was doing his best to appear unconcerned as he skated each day with the Princess in Regent's Park, the image of an affectionate husband.

On 16 February, the day that the trial opened, additional police were assigned to Westminster Hall where the court was to be held. A large crowd had converged on the Hall in anticipation of the expected revelations of scandal 'in the very highest circles'. Inside there was hardly enough space to accommodate the jury, the witnesses and the lawyers, let alone the large number of newspaper reporters and a posse of barristers, many of them of the 'briefless junior variety', who were crammed into the main body of the Hall. The gallery which ran round three sides of the building was equally crowded with members of the two families and their friends, a 'strong force of locals' and a large number of other 'interested spectators'. The only places undisturbed by the crowd were the jury box and the bench, where the judge sat alone, and the witness-box, which was a small platform surrounded by a rail and situated just inside the door.

As the respondent's case was the first to be presented to the court, it was pointed out on her behalf that the issue to be tried was not the guilt or innocence of Lady Mordaunt in respect of adultery with the co-respondents.

Dr Deane, for Sir Thomas, Lady Mordaunt's guardian *ad litem*, then proceeded to state the case. Since the question being asked was whether Lady Mordaunt was still insane and therefore unable to defend herself, he was strongly of the opinion that the present inquiry should only deal with events from 30 April 1869 when she had been presented with the petition. He impressed on his hearers the eminence and experience of the medical men who had examined her, dismissing Orford and Jones as unimportant, and reminding everybody that Sir James Simpson had a reputation which reached far beyond the United Kingdom. Dr Deane then listed the symptoms noted by the medical witnesses, and described how Lady Mordaunt's condition had over the months become worse and worse, and yet it was alleged that every symptom was feigned. Was it possible, he asked

that this young woman, not yet twenty-two years old, should have sufficient strength of will through ten long and dreary months, to keep up this play of madness? Giving her full credit for practice and art, by what stratagem could she govern the beat of her pulse and the throb of her heart so as to deceive all the medical men who examined her? By what drugs and devices could she regulate the appearance of her skin, and produce at will the clammy perspiration of disease? How moderate the temperature of her body so that the head be hot and the feet cold at the same time?

Dr Deane then called his first four witnesses, a formidable female team made up of Jane Laing, Mrs Carruthers, Miss Keddell and Sarah Barker. They opened strongly, building up one after the other the image of a lunatic lady who did her best to throw herself out of the carriage when it was in motion, who had to be bribed with pennies to go to bed, who was immodest, indecent, altogether crazy, with her screams in the night, her destructiveness, her bad behaviour at the table, her tendency to spit on the carpet. The hushed court was told how she had hammered on locked doors demanding that her husband should come out.

When Dr Deane had finished, it was Serjeant Ballantine's turn to cross-examine the witnesses, and he subjected Jane Laing to a barrage of questions, interrogating her about her conversations with Lady Mordaunt at the house in Worthing and in particular asking what Lady Mordaunt had told her about her married life. He also wanted to know whether Lady Louisa Moncreiffe had given her any indication of what had happened at, and after, the birth of her child. Miss Laing replied that Lady Mordaunt herself had spoken of her confinement and had indeed talked about 'all the people that she knew'. Serjeant Ballantine then asked her if Lady Mordaunt had said anything about being accused of impropriety with anyone. This provoked an objection from Dr Deane, who thought that the question should not be allowed as it had no bearing on the issue. Lord Penzance, however, quickly silenced him, maintaining that because everything Lady Mordaunt had said would have a relevance to the state of her intelligence, it was not a question that could be in any way 'eschewed'. Serjeant Ballantine did not hesitate to take advantage of the opportunity this gave him to press on ruthlessly with an examination which the witness was probably not expecting and would certainly have liked to avoid.

– I want, if possible to avoid mentioning names but did Lady Mordaunt accuse herself of any improper conduct with these persons? – No.
– You say she did refer to acquaintances, but never mentioned any impropriety?
– She talked of inviting people to a party, so as to make life less dull.
– Did she ever allude to Sir Charles's visit to Norway?

– Yes she did. She said she thought at one time of going with him. She talked of his going to Norway and of a proposal that she should go.
– Did she say why she did not go?

Miss Laing made no reply. By now the atmosphere in the Hall had become stifling. Under pressure from the heat, and from Serjeant Ballantine's questioning, Jane Laing had become increasingly agitated. She began to falter. 'I do not remember' she said, and then collapsed, apparently in a dead faint.

People rushed to her assistance. Restoratives were administered and she gradually came round. She was allowed to remain seated, as the proceedings continued.

– Did Lady Moncreiffe tell you of certain statements by Lady Mordaunt, a few days after her confinement? – She did.
– Did you ever refer to the statements or mention the names to Lady Mordaunt?
– I never mentioned the names. I asked her if she remembered making the statements. She said she remembered what was said about her having made them, but that she did not make them. I did not ask her anything further upon that. I think she understood what I referred to.

When it was her turn, Mrs Carruthers told the court that she was used to looking after people of a weak mind, explaining that she went to Worthing with the impression that Lady Mordaunt was a lunatic, and prepared to treat her as such.

Jane Keddell, who was called next, told the court that she had kept a diary, but added that she had destroyed it as she did not want the 'acts of indecency' to be read. She was questioned about Lady Mordaunt's behaviour with her baby, saying that she hardly seemed to care for it.

Sarah Barker, not in the least overawed by the crowded court, spoke confidently when she was in the witness-box. She insisted that in all the time she had been at Bickley she had never had a proper conversation with Lady Mordaunt. Like the others she described her extraordinary behaviour when out driving, and she said that sometimes, when she had taken Lady Mordaunt shopping, force was needed to get her to come home.

Serjeant Ballantine, cross-examining, asked Barker whose service she had been in before, and she inquired somewhat pertly what this had to do with the present case. When asked about her diary, she like Jane Laing said that she had destroyed it, as Sir Charles Mordaunt's lawyer had told her she would not be wanted.

When Serjeant Ballantine had finished with Barker, it was the turn of the doctors to stand up in court. Dr Priestley, Dr Tuke, Dr Gull, Dr Alderson, Sir James Simpson, Dr Burrowes and Dr Reynolds were all questioned in turn about their visits to Lady Mordaunt at Walton, Worthing or Bickley. They were asked to define puerperal mania and catalepsy, and to describe the symptoms which had led them to believe that Lady Mordaunt was mad.

Serjeant Ballantine asked Dr Priestley whether it would affect his judgement on the insanity issue if he were to find that Lady Mordaunt's statements concerning her 'improprieties' with certain gentlemen turned out to be true. Before he had time to reply to this rather tricky question, Lord Penzance intervened saying that a medical gentleman should not have to investigate the question of whether such statements were true or not. It was a different matter, however, when Dr Deane tried to prevent Serjeant Ballantine questioning Dr Priestley as to whether or not he had attended Lady Mordaunt prior to the birth of her baby.

Dr Deane (objecting) – Your Lordship knows what is coming.
Lord Penzance – I have not the least idea.

Serjeant Ballantine then explained to the judge that he proposed going into the circumstances of Lady Mordaunt's confinement and of her health previous to the birth of her baby.

The judge's response to this proposal was crucial. From the start, the Moncreiffe lawyers had based their case on the belief that they would be able to exclude anything that had happened before 30 April. Dr Deane now urgently pointed out the danger of prejudicing the main issue as well of involving 'persons outside' by going too far back in time.

Lord Penzance replied that as he had understood it from Dr Deane himself, the case being brought by Lady Mordaunt's guardian, Sir Thomas, was that Lady Mordaunt was affected with insanity, whereas the other side held that she was only 'simulating' the condition. Lord Penzance then said that if Lady Mordaunt were simulating, it followed that she must have a motive for so doing and this would have to be established. In order to do so, the facts of her past life would have to be put before the jury so that they could decide whether or not she had a good reason for pretending to be mad.

The judge's decision allowing the introduction into the inquiry of events previous to 30 April 1869 could be seen as a turning point. Sir Thomas's counsel did not let it go unchallenged. He pointed out that although the line was a delicate one to draw, he felt that it should be drawn, reminding the court that in a murder case no evidence would be allowed if there were a question of insanity. But Lord Penzance insisted that as Lady Mordaunt's condition apparently depended on what took place at her confinement, events at the time of the birth would have to be taken into account. Since this was so, and the one side was allowed to prove what took place then, why should the other side be forbidden to go back even earlier than that? Refusing to rule out all the facts and circumstances that had happened before 30 April, Lord Penzance allowed Serjeant Ballantine to continue questioning Dr Priestley about the medicines he had given Lady Mordaunt prior to the birth, and about the trouble with the baby's eyes in the weeks following the confinement.

Dr Tuke then told the court that he had come to the conclusion that Lady Mordaunt was suffering from puerperal insanity. He said that he regarded her confessions as the typical delusions of a patient suffering from that disease. If Lady Mordaunt had confessed to adultery with only one person it might have been different, but it seemed to him incredible that she should have behaved in that way, and according to her own admission, with half a dozen men, up to a few weeks before the birth of her child.

Next to appear in the witness-box was Dr James Alderson. He became impatient when questioned by Serjeant Ballantine about the details of Lady Mordaunt's condition, hinting that the word of an eminent physician like himself should be accepted without further probing. 'I think I could distinguish an insane person in the dark by the smell' he declared.

Sir James Simpson was then called. He listed his impressive qualifications and said that he had attended the Moncreiffe family 'for many long years'. When asked what state he had found Lady Mordaunt in the previous Saturday when he had gone down to Bickley, he testified that he had found her perfectly insane, 'a mere wreck and ruin of the mind'.

Questioned by Dr Deane about a woman's chances of recovering from puerperal fever Sir James replied that recovery was usual within the year, but after that the chances of getting over it began to diminish. 'It is said in our books' said Sir James 'that almost one third remain insane.' He had seen many cases of the disease, and this helped him to make his firm diagnosis. He had no hesitation in saying that she was utterly insane.

Lord Penzance – Permanently insane?
Sir James – Time alone can determine.

Cross-examined by Serjeant Ballantine, Sir James admitted that he was not quite sure when Lady Mordaunt's madness had first begun, but he believed it had started at a very early date, certainly within two or three days of the confinement, and perhaps during labour or even earlier. He based this last theory on the fact that after the waters had broken at the Parsonage, Lady Mordaunt had driven home, changed her dress and then immediately gone out again, alone and driving herself. He found this very odd behaviour in a woman who had probably already started to suffer labour pains. He then said he had been told by Mrs Forbes that about three days after her confinement, Lady Mordaunt had pointed out things that she thought were running on the wall. 'Any doctor would suppose insanity from that' said Sir James. He added that Mrs Forbes had also told him about the dead bodies in the room and Lady Mordaunt's fears of being pursued or poisoned. He agreed with the other doctors that delusions of impropriety were very common in puerperal cases and he quoted a specific example. He had, he recalled, sent out Dr Priestley, who had in his younger days been his assistant in Edinburgh, to examine just such a case, and the moment the lady suffering from delusions had seen him, she had cried out 'There is the father of my child!'

This revelation caused an outburst of laughter among the spectators.

It was Dr Gull's turn next. He recalled that he had seen Lady Mordaunt on six different occasions, and had found 'remarkable uniformity' on each. He dwelt on the 'absent' expression and the meaningless laugh. He told the court that he had 'questioned her in every way' and had even alluded to her unfortunate position, but all she could say to that was that 'a dose of castor oil would put it all right'. When he had talked to her about her child, her husband, and the condition she was in before the world, he said that he might as well have been talking to a piece of wood. It seemed to him that the best proof of her insanity was 'the uniformity of her absence of mind'. He was unable to see any evidence that she was shamming.

Dr Burrowes and Dr Reynolds were then questioned, after which the court adjourned.

That evening there were anxious consultations. For Sir Thomas and for the gentlemen who had been named in the confessions, the fact that Lord Penzance had allowed events previous to Lady Mordaunt's confinement to be discussed gave much cause for concern. Most important of all, the judgement had opened up the possibility that the Prince might after all be subpoenaed to appear in court. This was what so many people, not least the Queen, had most dreaded. For the heir to the throne to be called into the witness-box, to be questioned like anybody else, could only spell danger for the monarchy. As for the Prince, the prospect of being cross-examined by Serjeant Ballantine put him into a state of panic, realising as he did that the brilliant lawyer would naturally try and twist everything he said in order to compromise him. 'On the other hand, if I do not appear,' he told his mother, 'the public may suppose that I shrink from answering these imputations which have been cast upon me. Under either circumstance I am in a very awkward position, and you can easily imagine how I am worried, dearest Mama.'

For Sir Charles the proceedings had been reasonably encouraging, as Serjeant Ballantine's probing had already done much to reveal the triviality of some of the symptoms quoted by the doctors. At the same time, Sir James Simpson's description of his recent visit to Bickley with Lady Louisa seemed to suggest that Lady Mordaunt's behaviour had by now reached new extremes and Sir Charles's lawyers were afraid this might affect the testimony of Dr Orford if he continued to insist that he had never seen any symptoms of genuine madness. Serjeant Ballantine, scenting trouble, decided that it would be wise for the Warwickshire doctors to visit Bickley before they appeared in court in order draw their own conclusions as to her present state. Dr Orford and Dr Jones accordingly went down to Page Heath the following day.

Both Dr Jones and Dr Orford were astonished by the change in Lady Mordaunt's condition. Dr Orford arrived first and was shown into the drawing-room where she was sitting by the fireplace. He went straight up to her and said 'How do you do, my lady' and she looked up at him and said 'How do you do.' He was impressed by the 'dull sort of way' in which she spoke these words, so different from the natural vivacity he remembered from previous times. Sitting down at her side, he began to talk to her about Walton, recalling the hunt breakfasts, and particularly the time when she had been laid up after her miscarriage and he had forbidden her to go downstairs and join those breakfasting in the hall below. He asked if she could remember how 'vexed she had been', but she did not reply or react in any kind of way. Always, when he had seen her in the past, she had shown some spark of interest, but this time there was nothing. What struck him most were her eyes, which had always seemed so bright and intelligent. Now there was a deadness in them which had never been there before.

Dr Jones arrived later and at first he did not recognise this 'stout-looking' person who came out into the hall to greet him.

'I am sorry to disturb you at luncheon' he said, adding, after he had sat down, 'I have got a great deal to talk to you about.' He went on conversing in what he described as a 'familiar' manner, attempting to put her at her ease, but he could not get a word out of her, and suddenly she got up and threw herself on the rug in front of the fire.

'Lady Mordaunt, do you like lying there instead of sitting upon a chair?' he asked her.

'Sometimes' she replied. She then got up and moved to the other side of the room, 'dallying about there' as the doctor put it. He went over to her, and asked her to show him the drawing-room, putting her arm under his and leading her through as he would have taken a lady in to dinner. He hoped to make her feel quite at home with him in this way but she still refused to speak. He appealed to her, talked to her and did everything he possibly could, but she remained silent, and realising that he was making no progress, he cut short his visit. Both he and Dr Orford had seen enough to convince them that the obvious deterioration in Lady Mordaunt's condition now made it difficult to say conclusively that her mind was unimpaired.

On the second day of the trial, the atmosphere was even more tense than it had been the day before, as an increased number of visitors, crammed into the gallery and on the floor below, sat or stood waiting for the proceedings to begin.

Serjeant Ballantine opened by announcing that Mr Haynes had been taken very ill on his arrival from Leamington at the Brunswick

Hotel in Hanover Square. It was therefore requested that his evidence should be taken by commission, and it was arranged that this should be done later in the day.

The examination of the doctors then continued, Dr Harris and Dr Hughes describing how they had been given ample opportunity to observe Lady Mordaunt on a day-to-day basis at Worthing or Bickley. They both agreed with the diagnosis of puerperal mania given by the other doctors, Dr Harris assuring the court that no medical man could possibly mistake the basic symptoms – the hot and painful head, the 'muttering' deliriums and feverish pulse. He added that he himself would attach very little importance to any statements made by a patient suffering in that way.

Dr Hughes described Lady Mordaunt as 'a complete wreck', but Lord Penzance descended on him heavily for using a 'figurative' term. He hastily corrected himself and said that in his opinion Lady Mordaunt had no mind at all. Asked if he had witnessed any of the shocking and 'unwomanly' acts described by Lady Mordaunt's attendants, he admitted that he had not.

– I have not seen anything particularly indelicate. I have seen her Ladyship throw herself on a couch, and the question was how low or how high her legs might go up, but nothing worse than that.

Dr Hughes was also questioned about her eating habits. He described them as 'capricious'. Sometimes, he said, 'she eats not at all, sometimes most ravenously, putting in one mouthful after another, packing her mouth as full as it would hold.' He mentioned the time when she had eaten three or four mince pies at a sitting and added that she had put on so much weight that her dresses had been taken out by two inches.

Dr Hughes said he found it difficult to convey adequately to the court the 'vacantness' of her mind. He cited the time when she had complained of toothache and he had looked at the tooth and 'without a movement of her countenance' she had said, 'Oh it is nothing, it is baby cutting her eye-tooth.'

At other times Lady Mordaunt had grown excitable, and on these occasions he had administered bromide of potassium to very good effect. He was asked whether as a result of his fifty-two professional visits he had been able to decide whether Lady Mordaunt was in a happy or unhappy state of mind. He had seen her looking 'a perfect blank' over and over again. 'A few photographs would have told more than I can tell' he said.[109]

Next to enter the witness-box was Dr Wood, who described how he had arranged for Lady Mordaunt to be reunited with her baby as a means of affecting a cure. Much had changed since then, and although originally appointed as a 'referee', he had finally come down on the side of those who thought that Lady Mordaunt was irremediably insane. He used as an example of her unnatural 'docility' the episode when she had turned a china ornament upside down at his request, agreeing to do 'something purposeless and utterly unmeaning without the least appearance of irritation or annoyance at having been made such a fool of'.

Dr Wood now said he regretted stating that he had spoken 'roughly' to Lady Mordaunt in the course of one of his visits. Nobody, he felt, could possibly be rough with anyone 'so evidently helpless and in such a pitiable condition'. The word 'roughly' was therefore withdrawn and changed to 'strongly'.

Dr Wood described Lady Mordaunt's statue-like pose, as she stood fixed and passive, her mind apparently a blank 'as if a machine had been stopped in its action'. In his opinion these states did not add up to true catalepsy or rigor, as there was no apparent rigidity of the limbs but rather a 'simple suspension of mental manifestation'. He said that from first to last he had been struck by 'the remarkable consistency of her inconsistency'.

In his cross-examination, Mr Serjeant Ballantine concentrated on the game of whist, when Lady Mordaunt had played a wrong suit. He started off by asking Dr Wood what mistake she had made, pointing out that it was not an uncommon thing to happen. Dr Wood replied that she had played a wrong suit.

– Do you mean revoking? Are you a whist player? – Somewhat.
– Have you never revoked? – I dare say I have.
– I hope it is not an indication of insanity, I am sure.
– I should say that I do not take any one instance I have mentioned as proof of insanity.

Lord Penzance asked whether in his work at St Luke's Hospital Dr Wood had seen other people in the same state of mind as Lady Mordaunt. He replied that he had seen repeated instances of it. 'Do you call it dementia?' Lord Penzance asked him.

He replied that it was not true dementia, adding

– It is difficult to define it. It seems to be an arrest of mental power which does not strictly belong to the class of either imbeciles or demented persons.

Dr Wood admitted that he had at times detected some 'slight lights' occasionally appearing, but that on the whole Lady Mordaunt's 'darkened mind' had remained 'overshadowed, misty, and cloudy'.

The examination of the Moncreiffe doctors was now concluded. They had all stated, more or less categorically, that Lady Mordaunt had been, and still was, insane. Sir Thomas, who followed, agreed with them that to carry on a conversation with his daughter was quite impossible. He had the impression that she did not care whether she saw him at all, and when he was around she had shown no particular desire that he should stay longer. When the time had come to leave Walton, she did not appear to understand that she was going away, perhaps for good. He said that what had struck him most forcibly was her 'state of perfect indifference', although he did admit that when they got to London 'she got a little hysterical as she frequently used to do'.

Sir Thomas was then questioned about his visits to Worthing and Bickley. He said it was true that sometimes his daughter revealed a few gleams of understanding, whereas at others she appeared perfectly indifferent to everything, or else was 'excessively upset in her mind altogether and said the most extraordinary things'. For a while at Bickley she had seemed to be better, but she had then deteriorated, and her mind had gone right back to how it was when she was at Worthing.

When Mr Serjeant Ballantine came into the fray he cross-questioned Sir Thomas on the subject of Lady Louisa's visits to Walton after the confinement.

– Did you learn from Lady Louisa the statements that your daughter had been making to her?.
– I learnt from her partially, and from Sir Charles Mordaunt partially, very partially from him because he referred me to his brother.

Sir Thomas was asked about the conversations that had taken place about the paternity of the child, Lord Penzance intervening to inquire whether his wife, Lady Louisa, had been told by Lady

Mordaunt who was the father of her child. 'I think she told me that Lady Mordaunt had told her something of the sort' Sir Thomas replied. Dr Deane then intervened, challenging Lord Penzance to say how much of this was admissable. 'What is said to him is admissable in the evidence, though not as proof of the truth of it' Lord Penzance replied.

Reference was then made to the letter written by Harriett to her mother from Bickley on 8 October after the departure of Bird and 'Bunchey'. It seemed that Mr Benbow, Sir Thomas's lawyer, had been served a notice to produce it but he now said that he had no such letter. Mr Serjeant Ballantine asked Sir Thomas if he had seen it.

– Yes, I think I have.
– Do you remember its contents? – No.
– Should you remember them if you were reminded of them?
– No, it is a long time since I have seen it.
– Did you see it when Lady Louisa received it?
– No, I do not think I was at home when she received it.
– When did you receive it?
– Upon my word I really forget. I never thought anything more about it.
– It is a matter of very, very great importance, a letter from your daughter to her mother. Is it in existence?
– I am not aware. The letter was in existence when I saw it last.
– That is obvious.
Lord Penzance – When did you see it last ?
– About a week ago.
Serjeant Ballantine – In whose hands?
– I saw it at my Attorney's office.

Sir Thomas was then asked if he had read the letter.

– No, I do not recollect that I did. I was in a great hurry.

Serjeant Ballantine pointed out that it was only a week ago that he had seen the letter, at which Mr Deane found the letter among his papers and it was read out.

After that, Dr Deane said that he had no more witnesses to call and Sergeant Ballantine opened the case for Sir Charles, expressing the anxiety he felt at being entrusted with a case which could only create 'a feeling of compassion' in the minds of every well-regulated person. He spoke first of all of Sir Charles, whom he represented, a

man of honourable name, of honourable family, a man who had
represented his county in Parliament, and who had been looked up to
with respect. The contest now was to shut out an inquiry which if not
looked into could in the end entirely embitter Sir Charles's future life,
leaving undecided the question of whether he would be called upon
still to hold to the woman who he believed had been unfaithful to
him and to recognise a child that he believed not to be his own.
Ballantine refused to accept the analogy with a criminal case where
the offender's sanity was in question, and where the outcome of the
case could cost him his life. The question was whether Sir Charles
Mordaunt, who complained of a grievous and deadly injury, should
be shut out from any means whatever of redemption from it. 'That is
the question in this case' said Serjeant Ballantine.

Serjeant Ballantine devoted some time to Dr Wood's evidence and
in particular to the singing of the song 'Strangers Yet'. He described
how the unhappy girl, 'struggling unnaturally to maintain a false
appearance in many matters before those who were sent to examine
her', had broken down at last, memory rushing in, her situation
suddenly clear to her – her portion lost, her husband gone, abandoned by everybody – breaking down as any woman with a spark of
feeling would do under circumstances so frightful. 'There are some
things that do so speak to the human heart that man's words seem
almost unnecessary to strengthen them' Serjeant Ballantine concluded.

Next he considered the game of whist, saying that 'revokes will
happen in the very best regulated families' and to imagine for a moment that anything like insanity is to be deduced from a revoke is
strange indeed.

He went on to describe the marriage, a desirable one between
a 'superlatively beautiful girl of great personal attractions' and a
baronet of distinction, of exemplary character and conduct 'on
whose name there has never rested a stain'. Lady Mordaunt's parents
were well pleased with the match, and the settlements Sir Charles had
made were 'liberal in the extreme'.

There is no doubt whatever that the most perfect accord had
existed in the early days of the marriage and as far as he [Sir
Charles] knew and believed until these unhappy occurrences
burst upon him like a thunder clap, she was as pure a girl as ever
was embraced by a loving husband.

Serjeant Ballantine referred to Lady Mordaunt's history of hysteria, a term, he admitted, that few could define although 'probably there are few persons who in their circle are not acquainted with ladies who are suffering more or less from what is a very terrible disease'. He mentioned Lady Mordaunt's miscarriages which could have caused shock to her system. Referring to the trip to Norway, Serjeant Ballantine said he had heard it suggested that there was some inattention on the part of Sir Charles Mordaunt in leaving his wife for three or four weeks to go fishing. Sir Charles himself, Serjeant Ballantine maintained, had never dreamed of neglect. He had nothing but love, and love of the deepest kind, for the lady he was leaving.

Serjeant Ballantine then moved on to a discussion of dates, but Dr Deane immediately objected, saying that this was doubtful ground. Lord Penzance backed Ballantine up, saying that it was impossible to prevent him including such evidence. Dr Deane's reluctance to introduce third parties was understandable, but unwillingness, Lord Penzance pointed out, was not a legal ground. He himself would prefer that such matters should not be brought into court, but in the interests of common justice he could not refuse.

Given permission to proceed in the way he wished to go, Serjeant Ballantine spoke of Lady Mordaunt's shock on discovering the state of her child's eyes, which at once aroused a fear of discovery. Ballantine was told by Lord Penzance to omit the names involved until they were proved, so that he said Lady Mordaunt had confessed to wrong doing 'with A and B, with C and others and in open day'. She had used the expression 'I have been very wicked, I have done very wrong'. They would hear about the visits from the Prince and others, always without her husband's knowledge and against his wishes. 'Very wrong' was a term thoroughly applicable.

The question was whether or not Lady Mordaunt's confessions were the ravings of a lunatic or the true statements of a perfectly sane woman. 'That she was in company with the gentlemen I have mentioned we shall prove up to the hilt' Serjeant Ballantine claimed, saying that he would call in servants and others who had seen them together 'under circumstances in which if the inclination was present to them, the fact could be with great facility carried out'. He was sure that all the evidence he would bring before the court would leave 'no earthly doubt' that Lady Mordaunt was sane at the time she made her confessions, and Dr Orford, an experienced medical practitioner who would later be called, was ready to swear on oath that the existence of puerperal mania was 'a pure fable and a pure speculation'.

Serjeant Ballantine now confessed that he had exhausted himself, and as a result he did not propose to re-read the letter written on 8 November 1869 by Lady Mordaunt to her mother. He did not omit to point out, however, how hard Sir Thomas had tried to avoid having to produce it, knowing as he did that it appeared to have been written by a perfectly normal person, and not realising that it had been copied before Lady Mordaunt sent it off.

Now it was the turn of the Mordaunt retainers to give evidence, and the first to be called was Mrs Hancox. Totally devoid of any nerves, the midwife rattled off her evidence with relish and so fast that Dr Deane had on occasions to ask her to repeat what she had said as he could not keep up with her. She described the circumstances at and following the birth, keeping closely to the statements made in her affidavit. She told the court that Lady Mordaunt always used to cry when the baby was brought to her and she saw the state of its eyes.

– Did she make any remark at the time? asked Mr Ballantine.
– Yes, she made a remark each time.

Then there was the occasion when Lady Mordaunt had asked her to give the baby a dose of laudanum, saying that had she given birth in London the child never would have been brought to light at all as 'poor little miserable things like those were not allowed to be seen'.

Mrs Hancox insisted that at Bickley Lady Mordaunt would come up to the nursery in the evenings, staying for up to three quarters of an hour and talking quietly about the baby, about Walton, about Sir Charles and other subjects. Mrs Hancox was asked if she ever left the child alone with Lady Mordaunt, and she replied 'Certainly not.' She explained that this was because once Lady Mordaunt had suggested taking the child's life away.

– Did she ask if you would leave the child with her?
– Yes, she would say 'Shall I stay with this child for half-an–hour while you go downstairs?' and I would say 'No thank you, my lady'.
– In that tone of voice?
– In that tone of voice.

Re-examined by Mr Serjeant Ballantine, Mrs Hancox said that

she had always asked Lady Mordaunt 'natural' questions, not silly
ones like the doctors. That was probably the reason why she had
always talked freely with her, however reserved she was with everybody else.

On the subject of Lady Mordaunt's fit of hysterics on the day that
her mother had left her a week after the birth, Serjeant Ballantine
questioned her closely.

> – You say when Lady Moncreiffe went away that Lady Mor-
> daunt went into something that you described as hysterical. Is
> that so?
> – Yes.
> – And that Lady Louisa made some observation?
> – When she came into the room –
> – Just answer the question. What was the observation?
> – 'My dear, this is just like your own old self. I have not seen you
> in hysterics for a long time'.
> – Did Lady Mordaunt appear to be agitated at it?
> – Not in the least.
> – You are quite sure Lady Louisa said that?
> – I am quite certain that those were her ladyship's words.

Mrs Hancox was re-examined about the question of Lady Mordaunt saying she would be 'poorly'. She said that it had been entirely
Lady Mordaunt's idea to pretend to be ill, thinking she could soften
her husband that way, hoping to make him deal mildly with her and
not expose her to the world.

That evening, after the court had adjourned, urgent discussions took
place among the Prince's advisers as they tried to decide if it would be
better for him to appear in court whether he was called or not. Now
that the judge had allowed evidence referring to events before Lady
Mordaunt's confinement to be brought forward, it could be that he
should take the chance to clear his name. At the same time, in order
to stand up to cross-questioning he would have to be very sure that
his conscience was clear on the 'main issue', the question of adultery,
since it was most important that he should tell the truth, even if it
meant owning up to something that could be regarded as nothing
more than a youthful transgression with a lady of fragile virtue. He
had to remember that he would one day become 'the fountain of
justice', and he would certainly gain the respect of the nation if he

could go into the witness-box with a clear conscience and speak the truth in a way that was worthy of his illustrious name.[110]

The Queen, who still liked to believe that her son had stopped short of what she termed 'improper familiarity', redoubled her efforts to ensure that if he were to be called into the witness-box no 'improper questions' would be asked. The Prime Minister, William Gladstone, and high-ranking members of the judiciary were enlisted to make it clear to Lord Penzance that the Queen expected him to conduct the case discreetly, avoiding anything that could rebound unfavourably on the Crown.

One of the difficulties was that the press coverage at this time was far from sympathetic towards the Prince. Most of the newspapers had prejudged the Prince guilty of the crime Lady Mordaunt had imputed to him. 'If the Prince of Wales is an accomplice in bringing dishonour to the homestead of an English gentleman, if unbridled sensuality and lust have led him to violate the laws of honour and hospitality' thundered the report in *Reynolds Newspaper*, ' . . . then such a man, placed in the position he is, should not only be expelled from decent society, but is utterly unfit and unworthy to rule over this country.' It was certainly hard to believe in the innocence of a man who had been in the habit of visiting a young married woman at her home when her husband was out, and some felt that the trial had drawn back the veil on the worst excesses of society. An article in *Tomahawk* was less than polite about the high-class ladies with their berouged cheeks and dyed hair who with their 'brazen painted faces' appeared 'leering and gloating' each day in Westminster Hall. 'Hide your sin, Jezebel!' the newspaper added.

On the Wednesday night, at a dinner in the City, the toast to the Prince of Wales was greeted with the shouted and somewhat pointed reply, 'To the Princess!'

On resuming proceedings for the third day of what was described as 'this extraordinary cause', the court was again thronged, with several Members of Parliament and peers to be seen in the gallery listening intently to what was going on.

Both Mr and Mrs Cadogan had been persuaded to testify, although neither of them relished the prospect. As an intimate friend of Lady Mordaunt, a clergyman's wife and a mother of seven, Mrs Cadogan could be regarded as a convincing and reliable witness, but Dr Deane had no intention of giving her an easy ride. In an attempt to question her credibility, he asked her about the will of one of her relations, a Mrs Thwaites, in which she had stood to benefit from a legacy of £10,000. Mrs Thwaites had been declared insane and Mrs Cadogan had never received any money, but Dr Deane did his best to make her appear as somebody experienced in the art of manipulating insane people.

Once that subject was exhausted, Dr Deane questioned Mrs Cadogan very closely about her use of the word 'incoherently' when recalling how Lady Mordaunt expressed her intention of 'confessing all to Charlie'. She was asked what she meant by this and she said she had used the word to indicate that Lady Mordaunt was in great distress. This did not satisfy Dr Deane.

– Do you mean that 'in distress' and 'incoherently' are the same things? It was your own word.
– It was my own word, it was a bit of conversation that I heard.
– I want to know what you mean. I am speaking to a gentle-woman of education. I want to know what you mean by in-coherently.
– Well it had nothing to do with anything else that I heard.
– Then every scrap of conversation you hear a part of is in your judgment incoherent. Is that what you mean?
– I cannot say that, no.
– I did not make use of the word incoherently, you did. You cannot tell me why you made use of it. Very well, Mrs Cadogan, we will please leave it.

There followed some questions about Lady Mordaunt's state of mind on the two Saturdays, 6 and 13 March.

– You say she was hysterical on the 6th. Was she hysterical on the 13th?
– Not what I call hysterical. She was silent, she preserved si-lence.
– Did she seem as if she would cry if she could?
– She seemed in a wrapt state as if she were thinking.
– You mean with her eyes fixed?
– Oh dear no!
– What do you mean by a 'wrapt' state?
– She lay on the sofa and did not answer anything I asked.
– Did she turn her face toward you?

– Oh dear yes, and cried sometimes and cried bitterly when I sang to her.

Mr Cadogan, when it came to his turn, described his visits to Lady Mordaunt concerning the baptism of her baby. Under cross-examination he elaborated on his objections to the 'churching', saying that he could not do it while Lady Mordaunt was lying under 'this notorious scandal'.

The Dowager Lady Mordaunt, Mrs Smith, was then called. Her dignified appearance and the clarity of her speech aroused much admiration as she described her visit on 4 April when she again saw Lady Mordaunt in her boudoir.

– I found her on her sofa, dressed nicely and with a pretty cover upon the sofa and on a table near was her Prayer Book. I said that I hoped she would try and put a stop to the publicity of what must inevitably follow from her conduct. That was nearly all the conversation I can remember.
– Was there any indication to you that her mind was wandering and that she did not know what was said to her?
– None whatever.

The Dowager was then questioned about her visit on 9 May. This was the occasion when Lady Mordaunt had flung open the door of the housekeeper's room and had looked surprised at finding her mother-in-law there. She had then sat on the coal box, and the Dowager had remonstrated with her, thinking that she was 'shamming' and had said, 'We have had enough of this.' The next time she had visited they had walked in the garden and had what appeared to be a natural and normal conversation about the Dowager's son Arthur and his latest illness, about her daughter's governess, Miss Acton, and about Harriett's future brother-in-law Major Arbuthnot. 'I kissed her and that was the last time I ever saw her' said the Dowager.

On this note the court was adjourned for a few minutes. The Dowager's calm description of her walk in the garden with her daughter-in-law, mentioning the cowslips in the field and the honeysuckle, introduced a momentary sense of calm into the tense court room.

When the proceedings resumed, the Dowager under cross-examination firmly reiterated her opinion that any peculiarities in Lady Mordaunt's behaviour had all been assumed.

Sir Charles, who had been occupying a seat in the gallery, now came down into the witness-box. When questioned, he described what he believed to be the perfect happiness of his marriage, and he told the court that when he went to Norway this was the first time he and his wife had been apart for any length of time. Asked about her friends, Captain Farquhar, Sir Frederic Johnstone and Lord Cole, he said that she had spoken about them prior to her marriage and he knew that they were all friends of her family.

Serjeant Ballantine asked Sir Charles whether he had invited Sir Frederic to stay and he said he had, but that it was at his wife's request.

– Were you also aware that the Prince of Wales was an acquaintance of your wife? – I was.

– I believe you had no personal acquaintance with his Royal Highness?

– I cannot say I knew him well. I had spoken to him but beyond that he was never a friend of mine.

– But you were aware that he was acquainted with your wife's family, and in fact was on visiting terms with them?

– Certainly.

– Did he ever come to your house by any invitation of your own?

– Never.

– Did you ever express any desire to your wife in relation to His Royal Highness?

– I did. I warned her against continuing the acquaintance.

Lord Penzance – Tell us what you said to her upon the subject of His Royal Highness.

– I said that I had heard in various quarters certain circumstances connected with his previous character which caused me to make this remark. I did not enter into full particulars.

Serjeant Ballantine – At the time you expressed that desire to Lady Mordaunt had he to your knowledge been on one or two occasions to your house?

– I never saw him but once.

– And was that after you expressed your wish to Lady Mordaunt?

– Yes.

– Were you aware than any correspondence, written correspondence, existed between your wife and the Prince?

– No, I was not.

– Are you saying literally, that you were not aware of any letters passing between them, or might there have been any letters of a proper character?

– I cannot recall having seen any letters.

– It is not the question whether you were aware of her having received any letters.

Lord Penzance – The question is were you aware of the fact that any correspondence of any sort was going on between your wife and the Prince of Wales?

– I knew of nothing.

Mr Serjeant Ballantine – And supposing the Prince of Wales had been at your house whilst you were attending to your duties in the House of Commons or elsewhwere, were you made acquainted with the fact?

– I was not.

– Lord Penzance – Did you know from any source that he ever called at your house?

– No, I never heard of his frequent visits.

– That is not the question. Surely you can answer a simple question like that. Did you know from any source that the Prince of Wales ever called at your house?

– I had heard that he called, but I never saw him.

Mr Serjeant Ballantine – Had you heard that he had called frequently?

– No, not frequently. I heard that he called occasionally.

– From whom did you hear that? From Lady Mordaunt? – No.

– Had the fact of his calling been mentioned by connections of your family? – Yes.

– Did you speak to Lady Mordaunt on the subject after you had had that communication? – I did.

– And was it upon that or upon the second occasion that you gave her advice?

– It was upon the occasion I have already mentioned. I warned her and told her what my wishes were upon the subject.

Questions were then asked about Lady Mordaunt's visit to the Palace Hotel in November 1868, and Sir Charles stated that she had never mentioned that she had met Captain Farquhar there. He was also examined on the subject of his visit to Norway. He described how he had booked on a special steamer which had better accommodation than the normal ones.

Serjeant Ballantine – How did it happen that she did not go?
Sir Charles – She seemed not to wish to go. I had a conversation with Sir Thomas Moncreiffe about her going, but he did not agree with it.

Sir Charles said that he believed his wife had gone down to Walton accompanied by her sister and by Louisa Scott, the greatest confidante she had. He went on to relate how he went to Walton immediately he returned from Norway, but no mention was made of the presence there of the Prince, although Dr Deane, during the cross-examination, did question him briefly about the ponies.

– Did not you, or she with your knowledge, buy two ponies off the Prince of Wales ?
– No, I did not buy them off the Prince; they were bought off the Prince of Wales's coachman by me.

Sir Charles said after he returned from Norway, he and his wife had cohabited as usual and had proceeded to Scotland in August, by which time she had told him that she was 'in the family way'.

– That excited no suspicion in your mind ?
– Not at the time.

Mention was now made of Sir Frederic Johnstone's visits to Walton and the question his wife had asked as to why a man of his fortune and position had not married.

– My answer was that I had heard there was a rumour why he had not. She pressed me to tell her the reason, but I was most reluctant to say anything. I ultimately told her. I do not think she said anything in reply.

The events following the birth were described in detail by Sir Charles, culminating in the confession on Monday 8 March.

– She first said 'Charlie, you are not the father of that child, but Lord Cole is that father, and I, myself am the cause of its blindness.' She did not speak again for about a quarter of an hour.
– When she spoke again, what did she say ?
– She burst into tears, and said 'Charlie I have been very wicked. I have done wrong.' I said to her 'With whom ?' and she replied, 'With Lord Cole, Sir Frederic Johnstone, the Prince of Wales, and others, and often in open day.' I did not credit what she

said, but I saw nothing to indicate that she was under any delusion. She spoke in tones of deep distress, with apparent remorse
and repentance. I could not make any reply for I was too much
distressed.

Lord Penzance – Did you believe what she said?
– No, I did not even then.

The fact that Sir Charles had been able to mention the Prince
and others by name passed without comment and he then described
how he had opened his wife's locked desk and found the letters and
flowers from the bouquet given her by the Prince. These, together
with the Prince's handkerchief, were put on view.

Dr Deane cross-examined Sir Charles on the subject of his encounter with the Prince at his house in Chesham Place.

– I had been pigeon-shooting and when I came home I went to
lay down upon the bed as I was tired, and the witness Bird,
who will be called, told me that His Royal Highness was in the
house, and I came in and saw him. I was not with him for long
as he went away shortly afterwards.

Now Sir Charles had to face up to some hard questioning concerning his wife's health. Dr Deane asked him whether she had seemed
hysterical at times.

– I saw her at times distressed and nervous.
– Do you know the meaning of hysterics?
– Well, I believe it means crying. When a man cries, it is called
crying; when a woman cries it is called hysterics.

This remark was greeted with loud laughter in the court.

Sir Charles said that his wife's physical health had given cause for
concern in the summer of 1867, which was why he had taken her
away to Switzerland, and he knew that she had frequently consulted
Dr Priestley. Ill health, however, had not had anything to do with her
remaining at home while he went to Norway. As for her condition
following the birth, she had appeared to be making a full recovery,
but he had been more than perplexed by her confessions, believing at
first that they could have been caused by 'some irregularity connected
with her confinement'. For this reason he had called in Dr Jones, but
although he and Dr Orford found her distressed and at times silent,
they never suggested that she was out of her mind.

Counsel then produced the letters Sir Charles had written to Lady Louisa after the confinement. These were thought to show that at the time he believed his wife was in an unsound state of mind, since he had said that he found it difficult to make her understand what was said to her, that she did not know her child, that it was difficult to keep her quiet, and that, though not at all feverish, her mind wandered. Gradually, however, he had been forced to accept the fact that all these symptoms were caused not by feverishness but by remorse.

Lord Newport's letters and those from George Forbes were also mentioned, although they were not produced. Sir Charles said that he was aware that his wife was on terms of intimacy with Lord Newport, which was warranted, he thought, by the fact that they were cousins. As to Lord Cole, he had not been concerned about his friendship with his wife believing him to be 'conditionally engaged to one of her sisters'. There was, he believed, great intimacy between the Moncreiffes and Lord Cole.

Mr Serjeant Ballantine – Now it is a painful question, but I must put it to you, Sir Charles; had you any disease upon you when you returned from Norway ? – No.
– Nor at any other period ? – None whatever. Never during my whole life.
Lord Penzance – It has been intimated to me that His Royal Highness the Prince of Wales has received a subpoena to attend as a witness on the part of Sir Charles Mordaunt, and that he has expressed his entire willingness to do so. Now for that purpose I think it right that we should consult His Royal Highness's convenience, and appoint a day for him to attend.

To this Mr Serjeant Ballantine answered with some warmth that he knew the Prince had never been subpoenaed. 'All that we wish' he said

is that the Prince should put himself in communication with the solicitor conducting the petitioner's case, so as to enable him to give formal proof as to the authenticity of the letters which have been handed in. We do not desire that his Royal Highness should be compelled to attend as a witness.

Ballantine said he was surprised at the misunderstanding, and very sorry it had occurred, as it was his express wish that the Prince should not be required to attend.

The subject was then dropped, and the court adjourned until the next day, Saturday 19 February, the fourth day of proceedings. Rumours were by now circulating that although Serjeant Ballantine had made it clear he would not be subpoenaed, the Prince intended to appear voluntarily in the witness-box that afternoon to clear his name now that it had openly been mentioned by Sir Charles in connection with his wife's confessions.

It seemed that public interest in the appearance of 'exalted personages' was, as the *Birmingham Daily Post* reported, at last to be gratified. As a result an even larger crowd than on the previous days was waiting outside Westminster Hall hoping to gain admittance.

There had been some attempt to limit the numbers in the Hall by letting in only those who had been there when the court opened. It had been given out that as the gallery had not been designed to hold a great number of people, a survey would have to be carried out that evening to see how many could be safely accommodated.

Serjeant Ballantine, continuing from where he had left off the previous day, produced the letter which had been served on the solicitor to the Prince of Wales, and this expressly stated that there would be no occasion whatever for his Royal Highness's presence in court.

Ballantine then explained that after hearing Sir James Simpson's evidence, he had asked Dr Orford and Dr Jones to go down to Bickley in order to assess Lady Mordaunt's current mental state. Their report, he told the court, had convinced him that he could not contradict the evidence given by Sir James concerning Lady Mordaunt's present state of health as he had observed it on his most recent visit.

Lord Penzance – You do not wish, then, to prolong the controversy on that head ?
Mr Serjeant Ballantine – That is so; but I shall take the opinion of the jury as to the state of her mind on the 30 April, and subsequently to that date.

This statement brought a new element into the case which Lord Penzance did his best to evaluate. He accepted that Sir Charles's medical advisers would not 'prolong the conflict' about her present state of mind. But this, the judge ruled, was not enough. He pointed out that it must also be established whether or not Lady Mordaunt had been incapable of instructing her solicitor when the citation had been served on her the previous April. Lord Penzance added that if the suit was to go on at all, the condition of the lady's mind at and after her confinement would also have to be determined.

Dr Deane then rose, complaining that such a course would be extremely unfair, because if the jury should find that Lady Mordaunt was of sound mind at the date of her confinement, and when she made certain confessions, these confessions might be taken against her in the main suit. 'One word from her might clear up the whole matter, but she is not now in a position to pronounce it' said Dr Deane. He then attacked Serjeant Ballantine for delaying the admission about Lady Mordaunt's present state of mind until the last possible moment, which caused Lord Penzance to comment wryly, 'It may be a source of regret to you that the enemy has not fought longer, that you might have slaughtered him.' This remark was greeted with laughter from the crowded court, and there were further outbursts of mirth when Dr Deane replied that he would have liked to have slaughtered a good many of the persons who had been about the lady of late. 'I accept the victory, however. But I did expect, and – I won't say what I do expect' he added, his remark causing further laughter.

Now came the turn of Sir Charles's servants and the excitement mounted as lady's maid, footman, butler and housekeeper were questioned in turn, starting with Jessie Clarke, who confirmed that she had first noticed something going on between Captain Farquhar and her mistress in the summer of 1867.

– The day before he went away on the occasion of his visit in the autumn of 1867, did you notice anything which excited your suspicion – I did.
Lord Penzance – We are now going into the question of adultery with Captain Farquhar. Is that not so?
Mr Serjeant Ballantine – Yes.

Lord Penzance then said that such evidence could be inadmissable, since Lady Mordaunt had made no statement about Captain Farquhar; however, he allowed it, and Jessie was questioned about the marks on the linen, the events at the Palace Hotel, and the letter which she had subsequently found on Lady Mordaunt's dressing–table and had shown to Bird.

Cross-examining, Dr Deane asked Jessie when she had first mentioned the relationship between Lady Mordaunt and Captain Farquhar. Jessie replied that it had often been the subject of conversation

between herself, Mrs Caborn and Bird. After the confinement she had
spoken to Lady Louisa on the subject, and had then given the particulars to Mr Haynes, without mentioning the letter from the Tower.
She said that she had withheld the information about the letter from
Captain Farquhar because she did not wish to expose Lady Mordaunt more than she could help.

> Dr Deane – How came you to tell Mr Haynes more in October
> than in March?
> – Because the butler induced me to do so.

At this there was more laughter from the gallery.

> Lord Penzance (sharply) – Did you tell the lawyer you had not
> seen any letter? – Yes.
> – Then that was not true? – No.
> – It was false? – Yes.

Jessie was asked what had happened during Sir Charles's absence
in Norway and she described how Lord Cole stayed late at the house
on the 27 July, and detailed the events at Paddington when they had
caught the 3.40 train, non-stop to Reading.
Dr Deane – From 10 – 14 July 1868, who stayed in the house [Walton
Hall] besides Lord Cole ?
Jessie Clarke – Mr George Forbes and Miss Louisa Scott.
– Was there not a sister of Lady Mordaunt? – No.
– You swear that? – I do.

Jessie Clarke's ordeal in the witness-box lasted a long time and at
the end of it she had to stand up to some severe cross-questioning
from Dr Deane who at one point asked her to speak up. He inter-
rogated her about her conversations with Lady Mordaunt, telling her
how inconsistent it was of her to say that Lady Mordaunt was sane
and had never even feigned insanity. How did this fit in with Jessie's
remark 'My lady, it is no use deceiving me' delivered when Lady
Mordaunt had been 'assuming' silence?
When Serjeant Ballantine came back into the fray, he did his best to
clear up this apparent inconsistency.

> – You meant to imply it was no use your mistress pretending not
> to be right in her mind because you knew better. Is that what
> you meant?
> – I did not think Lady Mordaunt was not right in her mind.

– Did you think she was pretending to be of unsound mind?
– I really cannot explain to you any further.

There was then a short adjournment after which Mr Haynes's evidence was taken by commission as he was still too ill to attend the court. In his statement he recounted how he had served the petitioner's citation at Walton Hall on 30 April 1869. He described how 'pitiful' Lady Mordaunt had looked when he had handed her the document.

After this, Henry Bird was called and examined by Mr Inderwick. He stated that he was butler to Sir Charles and had also been butler to his father, having been in the service of the family for thirty years. He had first noticed the intimacy between Captain Farquhar and Lady Mordaunt when they were staying at various houses in Scotland during the autumn of 1867, and saw that this had continued when Captain Farquhar came to Walton Hall. He noticed that when Sir Charles was out shooting they were often together, particularly in her ladyship's sitting-room. Bird also recalled going into the billiard-room and finding them there.

– They seemed to have been close together, and appeared startled when I entered.
– Tell me what you mean by 'standing close together'. Do you mean that they were close enough to be touching?
– Yes, they were quite close enough to be touching, and when the door opened they seemed to go away from one another.

Lord Cole's visits were also described, particularly the one at Chesham Place on 27 June, when he had stayed on in the drawing-room until nearly one o'clock in the morning, the rest of the party having left soon after eleven. Bird recalled how he had seen Lady Mordaunt's candle, which she would have eventually used to light her way upstairs, and Lord Cole's hat and coat still there on the hall table, and how eventually, after hearing the front door 'go bang' he had gone through to the hall and found that all these items had gone.

The judge now allowed Bird to give his version of the Prince of Wales's involvement. He confirmed that the Prince had called at Sir Charles's house during the summers of 1867 and 1868, arriving at about four o'clock in the afternoons and staying for an hour or two.

– Was Sir Charles at home on those occasions?
– No, he was either at the House of Commons or pigeon-shooting.

– Did you receive instructions from Lady Mordaunt in relation
to his Royal Highness's visits? – I did.
– What were they? – That no one else was to be admitted after
His Royal Highness came.
– Were those instructions followed? – Yes.

Finally Bird was questioned about Lady Mordaunt's sanity. He
said that he had talked to her on many occasions in the weeks following her confinement and she had always appeared to speak rationally.
He admitted however that at Bickley he had begun to notice some
peculiarities, particularly her 'absent' fits and her tendency to wander
about the house. He mentioned the time when she had come into his
room and had told him afterwards that it was a mistake. There was
no good reason, he said, for her coming in at that time, although she
did have to pass his room to go to the water closet.

Bird told the court that he had not observed any of the acts of
indecency described by other witnesses. All the same he had his
doubts about Lady Mordaunt's state of mind; sometimes he thought
she was shamming, at other times he felt less sure. 'I could not make
up my mind either way' he said.

Alfred Brett, the porter at the Palace Hotel, described how he had
'scratched out' the name 'Farmer' in the arrivals book on finding it
was a mistake and had written in the name 'Farquhar', which he had
by then noticed on the Captain's portmanteau. George Jeffreys of the
same hotel said that the entry concerning the Captain's departure had
been in his handwriting, and confirmed that this was not done until
the luggage was taken out of the room. There was nothing to show
where the Captain had actually slept in the hotel the night before.

The footman Frederick Johnson was the next to be called and he
was questioned about Captain Farquhar's visit to Walton during the
shooting season of 1867. He said that he had observed a certain
imtimacy between the Captain and Lady Mordaunt and in particular
cited the time when he had disturbed them together in Lady Mordaunt's boudoir.

Johnson – I think there was a note sent down from Mrs
Cadogan's and I went into the sitting-room with it. Her Ladyship
was there with Captain Farquhar. There was much confusion and
I heard a rustling of dresses and that sort of thing going on.
Mr Inderwick – When you got in what did you say? Did Lady
Mordaunt say anything to you?

– She said I hadn't ought to come in without knocking.

Johnson was then questioned about the correspondence between Lady Mordaunt and the Prince.

Lord Penzance – You must have posted hundreds, I suppose.
– In my time.
– I mean while you were with Lady Mordaunt?
– I should think so.

The inquiry moved on to the time when the Prince had visited Lady Kinnoull's house when Lady Mordaunt was down with measles.

– Did he inquire for Lady Mordaunt?
– I don't know; the hall porter answers the door, the footman takes in the name and the groom of the chamber shows persons in.

Johnson found it hard to be precise about dates, however he said he could check with the paper that he had in his hand. He was told by Dr Deane to answer the questions without referring to his notes, and Lord Penzance said sharply, 'Put that paper up.' Johnson then said that he thought his lordship had given him leave to consult it.

Mrs Caborn was the next to appear. Mr Inderwick questioned her closely about the cheque that Lady Mordaunt had written prior to her departure from Walton the previous May, and she described how she had offered to lend Lady Mordaunt some notes as Mr Cobb had not been able to cash the cheque.

Mr Inderwick – You say she did not appear to like the notes?
– No she did not.
– Were they Bank of England notes or country notes?
– I cannot say. I do not remember.

Mrs Caborn insisted that there had been no signs of madness at that time. She said that before her departure Lady Mordaunt had sent for Mrs Caborn and talked quite normally about taking a wrapper or a railway rug for her journey.

In answer to Dr Deane's cross-examination, which concentrated on Lady Mordaunt's state of mind during her stay at Bickley, Mrs Caborn said that as soon as she saw her there she felt that she had changed. Although she could appear to be normal and was able to answer questions rationally, yet there was something odd in her behaviour which had not been evident before. But the real change had set in during the previous three months, when her mind had weakened rapidly.

Mrs Caborn herself seemed vague when questioned about details, and her recollections about the letter Lady Mordaunt had written to her mother the previous October were so hazy that in the end Lord Penzance gave up, simply saying 'I do not understand you.' She was then questioned about one of the cheques that Lady Mordaunt had written, and on this subject her memories were clear.

– Did you suggest to her that she should write a cheque?
– I did.
– To what purpose?
– To pay her ladyship's bills. She sat down to write; previous to her writing she sat down on the floor and then she got up and sat on the sofa and there she wrote the cheque.

There was further inconclusive questioning on the subject of other cheques, the lawyers themselves in the end becoming confused about the various numbers. Lord Penzance remarked that 'ladies do some-times draw cheques and make a mistake and tear the whole thing up'.

The next witness was Mrs Murray's father, General Arbuthnot. He described his meeting with Lady Mordaunt at his daughter's house in Chester Square. When Serjeant Ballantine asked him whether he had noticed anything during her conversation with him that could indi-cate derangement of mind, he replied 'Decidedly not' and added that she was very agreeable, altogether pleasing in her manners, and per-fectly sensible as to what had passed between them.

Dr Deane, cross-examining, asked whether during the course of their conversation there had been any silence or hesitation, and General Arbuthnot replied that during the time he was in the room there was no silence at all as everybody was talking. This remark provoked some laughter.

– Had you the greater part of the conversation, or she?
– Oh generally, when I talk to a pretty lady, I like to hear her observations as much as I can rather than my own.

There was more laughter at this, and Dr Deane remarked that he thought this was very gallant on the General's part.

Under cross-examination the General continued to insist that Lady Mordaunt had talked normally.

Dr Deane – So, as you have told us, you took her to be just such a person as one would meet in society? – Quite so.
– There was nothing the matter with her mind? – I did not perceive anything the matter with her.

General Arbuthnot then left the witness-box after a low bow.

The last witness of the day was Dr Solomon who confirmed that he had very considerable experience and a large practice in his particular branch of the profession, having been for twenty years surgeon to the Birmingham and Midland Eye Hospital, one of the largest eye hospitals in England. He then described his visit to Walton to examine the baby's eyes. He reported that he had found it labouring under what was termed purulent ophthalmia and he was then questioned as to whether the disease was of a 'specific' character. He replied that judging by the history of the case he would say that it was specific.

Lord Penzance – No, no, you must tell us in your opinion as formed from the appearances you then saw quite independently of what people have told you.
– There are no appearances which are diagnostic of the two in an infant.

Under further questioning, Dr Solomon confirmed that the treatment with astringent applications in both diseases was the same, although the gonorrhoeal version tended to be more obstinate in clearing up, and more destructive in leaving a permanent effect, in some cases destroying the eye altogether.

Serjeant Ballantine had saved his most favourable witnesses until last, hoping to leave a good impression on the jury by bringing forward the Murrays and Mrs Stephens, who had all treated Lady Mordaunt as a ordinary human being and had been rewarded in return with a show of more or less normal behaviour. Dr Orford and Dr Jones also remained to be questioned.

Mrs Murray, for her part, seemed totally overawed, and she gave her answers in such a low tone that it was difficult to catch her words. Quoting from conversations with her young friend, she recalled such sad but succinct remarks as 'We bear all the ignominy' or 'Never marry your daughter to a man she does not care for'. Mrs Murray also recounted how Lady Mordaunt had said 'I know that I have been very wicked but I did not know it at the time.'

Lady Mordaunt's conversation showed that her mind was not as capable as it would have been in perfect health, but although her manner was odd, as far as Mrs Murray was concerned, her acts were always sensible.

Lord Penzance – Do you call sitting on the ground sensible?
Mrs Murray – When you are tired, and no seat is near except the weighing chair, yes.
Serjeant Ballantine – Suppose there had been no question of sanity or insanity?
– I should have thought Lady Mordaunt was hysterical with those fits of laughter.

Mrs Murray then spoke of Lady Mordaunt's behaviour when Dr Wood stayed to dinner.

Serjeant Ballantine – How had she been in the morning?
– Perfectly sensisble.
– Was there any alteration when he came?
– Yes. I was reading a book of Lord Desart's. She appeared interested in one or two passages, and she laughed. She and I both laughed. She had work in her hand, but was not working. She got up to get some more wool. Then Dr Wood and Mr Hughes came in, and she would hardly answer a question.

Herbert Murray was called after his wife had left the witness-box and he gave details of his first visit to Bickley the previous September, when he had walked with Lady Mordaunt in the garden and she had conversed with him naturally and easily.

Questioned about her state of mind, Herbert Murray told the court that on the whole Lady Mordaunt had behaved very well with him and as a rule was rational, although her manner could change, as it had, for example, when Dr Wood or Miss Parsons arrived. He made the distinction between her laughter at the right moments, and her hysterical laughter at the wrong moments. When asked whether he thought that Lady Mordaunt was shamming, he said

– I will say so if you like.
Lord Penzance – It is not a question of if you like. Do you think so in your own mind ?
– Well, my lord, I think it was so.

He was sure that her fits of the 'blues' were genuine, hinting that these were understandable in view of the dull life she led, with no amusements except driving about. He pointed out to the court that Bickley was not a very lively place in September.

Mrs Stephens was then interviewed, and she described how during her ten days at Bickley she had taken the orders for lunch and dinner from Lady Mordaunt, just as she had always done at Walton before the confinement. She would draw out the list for dinner on a slate and submit it to Lady Mordaunt, who would either agree or alter what she had put down. The next day she would tell Mrs Stephens what she had liked and disliked the day before. On the Sunday Mrs Stephens had put rabbit on the menu, but she said she would not have that but the two grouse which had been sent the day before.

Dr Deane – Were her observations about these things sensible?
– Very.
– From what you saw while at Bickley did you believe that she was of unsound mind?
– No, she seemed to understand thoroughly what she was doing.

Those listening intently in the court now had a picture that was quite different from the maniac portrait painted by the nurses and doctors. With disarming simplicity Florence Stephens told them of a young woman who was thoughtful and considerate, making sure that her cook was able to work in the small kitchen without the help of a scullery maid, a young woman who had a right to be melancholy, cut off as she was from all communication with the outside world, so much so that, as she said, she often thought the postman must be dead.

Dr Orford now came into the witness-box. Composed, quite sure of himself, and determined to defy the medical establishment, he answered Serjeant Ballantine's questions firmly and clearly. He said that at the time of the birth Lady Mordaunt had first been placed under chloroform on the Sunday afternoon.

– And she was ultimately delivered of a child? – Yes.
– Did she suffer more than women usually do?
– Rather less, I should say.

Dr Orford then answered questions about the child's condition, and he was also asked about puerperal fever and puerperal mania.

He said that he had come across several cases of the former in his practice, but none of the latter.

– Had she any symptoms from the time you commenced attendance upon her until she left her bed, of puerperal fever?
– Certainly not.
– Had she any symptom whatever of mania? – I should say certainly not.
– Excluding matters that she stated in relation to particular men, and confining your attention entirely to the matters upon which she conversed with you, did she show any sign whatever of delusion? – None whatever.
– Did she require any unusual amount of medicine, or anything of that sort? – Rather less than usual.
– Was there any appearance of a hot head? – Not to my knowledge.
– Was there any sign whatever of madness about her?
– None whatever. I never saw anything the matter with her mind at all during the time I attended her.
– Did you ever hear of her raving? – I did not.
– Was she incoherent in her speech?
– Well, she spoke in monosyllables; and if that be incoherent, she was. I did not consider her incoherent.
– How did she sleep? – She slept very well.
– Was she hysterical? – She was not.
– Did you tell Sir Charles Mordaunt that her state was entirely hysterical, and not in the least dangerous? – I did not.
– Reflect. Did you not tell Sir Charles on the 3rd of March?
– I did not. Lady Mordaunt did not suffer from cataleptic hysteria. I did not tell Sir Charles that she did. I may have heard that Dr Jones said she did. I told Sir Charles I did not agree with Dr Jones.

Cross-examined by Dr Deane, Dr Orford said that he had seen Lady Mordaunt the previous Thursday.

– What state did you find her in?
– In such a state as I consider her mind gone.
Lord Penzance – Incurably so ? – No.

Dr Orford told the court that he had virtually refused to give any information to Sir James Simpson or Dr Priestley because he knew that there were two sides to the question and he wanted to keep to his own side. As far as he was concerned, Lady Mordaunt appeared to be shamming. He had first noticed it on the Monday after her confinement, when she had refused to speak. 'I thought she could speak if she liked, but she would not. I noticed nothing but silence and a fixed look.' When he saw her at Bickley, he was aware that she had changed.

> – The difference between her state at Walton and at Bickley was in her eyes. At Walton, there would have been a flicker of understanding, but at Bickley the eyes had seemed totally dead and I was not able to make the slightest impression upon her.

When Lord Penzance read extracts from Sir Charles's letters to Lady Mordaunt's family saying that she was prostrate and unable to recognise him, Dr Orford said that he thought that Lady Mordaunt was playing up to her husband.

He was questioned about the child's eyes and said that he felt they had taken an exceptionally long time to clear up. He had called in Dr Solomon because the case seemed more severe than others he had seen.

> Mr Serjeant Ballantine – What made you call in Dr Jones?
> Dr Orford – I did not like the responsibility of the case.
> Serjeant Ballantine – But you told us she was going on very well?
> – So I did.
> Lord Penzance – What, then, was the responsibility ?
> – I thought, my Lord, that a there was a great deal going on that would come out afterwards, and I should like to have somebody at my back.

Dr Jones was the next to be examined. Older than Dr Orford, with forty years of experience to Orford's thirteen, he was more cautious than his colleague, but he was equally adamant that he had never noticed any signs of puerperal mania, a disease which, he said, was 'easily distinguishable'. He said that he had realised from Dr Orford's manner that here was some mystery about the case. He had not heard anything about the statements Lady Mordaunt was alleged to have made, but all the same he came to the conclusion that 'there was a hysterical condition arising from mental emotion', and he thought it was extremely probable that Lady Mordaunt had something on her mind. He was sure that she was not suffering from insanity as she was perfectly capable of understanding what was said to her, and was intelligent in her replies when she made them. Like the others, he found that sometimes she did not reply, but when he had visited her on 26 March she had answered all his questions 'rationally and unaffectedly'. He remembered particularly how she had asked him where Sir Charles was and when he said he did not know, she had burst into tears.

Dr Deane questioned Dr Jones about his conviction that her state of mind was caused by nothing more than the crushing weight of affliction caused by the circumstances in which she had found herself. Dr Jones said that in his opinion the peculiarity of her manner was totally inconsistent with disease of the brain. When Dr Deane asked him what hysterical catalepsy was, Dr Jones put him right, replying 'Excuse me, cataleptic hysteria. It makes all the difference whether the substantive is placed before the adjective, or the contrary.'

'We will attend to our grammar' promised Dr Deane.

Dr Jones went on to explain that cataleptic hysteria could be described as a condition of the nervous system 'where there is a nerve force acting independently of voluntary force', a functional disturbance, in which the spinal cord was not affected except by reflex action. He denied that he had told Sir Charles that his wife's nervous system was so prostrate that she could not even be persuaded to take food, pointing out that he had in fact recommended her to get up, and when she had followed his advice, this had made her feel much better. He had been sure all along that if she continued to sleep for eight hours at night, her nervous system, affected though it was by hysteria, was bound to get better. As to the suggestion that she might be shamming, he believed that she tried not to be rational in front of him because that would destroy the effect she wanted to produce. He ruled out insanity or any form of mania, but stuck to his diagnosis of cataleptic hysteria.

Dr Jones described how he had gone upstairs when he had first heard Sir Charles say, 'The child is not mine', expecting to find Lady Mordaunt in a state of delirious excitement consequent upon fever, but he found no sign of any fever, and, as a result, no delirium. He was asked if there was necessarily a fever prior to the onset of puerperal mania. 'As a precursor,' he replied, 'I should think so. I have never seen it without it.'

Summing up, Dr Jones insisted that all the peculiarities he had witnessed could be accounted for by the unhappy circumstances under which Lady Mordaunt was placed, and that now, at Bickley, it seemed that Lady Mordaunt's mind was quite broken down by the terrible situation in which she found herself.

Dr Tyler Smith was questioned next, and he described his two visits to Bickley before Christmas, when he had found Lady Mordaunt looking very unhealthy, with her bad circulation and chilblains. He confirmed that having heard the evidence given by the two Warwickshire doctors he did not think that Lady Mordaunt had ever suffered from puerperal mania, none of the recognisable symptoms having been observed by the doctors attendant on her at the time of her confinement. She gave the appearance of suffering from dementia, although there was nothing he had seen or heard about that could not have been easily feigned. It was true that she seemed very reserved, but that was hardly a sign of madness. Dr Deane questioned him about catalepsy, which he described as 'one of the highest forms of hysteria'.

– May I not take it that the two combined in certain proportions will end in insanity ?
– They may do so, but that is not puerperal insanity.

It was by now three o'clock in the afternoon. The gallery having been examined and pronounced safe, the court had become more crowded than ever. Barristers, solicitors and newspaper reporters were jostling for space with people 'indirectly concerned or intimately interested' in the case, as well as several of the ladies 'whose painful duty it had been to appear as witnesses'. Outside the court several policeman had been doing their best to keep a way clear through the large crowd which had gathered in the hope of seeing the Prince. And then, soon after two o'clock, the Prince himself arrived and was quickly taken to Lord Penzance's private room.

As Serjeant Ballantine sat down, Dr Deane rose and in low measured tones gave the announcement that everyone had been waiting for. He told the court that as the name of the Prince of Wales had been prominently brought forward, he thought it was his duty, having regard to the position of his Royal Highness, to call him as a witness. He also intended to call Sir Frederic Johnstone, whose name had been mixed up in the matter 'with the most odious charge ever introduced into any case'.

After this announcement had been made, there was a buzz of excitement in the court, which increased when the door at the back of the witness-box was opened and the Prince was shown in. As he appeared, silence fell.

The Prince stood calmly in the witness-box, with only a rail separating him from the bench and the jury-box. He bowed to the judge, quietly, maintaining his dignity, and with perfect self-possession took the Testament which was handed to him to be sworn upon. Everyone in court remained seated.

The Prince was given the same treatment as all the other witnesses, the only concession being that in taking the oath he was allowed to press the inside of the Testament instead of the putting the board to his lips. Before the proceedings resumed, Lord Penzance said he thought it was his duty to point out to the Prince his position under the Act of Parliament passed in the previous session.[111] The Prince bowed at this, and Lord Penzance continued

> – No witness in any proceeding, whether a party to the suit or not, would be liable to be asked or bound to answer, any question to show that he or she has been guilty of adultery. From the course the case is taking I think it right to point out the provision of that Act to your Royal Highness and to say that you are not bound or required by law to submit to any interrogations on the subject.

At this the Prince again bowed to the judge.

Dr Deane then started to put the questions. The tension and sense of expectancy in the court was extreme, and even Dr Deane, experienced though he was, seemed quite overwhelmed, as in subdued and respectful tones he began the examination.

> Dr Deane – I believe your Royal Highness has been for some years acquainted with the Moncreiffe family.

The Prince, although sounding somewhat hoarse, spoke out firmly and clearly. 'I have.'

His words fell into the intense silence, and were heard by everyone. His calm, untroubled demeanour won him immediate sympathy among the onlookers. The excitement mounted as each question led nearer to the main point – the real reason for the Prince's appearance.

> Dr Deane – Were you acquainted with Lady Mordaunt before her marriage? – I was.

– On Lady Mordaunt's marriage did you write to her and make her some wedding present? – I did.

– Previous to Lady Mordaunt's marriage has she visited at Marlborough House when your Royal Highness and the Princess of Wales were there? – She has.

– And has she gone to the theatre with both your Royal Highnesses? – She has.

– We are told that Lady Mordaunt was married at the end of the year 1866. In the year 1867 did you see much of her? – I did.

– And in the year 1868? – I did also.

– Were you acquainted with Sir Charles Mordaunt? – I was.

– Have you frequently met Sir Charles Mordaunt? – I have.

– And with Lady Mordaunt? – And with Lady Mordaunt.

– Does your Royal Highness know a place called Hurlingham? – I do.

– Have you been in the habit of meeting Sir Charles Mordaunt there? – I have.

– On one occasion, I think in June 1868, was there a pigeon match, Warwickshire and Norfolk? – There was.

– I believe your Royal Highness and Sir Charles Mordaunt were the Captains for the county? – I believe so.

– Was Lady Mordaunt there? – She was.

– And her husband ? – And her husband.

The Prince confirmed that Lady Mordaunt had kept the score for both sides, and Dr Deane asked him whether in the course of the match he had spoken to Lady Mordaunt with Sir Charles standing by. 'I believe so' he replied.

Dr Deane – We have heard in the course of this case that your Royal Highness used hansom cabs occasionally. I do not know whether this is so. – It is so.

– I have only one more question to trouble your Royal Highness with. Has there ever been any improper familiarity or criminal act between yourself and Lady Mordaunt?
– There has not.

The Prince's words rang out plainly and clearly, delivered with such an air of honesty that it was hard to doubt their truth. A murmur of satisfaction ran through the court, followed by some faint clapping, and finally a muted but cordial cheer which was checked by the judge. The murmuring grew louder as speculation mounted. All eyes were on Serjeant Ballantine as he rose to his feet. It was the general belief that he would now start to cross-examine the Prince. He took everyone by surprise, however, when he said, simply 'I have no questions to ask his Royal Highness.' At this there was some clapping, which gradually became louder and there was some vigorous cheering which eventually turned into an ovation as the Prince left the court.

When this had finally died down, Sir Frederic Johnstone entered the witness-box and was then sworn and examined. It was said that he had been called in consequence of demands made by his solicitors[112] who alleged that during the preliminary proceedings to try the issue of Lady Mordaunt's sanity, charges had been made against Sir Frederic Johnstone in an unjustifiable manner, and wholly without precedent. 'We say nothing' they had written

> of the hardship and injustice of having such foul imputations made against him in a proceeding to which he is no party, and in which his Counsel are precluded from interfering or uttering a word in his defence, which they have avowedly put forth without a tittle of evidence to support them.

Because of these allegations, the solicitors had asked on Sir Frederic's behalf that he should be called at the earliest possible moment. Lord Penzance gave him the same assurances as he had given the Prince, that he was not bound to submit himself to any question unless he liked. Dr Deane started by asking him whether he had been acquainted with the Moncreiffe family for many years.

> Sir Frederic – I have, for several years.
> Dr Deane – Did you know Lady Mordaunt from a child?
> – I did.
> – And have you from that time down to recent events kept up acquaintance with Lady Mordaunt and with her family?
> – I have.
> – Sir Charles Mordaunt and you were at school together, I believe, but you did not know him till his marriage.
> – No, he was senior to me at school.
> – You have visited, we are told, frequently at Walton Hall, and I believe you kept your horses in the hunting season at Walton in the village. – I did.

Sir Frederic was then questioned about the occasion when he had dined alone with Lady Mordaunt at the Alexandra Hotel, and he confirmed that he had left the hotel around midnight.

– Let me ask you first of all, from first to last has there been any improper familiarity or criminal act between you and Lady Mordaunt? – Certainly not.

– Now Sir Frederic, in the course of this case it has been stated that you have suffered severely from venereal disease. Is that true or is it not?

– I say a more unfounded statement was never made by any man to the prejudice of another behind his back.

Lord Penzance – Utterly untrue is it?

– Certainly, for many years.

Sir Frederic was then cross-examined by Mr Serjeant Ballantine.

– You do not mean to imply that you never did suffer.

– Certainly not.

– I am sure I do not want to enter more minutely into these matters than I am obliged. What I suppose Dr Deane really meant to ask I will ask you. You mean at this particular period at all events you were not suffering from any disease of the kind.

– No, nor for many years previously.

– You did not mean to imply that you never did suffer?

– Certainly not.

Serjeant Ballantine then pointed out that Sir Charles had mentioned the disease in a private conversation with his wife and had not expected his remarks to go any further.

It had already been a day rich in drama when a startling revelation caused a further stir. It had been the intention, at the end of the day's proceedings, to read out the letters written by the Prince to Lady Mordaunt, but Dr Deane now told the court that to everyone's astonishment they had all appeared in the newspaper that morning.

Lord Penzance – I may safely say the publication of the letters could not have proceeded from any of the officers of the court, therefore it must have proceeded from some other party. It was a great act of impropriety.

Mr Serjeant Ballantine – I can only say that I myself and all those who instruct me were quite as much surprised as your Lordship to see it.

Lord Penzance – The impropriety consisted in publishing them, before they were read. It was most material that they should be read and they must be read.

The letters proved to be something of a disappointment to those who had hoped to hear shocking improprieties. The most incriminating letter, undated, but evidently written when Sir Charles was in Norway, in which the Prince had suggested that there would be 'no harm' in Lady Mordaunt staying in London while her husband was away, was read out of order and aroused no particular interest or comment.

Serjeant Ballantine then asked the judge's permission not to address the jury until the following day as it was now well after three o'clock. The court was consequently adjourned until the next morning at eleven o'clock.

The Prince went home well satisfied with his performance and that evening he wrote a note to his mother. What he had said in court, he told her, would ensure that the gross imputations which had been so wantonly cast upon him were now cleared up. He had certainly given a good impression of truthfulness with his frank and confident manner, and both Mr Gladstone and the Lord Chancellor wrote to congratulate him on his performance. Lord Hatherley had read the letters and pronounced them 'unexceptional in every way', at best harmless, at worst as some 'friendly but rather unwise missives inadvisedly sent to a woman without her husband's knowledge'. All the same he did caution the Prince about his future behaviour, telling him that as his life was 'a city set on a hill', he must in future endeavour to provide a good example.

33
The Verdict

The following day Serjeant Ballantine proceeded to sum up, pointing out how Sir Charles had produced every single person of whatever rank who could contribute to the case. The other side, by contrast, had made what appeared to be a deliberate attempt to suppress material which might have helped the jury come to a just conclusion, overwhelming them instead by a 'swarm' of eminent medical men. The Moncreiffes were trying to prove that Lady Mordaunt had been insane from the time of her confinement onwards. It was up to them to prove their case and yet they had failed to produce any of the most important witnesses who had seen her at that stage. The absence of any members of the family except Sir Thomas suggested that they were suffering from some sort of epidemic which was keeping them away from court.

> Where is Lady Louisa Moncreiffe? She is in London, we know. She was in court, I believe. Where is Mrs Forbes? Where is Miss Blanche Moncreiffe, her sister? Where is Mr Fiennes, her uncle, to whom she was sent to obtain advice – where is he?

Serjeant Ballantine realised that it would be 'a fearful agony' for a mother to be called to give evidence, but he considered that the magnitude of the interests at stake should do away with 'anything like delicacy'. It seemed to him that since those who were most knowledgeable shrank from coming into the witness-box, it was easy to suspect that they kept away because they knew they could not support the other witnesses.

Apparently afraid to call the mother who had watched over her daughter in childhood and probably knew her better than anyone else, Dr Deane had relied on four witnesses, some of them from lunatic asylums who had talked of 'matters so incredible' that he simply put their evidence out of sight.

Ballantine then dealt with Sir Charles's letters to his wife's relations, in which he described her state before and after her two confessions.

As a country baronet he was probably not familiar with fashionable life – a man of considerable fortune, a man who probably, so far as we can judge by his manner, passed more time in the country than in the metropolis, except during the sittings of Parliament – at all events, a person thoroughly single-minded, devotedly attached to this lady, and who, in writing these letters was hoping and believing that his wife was true, even against his own conviction – in writing to her mother that she was poorly, very poorly up to the 13th [the date of the second confession] he was trying to believe that she was not guilty of the crime of which she accused herself. These letters came from Lady Moncreiffe's escritoire, who gives them up for the purpose of damning Sir Charles, though she dared not appear here herself to give evidence.

Who could blame Sir Charles for at first refusing to believe that the men who had been enjoying his hospitality could have behaved so treacherously? It was only after finding her letters and talking to the servants that he had become convinced of his wife's guilt, and had felt it necessary to say to her 'You are an adulteress; we must separate; you and I can never be one again.' Then Sir Thomas arrives on 20 March and sees his daughter for 'scarcely a minute'. What happened then? 'Up to that time no living being thought this lady insane. From that time it was set up.' As for the child, it was admitted to be Lord Cole's 'as plainly as if it were proclaimed trumpet-tongued from one end of London to the other'.

Then there were the discussions concerning 'the poor diseased child', and the terms on which Mrs Hancox should maintain it. Monthly nurses, Serjeant Ballantine understood, tended to be 'very positive in their statements', and this one was no exception – she had in fact treated his lordship, and himself, with little respect. 'I can hardly picture such a scene as this chaffering between the mother and nurse for the maintenance of this child.'

Serjeant Ballantine then dismissed the testimony of Sir Thomas's doctors, pointing out how flawed their arguments had been. He quoted Dr Tuke's words when he had gone down on his knees in front of Lady Mordaunt, saying 'What can we do for you? You would not like to go to a lunatic asylum would you?'

'What could they make of that? What did they think of it?' Serjeant Ballantine asked the jury. Much more convincing, in his opinion, was the Dowager Lady Mordaunt's telling description of her interviews with her daughter-in-law. The Dowager's evidence was, he thought, a 'terrible contrast' to the testimony of the medical men.

Next Serjeant Ballantine dealt with events in London after Sir Thomas had removed his daughter to Lady Kinnoull's house in Belgrave Square. There, he reminded the jury, Lady Mordaunt would have been surrounded by servants, by lady's maids, by grooms of the chamber and 'all the usual paraphernalia of wealth'.

> I suppose that Lady Mordaunt had her hair dressed, had the clothes fastened on, was assisted to dress, went to breakfast, to dinner, and to tea. She must have done all these things in the company of other people. But who are they? Echo answers. Gentlemen, is not all this a sham, is it not too bad?

The fact that the other side would not call a single person who could give an account of her behaviour during the time she was at Belgrave Square was, he thought, a crying shame. The reason, he guessed, was because nobody who had seen her there was able in all honesty to say that she was mad.

In the same way Lord Cole had failed to appear in court.

> Where is Lord Cole, and what is he doing now? Here is a child expected to bear Sir Charles Mordaunt's name and inherit his property. Lord Cole is the father of that child, and Lady Moncreiffe is seeking to prevent the divorce. When we get the plain English of it, how foul it is! Lady Mordaunt makes a memorandum in her pocket book, and the very day on which the child is born accords with the night Lord Cole slept with her. Neither Lord Cole nor Captain Farquhar is called to contradict the adultery, and yet my learned friend is here to ask you to shut out Sir Charles from a court of justice and oblige him, by the law of the land, to maintain the infant of Lord Cole, to give it his name, and to allow it to inherit his property.

The question of the Prince of Wales was now raised. Serjeant Ballantine said that he had not wished to call the Prince, never believing that he had in fact been guilty of any criminal act, and he did not intend to discuss his involvement any further, only saying that although he knew that Lady Mordaunt had been more intimate with his Royal Highness than her husband had wished, there was no more to it than that. 'If I thought it necessary to point out that which would be criminal in the highest in the land, I hope I have the firmness and honour enough to do it' he said. Sir Frederic Johnstone, for his part, was more concerned in denying 'that which was deemed ungentlemanly' than in rejecting the adultery accusation.

A guest of Sir Charles, received at his table, received with hospitality and consideration, meets with this unhappy girl and dines with her in a private room at a fashionable hotel. It is all very well to come here and say there is no criminality. What business had he to meet her – dining there alone from eight o'clock to twelve at night – a young man dining with a beautiful young woman at a fashionable hotel? Let us bring it home to ourselves. Bring it home to yourselves. But, forsooth, the waiter could come in; I dare say he did sometimes. If this had occurred in a bedroom it would have been conclusive. There was a young man with her in an hotel these four hours, and I say there is nothing in the nature of the case to lead you to believe that when she mentioned the name of Sir Frederic, the lady was not speaking the truth.

And so, after over three hours, Serjeant Ballantine's peroration drew to a close.

I have seen my client and described his position. I can understand that the representative of an old house, in a county where he is loved and looked up to, has gone through a bitter trial and has endured bitter agony. He has been libelled, he has been slandered, and it has been sought to fix upon him the illegitimate child of another by a mother who has betrayed him; and this inquiry is to determine what shall happen upon these subjects. I can only say that I trust in dealing with them you will be guided to a right conclusion by your honest hearts and minds, and by a sound and impartial judgment.

On this note Serjeant Ballantine finally sat down, quite exhausted by his efforts. There was some subdued applause. Dr Deane then rose to his feet and addressed the jury. He accused Serjeant Ballantine of having mixed up the issue, having 'so descanted upon the attractions of Lady Mordaunt and the affection which existed between her and her husband and of the handsome settlements she had received at his hands' that as a result it was easy to forget that the point at issue was Lady Mordaunt's sanity at a certain time. Serjeant Ballantine, he said, had spent much of his long address in pointing out the absence of certain witnesses. The simple answer to this was that he and his learned friends had decided to confine themselves to events from 30 April up to the present time. For this reason, the absence of Mrs Forbes was the only one he himself had touched upon, as it was she alone who had been with her sister when the petition was served. The reason she was unable to attend was that she had been confined three weeks before. Dr Deane said that it would have been 'utterly outside' to call any one who was present at the first illness. It was in any case unnecessary, as he himself was prepared to give links of such perfect workmanship, so well welded, so perfectly joined together, that he could put before the jury a chain of evidence without flaw, extending from 28 February down to the present moment.

> In this case I feel very deeply for the position in which Sir Charles Mordaunt is placed. I feel deeply for the family to which Lady Mordaunt belongs. I feel deeply for all those whose names have been mentioned in this case. But there are perhaps three or four episodes in these lamentable transactions in which one will have some difficulty in restraining the language which ought to be applied. I shall endeavour to speak as calmly as I can of what I believe to be the hideous origin of all the trouble which this unfortunate family is now brought to.

He was referring, of course, to the conversation concerning Sir Frederic Johnstone between Lady Mordaunt and her husband, when Sir Charles told her that he believed Sir Frederic was suffering from a complaint which might bring disease upon any child he had. Dr Deane's theory was that, mentally unbalanced as she was as a result of her pregnancy, this information had somehow preyed on Lady Mordaunt's mind, and he quoted Mrs Cadogan's testimony that she had seemed unusually agitated and nervous about her forthcoming confinement.

Dr Deane then produced details which he felt could help prove that Lady Mordaunt had in fact been suffering from puerperal mania. She had, for example, virtually sent her mother away on one occasion, displaying the typical symptom of disliking her most intimate relations. Silence and taciturnity, the other two symptoms mentioned, she had displayed, he considered, on a number of occasions. Evidence that the mind was 'off poise' had been provided by the fact that she had suggested that the child should be given a dose of laudanum.

Lady Mordaunt's statements were then considered, particularly with reference to the Prince of Wales. Lady Mordaunt had referred to him in exactly the same terms as the others. Dr Deane agreed with his learned friend that the highest as well as the lowest must be proceeded against. But, he said, 'sever the accusation of the Prince of Wales from that made against the others, and if there is a delusion in one case, I defy anybody to say it is not a delusion in the other cases.' It seemed that Serjeant Ballantine had been quite prepared to accept Sir Frederic's evidence concerning his state of health, 'but if he believed Sir Frederic's evidence in that particular, what right had he to disbelieve his evidence as to the charge of adultery?'

It was urged that he dined alone with Lady Mordaunt at the Alexandra Hotel. No doubt he did. But had it come to this that a gentleman could not accept an invitation to dine with a lady whom he had known from childhood, and with whose family he was intimate, without subjecting himself to the imputation of abusing the opportunity?

He believed, no matter what his learned friend might say, that there were people – men and woman – young and handsome – who could meet under such circumstances and spend the evening together, and yet remain virtuous.

The same kind of argument applied to Lord Cole. He had, it seemed, been engaged to Lady Mordaunt's sister. What more natural than that he should visit and dine at her house? And how could a conclusion of guilt be drawn from the fact of his accompanying her in the train down to Reading, and spending afterwards a few days at Walton?

Dr Deane remarked on the fact that it was not until the fourth day of the trial that 'the other side', that is Dr Orford and Dr Jones, had finally conceded that Lady Mordaunt's mind was impaired. But if she was mad now, when had she become insane? Mr Murray had talked of fits of the blues towards the end of the previous year, and at that time she had written coherently to her mother. Had she been capable of writing that herself, or had Miss Parsons stood at her elbow, telling her what to put? He agreed that Lady Mordaunt had a strong motive for feigning, but again, had she begun with that motive, or developed it later? Dr Deane said that he had been enabled to call the Prince of Wales and Sir Frederic Johnstone, and they had stated that what Lady Mordaunt had said against herself was a delusion. He had therefore shown to the jury the state of her mind at the time of her confinement, on 30 April, and at the present time. It was no business of theirs whether this case should end today or should be reopened another time. Nor was the question whether Lady Mordaunt could simply say guilty or not guilty, but whether she could instruct those who advised her.

If any blame attached to the policy of not calling Lady Moncreiffe, Dr Deane was prepared to take the blame. He reiterated that he had not thought it was necessary to go into events which had taken place prior to 30 April – the papers had anyway been full of such details for the last week.

> I was not even aware until Tuesday afternoon that Sir Frederic Johnstone would be called. I did not know until yesterday morning what his Royal Highness was going to say. Voluntarily, in consequence of the charges made against them, they came forward – the one bound by his high position to support his honour before the public when it is assailed even by the out-pourings of a diseased and disordered mind; the other anxious to refute the foulest calumny that could be cast upon a young man who may hope one day himself to contract an honourable and happy marriage. It is to be regretted that such a charge should have been made against him; it is to be rejoiced at that it has been so thoroughly rejected.

At this there was some applause, which was immediately suppressed.

Lord Penzance told Dr Deane that he would sum up the case the next day and the court then adjourned.

On the last day of the trial, the court and the galleries were as full as they had been all the week as everybody crowded in to hear the judge's address to the jury and his final verdict.

Lord Penzance began his summing up. 'We are now approaching, I am happy to say, the end of this inquiry.' He remarked on the excep-tional amount of time that the case had taken, and the public atten-tion it had caused.

> It may be said, and I dare say has been said, that the avidity of the public to take part in the interest of this trial is a thing that is to be deplored, as showing a desire to participate in the inves-tigation of immoral questions. But, gentlemen, I am not quite

sure whether that is a correct description of the reason why this
trial has occupied so much attention. It is on account of the
position in society held by those who are implicated in this
matter that it has excited and occupied so much of the public
attention.

The judge felt that the eminence of the people concerned had
caused the exceptional interest, rather than the details of the case.

'The Warwickshire Scandal', as I believe it has been called in
the newspapers, was by early June no longer a private matter.
Rumour had spread it throughout the country. Many tongued
rumour gave its own account of those who were implicated in it,
and while reports are spread around, floating about in all classes
of society, is it altogether an evil that we should come in the
open day into open court and investigate the matter, and so
remedy a part of the wrong that has been done?

He reminded the jury how the 'intrepid' Serjeant Ballantine, such 'a
consummate master of legal rhetoric', had brought forward everything and everybody who could properly be included. 'Gentleman, I
cannot help thinking, after all is said and done, that we are no losers
by this public investigation.'

The judge then went on to deal with the topic which he said had
been much pressed upon the jury by Serjeant Ballantine, and this was
concerned with the effect on Sir Charles of their finding that Lady
Mordaunt was not able to answer. He thought it would be wrong to
think that this would necessarily mean that Sir Charles would never
be able to divorce her; she could after all recover, in which case he
could proceed in his suit just as if she had never been ill, and even if
she did not, would that necessarily mean that he would be tied for
ever to a wife who had dishonoured his bed? Such a situation would
have to be argued out in court and was not now the matter under
discussion.

The other matter which had attracted so much attention was, of
course, the question of Lady Mordaunt's adultery, but Lord Penzance
pointed out that this had turned out to be a curious sort of inquiry, in
which the ordinary process of reasoning had been reversed, and the
adultery had been introduced to prove the truth of the statements.
For, if the fact is true it would go some way towards showing that she
was sane when she made the statements.

It was obvious that all the men named by Lady Mordaunt had acted with some impropriety, but the judge hoped that the jury would not consider them guilty just because they had dined with a lady or travelled on the train with her. He then moved on to the item everybody had been waiting for. 'I must not omit the Prince of Wales' he said. He went quickly over the evidence to hand, the fact that the Prince had visited Lady Mordaunt's house at an ordinary time, that he had sometimes stayed behind at a lunch party for a quarter of an hour after the other guests had left, and that he had written letters. The judge did not feel that much needed to be made of all that.

'And now' Lord Penzance went on 'with very much pleasure to myself, I will pass away from that branch of the inquiry.' The time had come to approach the real question of the case, namely, the sanity of the lady at a certain time. As to the question of insanity, he could not think of any subject where it was more difficult to find the exact words. 'You talk of a person of weak intellect, or unsound mind, or so on. Sometimes you call them maniacs, suggesting the idea almost of a man chained to the leg of a bed.'

As in the diseases of the body, there were many different diseases of the mind. 'I must ask you whether you consider this lady was in such a condition of mental disease as to be unable to give the necessary instructions for her defence, and I prefer using that to any other phrase, because that is the question we have to try.'

Tests had been resorted to by the petitioner to try to establish that Lady Mordaunt was sane – for example, were the admissions true, and, what reasonable things did she say and do? The judge was unsure of the validity of these tests.

Suppose it were true that Lady Mordaunt had dishonoured her husband to the full extent she said, does it follow that she was sane? Do insane people never refer to events that have really taken place? . . . It is said she made the confession because the child was diseased, and she knew she would be found out; and if that were so, it would go a great way to show she was sane. But, gentlemen, the facts deny that. She accused Lord Cole of being the father, and asked if anything was the matter with the child. She was told no; and although that was repeated on the Tuesday and Wednesday, she did not retract the confession as to Lord Cole. Was she acting as a reasonable woman in the full possession of her faculties? Why should she make the confession? She might think she should obtain the forgiveness of her husband.

But that, the judge pointed out, was not so, because when Mrs Cadogan advised her to ask her husband for forgiveness, she simply said she would humble herself to no man, and then there was her extraordinary reply when asked to apologise to her husband that she was not in fact at all sorry for what she had done.

His Lordship then proceeded to read and comment upon the principal facts given by the witnesses. He demolished Nurse Hancox's evidence by pointing out that she had said Lady Mordaunt had confessed to her that the child was Lord Cole's even before the eyes had begun to be bad, and he was struck by the fact that no questions had been asked concerning Lady Mordaunt's condition during the week before she had made the confession to Sir Charles. She had indeed been described as looking cheerful, despite the depressing circumstances, and at a time when a mother is usually fondly attached to her child she took no notice of it. At the same time as Sir Charles was writing to his wife's relations, saying that she was so ill she did not know the people about her, Dr Orford was saying that she was well, and that the statements of Sir Charles were not true. There in fact seemed to be strange contradictions about the case.

He then dealt with the question of why Lady Louisa had not been called. He dared say that it would be a very painful and a very trying position for Lady Moncreiffe to be placed in, but, on the other hand, if she could give a different account from that presented by the witnesses on the other side, she ought not, in the interests of her child, to shrink from that ordeal. It had been said that it would be no worse for Lady Louisa than for a lady's maid to undergo the ordeal of appearing in court. But as to Jessie Clarke, no witness could be found who gave her evidence with more cheerful alacrity, touching everything that concerned her mistress's dishonour; and, if she had a feeling of repugnance in the witness-box, she had certainly disguised it admirably. The question was, could Lady Moncreiffe controvert the statement made by the witness on the other side? To that extent, the remarks of the learned counsel for Sir Charles Mordaunt were well founded, but the jury should form their own opinion of the circumstance. What they had to try, however, was whether the respondent was of a nervous and disordered mind, and they had to base their decision not on the evidence of the witnesses who were not called, but on the testimony of those who were.

As to the question of shamming, would life be worth living if the unfortunate young woman had to continue feigning for the rest of her life? Or, if she ceased to sham and returned to society in order to enjoy its pleasures, at that moment Sir Charles Mordaunt might prosecute his suit and demand the relief he now sought.

The judge now told the jury that the time had come for them to weigh up all the evidence. The crucial issue was to decide when Lady Mordaunt had first begun to show those symptoms of silence and want of comprehension which she was now suffering from to a great degree. 'Who shall say' he inquired 'when was the first period when there were no signs of a diseased mind?'

'The evidence has been laid in detail before you' the judge told the jury. 'You have given the attention which a jury should give in the course of a long trial. I do not think I can assist you further. '

It was now twenty-five minutes past two. Members of the jury retired to discuss the lengthy proceedings and to come to their verdict. Those who waited in the court in trepidation, each in their way fearing the outcome, had no idea how long they would remain in anticipation. The complications of the case, the many unanswered questions, the differences of opinion, all suggested that it would be some time before the jury would reappear. But after deliberating for barely ten minutes, they returned into court.

Mr Billinge (the clerk)– Gentlemen of the jury, have you agreed upon your verdict?

The foreman – We have agreed.

Mr Billinge – Was the respondent upon the 30 April in such a condition of mental disorder as to be unable to answer the citation and instruct an attorney in her defence?

Foreman – She was totally unfit.

At this there was some attempt at applause.

Mr Billinge (to Lord Penzance) – The other question I need not put.

Lord Penzance (to Dr Deane) – The other question is immaterial?

Dr Deane – We shall be glad to have the verdict of the jury upon the second point.

Lord Penzance – The question is, did she upon any subsequent time become so?

Dr Deane – And has been ever since?

The foreman – We are equally of opinion on that subject, and say the same.

There were a few moments of silence before there was some clapping and cheering, which gradually developed into an ovation.

After that, within a few minutes, all the spectators had left, the court assumed its ordinary business-like aspect, and another trial began.

34
The Aftermath

There were many people who felt that whether or not Lady Mordaunt had justly been declared insane, the trial had most of all demonstrated how easily a young lady could be raped within the confines of her own home, even in her own drawing-room, in the short time that a man lingers behind after a dinner-party when the other guests have left. Watchful parents, shocked to hear how mild flirtations had led to quick seductions, were more careful than ever to ensure that their daughters dressed with seemly modesty and never found themselves left alone with a man. This applied equally to married women: the Queen told her daughter Louise never to go out when her husband was away without making sure that she was accompanied by '*some* lady or other'.[113] Lillie Langtry recalled how angry Lord Malmesbury had been when she rode out from his house unchaperoned with one of his relations. She thought he was exaggerating the dangers which beset young people, but others would not have agreed. The Mordaunt case did much to reinforce the proprieties which the Prince and his set seemed to be doing their best to undermine.

Throughout the trial, detailed reports of the proceedings had appeared in all the major newspapers, and the day after the Prince's appearance in court *The Times* had written strongly in his favour. Once the proceedings had been concluded, other newspapers commented at length on the outcome, stressing the importance of the case. As the *Pall Mall Gazette* put it, there had been more at stake than the punishment of a guilty woman. Important rights of property and inheritance were involved and the question of a child whose legitimacy was in dispute.

There was a general feeling that, important though it was, the case had been presented in a way that was far from satisfactory. *The Times* thought that the legal procedure had been 'insufficiently considered', and it seemed to some that the whole affair had been surrounded by mysteries. Although the *Morning Post* was of the opinion that the verdict of madness was probably right, many other commentators remained uncertain. The *Daily News* believed that Lady Mordaunt's counsel had raised nothing more than 'a technical objection' when declaring that her insanity was a bar to further proceedings. It could after all be said that the same principle would preclude a debtor from collecting his debt if the debtor became insane after the debt was incurred. This led on to the question of why Lady Mordaunt's advisers had chosen in the first place to base her defence on an admission which did nothing to clear her name. Anyone would have thought that they, guided by her relations, would have seized every opportunity of vindicating 'her fair fame'. Since they had not, the question of Lady Mordaunt's guilt or innocence had been left undecided, and it followed that a cruel wrong had been inflicted on one or other of the parties involved. Sir Charles remained bound to a wife he believed to be unfaithful, and as for Lady Mordaunt, 'this poor creature has been driven out of her senses by the foul suspicion of a most unmerited wrong . . . and the brand of supposed illegitimacy fastened upon her child.' Then there was the plight of the men whose names had been 'bruited about', as the *Standard* put it, but who were unable to appear, Captain Farquhar, for one, now being far away in India.

It was all part of what the *Observer* described as 'the mistaken character of the enquiry'. The pleas which the jury accepted as valid had no bearing on the issue as to whether Lady Mordaunt had committed adultery or whether she was in any way the 'profligate creature' she had represented herself to be. As the *Standard* put it, the unfortunate lady would now suffer 'perpetual ostracism from everything that makes life worth having', condemned at the age of twenty-two to a living death for the rest of her days. At the same time, whether Lady Mordaunt was *compos mentis* or not, Sir Charles still did not know whether he would be able to continue his suit in the divorce court. If this had been settled at the outset, the court might have been spared 'a week's surfeit of details' which had led to 'no result save that of injury to public morality'.

The *Daily Telegraph* at least felt 'unspeakable relief' that those views of modern morality 'which would have been forced upon us if the unhappy respondent had been pronounced sane, may now be dismissed as founded only on the frenzies of a mind jangled and out of tune. The newspaper expressed sympathy for Lady Mordaunt, whose 'honour and status' had been threatened by the ravings of the puerperal mania she suffered from. There was altogether a 'tragic complexity' about the whole affair, with a 'hapless gentleman whose deplorable household story' had been laid bare to the world by Serjeant Ballantine:

> the whole sad record of his shattered home, one of the most ancient in the historic midland region of England, while his wife was bound to him by the bond of insanity, and her child round whom hangs and may for ever hang, the gloom and wretchedness of those agonising twelve months. Thus he stands, ten times more pitiable, more desolate, more desperate than if he had borne his great anguish in silence. Could any man in his position have done otherwise?

The *Morning Post* did not blame Sir Charles for taking steps which he believed necessary for the vindication of his honour, but it did at the same time feel deep sympathy for the ill-fated Lady Mordaunt who had been 'surrounded by faithless inferiors and pitiless equals – medical men, clergyman of the parish, even her own maid – and refused even the consolation of religion'. It was small wonder that she had become mad, with 'her honour trampled in the dust, her young life broken'.

The *Pall Mall Gazette* treated Sir Charles rather less kindly, castigating him for treating his wife in such a typically English way. He had done his best to drag her through the divorce court when in a similar situation a Frenchman would have quietly left her and a Spaniard or an Italian would have gone off and shot himself.

Most of the leader writers agreed that the most welcome outcome of the trial had been the Prince's 'voluntary and straightforward disavowal of Lady Mordaunt's allegations' which had at last cleared his name from the scandal. *The Times* felt considerable sympathy for the two people who had been 'aspersed yet not accused' and for 'the eldest son of the Queen' who had also rested under 'this cloud of obloquy'. And then the surreptitious publication of the Prince's letters had provided 'the first gleam to lighten the darkness'. It was to be hoped, *The Times* declared, that the *Birmingham Daily Post* which had lifted the cloud, should receive 'light punishment for this impropriety'. Thanks to its action, the simple, gossiping, everyday and 'stupidly honest' character of the correspondence had been revealed, and the innocent nature of the Prince's relationship with Lady Mordaunt established. He was seen to be nothing more than a friend and 'Highland neighbour' of her family. As far as *The Times* was concerned, 'The Prince's error was simply this – that he had been too careless of his reputation. He acted as a young man who does not understand the passion far too many have for scandal.' It was not easy, the newspaper pointed out, for the younger members of the royal family to remember the 'fierce light that beats upon the throne'. At the same time, the Prince had before him the pattern of the Prince Consort with his carefully regulated life, and so it was to be hoped that in future he would show 'fidelity to this example' so that Englishmen would see in their future King 'a life purifed from even the semblance of levity'.

Whether or not the Queen nursed such high hopes of future probity, or whether the Prince himself appreciated having the example of his father put in front of him, there is no doubt that mother and son were considerably relieved by the verdict. All the same, the Queen, while appreciating the support for her son expressed in *The Times*, naturally wished that the whole episode had never taken place. She wrote to her daughter Vicky from Windsor on 2 March 1870 thanking her for writing sympathetically about the trial and agreeing that Bertie's appearance in the dock had caused a great deal of good. Still, this could not take away from the fact that it had all been 'a painful, lowering thing'. The Queen said that she had never doubted Bertie's innocence, and it was her opinion that

his name ought never to have been dragged in the dirt, or mixed up with such people. He did not know of, or admire, the unfortunate, crazy Lady Mordaunt more than he does or did other ladies. The husband is a fool urged on by a bad brother and mother who wished the property to come to them – and certainly B. has been vindictively and spitefully used – though why and wherefore I can't tell. He may have said something about Sir C.M.'s usage of his wife, which came back to him as poor B. is not very discreet. He has however received many warnings now. You read I hope *The Times* article of the 24th – and a still finer one in *The Daily Telegraph* of the 26th. Have you seen that? B. feels now that these visits to ladies and letter writing are a mistake – to say the least. But they [the Prince and Princesses] lead far too frivolous a life, and are far too intimate with a small set of not the best or wisest people who consider being fast the right thing!! I hope we shall get him to change but it is difficult; still I never give up reminding him of this dreadful trial.

The only comfort was that her beloved Prince Albert had been spared the ignominy of his son's involvement in such a sordid affair; if he had been alive she knew that he would have suffered dreadfully. 'Believe me,' wrote the Queen, 'children are a terrible anxiety and the sorrow they cause is far greater than the pleasure they give.'[114]

The crisis had at least cemented the relationship between the Queen and her daughter-in-law. On 5 March the Queen told Vicky that Alix had just left Windsor

> with increased love and affection and regard on my part. We agree so well, and she is so good and honest and right-minded. She is looking wonderfully well – quite fat for her. She has felt everything that passed lately, deeply -but she is I think quite easy as to Bertie's conduct; only regretting his being foolish and imprudent.

If the Prince and his mother were relieved by the verdict, Sir Charles, of course, was deeply disappointed. He felt even more aggrieved when on 8 March Lord Penzance delivered his judgment. Conscious of the hardship a woman who had been temporarily deranged would suffer if she returned to her senses only to find that she had been divorced without a chance to defend herself, the judge made an order that no further proceedings should be initiated until Lady Mordaunt had recovered her sanity.

Convinced as he was that the jury at the trial had been packed and that Lord Penzance had been primed, Sir Charles now had to face the reality of an order which effectively prevented him from taking any further action. All possible ways of procuring his divorce seemed to be blocked. The trial had proved to him how difficult it would be ever to prove that his wife had recovered her sanity, and at the same time the judge's latest order made no provision for him to continue the suit should she in the end be diagnosed as permanently mad.

All the same, if anybody believed that Sir Charles would be intimidated by the verdict and discouraged from pursuing the matter any further, they had seriously underestimated his righteous anger and his determination to battle on under the banner of justice. It soon became known that he intended to appeal against the order. By 15 March the rumours had already reached the Crown Princess in Germany, who wrote to her mother in some alarm. 'Is it really true that all that awful business about Lady Mordaunt is coming out again and that Bertie's name will be mixed up again?' she asked, adding 'I think it is shocking.' The Queen however was reassuring, saying that she did not have the slightest fear that Bertie would be involved. Meanwhile, she had received a 'very kind and sensible letter' from the Princess's mother, the Queen of Denmark, about the whole business. She felt very sorry for the Princess's parents. 'I think it is so dreadful for them both' she wrote.[115]

A few days after the trial ended, Sir Charles wrote to tell Mr Hannay he had heard that Sir Thomas and Lord Cole would fight hard if there were further proceedings and would engage a more eminent counsel than Mr Deane. This made Sir Charles himself seriously consider engaging a different counsel. He was sure Serjeant Ballantine had been subjected to strong pressure from the Queen and Mr Gladstone, and this explained why he had so unexpectedly failed to cross-examine the Prince. He was, it was true, a brilliant advocate, but Sir Charles now wrote to Mr Hannay questioning whether he would be capable of dealing with the next stage of the proceedings. He made the suggestion that 'a great technical lawyer', Mr Melluish Q.C., should be approached. Particularly important was the fact that Melluish 'was in no way connected either with the [royal] Court or the Government'. If this approach could be done without offending Serjeant Ballantine and without delaying the drawing up of the motion to proceed, Sir Charles was definitely in favour of such a move.

On 4 March Mr Hannay, who had by now taken over all the work on the case from Mr Haynes, wrote to Mr Hunt stressing that immediate steps should be made to obtain a discharge of the order of 5 August under which Lady Mordaunt had been detained at Bickley. 'This Sir Charles wishes done immediately' he wrote. Hannay then touched rather nervously on Sir Charles's plan to engage Mr Melluish. Serjeant Ballantine himself was of the opinion that in summing up at the trial he had made one of the most brilliant speeches of his career, and he would undoubtedly greatly resent any suggestion that he had been influenced by the court or the Government. 'This is a delicate point,' Hannay wrote, 'requiring your minute consideration and we think if you could see Mr Inderwick *privately* and ascertain his views it would be most desirable.'

Lord Penzance now issued a new order discharging the one he had made the previous August. Lady Mordaunt was in future to be looked after at Sir Charles's expense in an establishment recognised by the Lunacy Commmissioners. This new order at least enabled Sir

Charles to make arrangements for removing Lady Mordaunt from Page Heath, thus freeing himself from the expense of a second establishment and the inconvenience of having to staff it with his own servants.

The justification for detaining Lady Mordaunt under the Lunacy Act had to be provided by a medical certificate, and on 27 March Dr Wood was sent down to Page Heath to assess her present condition for this purpose. He was shown into the sitting-room which was now quite bare of ornaments. Some of the furniture had also been moved out for fear, Miss Keddell said, that Lady Mordaunt might injure herself if she threw herself violently onto the floor. Dr Wood thought that Lady Mordaunt's behaviour was extremely strange. She told him he was Charlie, and asked if he remembered some buttons he had given her. While he was attempting to attract her attention, she started trying to tear the covering off a chair, and then she suddenly threw herself into a sitting position on the floor before rushing towards him on her hands and knees and putting her head on his knee. She picked up his hat and threw it at him, laughing immoderately. As a result of all this, Dr Wood had no qualms about signing the certificate.

It was now crucial to choose an establishment where Lady Mordaunt would receive the kind of treatment most calculated to restore her to a more normal frame of mind. Sir Charles consulted Dr Tyler Smith, who like Dr Forbes Winslow believed that those who were only marginally mad should not be treated with sedatives and housed with violent maniacs. He was still sure that if Lady Mordaunt could be sent to a warmer, less isolated location than Page Heath and allowed to live a more normal existence, her physical and mental health would improve at once. Rather then recommend a private asylum where Lady Mordaunt would have been in daily contact with mad people, Dr Tyler Smith suggested that she should be looked after on her own as a private patient by Dr Andrew Wynter and his wife at their home, Chestnut Lodge in Chiswick. Dr Wynter was experienced in the care and treatment of people suffering from mental disease. For the last fourteen years he had been in the habit of looking after insane and 'nervous' patients in his house with the approval of the Board of Lunacy Commissioners which had been set up to help avoid the wrongful commital of patients and to ensure that they were humanely treated.[116]

The certificates signed by Dr Wood and one other doctor made it plain that Lady Mordaunt would have to be restrained and must not be allowed to escape from custody. There was nothing prison-like, however, about Chestnut Lodge. Mr Hannay had satisfied himself that the establishment was suitable for 'a lady' and that every arrangement necessary for Lady Mordaunt's comfort would be made. She was to have her own separate suite of rooms as well as her personal attendant, but she would be treated as one of the family and every effort would be made to avoid giving her the feeling that she was being watched. Dr Tyler Smith was retained as the visiting physician and he was asked to call frequently but informally.

35
Chestnut Lodge

On 27 March 1870 Lady Mordaunt was taken away from Page Heath. Mrs Caborn accompanied her to her new home, and they were shown into the upstairs room which was to be Lady Mordaunt's own private sitting-room. When she had settled in, Mrs Wynter went in to greet her and saw an unhealthily overweight young woman wearing a dress that was torn and stained. Lady Mordaunt shook hands and looked at Mrs Wynter with 'a dull kind of gaze'. Although she did not seem to be nearly as bad mentally as they had been led to expect, both the Wynters were rather shocked by her physical appearance. They came to the conclusion that she was in very poor health.

For the first few days Lady Mordaunt seemed subdued. She would sit in her room in what Mrs Wynter described as 'a state of stupor', but this gradually wore off as Mrs Wynter gained her confidence and began to have conversations with her. She told Mrs Wynter how pleased she was not to be at Page Heath any longer, saying how much she had disliked the place and had hated all the people there.

In the more relaxed family atmosphere of Chestnut Lodge, where she was treated with respect and was no longer given the sedative, bromide of potassium, which had been administered by Dr Hughes at Page Heath, her condition improved dramatically. She began to take more care of her appearance and her clothes, dressing neatly and simply, and always choosing the dress herself. Her eyes began to regain their former beauty and brightness. She seemed to enjoy the food that she was given and there was no sign of the eating disorders that had been such a feature at Page Heath. She was also sleeping extremely well. At first her legs and ankles would swell in the evenings, but this symptom wore off quickly and she soon began to lose weight so that before long she had regained her figure and her good looks. Sometimes Mrs Wynter asked her to join them in the evenings and she seemed pleased to do so, always dressing for dinner if they invited her to dine with them. Sometimes when the Wynters had friends in, they would ask Lady Mordaunt to join them, and she behaved well, often getting up to say 'Let me pour the coffee for you', or she would hand round the bread and butter. Indeed on occasions like these she would act so normally that the guests found it hard to believe there was anything wrong with her. Lady Mordaunt liked to watch when the Wynters were playing croquet with their friends, and she would often wander in the garden with Dr Wynter.

Mrs Wynter had quickly gained her confidence, and the Wynters' son, Cecil Delap Wynter, an Oxford undergraduate who was home for the vacation, also got on with her well. She would accompany his songs on the piano and have lengthy conversations with him, answering his questions without hesitation. There were times, admittedly, when she became what he described as 'taciturn' but this was not often. Cecil Wynter was impressed with her prowess at the piano. He said that she could play Scottish reels quite brilliantly. He himself, as well as his mother, often played duets with her, which she obviously enjoyed. Cecil was sure that she understood everything that went on and he never encountered any odd behaviour or observed the 'fixed attitudes' that other people talked about.

Lady Mordaunt may have got on well with the Wynters but she was far less friendly towards the new 'lunatic' nurse, Mrs Archer, who had been engaged to look after her. Although Archer was an improvement on Barker and the other companions, Lady Mordaunt remained wary of her, refusing to answer her questions and only talking in monosyllables. Nurse Archer told her that she should not sit and think so much, but she replied somewhat rudely 'Hold your row, I must be a fool or born an idiot if I did not think.' One day she said 'Damn and blast everything' and when Mrs Archer looked shocked she said 'I must swear at something,' She also asked the nurse if she was in the plot with the rest. 'I do not know what you mean' replied Nurse Archer. In spite of all this, Nurse Archer never saw her eat fluff off the carpet or anything similar. In the early days she did sometimes throw herself rather violently onto the ground when Archer was with her, but she eventually gave this up as nobody took much notice.

Dr Wynter, like Dr Tyler Smith, believed that the insane benefited from as much intercourse as possible with the saner part of the community and the Wynters encouraged Lady Mordaunt to go out and about in their company. One day they all had lunch at Dr Tyler Smith's house. Lady Mordaunt behaved very well, and afterwards Mrs Wynter took her to the Baker Street Bazaar, which she obviously enjoyed, looking at the stalls and asking the price of things. She was less impressed by Madame Tussaud's which they went to afterwards. 'We are both alike, we think it dreadfully slow' said Lady Mordaunt, and Mrs Wynter agreed. Lunching with Dr Tyler Smith and going to Madame Tussaud's in the company of a doctor's wife was all very well, but it was decidedly dull compared to the amusements she had once enjoyed.

On Sundays Lady Mordaunt went to church with the Wynters, who noticed 'nothing improper in her conduct' – in fact Dr Wynter reported that Lady Mordaunt always behaved 'with perfect decorum', following the service all the time. She did sometimes, however, seem 'moved', or even rather angry, when the clergyman preached a sermon which touched on her own predicament.

It was decided that in order to give Lady Mordaunt as natural an existence as possible she should once again be reunited with her child. On 28 April Mrs Hancox arrived at Chestnut Lodge with Violet and remained there all the summer. Lady Mordaunt seemed very pleased to have her daughter with her, and she would often play with her or feed her and help her to walk. When Mrs Wynter asked if she would like her child to come out for a drive with her, she obviously thought this was a silly question and replied rather tartly, 'Yes, I like mine with me, and you will like yours with you I suppose.'

From the start, the Wynters never saw any signs of the more dramatic actions that people had reported during the last days at Bickley. At first Lady Mordaunt did some spitting, but this soon ceased and she certainly did not seem to be suffering from delusions of any kind. The Wynters had the impression that now the trial was over their charge could not bring herself to stage the more dramatic actions like throwing herself down in the road or pretending to eat coal. She did still sometimes stop in the middle of a sentence and she would strike up an 'attitude' and hold it for a few minutes. But throwing ornaments about was no longer on the agenda.

On several occasions Mrs Wynter suggested that they should drive up to Hyde Park at those times of the day when the fashionable world would be out and about. Lady Mordaunt soon noticed some friends from the past, among them Georgie Forbes, but she seemed to have no desire to meet them and would often draw back into the corner of the carriage for fear of being recognised. One day the Princess of Wales drove by, passing quite close to them.

'There is the Princess, Lady Mordaunt' Mrs Wynter said.

'Of course I know' Lady Mordaunt replied, making sure that she kept well out of sight.

Since the carriage drives seemed to be a success, Dr Wynter and his wife decided to take Lady Mordaunt to see a play. She behaved very well during the first act, but spent more time looking at the people in the audience than at the actors on the stage, using the opera glass to see if she could pick out any of her friends in the boxes. Dr Wynter had planned that they would leave early to avoid the crush, but she grew very excited when she was told it was time to leave and said, 'I am Lady Mordaunt, I shall do as I like.' Mrs Wynter was afraid there was going to be a scene, but they managed to get her out and she calmed down as soon as they got outside. When they arrived home she seemed very upset and soon became quite hysterical. Mrs Wynter went in to her and told Nurse Archer and the maid Emma to leave the room. After a while she calmed down and Mrs Wynter asked her what was the matter. It seemed that the visit to the theatre had unsettled her, reminding her of the days when she had been 'somebody'. This had been made worse because on her return Nurse Archer had been very domineering and she explained how much she disliked having 'attendants' on top of her all the time, always telling her what to do.

After this Lady Mordaunt began increasingly to confide in Mrs Wynter about the difficulties she faced. She said that sometimes she felt as if she had fallen into a pit from which no one would help her get out. She went so far as to say that she wished everyone named at the trial as having been 'improperly intimate' with her had gone into the witness box like Sir Frederic Johnstone and the Prince of Wales in order to deny the accusations she had made against them. She would then have been cleared of the stigma of infidelity. She knew that unless this happened she would always feel ashamed of going back into society, even though she had done no worse than a lot of other people. There were times when it almost seemed as if she would like to defend her innocence, telling the Wynters that she could easily explain away the '280 days' in the almanack, although later admitting that she could not really give any convincing explanation.

Dr Tyler Smith, like the Wynters, soon managed to establish a good relationship with his patient and on one occasion he had even persuaded her to talk to him about her past life, going over all the events which had brought her into the position she was in, mentioning the confessions, the trial, and the 'dreadful exposure'. She seemed most attentive, especially when he spoke of her future, 'in which she was evidently very much interested'. He told her that he could see no way out of her troubles except by another trial, which would in the end probably happen whether she was considered mad or not. The best course was to allow a trial to take place 'privately'. In that case it would be possible to make an arrangement safeguarding her marriage portion. There would be a minimum of publicity and she would then be free to marry again and retrieve her position.

Throughout this conversation Lady Mordaunt followed with apparent interest, making remarks which showed that she understood what he said. But at the end he felt quite check-mated when she said she thought that it would be better to take the second course and allow the trial to go against her, adding emphatically that she did not intend ever to marry again.

'Then you have had enough of married life?' he asked.

'Yes' she replied simply.

When Lady Mordaunt was taken to see a play about Amy Robsart, the rejected wife of Queen Elizabeth's favourite, the Earl of Leicester, she was on excellent behaviour and obviously enjoyed herself very much, although she was apparently 'much affected' by passages which seemed to have a bearing on her own situation. Later, presumably during the interval, a young gentleman came and asked if he could speak to Lady Mordaunt. Nurse Archer went to the door of the box and refused to let him in. Lady Mordaunt knew at once who it was and grew angry when Archer sent him away. She explained to the nurse that he was a family friend who had in the past 'made an offer' to one of her sisters. This was probably a reference to Lord Cole's supposed engagement to Lady Mordaunt's sister, so that the visitor who had tried to push his way into the box was in all likelihood Lord Cole himself.

Lady Mordaunt's public appearances must by now have begun to cause something of a stir. When she visited the theatre, many eyes were on her as she had sat in her box raking the audience with her opera glasses, and looking as beautiful as ever. Was this the same girl who had so recently and so publicly been described as incontinent, who had been observed eating fluff from the carpet and laughing manically? It was hard to believe.

Reported sightings of his daughter looking normal may well have caused Sir Thomas some alarm, and now, apparently with the full permission of the Lunacy Commissioners, he and Lady Louisa began to visit Chestnut Lodge rather frequently. Mr Hunt had already filed a copy of Sir Charles's appeal against Lord Penzance's latest order and this was due to be heard in the near future and it was in the Moncreiffes' interests to make their daughter keep up the madness pretence at least until the hearing was over.

To counteract the influence wielded by her parents, the Wynters kept Lady Mordaunt in touch with the legal proceedings which were under way, explaining as best as they could what was likely to happen at the appeal. On one of his visits Dr Tyler Smith warned her that unless she could show signs of a complete cure she would certainly end up in an asylum. He asked Nurse Archer, who was in the room at the time, whether she thought that Lady Mordaunt would end up as an idiot if she were to be put in a madhouse and associated with mad people. Archer replied that she was sure this would happen and began to implore Lady Mordaunt to give in and save herself from such a fate. Dr Tyler Smith watched Lady Mordaunt closely while this conversation was going on, and he said that the scene affected her 'very visibly'. She raised her hand and then let it fall again with an expression of mute despair. Dr Tyler Smith knew that testing her in this way might have seemed cruel. But he was sure that if she had been a real lunatic a threat of this kind would not have affected her in the way it did.

If the current situation was worrying for Sir Thomas, it was equally so for the Prince. The outcome of the appeal was as important to both of them as it was to Sir Charles. If Lady Mordaunt was really showing signs of recovery, or if Sir Charles appealed successfully for permission to carry on with divorce proceedings in spite of the madness verdict, the Prince might well find himself once again in the witness-box and there was no guarantee that he would escape cross-questioning the second time round.

The Prince's reputation had undoubtedly suffered as a result of his involvement in the trial and his popularity was currently at its lowest ebb. One night when he went to the theatre with the Princess, he was loudly booed and this upset him. With the Prince so little respected and the Queen 'invisible' it really did seem at times as if the monarchy itself was in danger. There was further cause for concern when a report appeared in a Sheffield newspaper claiming that Lord Sefton intended to bring an action for divorce against his wife, citing the Prince of Wales as co-respondent. The Earl had married in July 1866 a daughter of Lord Hylton, who was related to Lord Berkeley Paget,

one of Lady Mordaunt's friends and a member of 'the set'.[117] Lord
Sefton's house, Croxteth Hall near Liverpool, was conveniently close
to Aintree, while his magnificent shooting lodge, Abbeystead in Lan-
cashire, completed soon after his marriage, was just the kind of place
where the Prince liked to stay. The report was soon denied, and
nothing came of the accusation, but there were many people who
believed that there was no smoke without fire.

At the end of May there was an even more worrying development for the Prince when a letter appeared in the *Indépendance Belge*
said to have been written by him to his brother Alfred, 'Affie', on 4
March. The Crown Princess, Vicky, was horrified when she heard
about it. 'Either the letter is not authentic or if it is how on earth has
it got into the papers?' she asked her mother.

> Really [she wrote] poor Bertie is very unlucky and what one
> brother may say quite naturally to another sounds very different
> when in print and before the public. Besides, the French transla-
> tion has to a certain degree altered the sense of the words sup-
> posing the letter to be real and not a work of fiction.

Prince Alfred was at this time in India, and the exchange of letters between the brothers had been leaked to the *Madras Mail*. A
report also appeared in an Irish paper. The Queen told Vicky that
she felt 'quite at a loss' to understand what had happened. She herself was sure the letters were fabrications, while Bertie denied their
authenticity 'absolutely and indignantly'. It seemed to her that things
were sometimes 'invented abroad', and taken far too seriously in
foreign countries. All the same, the details rang distressingly true;
there were references to the alterations at Sandringham, to Alix and
to their children, including their eldest son 'Bertiebus'. The Queen
was referred to by the brothers as 'la mère', and Bertie told Affie that
before the trial 'la mère' had done a deal with Sir Charles, begging
him to leave her son's name out of the proceedings. He complained
that the Queen was always holding up his father as an example,
telling him that he must not do this or that and 'must always be
goody because *he* was so good' adding that although it was nine years
since his father died, he was still expected to sit in sackcloth and
ashes and worship his memory.

The Times did its best to help, stating that the letters between the
Prince of Wales and the Duke of Edinburgh,

though written with a certain smartness, were so evidently intended as a hoax that it was scarcely necessary to deny their
authenticity as long as they were only circulated at home; but as
foreign readers cannot be expected to discriminate, it is necessary to declare, as we have authority for doing, that both letters
are forgeries.

The Crown Princess was relieved to hear about the stand made by
The Times, believing that the foreign papers would now be able to
follow suit. 'Really things of this kind are most mischievous to our
family and to English interests' she wrote to her mother on 8 June.[118]
  Certainly the Prince's complaints about his mother's continuing
reprimands could have been authentic. On 1 June she subjected him
to a typical broadside.

> Now that Ascot races are approaching, I wish to repeat *ear-*
> *nestly and seriously* . . . that I trust you will . . . as my Uncle
> William IV and Aunt, and we ourselves did, *confine* your visits
> to the Races to the two days *Tuesday* and *Thursday* and *not* go
> on *Wednesday* and *Friday* to which William IV never went, nor
> did we . . . Your example can do *much* for good, and may do an
> immense deal for evil, in the present day.

  Her son did not respond too well to his mother's admonitions. I
fear, dear Mama, he wrote, 'that no year goes round without your
giving me a jobation on the subject of racing.' He reminded her that
he was past twenty-eight years old and should be credited with some
considerable knowledge of the world and society. 'You will, I am
sure, at least I trust, allow me to use my own discretion in matters of
this kind' he added, with a certain finality.

On 2 June Sir Charles's appeal was heard by three judges sitting in
open court at Westminster. In addition to Lord Penzance, the judges
were Sir Fitzroy Kelly, the Lord Chief Baron of the Court of Exchequer, and Sir Henry Singer Keating, one of the judges of the Court of
Common Pleas. Unable to discover any precedents in the divorce
court except the much-quoted case of Bawden v. Bawden, when
Judge Cressell had permanently stopped a suit by a husband against
an insane wife on the ground of her cruelty, they debated at length
the question as to whether or not adultery could be described
as a criminal offence. Marriage, Lord Penzance pointed out, was

something more than an ordinary contract, similar, for example, to the sale of goods or the hire of a ship. He saw it as an institution which provided the very framework of civilised society, and both he and Sir Henry Keating were particularly aware of the status marriage conferred on a wife, the loss of which could prove 'incalculably more terrible' than the fine or imprisonment she might incur in a criminal court. With that in mind, it seemed contrary to all sense of natural justice that Lady Mordaunt should suffer such a punishment without being granted the fullest opportunity of making her defence. Both judges therefore believed that there should be no further proceedings until she had recovered sufficiently to be capable of exercising her right to defend herself.

Lord Justice Kelly on the other hand, while mindful of the evil suffered by the woman, balanced her anguish with the distress suffered by a husband who might find himself bound for ever to a wife he believed to be an adulteress, ending up 'denied for ever the redress that he had been taught to believe an Act of Parliament had secured to him'. The difficulty was that the original divorce legislation in the Act of 1857 simply had not been framed to cover a case of this kind, and in Lord Justice Kelly's opinion the legislature, in order to save trouble in the future, should be asked to amend the Act in a way that would provide justice for both husband and wife in a case where madness was involved. Meanwhile, as long as there was a reasonable hope that Lady Mordaunt might recover, Lord Justice Kelly thought that the court should review the situation from time to time, so that when and if all hopes of recovery ceased, Sir Charles would then be permitted to proceed with his suit.

Since neither Lord Penzance nor Sir Henry Keating agreed with this suggestion, Lord Justice Kelly was overruled, and the original order of 8 March, that no further proceeding be taken until the respondent had recovered her mental capacity, was allowed to stand.

This conclusion brought little comfort to Sir Charles, although Dr Wynter's fortnightly reports from Chestnut Lodge had by now become so encouraging that there was at least a glimmer of hope that his wife could in the end be classified as sane. Dr Wynter noted that in the same way as her 'dirty and indecent' habits had been left off from the moment she arrived at Chiswick, nowadays she only occasionally broke out into hysterical laughter or put on her old 'stage-struck' attitude. She behaved 'quite properly' when out walking or driving and often read aloud to her attendant, while the presence of her little daughter Violet obviously gave her great pleasure. The doctor had talked to her about her position and had asked her if she remembered things belonging to the past, especially since the birth of her child. She told him it was all gradually returning to her and she hoped she would soon be able to talk about it. But when he asked if she would be able to give any explanation of her conduct, she firmly replied 'No, never.'

As to the question of 'feigning', the doctors could not fathom it out at all. 'No test we have been able to apply has answered perfectly' wrote Dr Tyler Smith. He did think, however, that there had already been times when Lady Mordaunt had been on the point of dropping all reserve and confiding either in himself or in one of the Wynters.

Meanwhile all Sir Charles could do was to wait and hope for Lady Mordaunt's improvement to be maintained. All the time the expenses mounted up. Dr Wynter in his letter to Hannay had acknowledged the June cheque for £46. 6s. 10d, and monthly payments such as these were becoming a considerable strain on Sir Charles's resources.

The Wynters believed that Lady Mordaunt's parents were doing their best to halt her recovery. Sir Thomas and Lady Louisa had begun to visit her more frequently, and Mrs Wynter reported that when she remained in the room, Lady Mordaunt would go very quiet, refusing to answer any of their questions and looking about her with a fixed gaze. Nobody knew, of course, how she behaved when she was alone with her parents. Whether or not it was as a result of their influence, she had now, in August, become less enthusiastic about going out into the world, and Mrs Wynter herself was beginning to get embarrassed by the loud laughter which she affected when they were out and about. There had been a recent incident when their carriage had been passed by a bus on the Richmond Road and she had laughed quite inordinately. This kind of scene was happening so frequently that Mrs Wynter made a vow not to go out alone in future into any public place with her charge unless there was some improvement in her behaviour.

One day Dr Wynter and his sister-in-law took Lady Mordaunt to see her sister's portrait at the Royal Academy. When they got home, she seemed depressed. Mrs Wynter asked what she had thought of the picture and she replied unenthusiastically, 'Not much.' In general she seemed to be very unhappy, and one day Mrs Wynter came in and found her crying. Mrs Wynter asked her what was the matter, but she simply leant forward over her hands and said she was the most wretched woman in existence. It seemed to the doctor's wife that she was almost at the end of her tether, having kept up the strain of feigning for so many months, not knowing what it would all lead to or whether she would ever again be able to lead a normal life.

Believing that a change of scene might be beneficial, the Wynters decided that Lady Mordaunt should spend some time at Seaford, which was considered suitably quiet and unfashionable and where she was unlikely to meet any of her friends. One advantage was that it would be more difficult for her parents to visit her there. Lady Mordaunt seemed pleased with the idea, although she became very upset when she was told that Violet would not be going with her and was returning to Warwickshire with Mrs Hancox. 'I do not wish her to be brought up as a cottager's child' she said.

It is possible that she had discussed the question of Violet's upbringing with her mother because that autumn there was a sharp exchange of letters between the grandmothers. The Dowager had been surprised to receive a personal letter from Lady Louisa, suggesting that their grandchild should be brought up at Moncreiffe.

> I should like so much [wrote Lady Louisa], with the consent of Sir Charles Mordaunt and his family, to have the charge of my little grand-daughter. I cannot but feel now she is no longer an infant she would be so much better under my care than that of Mrs Hancox. I would bring her up and educate her with my own little ones until some other arrangements became necessary for her welfare.
>
> Believe me my dear Caroline
>
> > Your affectionate cousin
> >
> > LOUISA MONCREIFFE

The Dowager was taken by surprise. She showed the letter to Sir Charles at once, and they both felt amazed by what they saw as a complete change of feeling. 'You knew as fully as we did' the Dowager wrote in reply,

> the arrangements that the child should be consigned to the care of Mrs Hancox for ever for a sum stipulated by yourselves and that you were then quite satisfied with the expediency and justice of such an arrangement.
>
> It is not for me to give any reply to your present proposal and I cannot help expressing my astonishment that under the present

wrong done to Sir Charles by your family, you should have written to me at all on the subject. Therefore I think that if you wish to make any further suggestions or explanations you had better communicate with Sir Charles's lawyers.

Yours truly,

C. S. MORDAUNT

This produced an even more frosty reply from Lady Louisa, written in the third person.

The house in Seaford where Lady Mordaunt was to spend the next few weeks was comfortable enough and Cecil Wynter, who was with the party until it was time for him to go back to Oxford, thought that she seemed happy there. Mrs Wynter noticed that she began to settle down immediately, talking in quite an uninhibited way about her past life. She told Mrs Wynter, who had never been to the races, how exciting they were, adding that Sir Frederic Johnstone owned horses which had run in the Derby the previous year. She showed Cecil her precious photograph album, explaining all the pictures and telling him who the people were. They often went to church together and sometimes walked out along the promenade. One day she and Cecil sat on the beach with her maid in attendance, talking about shells. Another time he took Lady Mordaunt and his mother out in a sailing boat.

Cecil Wynter could hardly be described as an adequate substitute for her past admirers, but he was at least a young man of her own age who treated her as an equal. When he went back to Oxford she obviously missed him and her behaviour started to deteriorate.

Now Lady Mordaunt began to quarrel regularly with Nurse Archer. One day, after having 'words' with her, she took the stopper out of her hot water bottle and poured the contents into the bed. On another occasion she acted even more viciously, boxing Archer's ears and pushing her onto the sofa. She also used some bad language, and Mrs Wynter told her that she must not behave in that way and must remember she was a lady.

Hanging on the wall in the sitting-room at Seaford was a 'likeness' of the Prince of Wales which Harriett would play and sing to for hours at a time. But even this eventually began to pall and one day she startled the Wynters by throwing a cup of tea at the portrait, saying, 'That has been the ruin of me', adding 'You have been the curse of my life, damn you.'

Feeling that Seaford was no longer contributing to Lady Mordaunt's recovery, the Wynters took her back to London on 5 November. She seemed glad to be back and soon settled into the routine of life at Chestnut Lodge, joining in the festivities at Christmas and dancing in the quadrilles at a children's new year party.

Both Dr Wynter and Dr Tyler Smith were required by the Lunacy Commissioners to submit regular reports on Lady Mordaunt's progress and Dr Wynter had informed them that he thought Lady Mordaunt was now sane, even if she did sometimes become 'excited in temper', her moods on the whole being linked to her monthly cycle. Although she seemed to suffer more than most women at certain times of the month, he thought that at other times she was quite normal, and would be perfectly capable of instructing a solicitor.

Dr Tyler Smith was much less guarded than Dr Wynter. He was prepared to state categorically that Lady Mordaunt was in sound bodily health and showed no sign of paralysis or weakness of the nervous system. He thought that 'the play of her features, the expression of her eyes, her brilliant complexion and her perfect ease of self possession' all betokened a state of high physical health. He was quite sure that she was not insane, and to back up his belief, he wrote a detailed analysis of the 'machinery' of her feigning. Going right back to the time of the birth, and taking due note of the observations made by the local doctors, he examined the methods Lady Mordaunt had used throughout to keep up the pretence – the laughter, the frowning, the 'absent' looks, the absurd remarks. He had observed that she always gave herself time to reflect before making a remark, and this, he thought, was an important indication of feigning. Quoting from his own book on obstetrics, he described the conversation of lunatics as 'irregular as the changing shapes in a kaleidoscope', adding that he had never heard Lady Mordaunt run on incoherently in this way. He had gained the impression that she had really enjoyed duping the eminent physicians who came to examine her, but that once the trial was over she had realised that there was no need to keep up the more dramatic and 'irksome' performances she had once put on.

Dr Tyler Smith described how he had discreetly watched Lady Mordaunt during the time that she had been at Chestnut Lodge and had used various means of calling her bluff. For example, when she had one day relapsed into fits of apparently uncontrollable laughter, he had carried out a test to see if he could make her stop. At first she went on laughing, 'burst after burst'. Then he said, 'Do you know, Lady Mordaunt, that a discovery has been made about you – they have found out the meaning of the French umbrella you took so much trouble about in Paris.'

The effect of this remark was dramatic. Lady Mordaunt's attitude changed completely, the laughter died and her expression changed. Dr Tyler Smith then went out of the room for a while and when he came back he found her absorbed in thought. The nurse told him later that she did not know what he had said to Lady Mordaunt, but whatever it was it had produced a 'wonderful' effect, for she had stopped laughing immediately and had not laughed again that evening. This proved to Dr Tyler Smith that Lady Mordaunt was not as mad as she liked people to believe, since an insane person would not have reacted so quickly to his remark, indeed would probably not have reacted at all.

Dr Tyler Smith felt sure that before long Lady Mordaunt would drop her disguise completely, particularly if she could be assured that she could keep her marriage jointure intact even if a divorce verdict were to go against her. Equally, if she and her family could be made to realise that more and more conclusive evidence concerning her adultery was being collected and would be brought out against her in later proceedings, then she might feel that the game was up and that there was no point in going on to 'further simulation'. With such considerations on her mind, it was hardly surprising that at times she relapsed into silence, for as she herself had said to Mrs Wynter, she had plenty to think about concerning her future life.

Altogether, Dr Tyler Smith felt that Lady Mordaunt's behaviour was unlike any form of insanity he had seen or heard of before and, he added, 'The opinion that she is suffering from dementia is belied by the aspect of her bright face and her intelligent quick eye.'

Once again, it was the eyes which seemed to give the clue to her condition. Whereas Dr Orford had been struck by their complete deadness when he had visited her at Bickley, now, after almost a year under Dr Wynter's care, there was, in Dr Tyler Smith's opinion, no denying their intelligence and brightness.

After putting in his long and careful report Dr Tyler Smith decided to enrol two more doctors in the hope that they would be able to confirm his findings. He therefore approached Dr Maudsley, a well-known authority in the field of mental science, who lectured on insanity at two London hospitals, and Dr Barnes, a leading authority on puerperal mania. When these doctors were asked if they were prepared to visit Lady Mordaunt 'informally', they were at first reluctant to do so, but Dr Tyler Smith persuaded them to overcome their scruples.

Dr Maudsley was a dour Yorkshireman, bearded and impressive. He had built up a successful private practice and was widely respected by his fellow practitioners, so much so that the previous year, at the age of only thirty-five, he had been elected President of the Medico-Psychological Association. In spite of his high office, however, he had already become uneasy about current psychiatric practices, realising how few of those who were detained in asylums were ever likely to go back into the world, and becoming increasingly aware of the dangers of dispensing drugs such as bromide, chloral and digitalis. He had a strong belief that much mental illness was curable, if treated rightly.

He was asked to dinner at Chestnut Lodge on 14 February, St Valentine's Day. When he first arrived, Lady Mordaunt was still upstairs, but a little while later she entered the sitting-room. He found it something of a shock to discover that the alleged lunatic he had been sent to assess was a graceful young woman with a fresh and healthy complexion. He was introduced to her as a family friend and she looked at him with a steady and penetrating gaze, as if sizing him up. At supper she sat next to him, and at first she looked quite demure. Then suddenly, taking him off his guard, she gave him a quick sideways glance from under her half-closed lids, as if trying to catch his eye. When he turned to her, she blushed slightly, and looked away. The game continued when she again caught his eye, this time in a reflection in the mirror which hung above the sideboard. He 'chaffed' her a little about that, saying that the mirror gave her an advantage. The doctor found Lady Mordaunt's eyes very striking. They were so bright and watchful and also quite coquettish. And sometimes they lit up with genuine amusement.

When the soup was served Lady Mordaunt put a spoonful to her lips and then suddenly started back as if it were hot and, 'laughing naturally', put down the spoon. Dr Maudsley particularly noticed this because in his experience demented patients would often take things remarkably hot 'without apparent inconvenience'.

After dinner, when the gentlemen had joined the ladies in the sitting-room, Mrs Wynter and Lady Mordaunt played some duets together.

'Is your friend fond of music?' she asked Mrs Wynter.

'Of course he is. Do you have any objection?' said Mrs Wynter.

'No, well, no' said Lady Mordaunt in an indifferent kind of way.

It did seem that already Lady Mordaunt was suspicious of the new-comer, and when he next visited, he saw the bright-eyed look replaced by the vacant stare that had been noted by other medical observers. He also heard the outbursts of loud and unnatural laughter. Sometimes, he noted, she laughed 'in a not unmeaning way' but prolonged the laugh unduly, and when anything amusing was said, she would laugh naturally at first, if rather loudly, beginning a fresh outburst when others had stopped. The normal tone of her voice would change and become loud and drawling, as she made inane remarks such as 'I like the Russians', or asked the doctor if he had been out in the rain that day, when in fact there had been no rain, or stated that there had been no ice that year when everybody had just been talking about all the skating there had been during the exceptionally long cold spell that had recently finished. If asked to elaborate her remarks, she would remain silent, and she refused to answer questions. When the sauce was handed to her at dinner, she took no notice of it at first, then when asked to take some, said abruptly 'What's this?', and when the maid told her, she said, looking up into the servant's face, 'I know what sauce is.' When it came to the dessert, Dr Maudsley handed her the biscuits, and she put her hand out quite normally to take one, but stopped midway. He then begged her to make up her mind quickly because his arm was getting tired, seeing that he was not a Samson or a Hercules. She laughed and took a biscuit, but after eating some of it she put the rest abruptly down, and darting her hand suddenly into the basket with a laugh, took two more biscuits which she began to eat together, as a child might do. Then, quite suddenly in the middle of a conversation, she flung the biscuits down onto the hearth rug in front of the Wynters' little dog that was lying there.

'Could you have done that?' she asked the doctor.

'No, Lady Mordaunt, it is improbable that I could, and I think improbabilities should never be made too improbable' he replied cryptically.

The second doctor who had been asked to call, Dr Barnes, had much the same experiences as Dr Maudsley. During his first visit Lady Mordaunt behaved on the whole rationally, but the second time he saw her she often seemed 'distraite', staring at people fixedly and stopping halfway through a sentence.

Dr Maudsley and Dr Barnes agreed that Lady Mordaunt's general aspect of intelligence and brilliant health was inconsistent with any form of insanity. They were sure that she was far too clever to be taken in by the pretence that they were friends of the family. Dr Barnes knew she had seen through him when on his second visit she had suddenly addressed him as 'Dr Barclay' and had held out her hand as if expecting him to feel her pulse. The doctors had no difficulty in agreeing that her odd behaviour was what they described as 'artificial and designed to attract notice'. Both were ready to swear that Lady Mordaunt was quite capable of instructing her solicitor. At the same time, they still felt that they could not make any definite diagnosis of her medical state without formally examining her in their acknowledged capacity as physicians. In the end, however, Dr Wynter managed to persuade them that if they paid a formal, professional visit, announcing that they were doctors, Lady Mordaunt would be 'armed at all points' and would probably refuse to say a word. They therefore agreed to report on what they had observed on their informal visits, and what they said prompted Serjeant Ballantine and Mr Inderwick to proceed on the basis that Lady Mordaunt no longer appeared to be mad.

There was one further aspect of the case which had troubled Dr Tyler Smith. At the trial Serjeant Ballantine had suggested that Lady Mordaunt could have been suffering from what was termed 'moral madness', a condition connected with the sexual appetites. It certainly did seem that Lady Mordaunt had been affected with 'erotic inclinations' so far approaching to nymphomania that it had led to her having sexual intercourse with many men, instead of being, as is commonly the case when women go astray, the victim of seduction by one man for whom she had formed a strong affection. Dr Tyler Smith wrote that he knew of

> several women of high rank in almost precisely the same condition of 'Free Love', to use the words of Mr Hepworth Dixon, and who really as Lady Mordaunt said 'think nothing of it' but who escape exposure from having husbands who for various reasons wink at the almost open adulteries of their wives.

Dr Maudsley was inclined to agree that Lady Mordaunt could come into this category. He was perhaps influenced by the coquettish look in her eye he had noticed during the dinner at Chestnut Lodge. He was known for his strong disapproval of sexual over-indulgence which he categorised as a kind of 'moral madness', although his colleagues liked to think that his preoccupation with this subject could have had something to do with the fact that he himself had not succeeded in fathering any children. In any case he did not enlarge on the question of moral madness in his report, and on the basis of what Dr Wynter, Dr Tyler Smith, Dr Maudsley and Dr Barnes all had to say, Serjeant Ballantine and Mr Inderwick agreed to proceed on the basis that Lady Mordaunt could no longer be described as mad. They advised Sir Charles that he must break free from the control of the Lunacy Commissioners. This meant that Lady Mordaunt would have to be treated as a thoroughly sane person in control of her own destiny. He must no longer undertake to maintain her, and notice would have to be given to Dr Wynter that after a certain date he would cease to be responsible for her care. It would be Dr Wynter's task to tell the Lunacy Commissioners that after careful scrutiny he had become convinced that Lady Mordaunt's symptoms were the result of feigning and not of disease.

The lawyers all agreed that if this action were taken, the burden of reopening litigation would be thrown onto Lady Mordaunt's own family as they would of necessity have to try and obtain an 'allotment' of alimony or pin money.

It was a drastic measure and even Sir Charles felt uneasy about the boldness of it. And when Mr Hannay went down to Chestnut Lodge on 10 May, he found Dr Wynter in a state of panic. It seemed that Sir Thomas had arrived the day before, and had pointed out to Dr Wynter the dangers of alienating the Lunacy Commissioners. He had stressed that the Commissioners wielded extensive powers and could make life extremely difficult for Dr Wynter as a professional man caring for insane people in his own home. Now thoroughly frightened, Dr Wynter categorically refused to make any statement about Lady Mordaunt's condition, claiming that Sir Charles's counsel had misinterpreted his previous reports. He made it plain that he felt disinclined to help Sir Charles, even if he could.

The next day Mr Hannay went to see Mr Inderwick in despair. They had known that it would be impossible to put pressure on Dr Wynter. All the same it was of crucial importance that he should write to the Commissioners if their plan was to succeed, and so Mr Hannay went down to Chestnut Lodge for a second visit and this time managed to persuade Dr Wynter to cooperate.

On 15 May Dr Wynter received a letter, written from the Office of the Commissioners in Lunacy at 19 Whitehall Place by the chairman, Lord Shaftesbury, who admitted that Mr Hannay, acting on the advice of two medical gentlemen, did have full power to discharge Lady Mordaunt if he saw fit. All the same, he wrote, the Commissioners felt that the evidence provided by the medical gentlemen in the case hardly inspired confidence, especially as in his previous communications Dr Wynter had never so much as mentioned the subject of 'feigning'. 'In these circumstances', Lord Shaftesbury continued, 'the Commissioners decline altogether to comply with the suggestion of your letter, leaving to yourself, Dr Tyler Smith and Mr Hannay the entire responsibility of the course which is proposed to be taken.'

Mr Inderwick read the letter and wrote immediately to Sir Thomas's solicitors, informing them that although Sir Charles was as convinced as ever of Lady Mordaunt's infidelity, he was not contemplating any further proceedings at this stage, 'being undisposed to undergo the anxiety and expense of a second investigation into the lady's state of mind'. He added that Lady Mordaunt was now at liberty to join her family or any of her friends, who would have to take the responsibility of maintaining her as Sir Charles was no longer prepared to do so.

Benbow and Saltwell replied at once, saying that Sir Thomas was not prepared to relieve Sir Charles from the legal responsibility of taking care of and providing for Lady Mordaunt, which appeared to be more than ordinarily binding considering her present condition.

Mr Hannay then received a letter from Dr Wynter saying that he had arranged for Sir Thomas to interview Lady Mordaunt the following Monday, 29 May. He had managed to postpone the visit for Lady Mordaunt's sake as she was 'unwell' and he was sure that if she were to see her father at this time she would become very upset, which would give him the opportunity of saying all over again that she was mad. It was apparent that matters had now come to a head and it was important to act before Sir Thomas had a chance to see, and to influence, his daughter. Mr Inderwick wanted to make sure that Dr Wynter had consulted Lady Mordaunt herself about her future, giving her the chance to say what she wanted to do. Dr Wynter replied that he had told her she would be free to go home with her father and she had seemed pleased, even asking Mrs Archer to bring her a timetable so that she could look up the trains to Perth. Fortified by this reassurance, the lawyers decided that Lady Mordaunt should be discharged on the last day of the month when Dr Wynter was due to receive his monthly payment, and that she should then be taken to her father's house in London and left there.

On 1 June the formal discharge was issued. Mrs Wynter then told Lady Mordaunt the news and informed her that as she was now a free agent she could do as she liked. It would be as well, Mrs Wynter said, if she could rouse herself and clear matters up for good, because if she did not she would certainly end up in an asylum. At that, Mrs Wynter reported, Lady Mordaunt jumped up in a rage and dashed her foot against the table, saying 'They dare not and I will never go into an asylum.' After a while, however, she calmed down and told Mrs Wynter that she would like to go home. When she was asked what she called home, she replied, 'Walton.' But a day or two later she told Mrs Archer that she was going back to Moncreiffe and asked the nurse whether she would like to go with her. 'We shall see' Mrs Archer replied.

When the maid intercepted a letter from Lady Mordaunt addressed to her father at White's Club, Dr Wynter handed it back to Lady Mordaunt unopened, saying that he had no wish to pry, and that she was free to post it herself, which she did.

All the same, Dr Wynter remained extremely uneasy about the whole situation, especially as it seemed that the lawyers expected him to deliver Lady Mordaunt to her father's house in person. Nobody had told him as yet whether Sir Thomas would be prepared to receive her and he could foresee an ugly situation developing and wondered how he would stand legally if Sir Thomas refused to take her on. Sir Charles's lawyer, Mr Hunt, refused to advise him on this point so he decided that the best thing would be to ask Sir Thomas to come and fetch Lady Mordaunt himself. Dr Wynter then left a note at White's Club, saying that he would call for the reply at five o'clock that evening. After some delay, Sir Thomas provided his reply in the shape of a copy of the letter written on 23 May by Benbow and Saltwell saying that they were not prepared to relieve Sir Charles from the legal responsibility of taking care of Lady Mordaunt.

It was obvious that an alternative plan would have to be made, and Dr Wynter now came up with the idea of giving Mrs Caborn the task of delivering Lady Mordaunt to her relations. She had after all brought Lady Mordaunt to Chestnut Lodge in the first place, and she seemed in every way a 'proper person' for the task. In addition she was trustworthy enough to take charge of Lady Mordaunt's very valuable jewellery, after checking all the items against the list that Dr Wynter had made.

Although the Lunacy Commissioners had agreed to an official discharge, they were now quibbling about the wording, telling Dr Wynter that he must alter it according to the Act of Parliament to say whether Lady Mordaunt was 'recovered, relieved, or not improved'. Mr Inderwick on being consulted told him to write back and say that the Act of Parliament had not been constructed to meet such a case as Lady Mordaunt's and to inform them that Mrs Caborn would be taking her to her father's house in Scotland. This was considered a better idea than sending her to Perth in the care of Nurse Archer who might, it was feared, 'take too strong a fancy to the place'.

On 14 June Mrs Caborn appeared and asked for Lady Mordaunt's instructions about the journey. At first Lady Mordaunt seemed hesitant, saying that she did not want to go to Scotland 'as she was feeling too seedy'. The Wynters told Mrs Caborn to call back the following morning. When she arrived, Mrs Wynter left the room and eventually Dr Wynter went up to find out how things were going and was told that Lady Mordaunt had after all decided to leave. 'There is nothing else I can do' she said.

Mrs Caborn then started the packing and it was agreed that they should depart that evening. Lady Mordaunt seemed quite bright and cheerful when the time came to go. Dr Wynter went with her in the carriage to King's Cross Station where, with Mrs Caborn, she boarded the night train for Perth.

The next day Haynes, Hannay and Haynes informed Benbow and Saltwell that Lady Mordaunt had expressed a desire to go to her father's residence in Scotland, and that they had subsequently received a telegram stating that she had left for Perth accompanied by Mrs Caborn, who would remain with her until she had secured the services of another maid. Benbow's retort was that although Lady Mordaunt could not of course be denied admittance into her father's house, at the same time they most strongly protested against her 'being considered to be capable of exercising any discretion or giving directions upon this or any other subject and we repeat that as it is not the intention of Sir Thomas Moncreiffe to relieve Sir Charles Mordaunt from his legal responsibility.' The only point on which Sir Thomas found himself able to agree with Sir Charles was that the anxiety and expense of a second investigation into the lady's state of mind was to be avoided, and he therefore expressed himself willing to take charge of Lady Mordaunt and her child provided Sir Charles gave him a written assurance that he would not prosecute or revive the suit in the divorce court.

Sir Charles was incensed by this proposal. How could he give an undertaking that he would not pursue his suit in the divorce court? Was he to be saddled for the rest of his life with an unfaithful wife and no hopes of an heir?

Always ready to dictate to the lawyers, Sir Charles proceeded to tell them that he would like to renew the offer made to Lady Louisa in March 1869 after the confinement. He was now, as then, prepared to pay his wife £400 per annum following a divorce which seemed to him a very generous offer, considering she would not be due to receive anything if her adultery could be proved. The possibility had to be faced that she might be able to conduct a successful defence if the divorce trial went ahead, but Sir Charles was not too worried about this. 'I am prepared to run the risk,' he told Mr Haynes, 'if there is any risk at all.' It seemed to him that Sir Thomas could well accept his offer of a compromise because he would not be able to afford to keep her if she were divorced and without means. 'He only offers to maintain her as insane' wrote Sir Charles 'because he no doubt can do so with the Prince of Wales's money or at all events money found by the co-respondents or someone else for the purpose.'

Mr Inderwick ignored the reference to the Prince of Wales and simply told Sir Charles, to his chagrin, that the offer was not practicable. The danger was that he might stand accused of collusion and might also run into trouble with the Queen's proctor. Mr Hannay then informed Mr Benbow that Sir Charles was unable to give any assurance that he would not at some time in the future revive his claim to contest the truth of Lady Mordaunt's sanity, or to pursue the divorce. In August Mr Benbow was informed that as Sir Charles was satisfied as to the illegitimacy of Lady Mordaunt's child, he declined to maintain it and would give instructions at once for it to be sent to Lady Mordaunt. The letter went on 'As we understood from you that it was the family's wish to bring up and educate the child, we presume the suggestion now made will be quite in accordance with their views and Lady Mordaunt's wishes.'

On 18 August another letter provided the information that Sir Thomas, while not refusing to provide for the child for the present, reserved the right at the proper time to establish her legitimacy – 'a right he will certainly exercise'. Benbow ended with a reminder that they were acting entirely for Sir Thomas and that Lady Mordaunt was now and had been ever since the trial 'quite unable to give him any instructions'.

The unfortunate Violet, referred to throughout the correspondence as 'it', a genderless and rejected legal object, was despatched to her grandfather's house early in September, a terse letter from the lawyers giving the information that she would leave on the Friday night, arriving in Perth on Saturday morning at 8.59. This produced a furious response from Benbow, complaining about the child, now falsely labelled illegitimate, being sent on 'a midnight journey' with the aim of forcing Sir Thomas to maintain her.

36

Dr Tuke's Asylum

In the autumn of 1871 Dr Tuke was asked whether he would be willing to accommodate Lady Mordaunt in his private asylum at the Manor House, Chiswick. Wondering whether anyone would be prepared to pay the bill, he was at first hesitant, but when he was assured that Lady Mordaunt's maintenance had been guaranteed by 'a person unknown' he expressed his willingness to receive her. On 11 November her mother and one of her brothers brought her down from Scotland.

Dr Tuke noted down her particulars in his Case Book, describing her as 'of middle height and much personal beauty'. He recorded that her physical health was good, although she still suffered from a weak pulse and cold hands and feet. Her general appearance was one of 'vacant imbecility'.[120]

Dr Tuke arranged for Lady Mordaunt to be looked after in a homely atmosphere at a cottage in the grounds of the asylum. After visiting her for a few days, he came to the conclusion that she was suffering from a more advanced form of the dementia than the one he had diagnosed two years before. He had little doubt that her condition was genuine and that her reason had 'fled'. 'There could no possibility of deception' he wrote.

A few days later Lady Mordaunt was examined by Sir James Alderson, recently knighted, by Dr Gull, by a Dr Boyd, by Dr Priestley and another Scottish doctor, Dr Tweedie. They all confirmed Dr Tuke's opinion and agreed to sign the madness certificate.

For the next few weeks Dr Tuke watched Lady Mordaunt closely, noticing that she had no occupation of any kind, that she did not read, had no 'work' and did not ask for anything. Occasionally she would look at picture books, or play the piano for a few bars. She apparently had no religious feeling of any kind and made no attempt to pray. Although she sometimes made 'pertinent' remarks, Dr Tuke considered her incapable of carrying on a conversation. She did not appear to have any delusions, although at times she seemed to be under the impression that Dr Tuke was her brother.

There were times when Lady Mordaunt seemed unsettled and there was 'a wild look' in her eyes. To counteract this, Dr Tuke administered the 'grim and baleful, hideous-tasting' drug chloral,[121] and he encouraged her to take regular exercise and to walk in the garden or along the road, whatever the weather. He did not prescribe any other medicines, except a mild aperient.

Sometimes Lady Mordaunt was allowed to drive into London which she appeared to enjoy, although only 'in the way that a child would do'. She was encouraged to go up to the main house for an hour or two to see Dr Tuke and to join with the other patients in any of the entertainments that were going on there. She seemed pleased with what was provided, although she did not take any notice of the other inmates. In the same way when she was out walking, she took little notice of anybody although she did show interest if she met any children or babies.

Her mind, Dr Tuke came to the conclusion, was 'that of a child', an intelligent child of say six years old. As an example of her immature behaviour, he cited the fact that when they brought her some water she would play with it, but never use it to wash in, always expecting other people to wash and dress her. As she settled down at Chiswick, she did, however, become more communicative. She began to talk about the friends she had known in earlier times including the Prince of Wales. Then one day her attendants broke it to her that the Prince had fallen dangerously ill. Dr Tuke recorded that she listened to what they had to say and then repeated what she had heard, word for word, exactly like a parrot. She then broke out into 'unmeaning' laughter.

The Prince had in fact gone down with typhoid at Sandringham and there was widespread anxiety about his condition. An army of journalists was mounting a vigil outside the grounds, besieging the small telegraph office at Lynn when there was anything to report.

Dr Gull, who had so recently signed Lady Mordaunt's madness certificate, now took charge of the royal invalid, nursing him, washing him with vinegar and moving his wasted body from bed to bed. 'We have *nice* Dr Gull here whom he likes and in whom we have the *greatest confidence*' the Queen wrote to Princess Louise. She explained to Vicky that although Dr Gull was a 'fashionable' doctor, he appeared to be very clever and religious into the bargain. It pleased the Queen that he seemed to be as anxious about her dear Bertie's moral welfare as he was concerned for his physical well-being.

The Prince submitted to his treatment with a mixture of meekness and bonhomie. 'That's right, old Gull,' he was heard to say as the doctor gingerly spooned some liquid down his throat, 'that's good, two or three more spoonsful, old Gull.'

When the disease really took hold, the Prince became delirious. For thirty-six hours the agonised onlookers were treated to 'the wildest, loudest, incessant talking, in all languages' with occasional bouts of whistling and singing. Princess Alexandra told Princess Louise that at times Bertie hardly knew her; he had called her 'his good boy' and when she said she was his little wife he replied 'That *was* once but is *no more*, you have broken your vows', an ironic remark, in the circumstances. The turning point came on 14 December, the anniversary of Prince Albert's death. The fever died down, and, weak though he was, the Prince suddenly sat up and arranged his own pillows. Subsequently, when he was feeling more like his old self, he took the pillows one by one and threw them about the room, even targeting the Princess with one of them. Soon, to the relief of his mother, his wife, his friends and relations and the nation as a whole, he was declared to be out of danger. In the minds of many, however, relief was mixed with the hope that he would emerge from his ordeal a wiser man. All the papers, the Queen told Vicky, as well as many sermons, expressed the same kind of sentiments. 'We all feel that if God has spared his life,' she wrote; 'it is to enable him to lead a new life – and if this great warning is not taken, and the wonderful sympathy and devotion of the whole nation does not make a great change in him, it will be worse than before and his utter ruin.' He had throughout his illness been as kind and courteous as ever, and it was hoped that to this would be added the sense of responsibility that had so far been remarkably lacking.[122]

For the Princess, her husband's convalescence proved to be a very happy time. Everything, she wrote, seemed bright and beautiful around her, when only recently it had threatened to become dark for ever. 'We are never apart, and are now enjoying our second Honey Moon' she added.

The Queen was worried because Bertie had lost so much weight. She told Vicky that his hair had 'come out dreadfully' so that the top of his head was now quite bald. His leg had swollen so badly that there was some doubt as to whether he would be able to attend the service of thanksgiving for his recovery due to be held at St Paul's Cathedral.

The Queen dreaded the service which she called 'this dreadful affair', regarding it as 'a great, great trial'. In the end, however, even she had to admit that it was a success. 'Millions must have been out and the decorations were really beautiful – the cheering deafening' she wrote.

What the Queen and her subjects did not know was that the Prince whose recovery they were celebrating had altogether ignored the good advice given to him by his mother, the Prime Minister and the Lord Chancellor after the Mordaunt trial and had once again been playing with fire. As a result, the previous spring, Lady Susan Vane-Tempest, the Duke of Newcastle's daughter, had told him that she was bearing his child. He told her callously to get rid of it, recommending Dr Clayton as the best man to go to. When Dr Clayton told her he could do nothing as it would be '*too late* and *too dangerous*', the Prince went so far as to give her £250 to cover the expenses of the confinement and to buy the secrecy of the servants who would accompany her into hiding at Ramsgate. Now, to placate her further, he offered her two tickets for the thanksgiving ceremony, which she graciously refused, saying that she had felt unwell ever since the birth of her child.[123]

On the day after the thanksgiving service Dr Tuke took Lady Mordaunt up to London and they drove through the principal streets looking at the decorations. He found it hard to explain to her what the decorations were there for, but he reported that she did seem 'very delighted at recognising the portrait of the Prince of Wales in one of the streets'.[124]

In the new year Dr Tuke reported a slight improvement in Lady Mordaunt's condition; she no longer suffered from cataleptic seizures although he frequently noticed what he described as a minor form of the same malady. On these occasions she would go almost crimson, her eyes would for a moment be fixed, and then would come 'a passion of tears'. He had to admit that most of the time there was much vivacity and 'apparent intelligence' in her expression, 'marking' as he put it, a 'type of dementia as distinguished from imbecility'. What struck him most was her extraordinary 'equilibrium'. Nothing seemed to upset her. When her relations came to visit her she met and parted with them without any apparent emotion, and she remained convinced that 'Charlie' would come and see her soon.

Throughout the summer Sir Charles had been left in the dark about his wife's condition. It came as a shock to him when Mr Hannay sent him a newspaper cutting which reported that she had been admitted to Dr Tuke's asylum suffering from dementia. He at once consulted Dr Wynter who assured him that there had been no sign of dementia during Lady Mordaunt's stay at Chestnut Lodge. If this condition existed, Dr Wynter wrote, then it must have developed after she left for Scotland.

Sir Charles now had to decide whether he should send his own doctors down to Chiswick to assess her current condition. Serjeant Ballantine advised him against such a course. He thought it unwise to embark on another inconclusive round of arguments about Lady Mordaunt's mental state. As almost two years had elapsed since the madness trial there had been a fair opportunity of ascertaining whether she was ever likely to recover. The time had now come to establish whether permanent insanity, if it could be proved, would prevent Sir Charles going on with his case.

As a result, on 29 February 1872, Sir Thomas Moncreiffe received a summons to attend the court on 5 March, to report on his daughter's condition. On 4 March Dr Tuke filed an affidavit on behalf of Sir Thomas, describing Lady Mordaunt's mental state in very strong terms. He stated that after Lady Mordaunt had been placed under his care he found that

> her mind had become an almost entire blank, her memory had gone, her actions were those of a child, her answers to questions – though sometimes sensible – were usually entirely irrelevant; she burst at intervals into fits of unmeaning laughter; if her attention was for a moment caught she would appear rational, but this condition never lasted for more than a few minutes.

This brought him to the conclusion that Lady Mordaunt was labouring under the symptoms of secondary puerperal dementia, and that her disorder was not feigned. Although he had made no reference to this in his Case Book, Dr Tuke did add that at first there had been occasional outbursts of violence, although these had now ceased. Lady Mordaunt slept well and placidly, and never made any reference to her 'history'. Dr Tuke remained convinced that Lady Mordaunt would not be capable of understanding the nature of the charge brought before her, or of managing the most ordinary affairs of life, or of distinguishing between right and wrong. As to her recovery, although at the outset there had been some grounds for hope, he felt that now there was nothing more than a remote probability of restoration to her mental capacity.

When the proceedings opened on 5 March, Serjeant Ballantine explained that Dr Tuke's testimony had convinced him that they had arrived at the stage when permanent insanity could be proved. He therefore wished to find out whether if this were so, it would be possible for Sir Charles to appeal to the House of Lords for leave to continue his case in the Divorce Court. He felt that as there had been a difference of opinion when the order had been made in the full court in 1870, there were good grounds for bringing the matter up now that two years had elapsed.

Lord Penzance recalled that in his judgment after the trial he had himself stated that if the form of the order should create any difficulty in the way of the petitioner appealing to the House of Lords, then a dismissal of the original petition would remove that difficulty.

Fortified by this assurance, Sir Charles immediately appealed to the Lords for a reversal of all the previous decrees and orders which were in his opinion 'erroneous and contrary to equity and justice', and to remit his cause to the Court for Divorce.

On 9 April Sir Thomas, as Lady Mordaunt's guardian, was given a copy of Sir Charles's appeal and told that he should put his answer in writing. He and his lawyers were taken aback by this new development and particularly by Sir Charles's sudden capitulation on the subject of his wife's sanity. They had expected the feigning debate to continue indefinitely. And although they were confident that Sir Charles's appeal to the Lords would be as unsuccessful as all his previous efforts, there was nevertheless a lurking doubt that he might accomplish his aim, which could prove very serious for the men Lady Mordaunt had named and particularly for the Prince.

The Prince himself seemed unconcerned. Now that he had recovered his health, he was secretly planning a trip to Rome *en garçon*. To his chagrin the Princess, less willing than he was to accept that their second honeymoon was over, insisted on going with him, inviting her mother and father as well as a brother and sister, to join them for good measure. The Queen, meanwhile, set off for Balmoral where, as Prince Leopold told his sister on 21 May, it had rained, hailed and snowed unceasingly ever since their arrival.

If Sir Charles had expected that his appeal would be dealt with immediately, he was to be disappointed. The months went by and it was well into 1874 before his case was heard. His wife remained in the asylum at Chiswick, bereft of any right to appeal or to defend herself. The quiet routine of her life went on. She continued her regular exercise, walking 'strongly and well', and behaving in the street or the garden with what Dr Tuke described as 'equal nonchalance'. The only things she seemed to notice were the flowers and similar things 'as a child would do'. She visited Dr Tuke every day, sometimes addressing him by his own name, but at others calling him 'Moncreiffe' or 'Mackenzie', or even 'grandmama'. When Dr Tuke drove with her to London, as he sometimes did, he reported that she never betrayed 'any interest in anybody or any place'. He thought it strange the way she talked in the same way to everybody, whether they were doctors, gardeners, nurses or patients, without distinction of rank. She still did not read, or pray or do any 'work'. She did, however, play the piano better than she had done before, constantly practising the same tunes. Cut off from the world, she seemed to have no idea of the passing of time except that she did not play the piano on Sundays, 'sometimes, however, declaring that it was Sunday when it was not'. Dr Tuke reported that she was 'much delighted with a large music box' which she would listen to for hours at a time, constantly asking to have another 'drum'. She was probably reminded of the large automatic organ in the hall at Walton which would play 'The Blue Danube' and other tunes when the footman brought in a drum and set it going.

Lady Mordaunt's general health remained good. She was still sleeping well and had put on weight. She had grown fond of the nurse who looked after her, showing great affection towards her as a child might do, and she seemed to be able to relate to the children she met when out walking, learning their names and liking to walk with them. 'Although neither saying or doing anything absolutely wrong, she never does anything right' was how Dr Tuke summed it up.

In 1874, in one of the monthly reports which he had to write for the benefit of the visiting Lunacy Commissioners, Dr Tuke noted that the nurse had said that Lady Mordaunt had taken to accusing people of 'intriguing with her', and had declared that Dr Tuke slept with her. On the whole, however, she remained as always 'cheerful but quite imbecile', in a state of a childish content, at times making pertinent remarks but still unable to sustain any coherent train of thought.

37

The Appeal to the Lords

On 15 May 1874, two years after Sir Charles had first applied for his appeal, the question was debated in the presence of Lord Chief Baron Kelly, Mr Baron Martin, Mr Justice Keating, Mr Justice Brett, and Mr Justice Denman, as to whether a husband could obtain a decree for divorce assuming his wife to be guilty of adultery and to be permanently insane.

The outcome was by no means certain and a decision was only reached after careful and lengthy discussions. The distinguished lawyers mulled over the differences between civil and criminal cases. They pontificated on the subject of adultery, stating that it was a grievous sin but not a crime. They searched through the statutes and pointed out the uncertainties that troubled the 'newly created' Divorce Court. Once again they complained about the lack of precedents. Fully aware that their final judgment could influence the outcome of other cases for many years to come, they moved warily, weighing up the pros and cons with extra care.

The consequences of a divorce for the wife were thoroughly worked over, with much emphasis being placed on the penal loss of status and the lack of maintenance which could prove particularly serious for a lunatic woman. Mr Justice Keating and Mr Justice Brett were in agreement on the point that a decree should not be granted if the respondent was mad and unable to reply to the charge.

Lord Chief Baron Kelly, on the other hand, spoke strongly, as he had done at the earlier appeal, in support of the husband who, without any fault on his side, might end up condemned to maintain an unfaithful wife and her 'spurious' children, at the same time being precluded for ever from marrying another woman. The law as it stood decreed that a dissolution must be granted if the petition was backed up by certain facts. Since this was the case, what right had anybody to withhold that decree, whether or not the respondent was mad?

The two other judges agreed with Lord Kelly. Surely, they argued, evidence could be accepted from other sources. It simply meant that one witness, the woman herself, was missing.

In his summing up, the Judge Ordinary agreed that there had been differences of opinion, but a majority of three to two had declared that lunacy was no bar to further proceedings. Having weighed it all up, the judge concluded that there was no justification for prolonging the discussions concerning 'this already painfully protracted case'. He therefore issued the order allowing Sir Charles to proceed in the Court of Divorce.

The Prince and the Moncreiffes now had to face the fact that Sir Charles would be able to go the full distance in his attempt to prove that his wife's confessions had in fact been true.

38

Further Proceedings

As soon as the outcome of the appeal became known, Sir Charles started urging his lawyers to press on with the divorce. It was his wish that the names of Captain Farquhar and the Prince should this time be included. He was less than pleased when the lawyers told him not only that it would be unwise to accuse Captain Farquhar and the Prince, but also strongly advised him that no further proceedings should be taken against Sir Frederic Johnstone. The lawyers intended to lay as little stress as possible on Lady Mordaunt's confession with its catalogue of names, although they admitted that in view of the notoriety the case had obtained, this could prove to be difficult. They stated very firmly that no case for damages should be contemplated.

Sir Charles understood the reasoning behind the decision to drop Sir Frederic's name from the list. There was always the danger that, wealthy as he was, he could afford to defend his case strongly and even put in a counter-charge. But Farquhar was different. Sir Charles believed that he was far too impoverished to put up a fight, his father having recently refused categorically to pay off his debts. But the lawyers would not listen and they insisted that only Lord Cole should be cited.

Nothing, of course, happened in a hurry. Sir James Hannen, the judge appointed to take charge of the case in the Divorce Court, announced that he would not be able to pronounce judgment until he had been given the opportunity of studying the opinion of the Lords. This had not as yet been published. He therefore moved that the matter should stand over until the end of the vacation. Sir Thomas Moncreiffe was in Scotland and he certainly did not rush down south to put in an answer on his daughter's behalf. Meanwhile, Sir Charles's lawyers were busy collecting new evidence and sorting out what should be used at the trial. Sir Charles reminded them that there were many passages marked in red on the original affidavits which had not been relevant to the insanity issue but which could now be brought forward. This time no mercy would be shown towards Lady Louisa and Helen Forbes. They would most certainly be subpoenaed, and both John and Osbert Mordaunt would be called to give evidence concerning the conversations that had taken place before Sir Thomas had come down to Walton and launched the madness theory.

Sir Charles made it clear he would not scruple to tell the court how he had warned his wife about the Prince's reputation, nor would he omit to repeat the warning Lord Dudley had given him about his wife's 'improper' relationship with the Prince before her marriage. There were many similar details, such as Harriett's anger when Bird had taken her blotting-paper to the stationers, or Lady Louisa's anxious remark that she hoped Harriett 'would go on all right' when Sir Charles was away in Norway. All this could now be introduced. Some of the servants were interviewed again to see if they could remember any further incriminating details.

Perhaps most interesting of all the new additions was the testimony from William Broadbridge the gardener. His name had been crossed off the list of possible witnesses before the madness trial, perhaps because his evidence was not considered relevant at that time. He now revealed, however, that he could remember seeing Lord Cole and Lady Mordaunt with Mr George Forbes and Miss Scott walking together near the church gate at about nine o'clock one evening in July 1868. Later he had caught sight of the shadowy figures of Lord Cole and Lady Mordaunt, alone in the dusk, going out of the gate at the top of the pleasure grounds and along the shady walk through the trees towards the Bath House. He did not see them come back.

We do not know what anxious consultations went on during the last weeks of the year as Sir Charles and his lawyers pressed on with their preparations for the divorce case. The Prince was undoubtedly worried, knowing as he did that this time there would be no holds barred. Sir Charles would not scruple to include any details that might incriminate him and Serjeant Ballantine would show him no mercy if he were to appear again in the witness box.

It was probably to save the Prince from all the dangers of a possible cross-examination at the hands of Serjeant Ballantine that Lord Cole suddenly announced, in the new year of 1875, that he would, despite all his former denials, now plead guilty.

Sir Charles should, perhaps, have been overjoyed when he heard about this volte-face, but instead he felt totally cheated. He had believed that at last, after five long years of needless litigation, he was to have his chance to expose the Prince and to reveal the corruption that existed in high places. There was little doubt in Sir Charles's mind that Lord Cole had been bribed to take all the guilt on himself by the Prince and the other men named in Lady Mordaunt's confessions. And if the man could confess to his guilt now, why could he not have done so all those years ago? Thousands of pounds unnecessarily spent on lawyers' fees could have been saved, and Lady Mordaunt herself could have been spared the dreadful fate of being shut away in an asylum.

Sir Charles's bitterness spilled over on paper in an impassioned letter to Mr Hannay. He begged that his counsel should be reminded of all that had gone before, in order to 'satisfy the general public' and to make sure that the truth was not buried for ever. What he described as Lord Cole's 'ordinary guilt' was as nothing when compared with the 'enormous wrongs' done to him by Sir Thomas in depriving him of the decree nisi which should have been his by right six years before. To obtain the decree alone was not all the justice due in the case, and he wished to point out how Sir Thomas had been aided all along, step by step, by Lord Penzance. He was sure that the original summons to stay the proceedings had been taken out on a fraudulent issue, since it was evident that Lady Mordaunt had been sane up to the day that Mr Haynes had served the citation and for some time afterwards. If at last reason had left her, there was plenty of evidence to suggest that her treatment when under the charge of Sir Thomas at Worthing was such as to lay the foundation of insanity in any woman in her position. But the Moncreiffes had seen fit to tell the world that he himself had taken proceedings against an innocent wife, that she had been ill-treated before and during her confinement and that it was this treatment which had driven her out of her mind.

Sir Charles went on to rage against the injustice of the insanity trial, noting how Lord Penzance had glossed over the absence of Lady Louisa and Mrs Forbes as witnesses. 'The course adopted by Sir T. Moncreiffe' wrote Sir Charles 'from the first has been one of conspiracy and fraud for which I hope he will be exposed on the present occasion.' It was not surprising that Sir Charles felt bitter and indignant. His expenses had mounted inexorably as a result of Sir Thomas's 'fraudulence', and if only Lord Cole had confessed his guilt in the first place, none of this would have been necessary.

On 11 March 1875 the case came up for trial before a special jury in the Divorce Court who by their verdict found that the respondent Harriett Sarah Mordaunt had committed adultery with

Lowry Egerton Cole. The Judge Ordinary then made the usual decree nisi that the marriage between the petitioner and the respondent be dissolved, condemning the co-respondent in costs. All that Sir Charles had hoped to reveal was omitted, and the Prince escaped unmentioned and unscathed.

In November 1875 the decree was made absolute. It seemed that the end was at last in sight. But still the costs mounted as the argument about Lady Mordaunt's maintenance and medical fees continued. Sir Charles begged the lawyers to hurry, telling them that the only way he would be able to pay off expenses amounting to nearly £10,000 would be to sell one of the largest farms on his Northamptonshire estate. This had recently come in hand, with a prospective buyer, Lord Penrhyn, keen to purchase.

Sir Charles was doing his best to vary his marriage settlement in order to pay Lady Mordaunt a much smaller sum than she would have been due had she been widowed. Sir Thomas fought back, pointing out that his daughter was one of fourteen children and so was entitled to no more than a thirteenth of his property. Then there was Lady Mordaunt's child Violet, who had remained at Moncreiffe after her mother's departure for Chiswick without any help from Sir Charles, and she too would have to be taken into account.

Mr Hannay was of the opinion that the less said about the child the better. Sir Charles certainly felt aggrieved at having to provide for her. Mr Inderwick, however, told him that he had no choice, since the child would have to be regarded as legal issue of the marriage. The only evidence of illegitimacy was in Lady Mordaunt's statements to that effect, admissible in evidence, but not for the purpose of bastardising the child, who could just as well have been fathered by Sir Charles on his return from Norway.

As to Lady Mordaunt being without means of support, this was a different matter. There was no doubt in Mr Hannay's mind that she would be amply provided for by the 'person unknown'. He himself mentioned Lord Dudley, although Sir Charles was always ready to believe the Prince would pay his share. However, recognising the need for amicable arrangements, Sir Charles was prepared to offer £300 per annum for Lady Mordaunt's maintenance, adding that in order to expedite matters he would agree to return the wedding presents.

Mr Hannay wrote to Mr Hunt setting out these terms and expressing the hope that the judge would settle quickly to avoid publicity.

After further negotations it was agreed that in addition to the £300 a year to be paid to Lady Mordaunt, a further £100 should be included for her daughter, which was exactly what Sir Charles himself had suggested to Lady Louisa many years before. Finally, in January 1877, the divorce settlement was completed and a bond was issued for securing the sums to be paid to Lady Mordaunt and her daughter.

Lady Mordaunt had remained at Chiswick while all the negotiations were going on. Dr Tuke's reports were by now becoming increasingly terse, and he repeatedly wrote nothing more than 'No change'. Then, early in 1877, a few weeks after the settlement had been completed, he noted that she had been removed from Chiswick House to Hayes Park where, to be known from now on as Miss Moncreiffe, she would remain under the care of Dr Benbow, a surgeon, who had recently set up a private asylum there.[125]

39
A New Start

With the settlement finally concluded, Sir Charles now felt that he could put the whole long nightmare behind him. Soon he was casting his eye around for a suitable young lady to fill the gap left by the precipitate departure of his wayward wife from Walton Hall in the early summer of 1869. He first paid his court to Helen, 'Nell', Amphlett, a striking girl who shared many of his interests. She was known for her fearless riding in the hunting field, as well as for her outstanding fishing achievements, which often achieved a mention in *The Field*. Her father was Edward Amphlett who owned the Horseley Iron Works in Shropshire. But she turned Sir Charles down, marrying instead a widowed composer, Sir John Bridge, who was the organist at Westminster Abbey. Some members of her family felt that this was rather a come-down for somebody who had been offered all the grandeur of Walton Hall and the status in the county that this would have brought to her.[126]

Sir Charles next turned his attention to Mary Louisa, the second daughter of the Hon. Henry Pitt Cholmondeley, who was the rector of Adlestrop in Gloucestershire. She was the granddaughter of two barons, Lord Delamere and Lord Leigh. Along with her five brothers and three sisters, all remembered by one of their older cousins as 'a number of little boys and girls all much the same in length, breadth and thickness', Mary had been brought up in a happy atmosphere at the rectory near the Norman church where five bells in the old tower rang out on Sundays to call the 200 souls in the village to prayer.

The Cholmondeley children lived a rural life. When they were older, the girls played the harmonium in church, went to choir practices, tea parties and school concerts, and helped with the church decorating. Their father was a kindly parson who loved to fish and occasionally to go out hunting. He doted on his daughters, particularly the petite and pretty Mary. Not for nothing had Mary earned herself the nickname 'M'aimée', for everybody loved her. On her fifteenth birthday her father wrote wishing her many happy returns and telling her that he had not forgotten to thank God for giving him 'a treasure that he loved so well'. On one of the rare occasions when he reproved her, it was because she had told him in a letter that she was suffering from 'dullness'. That, he thought, was a bad complaint. 'I should try to cure it if I was you' he advised her 'by writing a book or by painting a large picture to astonish our minds when we come home.'

Maimée had reached the age of twenty-six when Sir Charles first began to court her. If she had any scruples about marrying a divorced man, she overcame them. Charlie was made welcome at the Adlestrop rectory and he got on well with his future in-laws, much as he had done with Lady Louisa in the earlier and happier days of his first marriage. The wedding took place at Adlestrop on the 24 April 1878 and it was described as 'a bright episode in the history of this pretty village'. In honour of the occasion, nearly every house was adorned with flowers, flags or evergreens and there were triumphal arches across the street. In the evening, after Charlie and Maimée had left, a dance was held in the barn and Lord Leigh headed a country dance with Mrs Cholmondeley.[127] That evening Sir Charles's tenantry dined at the Talbot Hotel in Wellesbourne and a distribution of beef was made to all the Walton cottagers.

When Sir Charles and his new wife arrived at Walton they drove over the impressive new bridge built in Yorkshire stone which spanned the lake Sir Charles had recently created. Many of the old retainers, Cobb, Bird, Mrs Stephens and Broadbridge, were still there to greet the bride.

The second Lady Mordaunt made a good impression on all who met her, especially as she showed none of the 'fast' tendencies of her predecessor. Before very long it became known that she was 'in the family way' and on 27 January 1879, almost exactly nine months (or '280 days') from her wedding night she gave birth to a daughter, the happy event proving the falseness of those rumours which had once so unkindly deemed Sir Charles incapable of fathering a child.

40
The Second Time

While Sir Charles settled down to married life with a new wife, the Prince carried on in much the same way as he had always done. He frequented weekend parties as before, and showed no signs of replacing the companions so disapproved of by his mother. In her opinion his '*soi disant*' friends were nothing more than a collection of 'dreadful and very fatiguing bores'. The Prince for his part was openly critical of her relationship with the husky Highland retainer John Brown, whom he described unceremoniously as 'that brute J.B.'.[128]

The Queen did her best to discourage her son from continuing to bestow his favours on a succession of ladies. It was said that when she saw a photographic portrait of Lillie Langtry above her son Prince Leopold's bed, she removed it at once, standing on a chair to do so. Such was Lillie's charm, however, that the Queen herself in the end allowed her to be presented at Court, some said because she wanted to see the famous beauty for herself. There was anyway little she could do to prevent her susceptible eldest son from entering into a liaison with Lillie, who was just the kind of tomboyish woman he admired. Used as she was to the teasing ways of her many brothers, she was always delightfully ready to respond to his 'chaff'. There was the added advantage of an amenable husband who was happy to spend much of his time out of the way 'beguiling salmon' to use Lillie's own phrase.

The Mordaunt affair had provided some salutary lessons. It had highlighted for husbands the dangers of stirring up trouble as well as the difficulty of proving paternity in cases where husband and wife still cohabited. The Prince, although still directing his attentions towards young married women, had learned that in order to prevent his misdemeanours being brought before the public eye, he must in future act more discreetly.

But however hard he tried to limit the less admirable aspects of his life to those circles where he was surrounded by people he could trust, there were times when danger threatened. Even the long-suffering Langtry had on one occasion threatened divorce proceedings when his wife committed the classic indiscretion of failing to throw away the blotting paper after she had written a letter to the Prince. But always the threat receded, and for twenty years the Prince pursued his usual course without causing a public scandal. It was not until the summer of 1891 that his indulgences were once again brought out into the open when he was subpoenaed to appear in court in a slander case brought against him by one of his cronies, Sir William Gordon-Cumming. Sir William had been accused of cheating at the baccarat table during the famous house party at Tranby Croft where the Prince had been staying for the Doncaster races. He had signed a confession in return for a promise that nothing more would be said about the matter, but when the incident became common knowledge he had decided to sue for libel.

The Prince's advisers were alarmed by the prospect of a trial, and the Queen told Vicky that it was 'a fearful humiliation to see the future King of this country dragged (and for the second time) through the dirt, just like anyone else, in a Court of Justice'.[129] All the same she once again used every method in her power to help him, reserving all her venom for the man she described as 'this horrible Mr Cumming'.

Although ostensibly about a game of cards, and therefore less salacious than the Mordaunt case, the proceedings nevertheless engendered considerable public excitement. The Lord Chief Justice's court was full to overflowing with interested spectators, many of them society ladies who were brightly dressed as if for an outing on the river at Maidenhead. Junior members of the Bar crowded in just as they had done eleven years before, in February 1870, to hear the Mordaunt case.

Rumour had it that there was more to the baccarat story than met the eye and it was said that there had been a certain amount of horseplay between the ladies of the house and some of the guests, notably the Prince. But Sir William Gordon-Cumming's counsel, Sir Edward Clarke, was quickly reprimanded by the judge, Lord Coleridge, when he suggested that there were more matters at stake than a simple game of cards. Lord Coleridge did not intend to open the floodgates as Lord Penzance had done in the Mordaunt case by allowing evidence pointing to sexual misbehaviour on the part of the Prince. Adultery, Lord Coleridge was at pains to point out, was not the issue.

It had been understood from the start that Sir Edward Clarke would not be as merciful to the Prince as Serjeant Ballantine had been in 1870. Sir Edward in fact subjected him to a punishing cross-examination. Lacking the assurance that he had shown at the Mordaunt trial, the Prince looked anxious and worn, answering hesitantly. He admitted that he did not feel at all confident about the outcome.

Summing up at the end of the trial, Sir Edward made a brilliant speech, in his own opinion the finest in his whole career. He sincerely believed in his client's innocence, maintaining that Sir William had been tricked into signing an admission that he had cheated, simply to conceal from the world the fact that the Prince had been involved in the wicked game of baccarat. Such things, Sir Edward said, had in the past prompted men of otherwise exemplary character to sacrifice their honour 'in order to serve the interests of a dynasty or to conceal the foibles of a Prince'.

Sir Edward, like Serjeant Ballantine before him, believed that he would have won the day if the judge in his summing up had given due weight to the points he had made. Instead the jury brought in a verdict in favour of the defendants after going out for just thirteen minutes. There was uproar in the court, and the Prince himself was hissed and booed as he drove up the course at Ascot a few days later. Although naturally pleased with the verdict, he felt aggrieved at the way he had been treated. It seemed to him that the press coverage had been 'unkind and cruel' and he also thought that Sir Edward Clarke had been unnecessarily spiteful. The Prince remembered how at the Mordaunt trial, Sir William Gladstone had taken 'all the in-direct means in his power (and *successfully*)' to prevent anything injurious being brought out' and it seemed to him that somebody should have taken similar steps to muzzle Sir Edward Clarke.[130] As for Sir William Gordon-Cumming, he remained embittered for the rest of his life, banished as he was to Gordonstoun, his Scottish estate, and ostracised from the Prince's circle that had for so long been his natural habitat.[131]

Sir Charles Mordaunt could have felt equally bitter. He knew that he would never be able to introduce his new wife to royal circles. The fact had to be faced that none of the five daughters of his second marriage would ever be presented at Court, because as the Queen herself admitted, 'Bertie never forgets'. But Sir Charles had immunised himself against the hurtful sting of social ostracism by immersing himself in the country and the sporting life that it afforded. Neither he nor his second wife hankered after the hectic social round, and by now their married life had fallen into a regular pattern which they both enjoyed.

Each year, as autumn gave way to winter and the first snows of the season fell in Scotland, the family would return to Warwickshire from the shooting lodge at Glenfeshie where they spent the months of September and October,[132] and soon the hunting season would begin, Maimée often accompanying Charlie when he rode to hounds. They entertained members of the family, both at Walton and in Scotland, where their friend Lord Brooke, before his marriage to the beautiful Daisy Maynard, would often join them. In Scotland the children were able to enjoy walking and riding and scrambling about on the rocks along the river. Maimée kept 'dullness' at bay by sketching, writing up the game book, and going for walks. Sometimes in the evenings she would play dummy whist, or quietly do her knitting by candlelight while the men fell asleep, worn out after the day's stalking.

At home the Mordaunts lived a quiet life, remote from the glittering circle that had centred round the Castle at Warwick ever since Daisy, now Countess of Warwick, had begun to entertain the Prince. Sometimes Wellesbourne people would catch a glimpse of the Prince's new-fangled motor car as he drove through the village with Daisy at his side, on their way to visit the Prince's friend and financial adviser Ernest Cassel who had leased the house at nearby Compton Verney from Lord Willoughby de Broke.

The Prince also visited the Lows at Wellesbourne House which stood on the very margin of Sir Charles's Walton estate. The American Willie Low was a member of the Prince's set, sharing his interest in horses, gambling and the ladies. His attractive wife Juliette, from Savannah, Georgia, would entertain the Prince to dinner cooked by her coloured cook Mosianna Milledge and by the ever-popular Rosa Lewis who came along with her bevy of pretty helpers. The Prince was always happy to dine anywhere if he knew Rosa Lewis would be there and the Lows tickled his palate with unfamiliar delicacies such as sweet potatoes, waffles and peach-fed hams all imported from America. The Countess of Warwick would come too, lending Juliette a red carpet to put down in the Prince's honour.

The Prince was no doubt amused to think of his friend Willie bidding fair to oust Sir Charles Mordaunt from his traditional position in local society. Willie Low was an excellent shot, leased a top-class grouse moor from the Duke of Atholl, and out hunting was always to be seen up with the leaders. The Mordaunts for their part lived modestly, at Christmas time holding a family party in the dining room at Walton Hall, their daughters particularly enjoying the Scottish reels. The toasts that were proposed on those homely evenings were to the Mordaunts themselves, and to Mr Bird and Mrs Stephens.

41

The Younger Generation

After Lord Dudley died in 1886, his wife Georgina still continued the tradition of large Christmas parties at Witley Court, entertaining a new generation of Moncreiffe cousins, among them Evie, Helen Forbes's daughter, and her cousin Violet Mordaunt who had both reached the age when they were ready to be launched into society. Helen Forbes, now widowed, had already begun to take Evie round the country house circuit and in September 1887 she and Evie went to stay at Mar Lodge, where the Duke of Fife was entertaining the Prince and his usual entourage. Evie also went to house parties at the Rothschild houses, Ascott, Mentmore and Waddesdon. At one of these parties she met Willie James, one of the three rich James brothers from New York. In her album, along with a photograph of Ascott and the signatures of all the guests at a house party held there in February 1889, Evie drew a heart pierced with an arrow bearing the initials E. F. and W. J.[133]

The following month Evie and Willie were married. It was a good match. The James brothers had worked their way into the Prince's set with the help of their money and their charm, and the eldest had married Venetia Cavendish-Bentinck, one of the Prince's favourite ladies. Venetia knew how to provide the Prince with the right milieu for the kind of animated dinner parties he most enjoyed, and soon Evie and Willie followed suit, inviting him to stay at the flintstone mansion Willie had built at West Dean near Chichester.

Both Violet and Evie had inherited the Moncreiffe good looks, but Violet lacked the vivacity which had so appealed to the Prince of Wales in her mother and her aunts. She had grown up to be a serious-minded and religious girl, and it was even rumoured that she was gifted with second sight. Later her daughter-in law was to write that her bright eyes missed nothing that was going on, and what she did not see she knew by intuition. In addition she had an extraordinary rapport with animals and an occasionally mesmerising effect upon birds, which would lie in the palm of her hand.[134] Although she was undoubtedly a beauty, some may have wondered how good Violet

Mordaunt's wedding prospects were. Her aunts did what they could to compensate for the fact that her mother was unable to chaperone her and that her father preferred to forget that she existed. Unlike her Mordaunt half-sisters, she was presented at Court when her aunt Louisa took her to the Palace at the same time as some of the Atholl cousins.

It was at Witley Court that Violet first met her future husband, Lord Weymouth, the Marquess of Bath's eldest son, a shy and rather silent young man. Lady Dudley made sure that they sat next to each other at dinner and they soon found that they had much in common, for both of them preferred a quiet country life to the pleasures of the social round. It was not long before they became engaged, and at the Witley Christmas house party in 1889 the name H. Moncreiffe appears in Evie's album among the other signatures, which suggests that Violet's mother had been allowed out of the asylum on that occasion in order to meet her future son-in-law.

The wedding took place at Witley in April 1890, when Violet was just twenty-one years old. To his chagrin, Sir Charles was not invited to the wedding. The Moncreiffes were understandably of the opinion that since in the past he had never chosen to acknowledge the child, he could hardly expect to receive an invitation.

Sir Charles at first overlooked the fact that the divorce settlement had stated that Violet's allowance from him should be discontinued when she married. As a result the money went on being paid into her account. As soon as he realised what had happened, however, he demanded, not only that the allowance should be stopped, but that all Violet had received since her marriage must be repaid. Her husband pleaded poverty which he put down to the heavy expenses of running an estate, and he emphatically stated that neither he nor his wife could afford to pay back the arrears. The trustees were equally alarmed at the prospect of having to reimburse Sir Charles themselves. It was an unpleasant controversy that did little to endear Sir Charles to Violet or to her relations.[135]

Violet gave birth to daughters in 1891 and 1893, followed by a son, John, in 1895. In 1896 her husband inherited the estate after the death of his father, and Violet settled down to life as the chatelaine of Longleat. More serious-minded than her mother, she seemed to be searching for a deeper meaning in life, eventually finding the solace she sought in the Christian Science movement.

The shooting parties which gathered at Longleat every autumn always included some of Lord Weymouth's Thynne relations, but there was invariably a large gathering of Violet's family as well. She had been brought up in the nursery at Moncreiffe with her youngest uncles, John, born in 1866 just before her mother's marriage to Sir Charles, and Malcolm, born in August 1871. They had remained on affectionate terms, and John in particular was a frequent guest at Longleat. Then there was her cousin Gerald Arbuthnot, the son of her aunt Selina, as well as Evie Forbes's daughters Millicent and Alexandra James and their father Willie and Lord Tullibardine, the Duke of Atholl's heir. The game book included other names from the past – Netty Forbes, Georgie Forbes's widow, and Lord Newport, now the Earl of Bradford, and his heir.[136]

Not surprisingly the Prince never paid a visit to Longleat either before or after he became King. The Baths only once entertained royalty, when the future George V and his wife stayed with them for the reopening and consecration of Glastonbury Abbey in June 1909. By contrast the Prince and his family were frequent visitors at West Dean. Evie had known the royal Princesses from childhood and was particularly close to Maud, the youngest, born in 1869 after her parents returned from abroad to be met with the news of Lady Mordaunt's confession. The Prince found West Dean much to his taste, for the house was comfortable, it provided a convenient base for the Goodwood races and the shooting was excellent. Princess Maud shared her father's feelings. 'I *never* saw anything so beautifully arranged as West Dean' she told Evie 'and every room was pretty, not a *single* ugly thing to be seen.' Father and daughter were captivated by Evie's Moncreiffe good looks. 'You looked so sweet at the Devonshire Ball, and I such a monster' Princess Maud told Evie.

It was a sad fact that the Prince's three daughters, though remarkably pleasant and 'unstuck up', were also disappointingly plain. In photographs they stare out with their father's large eyes from heavy-featured faces. Princess Maud herself was only too aware that she had not inherited her mother's beauty, and when she and her sisters went to Torquay in 1886, she realised that Princess Alexandra was the only person the crowds wanted to see. Everyone, she told Evie, had been very disappointed because 'Mamma had a cold and did not appear, and only we three old hags. Oh lawks, I am sure you would have laughed at us!'

After Maud married the Prince of Denmark, her father, sometimes accompanied by his wife, continued his visits to West Dean. He wrote to 'My dear Evie' frequently, thanking her for her hospitality and making arrangements for future visits.[137]

42
The King

When Queen Victoria died in 1901 and her son at last came to the throne he immediately gained in public stature, just as Queen Victoria's ministers had always prophesied he would once he was given some responsibility. But hopes were disappointed if anyone had imagined that he would rid himself of his old habits and his less desirable companions. It soon became evident that nothing had changed. He continued to over-indulge himself, even though his friend Agnes Keyser, founder of the King Edward VII Hospital for Officers, did her best to help him control his eating and cut down his weight. He kept the same friends, continued his round of house parties, and openly consorted with his latest mistress, the Hon. Mrs George Keppel.

The James brothers and their wives remained much in favour. They often went down on the 'Monday special' from St Pancras to join the King's shooting parties at Sandringham. The founding of the King Edward VII Sanatorium for Consumption at Midhurst, which had been facilitated by a two million pound donation from Sir Ernest Cassel, gave the King a respectable excuse for paying return visits to Evie and Willie James at West Dean. Once he had done his duty at the hospital, he would be free to concentrate on the entertainments Evie could provide. Hilaire Belloc penned some lines which show what was on offer

> There will be bridge and booze till after three
> And after that, a lot of them will grope
> Along the corridor in *robes de nuit,*
> Pyjamas or some other other kind of dope . . .
> And Mrs James will entertain the King.[138]

The King, with his wife and Alice Keppel, paid his usual autumn visit to West Dean in 1906, arriving on 19 November. A month later Evie noted in her diary that she was unwell for several weeks afterwards. The following August, when she was up in Scotland, she gave birth to a son after many hours of severe pain. The baby was called

Edward, after his godfather, the King. 'I can well imagine your joy' the King wrote in his letter of congratulation, and in a telegram sent from Balmoral the Queen said that she was delighted to hear the good news and continued to ask tenderly after the 'darling little boy'.

'Never comment on a likeness' had been Lady Louisa Momcreiffe's advice to her daughters, but in this case it must have been tempting, and there certainly was some gossip about young Edward's paternity – as there had been at the time of Evie's own birth when people had counted back to a time when her mother and the Prince had seen a lot of each other in London when her husband's back was turned.

The King's visits to West Dean remained a regular part of his programme even after his health began to deteriorate. When he went down for the last time in the autumn of 1909 he seemed to be cheerful enough, although it was impossible to ignore the fact that the he was not at all well and that he was wheezing badly. In April 1910 he spent some time in Biarritz before returning to a deepening political crisis over the Home Rule Bill for Ireland. Much store was set on the King's ability to hold the balance and to calm the situation. Physically, he was hardly up to it; his stay in Biarritz had done him little good and his breathing difficulties seemed to be even more acute.

On 5 May Evie received a telegram telling her that the King was very ill. Venetia telephoned her later to say that there was little hope of a recovery. The next day Arthur James went down to West Dean to break the news that the King was dead. Willie was away from home but Arthur wrote to him immediately, begging him to return at once. 'Evie wants looking after' he told his brother.

The newspapers were full of tributes to the King and for days there was little talk of anything except the late monarch and the better aspects of his life. For Evie and many others there was a sense of irretrievable loss. As Arthur James put it:

> He goes at the height of his popularity and success and before he has been called upon to decide on the present crisis and before Socialism and anarchy take the country in their grasp. This however doesn't make those left behind feel his loss the less, but may help to explain why Providence has removed the man we all thought most essential for the welfare of the nation.[139]

Queen Alexandra, visiting Marlborough House for the first time after her husband's death, told her sister-in-law that it now seemed 'so sad and desolate without him, my beloved Bertie'.[140] Many remembered the King with affection. He had rewarded those who had been loyal to him with friendship and honours. Sir Frederic Johnstone, for example, was still receiving the Prince at his villa in Monte Carlo years after the Mordaunt scandal had blown over.[141] The King had created a bastion guarded by friends whose loyalty was unquestionable, friends like Sir Ernest Cassel 'so true and loyal and generous' or Christopher Sykes, paladin to the Prince's Charlemagne, who described himself as his master's 'obedient, loyal and most tried servant', with the accent, perhaps, on the 'tried'.

Anyone who helped the Prince out of a scrape could expect at the very least a title. Edward Hamilton, William Gladstone's private secretary, whose task it had been to sort out the honours lists, had not always felt happy about some of the names that went forward 'in deference to the Prince of Wales'. He noticed that the Prince sometimes 'persistently and somewhat questionably (if not fishily)' pressed his candidates on Mr Gladstone. For example, when the Prince suggested that a knighthood should be conferred on Oscar Clayton, the doctor recommended by the Prince to Lady Susan Vane-Tempest for carrying out an abortion, Hamilton expressed the hope that no 'disagreeable stories' would come out about him. Certainly Dr Gull received a baronetcy, and Dr Alderson was similarly honoured.[142]

For others, who received no honours, there was a residue of bitterness. Dr Orford, the Wellesbourne doctor, was one of them. Because of his courageous stand against the establishment he had been forced to move away from Wellesbourne, overwhelmed by all the publicity attached to the case.

There had been many for whom the heady pleasures of life in the Prince's circle had turned sour. Darkness had descended on the young lives of those whose indiscretions had condemned them to social ostracism. Harriett Mordaunt's case was especially pitiable, the living death of the asylum where she had remained until she finally died in 1906.

It was, of course, the women who fared worst. There was all too often a price to pay in the dismal aftermath of shame, rejection and unwanted pregnancy. 'We bear all the ignominy' Harriett had so rightly observed to Mrs Murray, and as Violet Effingham had put it in *Phineas Finn* 'the wrong side of the post for a woman is so very much the wrong side'.

The people who fared best in the aftermath of an involvement with the Prince were those who could turn cheerfully to another occupation, for example Lillie Langtry who had gone onto the stage and had changed, as she herself put it, 'from butterfly to busy bee', or Daisy, Countess of Warwick, who actively espoused the Socialist cause. As she thumbed through the old guest books, remembering the delightful parties of friends who had basked in the gardens, drawn the coverts and shot thousands of birds, Daisy could look back without rancour and say that it had all been 'a great game'.[143]

How different it all might have been for Sir Charles if he had been prepared to play the game, if he had ignored Lord Dudley's warnings and had invited the Prince to his house, accepting the consequences without complaint. To entertain the Prince, to accept his wife's adultery, might in the end have proved cheaper than having to pay the lawyers' fees. And had he done the gentlemanly thing and taken all the blame on himself, accepting the child as his own, he would at least have avoided being called a 'dirty tyke' by Rosa Lewis. That was many years later, when, an old lady by then, Rosa had visited Longleat and paused in front of a portrait of Violet, Marchioness of Bath, remembering the Warwickshire scandal. Rosa told Violet's daughter-in-law that in her opinion it would all have blown over if certain people had not written letters and if Sir Charles had not ignored basic decencies, calling in lawyers, and unlocking his wife's secret cabinet. 'No letters, no lawyers and kiss my baby's bottom' was Rosa's advice.[144]

She was right of course. How much would have been saved in terms of money and anguish, if only Sir Charles had never put the matter into the hands of the lawyers, and if the Prince had appreciated the dangers of 'intimacy on paper'. Writing letters, Queen Victoria had once admitted, was a family failing, and none more ill-advised than those billets-doux signed with the tell-tale initials, 'A.E.'.

43
Epilogue

Sir Charles did not live to see his old enemy become King. He had gone up to Arisaig on the West coast of Scotland in 1897 after the celebrations for the Queen's Jubilee, and had been thrown out of a trap while out driving with his brother Osbert. Although at first it had been thought that he was not too badly injured, he later developed an abscess on the liver and died after an operation in London.

They brought his coffin down and placed it in the library at Walton Hall. The following Wednesday, outside the little chapel where for so many years he had read the lesson on Sundays, the villagers gathered early and stood waiting silently. Many people were in tears. It was a day of brilliant sunshine. The coffin was brought over into the church which was far too small to accommodate all those who had come to mourn. Lady Mordaunt had specially requested that the service should be kept very simple, without pomp or show. She was accompanied by her five daughters, who watched with her as the coffin was lowered into its resting place by the south wall of the church.

The marks of respect speak volumes. All cub-hunting fixtures were cancelled, and at the Conservative Working Men's Club in Wellesbourne which had been founded by Sir Charles, it was decided to postpone indefinitely the entertainment fixed for the next month. The obituaries in the newspapers spoke of Sir Charles's prowess in the hunting field, of his love of the Highlands, of his interest in his estate and local affairs. It was noted that although he had shown little taste for the parliamentary life and had only served as an M.P. for two terms, he had been tireless in his support of the Conservative Party in the Division. Nobody, of course, mentioned the Warwickshire scandal which had shocked the nation nearly thirty years before.

Maimée was deeply distressed by the loss of her husband whose death had come so quickly and unexpectedly. Her whole way of life was abruptly changed. Now all the responsibilities were hers – the running of the estate, the bringing up of her mentally handicapped son, Osbert, the marrying off of her daughters. In the great house, gloom descended. The servants, the children, all were dressed in mourning clothes. Maimée herself was to wear black for the rest of her life.

Still grieving and ill, she felt unable to attend her parents' golden wedding anniversary at Adlestrop the following year. Her father had to admit how much he missed her. 'Well,' he wrote, 'it pleased God so to order it that we should not be together at this time, and what He orders must not only be submitted to, but we must try to teach ourselves that what He wills, has been ordered for the best.' And as Maimée's mother put it: 'I know that no one would have taken a greater interest in it all than your dear husband for he was always so good to us and so fond of your dear father.'

Gradually Maimée recovered her equilibrium. She took over the running of the estate with the help of the agent Mr Kibler, who had succeeded the indefatigable Mr Cobb, and she began to go hunting again.

Four years after the death of King Edward VII, the First World War broke out, interrupting the established round of house parties, shooting parties and the summer season. Longleat became a military hospital, and Lady Bath received many appreciative letters from the men she had cared for and befriended.

Violet's cousin Gerald Arbuthnot first went to the front with the 2nd Battalion of the Grenadier Guards in May 1916 and he wrote to tell her how his Moncreiffe blood revolted at all the petty inconveniences of army life. He described how beautiful the weather was and how he had been struck, on his journey to the railhead, by the peacefulness of the quiet French landscape. He had expected a gradual transition, but had been surprised by the sudden change to total devastation, with the screaming of shells, the rattle of machine guns, and the 'big fellow' crashing away, day and night.

John Moncreiffe, 'J. A.', was also at the front, serving with the Oxfordshire Hussars, and Violet often wrote to him. On 12 February 1916 he received a long letter from her which he put in his pocket and showed to her eldest son John, Lord Weymouth, when he came down to the dug-out that night. They had some tea and talked about Violet and about home. 'I don't think anyone could have had fewer cares or seemed more at peace with everyone and everything than he did' J.A. later told Violet in a letter, describing how he had passed him 'on the way up the trench from one of my guns to the other, sitting smoking a cigarette, and just had a word or two with him about midnight, and at three o'clock when I came back the same way someone told me he had been killed.' Lord Weymouth had been shot in the back of the head while standing exposed to enemy fire above the parapet. He was buried in a cemetery nearby, his grave marked by a simple wooden cross.

Every year Violet had prophesied that the war would be over in September, and when it finally came to an end, her health, which had never been good, deteriorated further and she became increasingly disabled. Her surviving son Henry came of age in 1926 and she was well enough to preside when a hundred guests were invited to Longleat to celebrate. Violet lived to see the day when Henry married Daphne, daughter of the 4th Baron Vivian.

Sir Osbert Mordaunt, Sir Charles's only son, died in 1934 at the age of fifty. After his death his mother lived on at Walton Hall with a reduced staff and by the time the Second World War broke out she had become bedridden following a fall from her horse. She continued to live in a wing of the house after it was requisitioned by the army. The furniture was put into store, and it was brought back to Walton in 1947 after Lady Mordaunt's death only to be sold.

In the will drawn up by Sir Charles, he had specified that after the death of his wife and his son Osbert, the Walton estate should be inherited by the eldest son of the eldest daughter of his second marriage. Adela had no children, and Irene was the next in line. She had married in 1907 the handsome Sir Robert Hamilton and it was on their eldest son Richard (the author's husband) that the estate devolved. When he came into the huge house it was dilapidated, and devoid of furniture. But among the rich collection of family papers in the muniment room were the four large boxes of documents relating to the divorce. There were the servants' diaries, the affidavits of lady's maid and midwife, doctors and clergyman, the bundles of legal correspondence, the shorthand writers' transcripts of the trial, carefully kept, perhaps, in the hope that someone would at a future date search through them and tell the world Sir Charles's side of the story.

The true story is as much about attraction and passion as it is about morals. Harriett, young and beautiful, inspired love in others and was also herself a prey to it. She fell for the Prince who had both the power to charm and the power to command. By contrast her husband was worthy, but uninteresting. 'Charlie is so good' she told the midwife, a quality which she had not valued enough until it was too late. Trollope summed it all up neatly when he put the question: 'Is it not a pity that people who are bright and clever should so often be exceedingly improper? And that those who are never improper should so often be dull and heavy?'

Reserved and shy Sir Charles certainly was, and perhaps excessively devoted to his sporting activities. But the documents stored for so many years in the muniment room do show that it was his wish that both he and Harriett should be given a second chance. It was not Sir Charles who had denied her the chance to speak out, putting her away out of reach of her friends. It was, as he himself believed, the treatment she received which caused her in the end to be pronounced by one of the most eminent 'mad' doctors in the land to have the mental age of a child of six.

At Walton Hall there are new structures now. There is a Leisure Centre where once the old vinery stood, timeshare apartments in place of peach houses, car parks where Captain Farquhar picked flowers to put in the young Lady Mordaunt's hair. Now visitors of many nationalities come thousands of miles to spend a few days in the bedroom where Violet was born, or in the boudoir where the lawyer delivered to the stricken Harriett the petition for divorce. Up in her room, now known as the Royal Suite, timesharers write their postcards home, looking out over the balcony to the woods beyond, just as Lady Mordaunt wrote the thank you letters for her wedding presents all those years before, surreptitiously planning her next meeting with the Prince. She had been adored then, by Charlie, by the Prince, and by her affectionate cousin Lord Newport. Some might say that she had died forgotten, shut away as she was from the world for so long. And yet the memory of her exploits has lived on to this day among Warwickshire people, together with the sad tale of the white ponies shot dead on the lawn at Walton Hall after the Prince had gone away.

Notes

1   *Your Dear Letter: Private Correspondence of Queen Victoria and the Crown Princess of Prussia (1861-1879)*, ed. Roger Fulford (1971), p. 165.
2   *My Dear Duchess: Social and Political Letters to the Duchess of Manchester 1858-1869*, ed. A. L. Kennedy (1956), p. 210.
3   Alice Miles, *Every Girl's Duty*, ed. Maggy Parsons (1992).
4   *Phineas Finn* was written in 1866-7 and first published serially from October 1867 to May 1869, and in book form in 1869.
5   Christopher Sykes, *Four Studies in Loyalty* (1946).
6   Frances, Countess of Warwick, *Life's Ebb and Flow* (1929), pp. 189-91.
7   Alice Miles, *op. cit.*, p. 123.
8   *Queen Victoria's Highland Journals*, ed. David Duff (1983), pp. 25, 52-3, 72, 73, 88; Sir Sidney Lee, *Edward VII*, vol. 1, p. 175. Sir Charles Forbes had been a captain in the 17th Lancers.
9   Anthony Trollope, *The Vicar of Bullhampton* (1870), pp. 85-6.
10   Founder of the East India House of Forbes, Forbes & Co.
11   *My Dear Duchess*, p. 133.
12   It was customary for ladies to knit garments for their friends. For example, the future Lady Paget knitted a waistcoat for the Prince of Wales, which he cordially thanked her for, saying that it had created quite a sensation when he wore it out hunting. *Personal Letters of King Edward VII*, ed. Lieut. Colonel Sewell (1931), p. 34.
13   *Framley Parsonage* was first published in 1861.
14   Lord Tyrone. Wilfrid Scawen Blunt, *My Diaries* (1920), vol. 2, p. 284.
15   Richard Hough, *Edward and Alexandra: their Private and Public Lives* (1992), p. 97.
16   *Can You Forgive Her?* (1868 ed.), pp. 148, 149.
17   *Your Dear Letter*, p. 44.
18   The original Corrour Lodge was bought by John Stirling Maxwell in 1890 who then built a second lodge three or four miles away at the head of Loch Ossian. This was burnt down in 1947. I am indebted to Donald Maxwell Macdonald for this information.
19   Helen Newport was the widow of Sir David Moncreiffe and the 3rd Earl of Bradford. She was Harriett's grandmother and George Newport's step-grandmother.
20   Anthony Trollope, *The Vicar of Bullhampton* (1870)

21 Robert Duff of Fetteresso Castle and Culter House, Kincardineshire. See below, note 69.

22 Edward Cadogan, aged 32, born in the East Indies, son of Edward Cadogan, of Travancore, Madras.

23 *Warwick Advertiser* 15 December; *Leamington Courier* 8 December 1866.

24 The Wise family lived at Woodcote, Leek Wootton in Warwickshire. Mr H. C. Wise was Sir Charles's fellow Member for South Warwickshire.

25 Elizabeth Hamilton, *The Old House at Walton* (1988), p. 223.

26 Francis Knollys (1837-1924) was the son of Sir William Knollys who had been appointed Comptroller and Treasurer to the Prince's household by Queen Victoria.

27 Princess Louise Victoria Alexandra Dagmar was christened in May. The Queen was disappointed that Victoria was only her second name. *Your Dear Letter*, p. 135.

28 Anita Leslie, *Edwardians in Love* (1973), pp. 63-4.

29 Maud and Edith, the two unmarried daughters of Charles, 2nd Baron Vivian. Their uncle John, who was a friend of Harriett's grandmother, Lady Kinnoull, was married to Florence Rowley who eloped with Lord Waterford in 1869 (see pp. 125-6). Louisa was the daughter of Sir William Scott of Ancrum, see note 37.

30 Lord Rendlesham was the great-grandson of Peter Thellusson, a rich city banker of Swiss origin. He rebuilt Rendlesham Hall in Norfolk to the design of William Burn in 1868. His cousin Charles Sabine Thellusson rebuilt Brodsworth in Yorkshire, the legal wrangling over this inheritance providing the model for the Jarndyce v. Jarndyce case in *Bleak House* by Charles Dickens.

31 Lady Filmer. Georgina Battiscombe, *Queen Alexandra* (1969), p. 86.

32 *ibid.*, p. 217.

33 This breed of doves was favoured as the birds were particularly quick and lively. They were released from boxes with collapsible sides and shot at from twenty-five yards' range. Later in the century the sport began to fall into disrepute, attracting, as Edward Hamilton recorded in his diary, 'gatherings of low-class people' and made the subject of extensive betting. In March 1883 Anderson's bill for preventing pigeon shooting was debated in the House, but Edward Hamilton felt that the cruelty argument did not altogether convince, as he thought it was no more cruel to shoot pigeons than pheasants, although it was certainly not nearly such a 'manly' exercise. 'All sport' he wrote 'is cruel and as such is indefensible.' The passing of the Captive Animals Act put an end to the sport. Edward Hamilton, *The Diary of Sir Edward Walter Hamilton 1880-1885*, 2 vols., ed. D. Bahlman (1972), p. 406.

34 *Your Dear Letter*, p. 91.

35 *Darling Loosy: Letters to Princess Louise 1856-1939*, ed. Elizabeth Longford (1991), p. 97.

36 Arthur Farquhar, a captain in the Coldstream Guards, b. 1843, was the second son of Sir Walter Farquhar of Cadogan House, Middlesex. His mother was a daughter of the 6th Duke of Beaufort. The family seats were at Gilminscroft in Ayrshire, and at Lenturk in Aberdeenshire. One of his ancestors had married Margaret Forbes of Newe; their son was minister of the chapel of Garioch 1738-87. Farquhar was a member of the Prince of Wales's set, as was his cousin Horace, created Baron Farquhar in 1898, who was a close friend of the Prince and became Master of the Royal Household. Arthur Farquhar ended up as a colonel in the Egyptian Army and Chief of Staff to Hicks Pasha. He was killed in the Sudan in 1883 having never married. Count Maffei was a popular member of London Society, and he became an honorary member of the Marlborough Club, founded in 1869 by the Prince for his own and his friends' entertainment. When the Prince was travelling in Italy in 1875 he visited the count in Brindisi. Sir Sidney Lee, *King Edward VII* (1925-7), vol. 1, pp. 177, 379.

37 Louisa was Sir William's third daughter. The Scotts of Ancrum were an old family said to be descended from Uchredus, filius Scoti who was witness to the foundation charters of the Abbeys of Holyrood House and Selkirk granted by David II in the years 1128 and 1130. Sir Michael Scott, the wizard, mentioned in Sir Walter Scott's *Lay of the Last Minstrel* was said to be one of their ancestors.

38 Elizabeth Hamilton, *The Old House at Walton*, p. 236 and note.

39 *Your Dear Letter*, p. 158, 9 November 1867.

40 Edward George Geoffrey Smith Stanley, 14th Earl of Derby (1799-1869). Leader of the Conservative Party from 1846 to 1868, and three times Prime Minister. Prince Albert had been disconcerted to find, when Stanley first assumed power in 1852, that he was a member of the 'fast set', that he was immersed in the world of racing, of which Prince Albert disapproved, and that he was a successful racehorse owner himself. Prince Albert, afraid that he would fill Court posts with 'Dandies and Roués of London and the Turf', spoke to him seriously about the moral obligations of Prime Ministers. He was, on the other hand, a man much to the taste of the Prince of Wales, although by the time this letter was written he was in failing health and suffering from gout. He resigned in February 1868 and was succeeded by Disraeli.

41 Frederick James Orford had been in practice for twelve years, having qualified as a member of the Royal College of Surgeons and Licentiate of the Society of Apothecaries in 1856. A native of Ipswich, he had worked in Birmingham and had been on the medical staff in the Crimean War. He lived at the house known as The Cottage in Church Street, Wellesbourne, with his wife and family of seven young

children. Dr Richard Pitt also worked in Wellesbourne, living in a house in Chestnut Square which is still known today as Pitt House.

42 Princess Mary of Teck, Duchess of Cambridge (1833-97), a cousin of the Queen, married in 1866 Francis, Duke of Teck. Their daughter Mary (May) was to marry George V.

43 Lord Berkeley Paget, fourth son of the 2nd Marquess of Anglesey. Louisa Scott wrote in April 1869 that he had been left very well off, getting a thousand a year which would enable him to rent a place for hunting.

44 Captain John Cranch Walker ('Johnny') Vivian was a close friend of the Moncreiffes, and in the 'Red Book' of 1869, his residence, along with the Countess of Kinnoull and Sir Thomas Moncreiffe, was listed as 14 Belgrave Square. Born in 1816, he became a captain in the 11th Hussars and an MP for Truro. His first wife Louisa Woodgate had died in 1855 and he had married Florence Grosvenor Rowley in 1861. She was 'having an affair' with Lord Waterford, see note 29.

45 *Warwick Advertiser*, 26 October 1867, 14 March 1868.

46 It was serialised in *St Paul's Magazine* from October 1867 -May 1869.

47 See p. 4 and note 3, above.

48 Alice Miles, *op. cit.*, pp. 15, 19-20.

49 The Hon. Oliver George Paulet Montagu, b. 18 October 1844 and d. 24 January 1893, fourth son of the 7th Earl of Sandwich. His elder brother Edward, who became 8th Earl, was born in 1839 and had been chosen by the Queen and Prince Albert as a suitable companion for Bertie in his youth, and they became near neighbours at Sandringham. Both brothers died unmarried.

50 Giles St Aubyn, *Edward VII* (1979), pp. 121-2. See also Battiscombe, *op. cit.*, pp. 83, 86.

51 Robert Murray, third son of Bishop Murray. Eleanor was his fourth daughter.

52 Alice Miles, *op. cit.*, p. 21.

53 Princess Victoria Alexandra Olga Marie, born Marlborough House 6 July 1868. The Queen, in a letter to Vicky on 10 July from Osborne, described the baby as 'a mere little red lump', and she thought that Alexandra looked pale and exhausted. 'I fear the seventh granddaughter and fourteenth grand-child becomes a very uninteresting thing – for it seems to me to go on like the rabbits in Windsor Park!' *Your Dear Letter*, pp. 200-1.

54 Alice Miles, *op. cit.*, pp. 24, 27, 30.

55 James Hamilton, 2nd Duke of Abercorn, 1838-1913, succeeded his father in 1885. He was Lord of the Bedchamber to the Prince of Wales from 1866 to 1886 and Groom of the Stole from 1886 to 1901, besides being one of his greatest friends.

56 Although Queen Victoria believed that duels were 'dreadful things', she did feel that the absence of them had led to a total want of chivalry and high tone amongst men, and a lack of respect towards women.

The Queen was convinced that there were positions which require duels, and had it not been that her son was involved, she might well have believed that this was one of the occasions.

57 Alice Miles, *op. cit.*, pp. 79-80.

58 John Hardy of Dunstall House, Burton-on-Trent, whose brother Gathorne Hardy was Chancellor of the Exchequer in the old Government.

59 Lord Hamilton married Lady Mary Anna Curzon on 7 January 1869.

60 Prince Alfred, second son of Victoria and Albert, known to the family as 'Affie'. He had always had an ambition to go to sea, and had been in naval service since 1858. The Queen tended to compare him unfavourably with Bertie, saying that he been a 'great, great, grief' to her as a result of his unpleasant behaviour, whereas Bertie, for all his faults, was always loving and affectionate, 'sometimes imprudent, but that is all'. *Your Dear Letter*, p. 204n.

61 Battiscombe, *op. cit.*, p. 96.

62 The Prince had bought Sandringham House with its shooting estate of 7,000 acres in 1860. Because it was comparatively small and inconvenient, the Prince soon embarked on alterations and additions as he tried to bring it up to the standard of many of the houses where he himself was invited to stay. Plans for large-scale rebuilding were initiated round about the time that this letter was written, to the design of the architect A. J. Humbert, who also carried out the work at Frogmore. Sir William Knollys lived near enough for the Prince to be able to stay with him and keep an eye on the works.

63 Francis Knollys, later Viscount, son of Sir William. He became the Prince's Private Secretary in 1870. The Queen disapproved of the appointment, believing Knollys to be 'a great deal too fond of the ladies and not over-discriminating in his choice of them'. She feared that he shared and would encourage her son's depraved tastes for late nights, cigars, the stage, frivolity and vice. Politically she distrusted his liberal sympathies, St Aubyn, *op. cit.*, pp. 88-9. He was described as an 'advanced Radical' by Sir Lionel Cust, and was appreciated by the Socialist Lady Warwick, who described him as 'that honest good man, good fellow, and model private secretary ... who was a liberal in politics and also in everything else'. According to St Aubyn, Knollys possessed almost all the qualities required of the perfect Private Secretary; in particular he was wise and discreet, although Alice Miles heard him described by her cousin Augustus as 'a little dark man, bearing a strong family resemblance to the *garçons* of Parisian restaurants', Alice Miles, *op. cit.*, p. 21.

64 In April 1867 the Queen sent Vicky £15 worth of goods for the bazaar she was holding in Berlin. She also talked of making a screen for the Queen Dowager.

65 Anthony Trollope, *He Knew He Was Right* (1869).

66 Elizabeth Hamilton, *The Old House at Walton*, pp. 224-7; John Pearson, *Edward the Rake* (1975), p. 19.

67 Geraldine, wife of Henry, 18th Baron Willoughby de Broke, daughter of James Barry of Fota Island, Queenstown, County Cork, and of Marbury Hall, Northwich, Cheshire, was married on 17 October 1867. Richard Greville Verney, Lord Willoughby de Broke, *The Passing Years* (1924), pp. 36-43.

68 *Your Dear Letter*, pp. 266-7.

69 Louisa was to marry Robert Duff of Fetteresso, Kincardineshire, in 1871.

70 Henrietta Maria, younger daughter of the Hon. Humble Dudley Ward.

71 Charlotte Baird was the daughter and co-heir of Douglas Baird of Thornhill, Dumfries, a brother of John Baird of Urie, Fetteresso, Kincardine. Douglas Baird had died the previous year.

72 Alice Miles, *op. cit.*, p. 105.

73 The introduction of pillar boxes had not only made it easier for lovers to carry on a clandestine correspondence, it had also facilitated the secret posting of Valentine messages, and over a million cards had been sent the year before.

74 James Vose or Vox Solomon of Birmingham in the county of Warwick, FRCS and Professor of Ophthalmic Surgery in the Queen's College, Birmingham, in practice since 1838.

75 Dr Richard Jones of 6 Waterloo Place, Leamington Spa, FRCS Eng. (Hon.) 1844, general surgeon, the Warneford Hospital, Leamington.

76 Lady Willoughby gave birth to a son a few weeks later, on 29 March, at 7 Rutland Gate. The son, Richard Greville, succeeded his father as 19th Lord Willoughby de Broke in 1902. 'Old Lady W.' was the widow of the 17th Baron who had died in 1862.

77 The Duchess of Montrose, Caroline Agnes, wife of 4th Duke of Montrose. Lord Graham was her son. Born in 1852, he did not in fact marry until 1876.

78 Alice Miles, *op. cit.*, p. 109. John Henry de la Poer, 5th Marquess of Waterford, 1844-95, succeeded his father 1866. Captain Vivian did succeed in divorcing his wife, Florence, née Rowley, in 1869, and she married Lord Waterford in July 1872, but she died the next year.

79 Lady Julia Holmesdale married William Viscount Holmesdale, later 3rd Earl Amherst, in 1862.

80 Arthur Haynes, of 9 Hamilton Terrace, Leamington Spa, was a respected local lawyer who had been in practice for thirty-five years. He held a large number, as many as eighteen, public appointments in Warwickshire under the magistracy of the county. He was in partnership with his son and with Mr Hannay, who later took over his work when he became ill.

81 Letters from Lady Louisa Moncreiffe and Mrs Forbes to the Duchess

of Atholl are reproduced by kind permission of the Blair Charitable Trust, Blair Castle, Perthshire.

82 Alice Miles, *op. cit.*, p. 110.

83 Sir James Simpson (1811-70) when in London stayed at 15 Clarges Street, Piccadilly. He was the youngest of a Linlithgowshire baker's seven sons. His career had been outstanding. He was particularly skilled in the use of forceps and wrote many papers on the puerperal conditions. His baronetcy was conferred on him in 1866. Dr Priestley was the co-editor of his *Obstetric Works*.

84 Dr Thomas Harrington Tuke, of Manor House, Chiswick and 37 Albemarle Street, Piccadilly, MD St Andrews 1849, Fellow of the Royal College of Physicians, of London and Edinburgh. He was a son-in-law of the famous John Connolly whose work at the Hanwell Asylum, and at his small private asylum, the Lawn House at Hanwell, had popularised a more sympathetic approach to the insane with less emphasis on restraint and a more positive approach to treatment, with the help of education and religious observance. Dr Harrington Tuke had himself set up a private asylum at his house in Chiswick. He was Hon. Secretary of the Medico-Psychological Association, becoming President in 1873. Several Tukes had made their name in the field of mental science at this time. William Tuke, member of a philanthropic Quaker family, had founded the Retreat at York, with the aim of helping the mentally ill to recover in a friendly and religious atmosphere. His son, Dr Daniel Hack Tuke (1827-95), contributed many articles to medical journals and travelled extensively studying methods of caring for the mentally sick in Europe and America. Dr John Batty Tuke, later Sir John (1835-1913), born in Beverley, Yorkshire, was superintendent of the Fife and Kinross District Asylum, where he developed the 'open door' system, and he introduced more enlightened methods of treatment when he later became Director of the Saughton Hall Asylum in Edinburgh.

85 Anita Leslie, *op. cit.*, p. 65.

86 This was later changed by the judge to 'some person to your petitioner unknown' as it was not considered possible for Sir Charles to commit adultery with his wife. Mr Inderwick added the clause in this form because, although convinced by Dr Orford's evidence that Lady Mordaunt had suffered from 'the disease', he had always felt that it would be dangerous to rely upon that alone as proof of her adultery. He did, however, feel that it might be possible to prove it independently of any of the co-respondents, and with this in mind he added the extra paragraph.

87 Dr James Alderson (1794-1882) of Berkeley Square, MD Oxon 1829, had succeeded to a large practice in Hull on the death of his father, but he later moved to London where he settled at 17 Berkeley Square and became senior physician at St Mary's Hospital on its foundation, a

post which he held until elected President of the College of Physicians in 1867. He was appointed physician extraordinary to the Queen in 1874.

88 William Gull was to read a paper to the Clinical Society of London in 1873 on the subject of anorexia nervosa, a disorder which had been newly identified. Elaine Showalter, *The Female Malady* (1985), p. 127.

89 The newspapers reported the death of a young girl from leprosy, contracted as a result of wearing an infected chignon; *Warwick Advertiser*, July 1869.

90 Alice Miles, *op. cit.*, pp. 119-20.

91 *ibid.*, p. 124.

92 *Your Dear Letter*, p. 238, 3 July 1869.

93 *Leamington Chronicle*, 31 July 1869.

94 A serjeant at law was a member of a superior order of barristers, from which until 1873 the Common Law judges were always chosen. The order was abolished in 1880.

95 Anthony Trollope, *The Vicar of Bullhampton* (1870), pp. 251, 261.

96 Prince Albert had appointed Dr William Jenner successor to Dr William Baly who was killed in a railway crash at Wimbledon in 1861. He was a pathologist who was well known for his research into typhus and typhoid.

97 Dr I. Russell Reynolds, Fellow of the Royal College of Physicians, Examiner in Medicine to the University of London, Professor of Medicine in University College and Physician to University College Hospital. Dr George Burrowes MD wrote from 18 Cavendish Square. His *Commentaries on Insanity* had been published in 1828.

98 Alice Miles, *op. cit.*, p. 124.

99 Lord Houghton wrote many poems, some of them sonnets. He had a house in Arlington Street and was described by Lillie Langtry as the most delightful host of his time. When she asked him if she could inspire him sufficiently to write a poem about her, he looked at her 'a wee bit pathetically' and said 'My dear, I am too old.' Lillie Langtry, *The Days I Knew* (1925).

100 In 1854 the Crystal Palace had been moved from Hyde Park, where it had originally been built to house the 1851 Exhibition, to Sydenham, only a few miles from Bromley. It had suffered a fire in 1866 and was finally burnt down in 1936.

101 John Fiennes, born 1830, succeeded his father in 1887 as 17th Lord Saye and Sele.

102 The lost village of Walton, to the south of Walton Hall, was known as Walton d'Eivile.

103 Dr Forbes Winslow was descended from Edward Winslow, one of the Pilgrim Fathers and the first Governor of Massachusetts. He had graduated as licentiate of the Society of Apothecaries in 1869. From a year old he had lived among the insane, his father having founded the

Sussex and Brandenburgh House Asylum at Hammersmith in 1844, the year of his birth. He felt that he had become a 'mental expert' long before he actually qualified. His father, who had one of the largest lunacy practices in England, helped to establish the recognition of the pleas of insanity in criminal cases in England, and he himself became involved in 'medical jurisprudence', being called as a witness in a number of celebrated murder cases. Dr Tyler Smith lived at 21 Upper Grosvenor Street. He was connected with several obstetrical institutions, lecturing in midwifery at St Mary's Hospital.

104 Dr Forbes Winslow, *Recollections of Forty Years* (1910), p. 97.

105 Eating disorders among women reached epidemic proportions from 1870 onwards, and were linked by psychiatrists to the emergence of the 'New Woman' with her demands for greater independence and a better education. Showalter, *op. cit.*, pp. 18, 121, 127, 137.

106 Philip Magnus, *King Edward the Seventh* (1964), pp. 107-8.

107 An article 'Feigned Insanity: with Cases' by Dr David Nicolson, Assistant Medical Officer at Portland prison, had recently appeared in the January 1870 number of *The Journal of Medical Science* and this was quoted by the lawyers. Nicolson started his article by quoting instances of 'counterfeiting' in Shakespeare's plays.

108 John Pearson, *Edward the Rake* (1975), pp. 55-6.

109 It had become fashionable in the medical profession to use photographs to illustrate hysterical states in women. J.-M.Charcot (1825-93) had just begun his work in Paris and the camera played an important part in his studies of hysterical women. He also gave popular public lectures illustrated by hysterical patients who would eat charcoal, crawl on the floor barking, or cradle a top hat as if it were a baby. Charcot experimented with hypnosis, and some felt that he 'coached' his subjects to act dramatically at his lectures and in front of the camera. Showalter, *op. cit.*, pp. 147-51.

110 St Aubyn, *op. cit.*, pp. 162-3.

111 Chapter 68, 3rd Section.

112 Baxter, Rose, Norton & Co.

113 *Darling Loosy*, p. 151, June 1871.

114 *Darling Child: Private Correspondence of Queen Victoria and the Crown Princess of Prussia 1871-1878*, ed. Roger Fulford (1976), pp. 262-3.

115 *ibid.*, pp. 266-7.

116 Dr Wynter was a Doctor of Medicine of the University of St Andrews and a member of the Royal College of Physicians. Chestnut Lodge was at 1 Bolton Road, Grove Park. In 1857 he had written an article on lunatic asylums in *The Quarterly Review* and his book *Borderlands of Insanity* was published in 1875. He was also editor of *The British Medical Journal*.

117 See above, p. 58 and note 3.

118 *Your Dear Letter*, pp. 279-82.

119 'Henry Maudsley, psychiatrist, philosopher and entrepreneur', Trevor Turner, *Psychological Medicine* 1988, 18, pp. 551-74. Dr Maudsley (1835-1918) had been joint editor of *The Journal of Medical Science* since 1863, physician at the West London Hospital since 1864, and lecturer on insanity at St Mary's Hospital since 1868. His book, *The Physiology and Pathology of the Mind*, was published in 1867. Like Dr Tuke, he was a son-in-law of Dr Connolly (see note 84). Maudsley later gave £30,000 for the foundation of the Maudsley Hospital for the 'early treatment of curable mental illness and for research and teaching in psychiatry'.

    Dr Barnes of 31 Grosvenor Street was obstetric physician to St Thomas's Hospital, Examiner in obstetric medicine to the University of London, and a Member of the Royal College of Physicians and the Royal College of Surgeons.

120 'Dr Tuke's Case Book, Chiswick House Asylum May 1870 – October 1884', the Wellcome Institute for the History of Medicine (Western Manuscripts Collection MS 5725). Dr John Batty Tuke had read a paper at the half-yearly meeting of the Medico-Psychological Association to the Royal College of Physicians in Edinburgh on 'The Cottage System of Management of Lunatics as Practised in Scotland, with Suggestions for its Elaboration and Improvement'. This was published in the January 1870 edition of *The Journal of Mental Science* edited by C. L. Robertson and Henry Maudsley. The housing of Lady Mordaunt in a cottage in the grounds of the Manor House was in line with the theory that harmless lunatics did better in a less institutionalised environment. Following the death of Dr Harrington Tuke, the asylum was run by his two sons, one of whom, Dr Thomas Seymour Tuke, had been the resident physician. The asylum was moved to Chiswick House, the Earl of Burlington's villa, in 1894.

121 Hydrate of chloral was described in this way by 'A Sane Patient' whose book *My Experiences in a Lunatic Asylum* was published in 1879. The dosage given by Dr Tuke was gr xii. At the Quarterly Meeting of the Medico-Psychological Association on 28 October 1869, there had been a clinical discussion on the administration of 'the new remedy', chloral, several doctors saying that they had found it useful in the treatment of delirium tremens and also in 'violent and destructive mania'. Dr Llewllyn Williams advised frequent doses, which he believed to be perfectly safe, recommending a solution prepared at Bell's in Oxford Street.

122 *The Times*; Longford, *Darling Loosy*, pp. 158-9; *Later Letters of Lady Augusta Stanley 1864-1876*, ed. the Dean of Windsor and Hector Bolitho (1929), pp. 147-51.

123 St Aubyn, *op. cit.*, pp. 154-9.

124 Dr Tuke's Case Book, *op. cit.*, p. 82.

125 It is probable that Dr Benbow was related to the Moncreiffes' lawyer. The house, which was situated north of the Uxbridge Road, had been rebuilt in 1820. It remained a private mental asylum until 1898 when the manorial estate was broken up on the death of Charles Mills, Lord Hillingdon. After this it was used as a private nursing home, and it was demolished in the 1960s after being bought by Heinz & Co. The Mills family were related to the Mordaunts.

126 I am indebted to Carolanne Hudson and John Stainer for this information.

127 William Henry, 2nd Baron Leigh, who had succeeded his father Chandos in 1850. He was well known for his exceptionally loud voice. A description of life in the village is to be found in Rose Cholmondeley's *Adlestrop: Its Cottages and Their Inmates 1876-1877* (1935), ed. by her brother Lionel Cholmondeley, vicar of the Edge, Gloucestershire.

128 *Darling Child*, p. 186; *Darling Loosy*, p. 169.

129 Magnus, *op. cit.*, pp. 227-8.

130 *ibid.*, pp. 228-9.

131 The Right Hon. Sir Robert Michael Havers QC, Edward Grayson and Peter Shankland, *The Royal Baccarat Scandal* (1977).

132 Glenfeshie was at that time part of the Ballindalloch estate owned by the Macpherson-Grants.

133 West Dean papers.

134 Daphne Fielding, *Mercury Presides* (1954), p. 110.

135 Longleat, Farrer papers 171,240. Lady Bath did receive the £200,000 inherited by her mother under the marriage settlement with Sir Charles.

136 Longleat Game Books NMR D 28 (6), (7), and (8); Visitors' books 5th Marquess 165, 01/01/1900, 18/11/1901, 01/06/1910, 01/06/1913.

137 West Dean Papers.

138 Quoted by Anita Leslie, *op. cit.*, p. 153.

139 Extracts from Evie James's diary and from Arthur James's letter: West Dean Papers.

140 *Your Dear Letter*, p. 273.

141 *Personal Letters of King Edward VII*, edited by J. Sewell (1931), p. 221.

142 Edward Hamilton, *The Diary of Sir Edward Hamilton 1880-1885*, ed. D. Bahlman (1972), pp. 128, 249, 254 and n.

143 Frances Countess of Warwick, *op. cit.*, pp. 81, 125-6, 178, 264.

144 Daphne Fielding, *The Duchess of Jermyn Street: the Life and Good Times of Rosa Lewis of the Cavendish Hotel* (1964), p. 191.

145 Longleat Papers: Correspondence of the 5th Marchioness: J. A. Moncreiffe, G. Moncreiffe and Violet Dickinson, 1916.

Index